Cloud Computing Technologies for Green Enterprises

Kashif Munir
University of Hafr Al-Batin, Saudi Arabia

A volume in the Advances in
Business Information Systems and
Analytics (ABISA) Book Series

Published in the United States of America by
    IGI Global
    Business Science Reference (an imprint of IGI Global)
    701 E. Chocolate Avenue
    Hershey PA, USA 17033
    Tel: 717-533-8845
    Fax: 717-533-8661
    E-mail: cust@igi-global.com
    Web site: http://www.igi-global.com

Library of Congress Cataloging-in-Publication Data

Names Munir, Kashif, 1976- editor.
Title Cloud computing technologies for green enterprises Kashif Munir,
    editor.
Description Hershey, PA Business Science Reference, [2018] Includes
    bibliographical references.
Identifiers LCCN 2017013425 ISBN 9781522530381 (hardcover) ISBN
    9781522530398 (ebook)
Subjects LCSH Cloud computing--Security measures.
    Telecommunication--Energy conservation--Case studies. Green movement.
    Sustainable development.
Classification LCC QA76.585 .C5845 2018 DDC 004.6782--dc23 LC record available at httpslccn.
loc.gov2017013425

This book is published in the IGI Global book series Advances in Business Information Systems and Analytics (ABISA) (ISSN: 2327-3275; eISSN: 2327-3283)

British Cataloguing in Publication Data
A Cataloguing in Publication record for this book is available from the British Library.

All work contributed to this book is new, previously-unpublished material.
The views expressed in this book are those of the authors, but not necessarily of the publisher.

For electronic access to this publication, please contact: eresources@igi-global.com.

Advances in Business Information Systems and Analytics (ABISA) Book Series

ISSN:2327-3275
EISSN:2327-3283

Editor-in-Chief: Madjid Tavana, La Salle University, USA

MISSION

The successful development and management of information systems and business analytics is crucial to the success of an organization. New technological developments and methods for data analysis have allowed organizations to not only improve their processes and allow for greater productivity, but have also provided businesses with a venue through which to cut costs, plan for the future, and maintain competitive advantage in the information age.

The **Advances in Business Information Systems and Analytics (ABISA) Book Series** aims to present diverse and timely research in the development, deployment, and management of business information systems and business analytics for continued organizational development and improved business value.

COVERAGE

- Data Strategy
- Data Analytics
- Algorithms
- Legal information systems
- Big Data
- Business Decision Making
- Performance Metrics
- Information Logistics
- Forecasting
- Business intelligence

IGI Global is currently accepting manuscripts for publication within this series. To submit a proposal for a volume in this series, please contact our Acquisition Editors at Acquisitions@igi-global.com or visit: http://www.igi-global.com/publish/.

Titles in this Series

For a list of additional titles in this series, please visit:
https://www.igi-global.com/book-series/advances-business-information-systems-analytics/37155

Smart Technology Applications in Business Environments
Tomayess Issa (Curtin University, Australia) Piet Kommers (University of Twente, The Netherlands) Theodora Issa (Curtin University, Australia) Pedro Isaías (Portuguese Open University, Portugal) and Touma B. Issa (Murdoch University, Ausralia)
Business Science Reference • ©2017 • 429pp • H/C (ISBN: 9781522524922) • US $210.00

Advanced Fashion Technology and Operations Management
Alessandra Vecchi (London College of Fashion, University of London Arts, UK)
Business Science Reference • ©2017 • 443pp • H/C (ISBN: 9781522518655) • US $200.00

Maximizing Business Performance and Efficiency Through Intelligent Systems
Om Prakash Rishi (University of Kota, India) and Anukrati Sharma (University of Kota, India)
Business Science Reference • ©2017 • 269pp • H/C (ISBN: 9781522522348) • US $175.00

Maximizing Information System Availability Through Bayesian Belief Network ...
Semir Ibrahimović (Bosna Bank International, Bosnia and Herzegovina) Lejla Turulja (University of Sarajevo, Bosnia and Herzegovina) and Nijaz Bajgorić (University of Sarajevo, Bosnia and Herzegovina)
Information Science Reference • ©2017 • 180pp • H/C (ISBN: 9781522522683) • US $140.00

Handbook of Research on Advanced Data Mining Techniques and Applications for ...
Shrawan Kumar Trivedi (BML Munjal University, India) Shubhamoy Dey (Indian Institute of Management Indore, India) Anil Kumar (BML Munjal University, India) and Tapan Kumar Panda (Jindal Global Business School, India)
Business Science Reference • ©2017 • 438pp • H/C (ISBN: 9781522520313) • US $260.00

For an enitre list of titles in this series, please visit:
https://www.igi-global.com/book-series/advances-business-information-systems-analytics/37155

701 East Chocolate Avenue, Hershey, PA 17033, USA
Tel: 717-533-8845 x100 • Fax: 717-533-8661
E-Mail: cust@igi-global.com • www.igi-global.com

Editorial Advisory Board

Sant Baba Bhag Singh, *University Village Khiala, India*
Navneet Singh, *University Village Khiala, India*
Abdellah Touhafi, *Vrije Universiteit Brussel, Belgium*
Samadi Yassir, *Mohammed V University, Morocco*
Mostapha Zbakh, *Mohamed V University, Morocco*

Table of Contents

Detailed Table of Contents

Chapter 1
Parkavi Ravi, Thiagarajar College of Engineering, India
Priyanka Chinnaiah, Thiagarajar College of Engineering, India
Sheik Adullah Abbas, Thiagarajar College of Engineering, India

Green computing, also called green equipment, is the environmentally sustainable
to use of computers and related resources like - monitors, printer, storage devices,
networking and communication systems - effectively with minimal or no impact on the
environment. Green cloud is a catchphrase that refers to the potential environmental
benefits that information technology (IT) services delivered over the Internet will
present society. The word combines the words green meaning environmentally
gracious and cloud, the traditional image for online and the shortened name for a
type of service delivery model known as cloud processing.

Chapter 2
Kijpokin Kasemsap, Suan Sunandha Rajabhat University, Thailand

This chapter reveals the overview of cloud computing; cloud computing, green
computing, green ICT, and data center utilization; the importance of cloud computing
in the digital age; the advanced issues of green computing; and the important
perspectives on green ICT. Cloud computing is computing based on the Internet.
Green computing and green ICT are the sustainable business practices of reducing
the environmental footprints of technology by efficiently using several resources.

Green computing and green ICT are the important perspectives for the businesses to improve their corporate image by meeting regulatory requirements and sustainability demands of both customers and employees. The chapter argues that cloud computing, green computing, and green ICT are the advanced technologies toward improving sustainability and sustainable development in the green economy.

Amjad Gawanmeh, Khalifa University, UAE
Ahmad Alomari, Ecole de Technologie Superieure, Canada
Alain April, Ecole de Technologie Superieure, Canada
Ali Alwadi, Auckland University of Technology, New Zealand
Sazia Parvin, University of New South Wales, Australia

The era of cloud computing allowed the instant scale up of provided services into massive capacities without the need for investing in any new on site infrastructure. Hence, the interest of this type of services has been increased, in particular, by medium scale entities who can afford to completely outsource their data-center and their infrastructure. In addition, large companies may wish to provide support for wide range of load capacities, including peak ones, however, this will require very higher costs in order to build larger data centers internally. Cloud services can provide services for these companies according to their need whether in peak load capacity of low ones. Therefore, resource sharing and provisioning is considered one of the most challenging problems in cloud based services since these services have become more numerous and dynamic. As a result, assigning tasks and services requests into available resources has become a persistent problem in cloud computing, given the large number of variables, and the increasing types of services, demand, and requirement. Scheduling services using a limited number of resources is problem that has been under study since the evolution of cloud computing. However, there are several open areas for improvements due to the large number of optimization variables. In general, the scheduling of services on available resources is considered NP complete. As a result, several heuristic based methods were proposed in order to enhance the efficiency of cloud systems. Since the problem has several optimization parameters, there are still several improvements that can be done in this area. This chapter discusses the formalization of the problem of scheduling multiple tasks by single user and multiple users, and then presents a proposed solution for each individual case. First, an algorithm is presented and evaluated for optimum schedule that allocates a number of subtasks on a given number of resources; the algorithm was shown to be linear vs. number of users. Then, an algorithm is presented to address the problem of multiple users allocations, each, with multiple subtasks. The algorithm was design using the single user allocation algorithm as a selection function. Since, this problem is known to be NP complete, heuristic based methods are usually used in order to provide better solutions. Therefore, a green evolutionary based algorithm is proposed in order to address the problem of resource allocation with large number of users. In addition, the algorithm presents allocation schedule with better utility, while the execution time is linear vs. different parameters. The results obtained in this work show that it overcomes the outcome of one of the most efficient algorithms presented in this regard that was based on game theory. Further, this method works with no restrictions on the problem parameters as opposed to game theory methods that require certain parameters restrictions on cost vector or compaction time matrix. On the other hand, the main limitation of the proposed algorithm is that it is only applicable to the scheduling problem of multiple tasks that has one price vector and one execution time vector. However, scheduling multiple users, each with subtasks that have their own price and execution time vector, is very complex problem and beyond the scope of this work, hence it will be addressed in future work.

Chapter 4
Amine Haouari, Mohammed V University, Morocco
Zbakh Mostapha, Mohammed V University, Morocco
Samadi Yassir, Mohammed V University, Morocco

In this paper, the authors present a state of art survey of cloud computing, highlighting its architectural principles, implementation as well as research directions in this increasingly important domain. They cover the different security issues that has emanated due to the nature of the service delivery models of a cloud computing system. Furthermore, in this survey the researchers highlight the concept of trust in digital environment as well as the use of containers like Docker, the block chain principle, artificial intelligence, last findings in the field of cryptography and other new concepts used in the domain of security and privacy related to cloud computing environments. They provide in the end an overview of the metrics which are mandatory in order to have a green flavor of cloud computing and the strategies that are currently used.

Chapter 5
Indira K., Thiagarajar College of Engineering, India
Thangavel M., Thiagarajar College of Engineering, India

Cloud computing is a highly scalable and cost-effective infrastructure for running HPC, enterprise and Web applications. However, the growing demand of Cloud infrastructure has drastically increased the energy consumption of data centers, which has become a critical issue. High energy consumption not only translates to high operational cost, which reduces the profit margin of Cloud providers, but also leads to high carbon emissions which is not environmentally friendly. Hence, energy-efficient solutions are required to minimize the impact of Cloud computing on the environment. Thus, in this chapter, we discuss various elements of Green Clouds which contribute to the total energy consumption. The chapter also explains the role of Green Cloud Performance metrics and Green Cloud Architecture.

Chapter 6
Thangavel M., Thiagarajar College of Engineering, India
Jeyapriya B., Thiagarajar College of Engineering, India
Suriya K. S., Thiagarajar College of Engineering, India

In recent years, computer worms are the remarkable difficulties found in the distributed computing. The location of worms turns out to be more unpredictable since they are changing quickly and much more refined. The difficulties in gathering worm's payload were recognized for identifying and gathering worm's payloads and the honey pot which is high-intelligent to gather the payload of zero-day polymorphic heterogeneous and homogeneous stages in distributed computing. The Signature-based discovery of worms strategies work with a low false-positive rate. We propose an irregularity based interruption location instrument for the cloud which specifically benefits from the virtualization advancements all in all. Our proposed abnormality location framework is detached from spreading computer worm contamination and it can recognize new computer worms. Utilizing our methodology, a spreading computer worm can be distinguished on the spreading conduct itself without getting to or straightforwardly affecting running virtual machines of the cloud.

Chapter 7
Abhishek Majumder, Tripura University, India
Samir Nath, Tripura University, India
Avijit Das, Tripura University, India

With the help of cloud computing Mobile Cloud Computing (MCC) overcomes the limitations of a mobile device such as security, performance and environment. But, security of the data stored in the cloud is a very challenging issue. Since the cloud cannot be fully trusted, data stored in the cloud is not fully secured. Integrity of the stored data is very important for the data owner. Therefore, it is a big problem to maintain the integrity of the data stored in the cloud environment. This chapter discusses existing schemes for data integrity in the mobile cloud environment. In this chapter a scheme has been proposed for enhancing data integrity in Mobile

Cloud Environment. To make integrity checking fast the size of the data file is used. It has also been shown that how fast the integrity loss can be detected if the file size is considered. Finally, the proposed scheme is compared with some of the existing scheme.

Chapter 8

Computing technology acting a very vital role in our day to day activities. Later the associated high volume of energy consumption has become a major concern every economically and environmentally. Green computing is associate rising application in computing effectively that leads to very important greenhouse gas reduction. In toughened computing has become an important half that has got to be thought of seriously by ordered generation data and communication technology designers. Green computing is to use computer and connected resources in atmosphere, friendly ways in which. Such practices embrace the implementation of energy-efficient central method unit (CPU), servers and peripheral any as finding innovative ways in which of reducing resource consumption and proper disposal of electronic waste. Many IT manufacturers and vendors endlessly invest in designing energy economical computing devices, reducing the use of dangerous material, and galvanizing the recyclability of digital devices and printing papers.

Size of the data used by enterprises has been growing at exponential rates since last few years; handling such huge data from various sources is a challenge for Businesses. In addition, Big Data becomes one of the major areas of research for Cloud Service providers due to a large amount of data produced every day, and the inefficiency of traditional algorithms and technologies to handle these large amounts of data. In order to resolve the aforementioned problems and to meet the increasing demand for high-speed and data-intensive computing, several solutions have been developed by researches and developers. Among these solutions, there are Cloud Computing tools such as Hadoop MapReduce and Apache Spark, which work on the principles of parallel computing. This chapter focuses on how big data processing challenges can be handled by using Cloud Computing frameworks and the importance of using Cloud Computing by businesses

Chapter 10

Rachid Cherkaoui, Mohammed V University, Morocco

Mostapha Zbakh, Mohammed V University, Morocco

An Braeken, Vrije Universiteit Brussel, Belgium

Abdellah Touhafi, Vrije Universiteit Brussel, Belgium

This chapter contains the state of the art of the latest security issues of cloud computing as well as security issues of internet of things (IoT) applications. It discusses the integration of IoT platforms with cloud computing services, security of the hosted data, intrusion and anomaly detection techniques used to detect attacks in virtualized networks. The chapter also discusses some of the lightweight anomaly detection techniques to use in integrated constrained devices' ecosystems with cloud computing environments. This chapter focuses on efficient integration of cloud hosting with IoT applications as well as integration of lightweight intrusion detection systems in the latter environments.

Chapter 11

Abdelghafour Harraz, Mohammed V University, Morocco

Mostapha Zbakh, Mohammed V University, Morocco

Artificial Intelligence allows to create engines that are able to explore, learn environments and therefore create policies that permit to control them in real time with no human intervention. It can be applied, through its Reinforcement Learning techniques component, using frameworks such as temporal differences, State-Action-Reward-State-Action (SARSA), Q Learning to name a few, to systems that are be perceived as a Markov Decision Process, this opens door in front of applying Reinforcement Learning to Cloud Load Balancing to be able to dispatch load dynamically to a given Cloud System. The authors will describe different techniques that can used to implement a Reinforcement Learning based engine in a cloud system.

Chapter 12

Anita Dashti, Foolad Institute of Technology, Iran

Mobile Cloud Computing (MCC) is a rich technology of mobile that offers cloud resources and network technology features like unlimited storage at any time via Ethernet or internet based on Pay-Per-Use method. In MCC all processes will be done in cloud servers and data is stored there too, thus mobile devices are just a tool for presenting events. MCC technology is completely different from previous traditional network technologies, so nowadays most impossible ways are becoming possible. MCC is a combination of cloud computing and mobile network. Being online and internet network brings some problems for users. One of the most popular challenges in this technology is building a secure architecture in mobile internet platform. Different security frameworks in different contexts of security challenges in MCC are recommended and compared in some common parameters to have better understanding of which one is the best for user's needs.

Chapter 13

The cloud computing is the term which have different services such as storage, servers, and applications which are delivered to an organization's computers and devices through the Internet for both technical and economical reasons. However they are many potential cloud users are reluctant to move to cloud computing on a large scale due to the unaddressed security issues present in cloud computing and so is increased the complexity of the infrastructures behind these services. So in this chapter, the challenges faced on both auditing and monitoring is identified. Accordingly it considers an investigation which uses to produce the major security audit issues present in cloud computing today based on a framework for security subsystems. To overcome the standards of auditing and process of auditing is briefly explained. There are also many platforms that provide cloud services also those domains are listed out with domain based monitoring process.

Trust relationships among multiple Cloud Service Providers is a concept in which multiple cloud service providers from multiple distributed Identity Provider can access resources of each other, only if they are trusted with their Identity Provider. In this chapter a scheme has been proposed to enhance the security of data in a multi-cloud environment by improving trust relationships among multiple clouds. The scheme is also designed to overcome interoperability problem between different clouds. In the proposed scheme concept of proxy is used. Client organization tries to communicate with multiple cloud service providers through proxy. Client organization send resource request to cloud service providers. On receiving the resource request the cloud service provider collect the authentication confirmation from proxy. Then it sends the reply and data to requested client organization. Numerical analysis and comparative study of the proposed scheme with some of the existing scheme has been carried out.

Foreword

Cloud Computing has emerged as a pervasive and consumer drive utility that is attracting a great interest from entrepreneurs, innovators and technology experts, as well as the 'connected' general public at large. Backed by the industry, Cloud Computing has become a useful paradigm for the financial and commercial sectors. Whereas, general public are moving from the traditional Information and Communication Technologies (ICT) to social media and mobile-based technologies, Industry are moving towards distributed computing based on virtualisation, networked grids and cluster technologies. The core benefits that Cloud paradigm is promising, is in terms of 24x7 availability of IT-related resources as and when required; scalability of enterprise applications; virtualisation of IT-related environments; and multi-tenancy of cloud-based infrastructures of varied varieties. For the business enterprises, in particular, Cloud technologies provide facilities and resources to process Bid Data to conduct Data Analytics to gain Business Intelligence to support timely decision making at the corporate level. Cloud related technologies are really proving to be the silver bullet.

Cloud paradigm is, in fact, also providing the foundation for many new developments for various sectors of the society - including commerce, education, health, and banking. One area where cloud-related technologies are being adopted is in the development and maintenance of Green Environments, including Green Enterprises and Green Enterprise Communities – where the ethos is that of usability, and preservation of resources including the environment. Here, *Green* refers to systems that are autonomic, self-developing, eco-friendly, and self-sustainable. Technologies are readily available; what is needed is the will and commitment; and further research and innovation. Developments of Digital Smart Cities, Smart Grids, and, in general, Smart Living are just some aspects of the Green Developments.

In the context of Green Enterprises, this book addresses the areas of technologies that underpin the associated developments, presents the case studies, and discusses the state of the art in terms of frameworks, methodologies, current practices, and future directions. This book is a useful source of information for enterprise architects, managers and directors of organisations, as well as students and researchers in the fields of Cloud Computing and Green Technologies. The book provides a thorough and timely investigation of the convergence of Cloud related technologies and Green technologies. It is a welcome addition to the existing body of knowledge in these fields and the new emerging technologies.

Professor Zaigham Mahmood
Debesis Education, UK
June 2017

Zaigham Mahmood is a researcher and published author/editor of 22 books on distributed computing including subjects such as Cloud Computing, Big Data, Software Engineering, Smart Cities, and E-Government (www.amazon.co.uk/Zaigham-Mahmood/e/B00B29OIK6). He holds positions as Professor Extraordinaire at the NW University, S Africa; Professor at Shijiazhuang Tiedao University, China; and as Foreign Professor at IIUI and NUST in Islamabad, Pakistan. He is currently a Senior Consultant in Teaching and Learning with Debesis Education in Derby, UK.

Preface

Cloud Computing has become a scalable services consumption and delivery platform in the field of Services Computing. The technical foundations of Cloud Computing include Service-Oriented Architecture (SOA) and Virtualizations of hardware and software. The goal of Cloud Computing is to share resources among the cloud service consumers, cloud partners, and cloud vendors in the cloud value chain.

According to the Research and Markets' Global Security Services Market 2015-2019 report, the market for security products and services is growing globally and demand for cloud-based security is leading the charge. In fact, the Cloud Security Market report by Markets and Markets predicts the market size at nearly $9 billion by 2019. Cloud computing helps enterprises transform business and technology. Companies have begun to look for solutions that would help reduce their infrastructures costs and improve profitability.

This book aims to bring together researchers and practitioners in all security aspects of cloud computing. This book project is set up to provide a platform for the researchers in cloud computing community to publish and report the recent advances in cloud computing technologies and services.

OBJECTIVES

The major objectives include the followings:

- Provide a snapshot on research advances of cloud computing Technologies for Green Enterprises.
- Discuss issues, solutions, challenges, and needs in securing cloud computing environment.
- Report secure cloud engineering experience and lessons as well as industry case studies.

TARGET AUDIENCE

Policy makers, academicians, researchers, advanced-level students, technology developers, and government officials will find this text useful in furthering their research exposure to pertinent topics in Cloud Computing Technologies for Green Enterprises and assisting in furthering their own research efforts in this field.

APPROACH

This book incorporates the concepts of cloud computing technologies as well as design techniques, architecture and application areas. It also addresses advanced security issues such as digital forensic, big data, access control and fault tolerance etc. The chapters are organized as follows:

Chapter 1, "Cloud Computing Technologies for Green Enterprises: Fundamentals of Cloud Computing for Green Enterprises," presents different approaches to green computing which includes recent trends framework and security implementation for green cloud.

Chapter 2, "Cloud Computing, Green Computing, and Green ICT," explained the overview of cloud computing; cloud computing, green computing, green ICT, and data center utilization; the importance of cloud computing in the digital age; the advanced issues of green computing; and the important perspectives on green ICT.

Chapter 3, "Green Evolutionary-Based Algorithm for Multiple Services Scheduling in Cloud Computing," presents a green computing scheduling method to solve the problem of resource allocation in which cloud services requesting the usage of resources across a cloud-based network, where the cost of computational service depends on the amount of computation.

Chapter 4, "Current State Survey and Future Opportunities for Trust and Security in Green Cloud Computing," discussed advantages in using a cloud-based system, practical problems which have to be solved and what should be done to have a green secure flavor in a computing environment.

Chapter 5, "Green Cloud Computing," discussed various elements of Green Clouds which contribute to the total energy consumption. The chapter also explains the role of Green Cloud Performance metrics and Green Cloud Architecture.

Chapter 6, "Detection of Worms Over Cloud Environment: A Literature Survey," presents that it is conceivable to utilize highlights offered by virtual machine reflection to identify and to contain the spreading of computer worms. This chapter also distinguished difficulties confronting current methodologies amid gathering polymorphic computer worms in distributed computing.

Chapter 7, "Data Integrity in Mobile Cloud Computing," discusses a mechanism to ensure the data integrity as well as the confidentiality of the user's data stored in cloud in MCC environment.

Chapter 8, "Cloud Computing Technologies for Green Enterprises," presents Green IT practices—including exciting new efforts within the major space of knowledge center power utilization, and implementation of these programs.

Chapter 9, "Big Data Processing on Cloud Computing Using Hadoop Mapreduce and Apache Spark," presents surveys on the state-of-the-art of Big Data and Cloud Computing, covering their essential concepts, prominent characteristics, key technologies as well as the issues and challenges of Big Data and solutions by using Cloud computational frameworks Hadoop Mapreduce and Apache Spark.

Chapter 10, "Anomaly Detection in Cloud Computing and Internet of Things Environments: Latest Technologies," presents lightweight intrusion detection and prevention systems and techniques to minimize the risks of getting hacked especially in critical systems.

Chapter 11, "Cloud Load Balancing and Reinforcement Learning," presents what Reinforcement Learning is, and propose a handful of different implementations that were studied throughout the literature to achieve control over systems that present the same symptoms as the problem of load balancing in cloud.

Chapter 12, "Mobile Cloud Computing Security Frameworks: A Review," discussed MCC and security issues in all parts, from infrastructure to front end, and other user concerns for using MCC resources.

Chapter 13, "Monitoring and Auditing in the Cloud," described the main platforms and services for Cloud monitoring, indicating how they relate with such properties and issues.

Chapter 14, "Trust Relationship Establishment Among Multiple Cloud Service Provider," proposes a proxy-based trust relationship establishment technique to overcome the problem of pre-agreement in federated cloud environment.

Acknowledgment

We extend our thanks to the many people who contributed to the preparation of this book. In particular, we heartily thanks all the contributing authors. We greatly appreciate reviewers for their helpful and insightful comments, thorough technical reviews, constructive criticisms, and many valuable suggestions.

We are indebted to the management and staff of IGI Global for their valuable contribution, suggestions, recommendations, and encouragements from inception of initial ideas to the final publication of the book. In particular, we would like to thanks Allison McGinniss for her initial contributions and support. And most importantly, we are grateful to Maria Rohde for the great help received from her throughout the final stages.

Deep appreciation goes to Dr. Zaigham Mahmood for providing us with constructive and comprehensive foreword.

The editors wish to acknowledge University of Hafr Al-Batin, Saudi Arabia for their support in providing the various facilities utilized in the process of production of this book.

This work was supported by Deanship of Scientific Research program of University of Hafr Al-Batin, Saudi Arabia.

Kashif Munir
University of Hafr Al-Batin, Saudi Arabia

Chapter 1
Cloud Computing Technologies for Green Enterprises:
Fundamentals of Cloud Computing for Green Enterprises

Parkavi Ravi
Thiagarajar College of Engineering, India

Priyanka Chinnaiah
Thiagarajar College of Engineering, India

Sheik Adullah Abbas
Thiagarajar College of Engineering, India

ABSTRACT

Green computing, also called green equipment, is the environmentally sustainable to use of computers and related resources like - monitors, printer, storage devices, networking and communication systems - effectively with minimal or no impact on the environment. Green cloud is a catchphrase that refers to the potential environmental benefits that information technology (IT) services delivered over the Internet will present society. The word combines the words green meaning environmentally gracious and cloud, the traditional image for online and the shortened name for a type of service delivery model known as cloud processing.

DOI: 10.4018/978-1-5225-3038-1.ch001

INTRODUCTION

Green Enterprise Computing refers to how business or corporate sectors can deal with the vision of Green computing to manage power utilization and boost energy efficiency. Green Computing or Green IT is the study and practice of using computing resources in an ecological manner to tone down the environmental impacts of computing. All these, in turn, bring up the issue of reducing immoral use of resource and power Green computing whose goals are to reduce the use of perilous materials, maximize energy efficiency during the product's lifetime, and promote the recoverability or biodegradability of redundant products and factory waste. Computers today not only used in offices but also at homes. This can be called as Green Computing. We use Green Computing because it reduced energy usage from green computing techniques translates into lower carbon dioxide emissions, stemming from a decline in the fossil fuel used in power plants and transportation, Conserving resources means less energy is required to produce, use, and order of products, saving energy and resources saves money. Green computing even includes changing government policy to promote recycling and lowering energy use by individuals and businesses.

Green Cloud computing can be used to manage efficient processing and utilization of computing infrastructure and reduce energy consumption. It is needed for ensuring that the future development of Cloud computing is supportable else, cloud computing with growing front-end client devices interacting with back-end data centers will begin a huge escalation of energy usage. Green Computing is also defined as designing, manufacturing/engineering, using and disposing of computing devices in a way that reduces their environmental impact. IT department is usually always the one department that uses the majority amount of power which in turn is an unnecessary amount of "Green computing" represents environmentally responsible way to reduce power and ecological e-waste. Virtualization, Green Data Centre, Cloud computing, grid computing, Power optimization are the technologies of green computing. Main goals of green computing are to condense the use of poisonous and hazards materials and progress the energy efficiency, recycling of factory waste. Cloud Computing is a model for delivering services in which resources are retrieved from the internet through web-based tools and applications, rather than a shortest connection to a server. Data is stored in servers. Cloud computing structure allows access to information as long as an electronic device has access to the web. This type of system allows human resources to work distantly. It enables hosting of applications from consumer, scientific and business domains. But data centers hosting cloud computing applications consume enormous amounts of energy, causal to high operational costs and carbon footprints to the environment. With energy shortages and global climate modify leading our concerns these days; the power consumption of data center has become a key issue. Therefore, green cloud computing solutions saves energy as well as reduces operational costs. The vision for power resourceful management of cloud computing environments. Such practice expert implementation of server and peripherals as well as decrease the power consumption. It shows how to use resources proficiently and how to reduce the waste Green computing is the requirement to save the energy with the operating cost.

GREEN COMPUTING

Green computing is the ecological use of computers and correlated resources. Such practices include the execution of energy-efficient central processing units, servers, peripherals as well as reduced resource expenditure and proper disposal of electronic waste. Green computing is a study and practice of designing, industrialized, using, and disposing of computers, servers, and associated subsystems such as monitors, printers, storage devices, and networking and interactions systems resourcefully and efficiently with minimal or no impact on the environment." The goals of green computing are similar to green chemistry; reduce the use of hazardous materials, make the most of energy efficiency during the product's lifetime, and promote the recyclability or bidegradability of defunct products and factory waste. Research continues into key areas such as making the use of computers as energy-efficient as possible, and designing algorithms and systems for efficiency-related computer technologies.

There are several approaches to green computing namely

- Algorithmic efficiency
- Resource allocation
- Virtualization
- Power management

NEED OF GREEN COMPUTING IN CLOUDS

Modern data centers, in service under the Cloud computing model are hosting a multiplicity of applications ranging from those that run for a few seconds to those that run for longer periods of time on collective hardware platforms. The need to manage multiple applications in a data center creates the challenge of on-demand reserve provisioning and allocation in response to time-varying workloads. Normally, data center capitals are statically allocated to applications, based on peak load characteristics, in order to maintain isolation and provide performance guarantees. Recently, high performance has been the individual concern in data center deployments and this require has been fulfilled without paying much deliberation to energy consumption. The average data center exhaust as much energy as 25,000 households. As energy costs are increasing while availability dwindles, there is a need to shift focus from optimizing data center resource management for sterilized performance to optimizing for energy efficiency while maintaining high service level performance.

Data centers are not only luxurious to maintain, but also unsociable to the environment. Data centers now drive more in carbon emissions than both Argentina and the Netherlands. High energy costs and huge carbon footprints are incurred due to huge amounts of electricity needed to power and cool numerous servers hosted in these data centers. Cloud service providers need to adopt measures to ensure that their profit margin is not considerably reduced due to high energy costs. For instance, Google, Microsoft, and Yahoo are building large data centers in unproductive desert land s the Columbia River, USA to exploit cheap and reliable hydroelectric power.

Lowering the energy convention of data centers is a demanding and composite issue because computing applications and data are increasing so quickly that progressively larger servers and disks are desirable to process them fast enough within the essential time period. Green Cloud computing is envisioned to achieve not only well-organized processing and utilization of computing infrastructure, but also minimize energy utilization. This is essential for ensuring that the future growth of Cloud computing is sustainable. Otherwise, Cloud computing with increasingly persistent front-end client devices interacting with back-end data centers will cause an huge acceleration of energy usage.

To address this problem, data center resources need to be managed in an energy well-organized manner to drive Green Cloud computing. In particular, Cloud resources need to be allocated not only to satisfy QoS requirements specific by users via Service Level Agreements (SLA), but also to decrease energy usage.

GREEN CLOUD SERVICES

- **Infrastructure as a Service (IaaS):** "Infrastructure as a Service (IaaS)", delivers computer infrastructure – A platform virtualization environment - as a service. Rather than purchasing servers, software, data-center space or network tackle, clients instead as a fully outsourced service.
- **Desktop as a Service (DaaS):** With DaaS, deployment and management of the desktop environment is beginner's. Data and applications are accessed from beginning to end a virtual environment, allowing businesses and providers to support, patch and maintain one environment rather than

managing personage desktops during an organization. And, with one central environment, data is more secure while still allowing users the elasticity to choose between working on desktop or mobile devices.

- **Software as a Service (SaaS):** "Software as a Service (SaaS), sometimes referred to as "software on demand," is software that is deployed over the internet and/or is deployed to run behind a firewall on a local area network or personal computer.
- **Disaster Recovery as a Service (DRaaS):** Serve Restore, our cloud disaster recovery solution for on-premise physical servers, is often called our better than backup solution. With Serve Restore, our engineers prebuilt a fully designed virtual environment for your data. When disaster strikes, we fully manage the recovery of your servers, construct them to run within our cloud environment in just a combine of hours.
- **Backup as a Service (BaaS):** Green Clouds backup solution powered provides a remote, secure, cloud based storage destination for obtainable server infrastructures.

ENERGY SAVINGS IN THE CLOUD

Here are some of the ways that the cloud can help a corporation cut its carbon footprint down to size:

- **Fewer Machines:** With the cloud, server deployment rates are typically 60-70%, while in many small business and industry environments, exploitation rates hover around 5 or 10%. As a result, shared data centers can employ small number machines to get the same capacity.
- **Equipment Efficiency:** Larger data centers frequently have the resources to allow them to improve to energy-saving equipment and building systems. Usually, this is not an option in smaller organizations where this good organization is not the focus.
- **Consolidated Climate Control Costs:** In order for a server to run at its the highest point performance, its temperature and humidity level must be suspiciously controlled, and cloud providers can use high density efficient layouts that are unbreakable for in-house centers to reproduce.
- **Dynamically Allocated Resources:** In-house data centers need extra servers to handle peak data loads, and cloud providers can enthusiastically allocate resources where fundamental in order for fewer machines to sit idle. Cloud computing has massive potential to transform the world of IT: reducing costs, improving efficiency and business agility, and s to a more sustainable world.

There are basically four main entities involved in the Green Cloud Computing Environment:

1. **Consumers:** Cloud consumers suggest service requirements from anywhere in the world to the Cloud. It is main to notice that there can be a difference between Cloud consumers and users of deployed services. For occurrence, a consumer can be a company deploying a Web application, which presents unreliable workload according to the number of users accessing it.

2. **Green Resource Allocator:** Acts as the interface between the Cloud infrastructure and consumers. It requires the communication of the following components to support energy-well-organized resource management:

    a. **Green Negotiator:** Negotiates with the consumers/brokers to complete the SLA with specified prices and penalties (for violations of SLA) between the Cloud provider and consumer depending on the consumer's QoS requirements and energy reduction schemes. In case of Web applications, for illustration, QoS metric can be 95% of requirements being served in less than 3 seconds.

    b. **Service Analyzer:** Interprets and analyses the service requirements of a submitted request before deciding whether to accept or reject it. Hence, it needs the most modern load and energy information from VM Manager and Energy Monitor respectively.

    c. **Consumer Profiler:** Gathers specific characteristics of customers so that important clients can be granted particular privileges and prioritized over other clients.

    d. **Pricing:** Decides how service requests are charged to manage the supply and demand of computing resources and facilitate in prioritizing service allocations effectively.

    e. **Energy Monitor:** Study and resolve which physical machines to power on/off.

    f. **Service Scheduler:** Assigns requests to VMs and determines resource privilege for allocated VMs. It also decides when VMs are to be added or uninvolved to meet demand.

    g. **VM Manager:** Keeps track of the availability of VMs and their resource privilege. It is also in charge of migrating VMs across physical machines.

    h. **6. Accounting:** Maintains the actual usage of resources by requests to compute usage costs. Historical usage information can also be used to improve service allocation decisions.

3. **VMs:** Multiple VMs can be enthusiastically started and stopped on a single physical machine to meet accepted requests, hence providing maximum flexibility to construct various partitions of resources on the same physical machine to different explicit requirements of service requests. Multiple VMs can also parallel run applications based on different operating system environments on a single physical machine. In addition, by dynamically migrating VMs crosswise physical machines, workloads can be consolidated and unexploited resources can be put on a low-power state, turned off or construct to operate at low-performance levels (e.g., using DVFS) in order to save energy.

4. **Physical Machines:** The underlying physical computing servers present hardware infrastructure for creating virtualized resources to meet service demands.

CLOUD COMPUTING MORE GREEN ENTERPRISES

Three approaches have been tried out to build cloud computing environments more environmental friendly. These approaches have been tried out in the data centers under experimental conditions. The methods are:

- **Dynamic Voltage Frequency Scaling Technique (DVFS):** Each electronic circuitry will have an operating clock related with it. The operating frequency of this clock is familiar so that the supply voltage is synchronized. Thus, this method heavily depends on the hardware and is not convenient according to the unreliable needs. The power savings are also low compared to other approaches. The power savings to cost acquire ratio is also low.
- **Resource Allocation or Virtual Machine Migration Techniques:** In a cloud computing environment, each physical machine hosts a number of virtual machines engaging which the applications are run. These virtual machines can be transferred across the hosts according to the varying needs and accessible resources. The VM migration method focuses on transferring VMs in such a way that the power increase is least. The most power well-organized nodes are selected and the VMs are transformed across to them. This method is dealt in detail later.
- **Algorithmic Approaches:** It has been experimentally resolute that an ideal server consumes about 70% of the power utilized by a fully utilized server.

Using a neural network interpreter, the green scheduling algorithms first estimates required dynamic workload on the servers. Then preventable servers are turned off in order to minimize the number of running servers, thus minimizing the energy use at the points of utilization to present benefits to all other levels. Also, several servers are added to help reassure service-level agreement. The bottom line is to protect the environment and to condense the total cost of ownership while ensuring quality of service.

VM Migration

The problem of VM distribution can be divided in two: the first part is admission of new requests for VM provisioning and placing the VMs on hosts, whereas the second part is optimization of current allocation of VMs.

Optimization of present allocation of VMs is carried out in two steps: at the first step, we select VMs that need to be migrated, at the second step chosen VMs are located on hosts using MBFD algorithm. We propose four analytical methods for choosing VMs to migrate. The first methodical, Single Threshold (ST), is based on the idea of setting upper utilization threshold for hosts and placing VMs while maintenance the total utilization of CPU below this threshold. The aim is to preserve free resources to prevent SLA violation due to consolidation in cases when exploitation by VMs increases. At each time frame all VMs are reallocated using MBFD algorithm with further condition of keeping the upper utilization threshold not violated. The new placement is achieved by live migration of VMs.

The other three analytical are based on the idea of setting upper and lower utilization thresholds for hosts and maintenance total utilization of CPU by all VMs between these thresholds. If the utilization of CPU for a host goes less than the lower threshold, all VMs have to be migrated from this host and the host has to be switched off in order to remove the idle power consumption. If the utilization goes over the upper threshold, some VMs have to be migrated from the host to reduce exploitation in order to prevent probable SLA violation. We propose three policies for choosing VMs that have to be migrated from the host.

- **Minimization of Migrations (MM):** Migrating the smallest number of VMs to minimize migration in the clouds.
- **Highest Potential Growth (HPG):** Migrating VMs that have the lowest usage of CPU reasonable to the requested in order to minimize total potential increase of the utilization and SLA violation.
- **Random Choice (RC):** Choosing the essential number of VMs by alternative them according to a uniformly distributed random variable.

FEATURES OF CLOUDS ENABLING GREEN COMPUTING

Cloud Infrastructure has developed to a key environmental disquiet keeping in view of energy consumption and carbon production. The key technology for power efficient Clouds is "Virtualization", development of presenting a logical grouping or subset of computing resources so that they can be accessed in ways that give benefits over the unusual configuration.

The following are the four key factors that have enabled the Cloud Computing to lower power usage and carbon radiation from ICT. In this way, organizations can reduce carbon radiation at last 30% per user by moving their applications to the cloud.

1. **Dynamic Provisioning:** In long-established settings, IT companies end up deploying far more infrastructure than desired. It is very difficult to forecast the demand at a time and to warranty availability of services and to maintain confident level of service quality to end users. The virtual machines in a Cloud infrastructure can be live migrated to another host in case user application requires more property. Cloud providers observe and expect the demand and thus allocate resources according to demand. Those applications that require less number of resources can be consolidated on the same server. Thus, datacenters always continue the active servers according to current demand, which results in low energy consumption than the traditional approach of over-provisioning.

2. **Multi-Tenancy:** Cloud computing infrastructure reduces on the whole energy usage and associated carbon emissions. The SaaS providers serve multiple companies on same infrastructure and software. This approach is obviously more energy efficient than multiple copies of software installed on different infrastructure, which can minimize the need for extra infrastructure. The smaller variation in demand results in better prediction and results in greater energy savings.

3. **Server Utilization:** Using virtualization technologies, several applications can be hosted and executed on the same server in separation, thus lead to utilization levels up to 70%. Even though high exploitation of servers results in more power consumption, server running at higher operation can process more workload with similar power usage.

4. **Datacenter Efficiency:** The power efficiency of datacenters has main impact on the total energy usage of Cloud computing. By using the most energy well-organized technologies, Cloud providers can considerably improve the Power Usage Effectiveness (PUE) of their datacenters. Cloud computing grant services to be moved involving multiple datacenter which are running with better PUE values. This is achieved by using high speed network, virtualized services and dimension, and monitoring and accounting of datacenter.

APPROACHES TO GREEN COMPUTING

Green Data Center

Practical requirement of data centers are as follows:

- Provide a physical secure position for server.
- Should provide all-time network connectivity in data center.
- Should provide essential power to operate all equipment.

Characteristics:

- Design must be simple.
- Design must be scalable.

The design should be scalable because once it is finalized it must work for any size of computer center:

- Design must be modular.
- Design must be flexible.

Virtualization

Virtualization, a term that used a variety of techniques, methods or approaches to create a virtual environment, such as a virtual hardware platform, virtual operating system (OS), storage device, or network resources.

Challenges

Complexities of licensing are the issue with virtualization. For instance, a Linux based server offers a virtualized windows server must satisfy licensing requirements. Because of this licensing issue flexibility of virtualization and benefits of on demand virtualization is in a weak position. Some venders of proprietary software have attempted to update licensing scheme to address the virtualization but flexibility and cost issues are opposing requirements. Virtualized desktop results in trust on centralized servers (for computing and SAN storage) and the network (and higher-bandwidth requirements). Dependency on centralized server and network leaves the end users vulnerable to server. The user able to operating locally through an outage, but when user logs off or reboots the machine it become dead This is in contrast with thick clients where the user locally operates continually until the connectivity can be restored:

1. **Product Longevity:** Gartner maintains that the PC developed process accounts for 70% of the natural resources used in the life cycle of a PC. Therefore, the biggest involvement to green computing usually is to broaden the equipment's lifetime. Another report from Gartner recommends to "Looking for product longevity, including upgradability and modularity. "For instance, manufacturing a new PC makes a far bigger environmental footprint than manufacturing a new RAM module to improve an existing one.

2. **Data Center Design:** Data center services are heavy consumers of energy. The U.S. Department of Energy estimates that data center services consume up to 100 to 200 times more energy than standard office buildings. According to the U.S. Department of Energy, Information technology (IT) systems, Environmental settings, Air management, Cooling systems and Electrical systems are the primary areas on which to focus energy proficient data center design best practices.

3. **Software and Deployment Optimization:** It includes algorithmic effectiveness, resource allocation, workstation servers and virtualization. The efficiency of algorithms has an impact on the amount of computer resources essential for any known computing function and there are many efficiency trade-offs in writing programs. Allocating resources according to the energy can be saved. With virtualization, a system administrator could merge a number of physical systems into virtual machines on one single, powerful system, by this means unplugging the original hardware and dropping power and cooling disbursement. Virtualization should be able to support distributing work so that servers are either busy or put in a low-power sleep state. Terminal servers have also been used in green computing. When using the system, users at a terminal connect to a central server; all of the authentic computing is done on the server, but the end user experiences the operating system on the terminal. These can be combined with thin clients, who use up to 1/8 the amount of energy of a common workstation, resulting in a decrease of energy costs and consumption.

4. **Power Management:** The Advanced design and Power Interface (ACPI), an open industry standard, allows an operating system to straight control the power-saving aspects of its fundamental hardware. This allows a system to automatically revolve off components such as monitors and hard drives after set periods of inactivity. In addition, a system may hibernate, when most components (including the CPU and the system RAM) are turned off. ACPI is a successor to an previous Intel-Microsoft standard called Advanced Power Management, which allows a computer's BIOS to control power management functions. Some

programs allow the user to physically adjust the voltages complete to the CPU, which reduces both the amount of heat produced and electricity consumed. This process is called under volt. Some CPUs can automatically under volt the processor, depending on the workload; this technology is called "SpeedStep" on Intel processors.

5. **Materials Recycling:** Recycling computing tools can keep destructive materials such as lead, mercury, and hexavalent chromium out of landfills, and can also replace equipment that otherwise would need to be pretend, saving further energy and emissions.

6. **Telecommuting:** Teleconferencing and telepresence technologies are often implemented in green computing resources. The advantages are many; improved worker satisfaction, decrease of greenhouse gas emissions related to travel, and increased income margins, resulting from lower overhead costs for office space, heat, lighting, etc.

7. **Telecommunication Network Devices Energy Indices:** The energy expenditure of information and communication technologies (ICTs) is today important even when compared with other industries. Recently some study tried to identify the key energy index that allows a relevant comparison between different devices (network elements). This analysis was focus on how to optimize device and network consumption for carrier telecommunication by itself. The target was to allow an immediate observation of the relationship between the arrangement technology and the environmental impact.

Need of Virtualization for Green Computing

Cloud computing cannot be always appropriate for ecology. The recent studies confirmed that rely on a server is in the main more environmentally friendly, although care must be taken to a entire sequence of parameters to compute the best real efficiency of the cloud. In other words, the data centers force on real environment by producing heat. It is also important to keep in mind that a data center has a more environmental collision than a system. The research was based on setups those include virtualization and without virtualization. It is found that on-site server with no virtualization will emit about 46kg of CO_2 per year. If data is stored on the public cloud whose servers are not that well-organized, those servers are not well used and use electricity from higher carbon-emitting sources. Thus, there will be some practices by which servers can be run with greener solutions. Also, studies also proved that cloud systems are more energy capable and carbon efficient than that of an ordinary system. It consists of a concept of use of virtualization. And thus, virtualization is critical to cloud computing. It simplifies the delivery of services by provided that a platform for optimizing complex IT resources in a scalable manner. That makes cloud computing so cost effective. In cloud computing it needs to support many different service environments, to manage the various aspects of virtualization in cloud computing most companies use hypervisors. A hypervisor, also called a virtual machine manager (VMM), is a program that allows multiple operating systems to share a on its own hardware host. Each operating system appears to have the host's processor, memory, and other property all to itself. However, the hypervisor is scheming the host processor and resources, allocating what is needed to each operating system in turn and making sure that the guest operating systems (called virtual machines) cannot disrupt each other. The hypervisors can support different operating system environment hence, the hypervisor becomes a perfect delivery mechanism by allowing you to show the similar application on lots of different systems. Because hypervisors can load multiple operating systems, they are a very practical way of getting things virtualized rapidly and efficiently.

Discussion on How Virtualization Works as in the Green Cloud Computing

Let's discuss about how virtualization makes cloud green or eco-friendly. We know, the data center consumes the power as enormous as that can be used to power thousands of homes. The environmentalists and computer scientists are working on reducing the huge amount of power used and make data centers additional energy-efficient than they currently are. The virtualization can be the solution for it. It can be used to decrease power consumption by data centers. The main purpose of the virtualization is that to make the most efficient use of available system possessions, including energy. A data center, installing virtual infrastructure allows several operating systems and applications to run on a lesser number of servers, it can help to reduce the in the main energy used for the data center and the energy consumed for its cooling. Once the number of servers is reduced, it also means that data center can decrease the building size as well. Some of the advantages of Virtualization which directly brunt efficiency and contributes to the environment include: Workload balancing across servers, Resource allocation and distribution are better monitored and managed and the Server utilization rates can be increased up to 80% as compared to initial 10-15%. The energy saved per server would be near about 7000 KWH per year. It means that there would be large saving of energy.

Green Computing Techniques to Manage Power in Computing System

These techniques can be classified at different levels:

1. Hardware and Firmware Level
2. Operating System Level
3. Virtualization Level
4. Data Center Level

Hardware and Firmware level techniques are applied at the developed time of a machine. These techniques control all the optimization methods that are applied at the time of scheming at the logic, circuit, architectural and organization levels. Operating System level techniques include methods which take care with reference to programs at operator level. Virtualization level techniques used the perception of Virtual Machines (VMs) to manage power. In this number of VM are created on a physical server, so that reduce the amount of hardware in use and improve the utilization of resources. Data Center level techniques are practical at data centers and embrace methods which are used to manage workload across physical nodes in data centers.

Adoption of Green Computing Practices

With the digital development, the IT industry has focused on the increase and use of IT products and services to satisfy the raising demands of business consumers. Due to this the following factors are impacting the IT industry and coercing the acceptance of Green Computing practices:

1. Rapid growth in the size and scale of data centers
2. Advancement in CPUs
3. Energy Cost
4. Server utilization
5. Impact on the environment.

Framework for Green Cloud Computing

Green cloud computing frameworks to supply energy capable services to the cloud users. There are mainly four components as described below:

1. **Users/Brokers:** At topmost layer the cloud users/brokers demand for services from anywhere around the world. APIs provides the capacity to store VM images and source files for web server mechanism.
2. **Green Service Request Manager:** It provides a crossing point between the cloud users and cloud infrastructure. It handles all the requests generated by

the cloud users and supports the energy efficient resources. It also uses various scheduling schemes for distribution of virtual machines.

3. **Virtual Machines:** Commonly known as Virtual appliances it includes software to create and deploy the applications. VMs are used to handle the service requests at the virtual machine layer.

4. **Physical Machines:** The lowest layer exhibits the physical objects or resource instances to map the services to particular machine so that the calculation of the particular task can be performed.

GREEN CLOUD COMPUTING BENCHMARKS

With the advancement of technology, where the cloud computing resources are being remotely controlled by the service providers It is necessary to provide the energy efficient services while maintaining the cost. To keep such performance tradeoffs various benchmarks were introduced previously to measure the rate of power consumption, energy efficiency, resource utilization etc. at the level of system, data centre and server. These benchmarks are listed with their brief formulation, level of usage and application discipline in Table.

VM MIGRATION

The problem of VM allocation can be divided in two: the first part is access of new requests for VM provisioning and insertion the VMs on hosts, whereas the second part is optimization of present allocation of VMs.

Optimization of current allocation of VMs is carried out in two steps: at the first step, we select VMs that require to be migrated, at the second step chosen VMs are located on hosts using MBFD algorithm. We propose four heuristics for choosing VMs to migrate. The first heuristic, Single Threshold (ST), is based on the idea of location upper consumption threshold for hosts and placing VMs while maintenance the total exploitation of CPU below this threshold. The aim is to protect free resources to prevent SLA destruction due to consolidation in cases when utilization by VMs increases. At each instance frame all VMs are reallocated using MBFD algorithm with extra condition of keeping the upper exploitation threshold not violated. The new assignment is realized by live migration of VMs.

The other three heuristics are based on the idea of setting upper and lower consumption thresholds for hosts and maintain total utilization of CPU by all VMs connecting these thresholds. If the utilization of CPU for a host goes under the lower threshold, all VMs have to be migrated starting this host and the host has to be switched off in order to remove the idle power consumption. If the utilization goes over the upper threshold, some VMs contain to be migrated from the host to reduce exploitation in order to check potential SLA violation. We propose three policies for choosing VMs that have to be migrated from the host.

- **Minimization of Migrations (MM):** Migrating the smallest amount of number of VMs to minimize migration overhead.
- **Highest Potential Growth (HPG):** Migrating VMs that have the lowest usage of CPU moderately to the requested in order to minimize total potential increase of the exploitation and SLA violation.
- **Random Choice (RC):** Choosing the required number of VMs by selection them according to a uniformly distributed random variable.

RECENT IMPLEMENTATIONS OF GREE COMPUTING

Blackle

Is a search-engine site motorized by Google Search. Blackle came into individual based on the concept that when a computer screen is white home, your computer exhausts 74W. When the screen is black it consumes only 59W. Based on this theory if each person switched from Google to Blackle, mother earth would save 750MW each year was a really good implementation of Green Computing. The principle behind Blackle is based on the information that the display of different colors consumes different amounts of energy on computer monitors.

Fit-PC

A tiny PC that draws only 5w: Fit-PC is the size of a book and extremely silent, yet fit sufficient to run Windows XP or Linux.fit-PC is projected to fit where a standard PC is too bulky, noisy and power hungry. you ever wished for a PC to be compact, quiet and green then fit- PC is the perfect fit for you. Fit-PC draws only5 Watts, consuming in a day less power than a conventional PC expend sin 1 hour. You can leave fit-PC to work 24/7 without making a dent in your electric.

Zonbu Computer

The Zonbu is a new, very energy well-organized PC. The Zonbu consumes just one third of the power of a distinctive light bulb. The tool runs the Linux operating system using a 1.2 gigahertz processor and 512 megs of RAM. It also contains no moving parts, and does even surround a fan. You can get one for as little as US$99, but it does involve to sign up for a two-year subscription

Sunray Thin Client

Sun Microsystems is exposure increased customer attention in its Sun Ray, a thin desktop client, as electricity prices scale, according to Subodh Bapat, vice president and chief engineer in the Eco liability office at Sun. Thin clients like the Sun Ray consume far less electricity than predictable desktops, he said. A Sun Ray on a desktop consumes 4 to 8 watts of power, because most of the important computation is performed by a server. Sun says Sunrays are mainly well suited for cost-sensitive environments such as call centers, education, healthcare, service providers, and finance. PCs have more controlling processors as well as hard drives, something thin clients don't have. Thus, expected PCs always consume a significantly larger amount of power. In the United States, desktops need to consume 50 watts or less in idle mode to succeed for new rigorous Energy Star certification

The Asus Eee PC and Other Ultra Portables

The "ultra-portable" class of personal computers is characterized by a small size, practically low power CPU, compact screen, low cost and innovations such as using flash memory for storage rather than hard drives with revolving platters. These factors combine to enable them to run more professionally and use less power than a standard form factor laptop. The Asus Eee PC is one example of an ultraportable. It is the size of a book, weighs less than a kilogram, has built-in Wi-Fi and uses flash memory as a substitute of a hard drive. It runs Linux too.

RESOURCE ALLOCATION STRATEGY

There are various Strategies which are related to Resource Allocation:

1. **Resource Allocation Strategy in Cloud Computing:** In cloud computing, Resource Allocation (RA)is the procedure of allocating accessible resources to the demanded cloud requirements above the internet. Resource allocation starves services if the allocation is not grasped accurately. Resource provisioning solves that impede by permitting the ability providers to grasp the resources for every single individual module. Resource Allocation Strategy (RAS) is all relating to incorporating cloud provider hobbies for employing and allocating manipulated resources inside the check of cloud nature so as to encounter the

needs of the cloud application. It needs the kind and number of resources demanded by every single request in order to finish a user job. The order and period of allocation of resources are furthermore an input for an optimal RAS.

2. **Task Scheduling Algorithms in Cloud Environment:** Cloud users join virtualization, computerized multimedia, and internet connectivity to furnish their services. A frank agent of the cloud nature is client, server, and web connectivity. A hybrid computing ideal permits client to impact both area and private computing services to expertise a extra flexible and cost-effective computing utility. The area cloud nature involves Web established request, Data as a ability (DaaS), Groundwork as a Service (IaaS), Multimedia as a ability (SaaS), and Email as a ability (EaaS). A confidential cloud accesses the resources from the area cloud association to furnish services to its clients.

3. **Policy and Job Scheduling Algorithms of Cloud Computing:** Job arranging of cloud computing mentions to the procedure of adjusting resources amid unrelated resource users according to specific laws of resource use below a given cloud environment. Resource organization and job arranging are the key technologies of cloud computing. At present, there is not a uniform standard for job arranging in cloud. Most algorithms focus on job correspondent that is nearly accountable for all the task allocations, replies and retransmissions.

4. **Resource Allocation Policies in Cloud Computing Environment:** Resource allocation is a subject that has been dispatch in many computing areas, such as operating systems, grid computing and datacenter management. A Resource Allocation System (RAS) in Cloud Computing can be seen as any device that aims to guarantee that the applications' requirements are attended to correctly by the provider's infrastructure. Along with this guarantee to the developer, resource allocation mechanisms should also consider the current status of each reserve in the Cloud environment, in order to apply algorithms to better distribute physical and/or virtual assets to developers' applications, thus minimizing the operational cost of the cloud location.

5. **Ant Colony Optimization Algorithm for Resource Allocation:** Cloud computing dispersed cluster uses a Master/Slaves structure. There is a Chief node responsible for manipulating and supervision all the Slave nodes. As the specific condition of resource is strange below cloud circumstance, and the webs do not have a fixed topology, the construction and the resource allocation of the complete cloud nature is unpredictable.

6. **Dynamic Resource Allocation Strategy in Cloud Computing Environment:** Cloud data centers can be a distributed web in construction that is composed of countless compute nodes, storage nodes, and web node. Every single node is industrialized by a sequence of resources such as CPU, recollection, web

18

bandwidth and countless more. These resources are shouted multidimensional resources. The number of contiguous mechanisms (VMs) used in a huge cloud data center every single date can be extremely colossal, and their placement familiarize a momentous burden on the data center web.

7. **Dynamic Resource Allocation using Migration in Cloud:** The cloud computing period guarantees subscribes that it sticks to the ability level concurrence by bestowing resources as ability and by needs. Though, date by date subscribers' needs are rising for computing resources and their needs have animated heterogeneity and period irrelevance. But in cloud computing nature, resources are public and if they are not accurately distributed next it will result into resource wastage.

Reducing Use of Paper

Much of our communication and documentation is still conducted via a paper shadow. Not only does this leave loads of paper to manage, there is the economic cost of all the ink and paper and, more importantly, there is also an environmental cost concerned with printing that we all bear as

"a society. The environmental impact of printing is significant and wide ranging. The printing business is one of the most polluting industries in the world for the following reasons:

- The printing industry uses important amounts of energy from heating and lighting to powering tools and final delivery.
- Large quantities of water are used in most printing processes. In most of the cases, infected water is liable without cleaning.
- Comparatively high levels of waste are generated in the print development. From printing plates and ink tins to pallets and packaging there is plenty of waste formed by the printing industry.
- Many volatile organic compounds (VOCs) are said to branch from the printing industry. As the ink dries, the isopropyl alcohol used as a damping solution, evaporates at room temperature, releasing VOCs. These are colorless, odorless gases that are dangerous to the surroundings; contribute to global warming and the making of ozone, as well as being harmful to pressroom workers.
- To make paper, pulpwood trees are cut down in large numbers and are then transported to document mills where pulpwood fibers are strong and dried into sheets. This process is particularly energy consuming and the polluted waste water produced pose a major environmental hazard. Further, the impact of deforestation on the environment is a greater reason for concern.

The following policies can be adopted to reduce paper wastes in the enterprise:

- Memos and newsletters that workers should see, but need not keep can be posted online.
- Document editing and formatting features of ubiquitous word processing software can be broken instead of making drafts on document.
- Information can be exchanged electronically via e-mails and formal online forums instead of fax or mailed letters when probable.
- An electronic filing system can be put in place for easy and well-organized storage and recovery of all electronic documents.

DESKTOPS VS. LAPTOPS

Laptop computers may require the absolute power of their desktop counterparts, but they are more feasible from a green computing perception.

The following points highlight some of the s of using laptops over desktops:

- **Energy Efficiency:** Laptops consume on average 20-50 watts of electricity (which can be further trimmed in power saving modes) whereas desktops consume about 60-200 watts. The conventional Cathode Ray Tube (CRT) monitors of desktops also use more power than the Liquid Crystal Display (LCD) monitors of current laptops.
- A laptop is always better to use than a desktop computer as it uses 1/3 of the energy and is portable thus taking up less room. The fundamental issue with present desktops is that they consume significant energy even in idle mode, but by their design, laptops use much less active power.
- **Battery Power:** Laptops benefit from energy efficiency as a necessary importance of their battery-powered design so much so that manufacturers often tout how long laptop computers can run on battery power as a selling position.

The prospect of extending the battery life of laptops can be approached from two perspectives:

- Adding a larger, higher-capacity battery to the laptop
- Designing the laptop hardware to use less energy.
- **Less Potential, Less Consumption:** Laptops contain a lower possible for maximum power consumption because they attribute smaller power supply units (PSUs). A piece desktop computer has the potential to draw 400Wh

energy at complete load with a larger PSU, whereas a performance laptop may be limited to 90Wh because of its smaller PSU. Laptops often include considerably slower performing but more energy well-organized processors and other components, compared to correspondingly-named desktop parts, so processes may take longer to complete. However, many firms such as Intel have already inhabited greener desktop computing in a big way with highly energy-efficient processors like Atom Businesses are more and more switching to or substituting on premise solutions with cloud-based models for resource and processing power constraint to tap benefits like faster scale up/scale-down of capacity, pay-per-use pricing, and access to various cloud-based applications. Cloud computing solutions also allow enterprises to —— virtual cloud servers. It eliminates the need to install and preserve bulky, energy consuming physical servers by relocating them on the Internet. In many small business and commercial environments, server utilization rates are around 5 or 10 percent, but with the cloud, consumption rates are typically 60-70 percent due to shared data centers that employ fewer machines to get an equivalent capacity. The cloud-based alternative can be used in areas such as data storage, networking, software applications and operating systems. As a result, business or business sectors can save a lot of money, time and resources on maintenance and support.

The cloud infrastructure addresses two significant elements of a green IT approach: resource efficiency and energy efficiency:

- **Resource Virtualization:** Virtualization is a initial technology for deploying cloud-based infrastructure that allows a particular physical server to run multiple operating system images concurrently. As an enabler of consolidation, server virtualization reduces the whole physical server footprint, which has intrinsic green benefits.
- From a resource-efficiency perception, less equipment is needed to run workloads, which proactively reduces data center space and the ultimate e-waste footprint. From an energy-efficiency perspective, with less physical tackle plugged in, a data center will use less electricity. It is attraction noting that server virtualization is the most extensively adopted green IT project implemented or planned, with 90 percent of all IT organizations worldwide adopting it by
- **Automation Software:** The presence of virtualization unaccompanied does not maximize energy and reserve efficiencies. To rapidly provision, move, and scale workloads, cloud-based infrastructure relies on computerization software. Combined with the right skills and prepared and architectural

standards, computerization allows IT professionals to make the most of their cloud-based infrastructure asset by approaching the limits of traditional consolidation and exploitation ratios. The higher these ratios are, the less physical infrastructure is needed, which in turn maximizes the energy and resource efficiencies from server virtualization.

- **Pay-Per-Use Self-Service:** The pay-per-use nature of cloud based communications encourages users to only consume what they need and not more. Shared with self-service, lifecycle management will improve, as users will ——turn off or transfer resources and infrastructure after use. The pay per-use self-service capability of the cloud thus drives resource and energy efficiencies simultaneously.

- **Multi-Tenancy:** Multi-tenancy allows lots of different organizations (public cloud) or many different business units inside the same organization (private cloud) to benefit from an ordinary cloud-based infrastructure.

- **Reduce Costs:** Consolidation means fewer servers, which in turn means lower cooling and space requirements, which means lower energy costs.

- **Fulfill Regulations:** By tapping more efficient and therefore lower-emitting resources, cloud customers can reduce their carbon emission and be better-positioned to meet regulatory standards.

- **Improve Resiliency:** Consolidation and improved exploitation create more space, more command, and more cooling capacity within the same facility. Tapping into the cloud offloads the management of those resources to the cloud provider.

THE SECURITY IMPLICATIONS OF GREEN ENTERPRISES

Virtualization

There is also anxiety that predictable information security controls cannot mark malevolent traffic passing between virtual machines (VMs). "In a virtual environment, if you contaminate one virtual server or one operating system, you peril infecting all the other systems and server management in that environment," says Doug Cooke, manager, system engineers at anti-virus firm McAfee's Canadian office. "There's no documentary confirmation that actual threats have got through all the operating systems in a virtual environment, but 'white-hat' groups have proved it's possible."

"A few firewall products have been ported to the VMware environment and they organize taps, so they are preliminary to see traffic between the VMs, but they can't block it", O'Higgins says. "So these controls are not for the most part effective. After all, you want firewalls to block assured traffic, not just look at it. The approach

Third Brigade uses is host security, so that each individual VM is confined, and malicious traffic connecting VMs can be detected and blocked."

Simple Measures

Consolidation isn't restricted just too broad operating systems, however. Information security vendors have been squeezing more functions into a single box though driving down power consumption. "As UTM appliances can perform multiple security functions such as firewall, spam / web filtering, IPS/IDS, and gateway anti-virus, firms can reduce the number of dissimilar security systems on their networks", Forti Green allows clients to approximation the potential annual energy savings of a UTM-based network security topology compared to a traditional architecture with multiple info security devices at each site. "You tell Forti Green the number of UTM boxes in the branch offices, and the totals at the head office and the regional offices," James says. "The branch devices can have fewer security functions than the regional office devices, which will in turn have less than the head office boxes."

Routers

Cisco has started putting numerous virtual security functions onto its routers, says Fred Kost, director of advertising, Cisco Virtual Office (CVO). "We offer content program on our ASR edge routers and contented filtering, firewalls and intrusion prevention on our ISR boxes", he says. "Cisco's Adaptive Security Appliances include firewall, IPSec and SSL VPN security, and email screening. The ASR can also run multiple virtual firewalls for divide partitioned networks."

Power Management

The effort made to decrease the power expenditure of servers and information security appliances doesn't eliminate the need to monitor and manage that energy use. Several initiatives are underway to measure and manage IT devices' influence consumption, although information security appliances cannot yet be mechanically powered down while their traffic flow is dormant.

Cloud Computing

Global service line lead for security move toward and hazard management at Accenture, says some cloud providers such a state in their SLA (service level agreement) where they store clients' data, but others don't do so. "I predict cloud providers that are not apparent being locked out of markets likes the European Union, where there are clear laws about how data is stored and transmitted. What's incident in the EU is that firms are looking for intra-European cloud solutions to avoid contravention EU data privacy laws."

Ashdown adds that firms using a cloud provider must insist in their SLA that the provider go through third-party security audits.

"If you store data on a third-party cloud, you could fall victim to a man-in-the-middle attack", says IDC's Senf. "It's vital to encrypt data sent to a cloud, and the provider must have an SLA specifying that they use good authentication."

The answer to man-in-the-middle is to use two-factor authentication in the form of hardware or software tokens, and to prove the IP address of PCs logging on to the cloud, There are clearly benefits for both the information security occupation and the broader IT department when it comes to using green technology. But apply it with care, and guarantee that your power saving efforts doesn't compromise your data.

Advantages of Green Computing:

- Reduced energy method from green computing techniques translates into lower carbon dioxide Emissions, stemming from a reduction in the vestige fuel used in power plants and transportation.
- Conserving resources means less energy is essential to produce, use, and arrange of products.
- Saving energy and possessions saves money.
- Green computing even includes changing government policy to promote recycling and Lowering energy use by individuals and businesses.
- Reduce the risk existing in the laptops such as chemical known to source cancer, nerve damage and immune reactions in humans.

Benefits of Cloud Computing for Green Enterprises

Reduce Paper Consumptions

The world uses over 300 million tons of documents every year. Businesses account for a very large split of the paper that is inspired. Smart businesses will look for ways to reduce paper expenditure to become promote sustainability. Cloud computing considerably reduces the need for paper, because it enables businesses to use digital technology for projects that may not have been a practicable otherwise. One example is sharing critical documents with organizational counterparts in other regions.

Reduce Server Dependence

While data storage is distant greener than retaining records on paper, it's still not 100% environmentally friendly. Servers involve a decent amount of energy to operate. If you are storing terabytes of data, then you'll likely need a superior server. However, it's much more reasonable to store data on a single large server than frequent hard drives. Since cloud computing allows you to store your data in a central database, you'll significantly decrease the number of servers that you rely on.

Cut Transportation Costs

Transportation and distribution are two other actions that leave a large carbon footprint. Cloud computing is significantly reduced, because your organization will not need to mail nearly as many documents.

Take Your Green Business to the Cloud

There is a diversity of reasons that smart companies are going green. The two most understandable benefits for their bottom line are that they can save on waste and progress their branding with customers that are disturbed about sustainability. They also get to see that they are doing their part to support a better world.

CONCLUSION

Cloud computing is prevailing as a considerable shift as today's organizations which are in front of extreme data overload and skyrocketing energy costs. Green Cloud architecture, which can help combine workload and attain significant energy saving for cloud computing environment, at the same time, guarantees the real-time recital for many performance-sensitive applications.

In the future, there are still a number of research behavior that we plan to carry out, which could improve the performance of Green Cloud and bring solid value to users to attain their business goals and their social dependability in Green IT Applying green technologies is highly fundamental for the sustainable development of cloud computing. Of the various green methodologies enquired, the DVFS technology is a highly hardware oriented approach and hence less supple. Green scheduling algorithms based on neural predictors can lead to a 70% power savings.

These policies also enable us to cut down data Centre energy costs, thus leading to a strong, aggressive cloud computing industry. End users will also benefit from the decreased energy bills. As a conclusion, Green Cloud effectively saves energy by dynamically support to workload leveraging live VM migrations, at the same time convention system SLAs.

REFERENCES

Agarwal, S., Ghosh, A., & Nath, A. (2016). Green Enterprise Computing- Approaches Towards a Greener IT. *Presented at the International Journal of Innovative Research in Advanced Engineering (IJIRAE).*

Blue and Green Tomorrow. (n. d.). Benefits of green cloud computing. Retrieved Dec 12, 2016 from http://blueandgreentomorrow.com/environment/benefits-of-cloud-computing-for-green enterprises/S

Bobby, S. (2015). A greener approach to computing and save energy. *International Journal of Advance Research in Science and Engineering.*

Computer Weekly. (n. d.). Security implications of green IT. Retrieved Dec 12, 2016 from http://www.computerweekly.com/feature/The-security-implications-of-green-IT

Jayanthi, S., & Babu, S. (2015). Green Cloud Computing - Resource Utilization with Respect to SLA and Power Consumption. *International Journal of Computer Science and Mobile Applications.*

Kamiya, S.N. (2013). Green Cloud Computing Resource Managing Policies a Survey.

Liu, L., Wang, H., Liu, X., Jin, X., He, W. B., Wang, Q. B., & Chen, Y. (2009) *GreenCloud: A New Architecture for Green Data Center.*

Nimje, A. R. V. T. Gaikwad, H. N. Datir (2013). Green Cloud Computing: A Virtualized Security Framework for Green Cloud Computing. *Presented at the International Journal of Advanced Research in Computer Science and Software Engineering.*

Pandya, S. S. (2014). Green Cloud computing.

Patel, Y. S., Jain, K., & Shukla, S. K. (2016). A Brief Survey on Benchmarks and Research Challenges for Green Cloud Computing. *Presented at the National Conference on Advancements in Computer & Information Technology.*

Patil, P. S., & Kharade, J. (2016). A Study on Green Cloud Computing Technologies. *Presented at the International Journal of Innovative Research in Computer Communication Engineering.*

Pragya, M. G. (2015). A Review on Energy Efficient Techniques in Green Cloud Computing. *International Journal of Advanced Research in Computer Science and Software Engineering.*

Prashant, D. (2014). Greening the Cloud Computing.

Chapter 2
Cloud Computing, Green Computing, and Green ICT

Kijpokin Kasemsap
Suan Sunandha Rajabhat University, Thailand

ABSTRACT

This chapter reveals the overview of cloud computing; cloud computing, green computing, green ICT, and data center utilization; the importance of cloud computing in the digital age; the advanced issues of green computing; and the important perspectives on green ICT. Cloud computing is computing based on the Internet. Green computing and green ICT are the sustainable business practices of reducing the environmental footprints of technology by efficiently using several resources. Green computing and green ICT are the important perspectives for the businesses to improve their corporate image by meeting regulatory requirements and sustainability demands of both customers and employees. The chapter argues that cloud computing, green computing, and green ICT are the advanced technologies toward improving sustainability and sustainable development in the green economy.

INTRODUCTION

Cloud computing is able to provide the huge resources and computing ability to users (Chen, Li, & Susilo, 2012). In cloud computing, the on-demand resource provisioning ensures the optimal resource allocation and is cost effective (Prasad & Rao, 2014). The major motivations to adopt cloud computing services include no upfront investment on infrastructure toward transferring responsibility of maintenance, backups, and license management to cloud service providers (Dastjerdi, Tabatabaei, & Buyya, 2012).

DOI: 10.4018/978-1-5225-3038-1.ch002

Computers require power to run (Adhikari & Roy, 2016). The consumers of electricity are responsible for the green production toward reducing overall carbon dioxide emission and greenhouse gases (Adhikari & Roy, 2016). Green computing is the environmental saving computing paradigm, which involve hardware, software, and people (Singh & Gond, 2017). The adoption of green computing involves many improvements, and provides the energy-efficiency services for data centers, power management, and cloud computing (Palanivel & Kuppuswami, 2017).

Nowadays, the information and communication technology (ICT) industry forms a complex group of hardware, software, networks, and its users so there must be the systematic classification for green computing approaches, which emphasize the sophisticated problems (Kesswani & Jain, 2017). The usage of cloud computing and its life cycle can produce the hazardous substances that need to be addressed in the efficient and green perspectives (Palanivel & Kuppuswami, 2017).

This chapter is based on a literature review of cloud computing, green computing, and green ICT. The extensive literature of cloud computing, green computing, and green ICT provides a contribution to practitioners and researchers by revealing the aspects of cloud computing, green computing, and green ICT in order to maximize the impact of cloud computing, green computing, and green ICT toward business sustainability.

BACKGROUND

Cloud computing technology is not a new concept for most of the sectors, such as banks, automobile, retail, health care, education, and logistics (Al-Hudhaif & Alkubeyyer, 2011). Cloud computing is an easy-to-adopt technology with simple and latest architecture (Hutchinson, Ward, & Castilon, 2009). This architecture presents information technology (IT) as a paid service in terms of deployment and maintenance (Sean, Zhi, Subhajyoti, Juheng, & Anand, 2011). Various deployment models of cloud computing make the adoption easy for any type of sector, depending on the need of usage (Singh, Mishra, Ali, Shukla, & Shankar, 2015). This innovative technology makes the collaboration easier among companies by the application of cloud computing (Xuan, 2012).

There has been rapid expansion of the IT due to contribution to the carbon dioxide emission (Khan, Shah, & Nusratullah, 2017). The major objective of the Energy Star program is to assign a voluntary label to the computer products, that were successful in minimizing energy consumption while maximizing efficiency (Jena & Dey, 2013). Green computing is recognized as a way for organizations and individuals to be efficient in resources (McWhorter & Delello, 2016), and considers the use of computers and related resources in an eco-friendly manner, such as the implementation of energy efficiency in the computing equipment (Adhikari & Roy, 2016).

ICT is rapidly growing, and has major influence in all fields of activity (Radu, 2014) toward delivering the intelligent products and services (Banerjee, Sing, Chowdhury, & Anwar, 2013). Green ICT emerges as a new perspective for designing, developing, and managing the computing infrastructure aiming for more efficient processes and mechanisms to avoid the waste of resources toward environmental sustainability (Moreno & Xu, 2013). Over the past few decades, the explosion of the ICT devices has led to a particular focus on the environmental impact in the ICT industry (Chitra, 2011). Green ICT is designed to conserve energy, compared to its conventional counterpart (Ryoo & Choi, 2011).

ASPECTS OF CLOUD COMPUTING, GREEN COMPUTING, AND GREEN ICT

This section provides the overview of cloud computing; cloud computing, green computing, green ICT, and data center utilization; the importance of cloud computing in the digital age; the advanced issues of green computing; and the important perspectives on green ICT.

Overview of Cloud Computing

Cloud service users have increased worldwide, and cloud service providers have been deploying and operating data centers to serve the globally distributed cloud users (Son, Jung, & Jun, 2013). Cloud computing allows business customers to elastically scale up and down their resource usage based on their requirements (Song & Xiao, 2013). Cloud computing offers a bulk of resources, such as networks, computer processing power, and data storage space (Thakur & Verma, 2015).

Cloud computing promises to increase innovation, improve business agility, and reduce costs (Sasikala, 2013). Business process complexity, entrepreneurial culture, and the degree to which existing information system (IS) functions embody application functionality significantly affect a company's propensity to adopt the cloud computing technologies (Wu, Cegielski, Hazen, & Hall, 2013). Efficient resource provision, which can guarantee the satisfactory cloud computing services to the end user, lays the foundation for the success of commercial competition (Zhang, Huang, & Wang, 2016).

Li (2015) indicated that hybrid cloud service-related selection optimization is distributed to and performed at two levels: hybrid cloud user agent (i.e., hybrid cloud service agent at hybrid cloud service layer) and hybrid cloud service agent (i.e., hybrid cloud agent at hybrid cloud resource layer). Interactions among hybrid cloud user agent, hybrid cloud service agent, public cloud agents, and private cloud agents are mediated by means of market mechanisms (Li, 2015).

Cloud Computing, Green Computing, Green ICT, and Data Center Utilization

Cloud computing becomes commercially attractive and its use is growing since it promises reducing the maintenance and management costs in comparison with traditional data centers (Moreno & Xu, 2013). Cloud computing provides on-demand access to computing resources for users across the world, and offers services on a pay-as-you-go model through data center sites that are scattered across diverse geographies (Khosravi & Buyya, 2017).

In large-scale data centers, tens of thousands of compute and storage nodes are connected by a data center network to deliver a single-purpose cloud service (Alshaer, 2015). However, these data centers equipped with high performance infrastructures significantly consume huge power causing global warming by emitting the carbon footprint, thus giving a serious environmental threat to today's world (Jeyarani, Nagaveni, Sadasivam, & Rajarathinam, 2011). The carbon footprint is one way to rate the environmental impacts of ICT (Kern, Dick, Naumann, & Hiller, 2015).

Cloud computing environments are available at a fraction of the time and effort when compared to traditional local data center-based solutions (Sanduja, Jewell, Aron, & Pharai, 2015). Cloud computing deals with handling virtualized instances of machines in different geographical locations (Anandharajan & Bhagyaveni, 2014), and provides the opportunity to migrate virtual machines to "follow-the-green" data centers (Sabry & Krause, 2013).

Data centers play a crucial role in the delivery of cloud computing services by enabling on-demand access to the shared resources, such as software, platform, and infrastructure (Kantarci, Foschini, Corradi, & Mouftah, 2015). Because data stored in the cloud computing may be lost or corrupted, users are suggested to verify data integrity before the utilization of cloud computing data (Wang, Li, Liu, Li, & Li, 2014).

Cloud infrastructures rely on numerous networked devices in data centers to provide the virtualization and sharing of resources (Voderhobli, 2015). However, data centers produce large amount of carbon dioxide emissions, which significantly contribute to the environmental issue of global warming (Cao, Zhu, & Wu, 2015). The energy consumption in the cloud is proportional to the resource utilization, and data centers are almost the world's highest consumers of electricity (Kumar, Sahoo, & Mandal, 2016). The complexity of the resource allocation problem increases with the size of cloud infrastructure, and becomes difficult to effectively solve (Kumar et al., 2016).

The recent development of distributed computing enables the creation of large-sized data centers, while the computational intensive applications in cloud computing require powerful processors, which generate lots of heat during the computation and command extra-cooling system (Wang & Huo, 2014). Large amount of energy is consumed by the data centers hosting cloud computing applications contributing high operational costs and carbon footprints to the environment (Ahuja & Muthiah, 2016).

The great amounts of energy consumed by large-scale computing and network systems (e.g., data centers and supercomputers) have been a major source of concern in a society concerning ICT systems. Data centers form the crucial part of an organization's overall strategy for reducing carbon dioxide emissions (Philipson, 2013). To improve the energy consumption of the data centers toward green ICT, it is important to understand the energy consumption pattern of the data centers (Gahlawat & Sharma, 2016). There are various factors contributing to the total energy consumption of the data centers, such as fixed energy consumption components regarding lighting and networking equipment; dynamic energy consumption components in terms of uninterruptible power supply (UPS) and power distribution unit (PDU), and servers (Gahlawat & Sharma, 2016).

Importance of Cloud Computing in the Digital Age

Cloud computing includes network access to storage, processing power, development platforms, and software (Kasemsap, 2015a). As an emerging technology, cloud computing changes the form and function of IT infrastructures in global supply chain (Kasemsap, 2015b). Cloud computing provides virtualized resources to the customers utilizing various technologies, such as Web 2.0 services, virtualization, and multi-tenancy. Multi-tenancy, the hosting of multiple customers by a single application instance, leads to improved efficiency, improved scalability, and less costs (Maenhaut, Moens, Ongenae, & de Turck, 2016).

To enable enterprises to benefit from migration while achieving cost-efficiency and keeping sensitive user data confidential against unreliable cloud servers, planning which cloud servers to migrate to the cloud and which to be hosted on-premise is a key problem (Huang, Yi, Song, Yang, & Zhang, 2014). Migrating legacy systems or deploying a new application to a cloud computing environment has recently become very trendy, because the number of cloud service providers available is still increasing (Quinton, Romero, & Duchien, 2016).

As cloud computing is becoming a mainstream platform, it has become important to understand the implications on customers' applications or systems when deployed on cloud computing (Garg & Buyya, 2013). Cloud computing services are delivered to the customer through the Internet (Duan, Yan, & Vasilakos, 2012). The Web 2.0 applications are used to access and manage cloud resources that makes Web 2.0 applications an important component of the cloud computing (Menzel, Ranjan, Wang, Khan, & Chen, 2014). Customers' processes are executed in virtualized environment that in turn utilize the physical resources (Guan, Wu, Wang, & Khan, 2014).

Guo et al. (2010) indicated that cloud computing is available for the computationally-intensive and data-intensive remote sensing services. Multiple virtual processes of various cloud computing users are allocated to same physical machines that are segregated logically (Ali, Khan, & Vasilakos, 2015). This gives rise to a multi-tenant environment in the cloud computing. Despite the provided advantages, the cloud computing is not exclusive of risks with security being the key risk. Virtual teams can be formed more often because cloud computing gives teams the useful tools they need to effectively collaborate and at a reduced cost to the organization. Leaders of virtual teams carry the responsibilities to satisfy their bosses, subordinates, and external customers in a complex distributed environment that is highly dependent on IT perspectives (Kasemsap, 2016).

With the development of IT and medical technology, many developed countries have established organizations to develop electronic medical standards in response to apply the development of technology information, and they gradually develop the emerging patterns of personal health records (PHRs). The sharing of PHRs in cloud computing is a promising platform of health information exchange (Liu, Huang, & Liu, 2015). As wearable devices are becoming more and more powerful, patients can learn more on their own health indicator at any place and any time (Liu et al., 2015). Patients can effectively upload their collected PHR to the cloud computing through mobile devices (Liu et al., 2015).

Advanced Issues of Green Computing

Green computing is a highly motivated smart computing, which tries to save energy and environment by minimizing the harmful impacts of the computing resource's production and utilization (Kesswani & Jain, 2017). Approach to developing green computing can be broadly divided into four parts: hardware device manufacturing, software techniques, people awareness, and standard policies (Singh & Gond, 2017).

Green computing is considered as the first wave of sustainability (Issa, Tolani, Chang, & Issa, 2015). Energy consumption is a key aspect in deploying distributed service in cloud networks within decentralized service delivery architectures (Sabry & Krause, 2013). Since cloud computing allows for sharing of resources, it reduces the need to deploy more hardware, thus reducing power consumption toward green computing (Voderhobli, 2015).

The essence of green computing lies in proximity with green chemistry (Yuvaraj, 2015), which is the practice of designing, manufacturing, using, and disposing of computers, servers, and associated subsystems for reducing the use of hazardous materials, maximizing energy efficiency, and promoting the recyclability or biodegradability of products (Hu & Kaabouch, 2012). To make cloud data centers greener, it is beneficial to limit the amount of active servers to minimize energy consumption (Yang, Kuo, & Yeh, 2011).

Power reduction and energy conservation are important in high-performance computing systems to minimize the operating cost (Zheng & Cai, 2010). Thus, the need for efficient workload schedulers, which are capable of minimizing the consumed energy, becomes increasingly important (Shojafar, Cordeschi, & Baccarelli, 2016). Performance features (e.g., speedup and CPU-intensiveness) enable the workload scheduler to make the trade-offs between power consumption and application performance (Mair, Huang, & Zhang, 2012). Efficient scheduling approaches show the promising ways to reduce the energy consumption of cloud computing platforms while ensuring the quality of service (QoS) requirements of tasks (Chen et al., 2015).

The excessive use of modern day appliances (e.g., laptops and personal computers) have contributed to environmental pollutants that are damaging the environment (Garg, Gupta, Goh, & Desouza, 2010). Power consumption of resources and amount of electronic waste can be reduced by implementing different eco friendly hardware (Bhadra & Kundu, 2016). Reduced energy usage from green computing techniques translates into the reduced carbon dioxide emission, stemming from a reduction in the fossil fuel used in power plants and transportation (Jena, 2013).

With the growing awareness and popularity of environmental preservation, research on green computing has gained recognition around the world (Ganesh & Anbuudayasankar, 2013). Green computing concept can be achieved by using several methods adopted by researchers including renewable energy, virtualization through cloud computing, proper cooling system, identifying suitable location to harvest energy while reducing the need for air conditioning systems and employing both suitable networking and IT infrastructure (Mardamutu, Ponnusamy, & Zaman, 2016).

While many computing systems come with power-saving settings, there are a wide variety of products that monitor and adjust the energy levels to increase energy performance and reduce wasted energy (Jena, 2013). The data over the cloud can be procured with the help of rough set-based methods, which can help conserve the energy (Shivalkar & Tripathy, 2015). In addition, teleworking technologies are variously implemented for green computing initiatives, and the advantages of teleworking technologies include reduced greenhouse gas emissions concerning transportation demand reduction, improved worker satisfaction, and reduced overhead office costs (Egbuta, Thomas, & Al-Hasan, 2014).

Important Perspectives on Green ICT

As human beings become increasingly dependent on technology, the relationship of ICT with the natural environment is continuously degrading (Bekaroo, Bokhoree, & Pattinson, 2016). Modern ICT systems are made up of a complicated mix of people, networks, hardware, and software toward increasing energy consumption and environmental concerns (Kamani, Kathiriya, Virparia, & Parsania, 2011).

ICT has a fundamental role in collaborating for a sustainable development by providing the services in an efficient way, however, its own structure should follow the sustainable principles by consuming reduced energy amount (di Salvo, Agostinho, Almeida, & Giannetti, 2017). Businesses and individuals should integrate sustainability in their ICT strategy and to include cloud computing technology as an important tool for sustainable work, especially in the IT departments to cut costs and increase productivity toward green ICT (Isaias, Issa, Chang, & Issa, 2015).

Green ICT is introduced to support the implementation of the green environment (Din, Haron, & Ahmad, 2013). The innovative activity in green ICT domains is characterized by high growth and high levels of technological pervasiveness, considerable entry of new innovators and a wide variety of actors with a prevalence of large ICT companies and universities (Cecere, Corrocher, Gossart, & Ozman, 2014).

The impacts of climate changes are significantly influencing the approaches of organizations and governments to utilize resources, develop appropriate environment-friendly frameworks, and adopt a holistic approach to understanding their operating environment (Gasmelseid, 2016). The socioeconomic and environmental challenge facing the leaders of tomorrow is how green ICT can be effectively applied by organizations to contribute to the global green revolution (Roodt & de Villiers, 2012).

Large-scale IT usage harms the environment during its life cycle, and this issues results in a threat to sustainability (Smeitink & Spruit, 2013). Green ICT is attributed to the initiatives and programs that directly or indirectly address environmental sustainability (Hernandez & Ona, 2016). Green ICT is an emerging area in the ICT management emphasizing on six dimensions namely raw material and resources, energy and climate, excess production, health and safety of mankind, management development, and invention through ICT (Khan, Honnutagi, & Khan, 2015).

Computer industry-related sustainability management includes design and development of energy efficient computer products, refurbishing of computer assets, purchasing of green or refurbished components, and providing sustainability metrics procedures (Rahman, 2016). The important driver for the adoption of energy-aware behavior toward green ICT is the development of corporate social responsibility (CSR) initiatives, by which organizations present themselves as socially responsible, and therefore improve their standing in the eyes of consumers (Pattinson, Oram, & Ross, 2013).

Information systems, computers, and computing significantly consume an immense amount of natural resources, the energy used to power them, and the problems that arise in the disposing of obsolete hardware (Raisinghani & Idemudia, 2016). Every server has a cooling mechanism to dissipate the heat generated by it (Deshmukh, Jothish, & Chandrasekaran, 2015). A major portion of the energy consumption of the server is taken up by this cooling mechanism (Deshmukh et al., 2015).

Enterprise architecture as a function can assist in driving green ICT initiatives because it is focused as the strategic practice in the long-term planning, development, and management of an organization's ICT environment (Curtis & Lingarchani, 2011). The success or failure of green ICT policies is determined by the way an organization manages the participation and social interactions of its employees and customers (Deshpande & Unhelkar, 2011).

Green ICT can help solve the problem in terms of introducing green innovations and applying ICT to increase the efficiency of energy management toward green organization (Thongmak, 2013). Green organization works on enhancing the data and information management within the organization that revolves around information systems, their databases, and their applications (Deshpande & Unhelkar, 2011).

FUTURE RESEARCH DIRECTIONS

The classification of the extensive literature in the domains of cloud computing, green computing, and green ICT will provide the potential opportunities for future research. Environmental sustainability is important because it ensures people have water and resources, and adopting its practices protects the environment and human health (Kasemsap, 2017a). Environmental management aims to prevent pollution, preserve natural resources, and reduce environmental risks toward creating an environmentally-friendly image with different stakeholders (Kasemsap, 2017b). Considering the associations among cloud computing, green computing, green ICT, environmental sustainability, and environmental management in the green economy should be further studied.

CONCLUSION

This chapter explained the overview of cloud computing; cloud computing, green computing, green ICT, and data center utilization; the importance of cloud computing in the digital age; the advanced issues of green computing; and the important perspectives on green ICT. Cloud computing is computing based on the Internet. Green computing and green ICT are the sustainable business practices of reducing the environmental footprints of technology by efficiently using several resources. Green computing and green ICT are the powerful approaches to utilizing various resources (e.g., office space, data centers, computers, and servers) in an environmentally friendly way. Green computing and green ICT are the important perspectives for the businesses to improve their corporate image by meeting regulatory requirements and sustainability demands of both customers and employees. Cloud computing, green computing, and green ICT are the advanced technologies toward improving sustainability and sustainable development in the green economy.

REFERENCES

Adhikari, M., & Roy, D. (2016). Green computing. In G. Deka, G. Siddesh, K. Srinivasa, & L. Patnaik (Eds.), *Emerging research surrounding power consumption and performance issues in utility computing* (pp. 84–108). Hershey, PA: IGI Global. doi:10.4018/978-1-4666-8853-7.ch005

Ahuja, S. P., & Muthiah, K. (2016). Survey of state-of-art in green cloud computing. *International Journal of Green Computing*, 7(1), 25–36. doi:10.4018/IJGC.2016010102

Al-Hudhaif, S., & Alkubeyyer, A. (2011). E-commerce adoption factors in Saudi Arabia. *International Journal of Business and Management*, 6(9), 122–133. doi:10.5539/ijbm.v6n9p122

Ali, M., Khan, S. U., & Vasilakos, A. V. (2015). Security in cloud computing: Opportunities and challenges. *Information Sciences*, 305(1), 357–383. doi:10.1016/j. ins.2015.01.025

Alshaer, H. (2015). An overview of network virtualization and cloud network as a service. *International Journal of Network Management*, 25(1), 1–30. doi:10.1002/nem.1882

Anandharajan, T., & Bhagyaveni, M. (2014). Minimum power performance-based virtual machine consolidation technique for green cloud datacenters. *International Journal of Green Computing*, 5(1), 24–43. doi:10.4018/ijgc.2014010103

Banerjee, S., Sing, T. Y., Chowdhury, A. R., & Anwar, H. (2013). Motivations to adopt green ICT: A tale of two organizations. *International Journal of Green Computing*, 4(2), 1–11. doi:10.4018/jgc.2013070101

Bekaroo, G., Bokhoree, C., & Pattinson, C. (2016). Impacts of ICT on the natural ecosystem: A grassroot analysis for promoting socio-environmental sustainability. *Renewable & Sustainable Energy Reviews, 57*, 1580–1595. doi:10.1016/j.rser.2015.12.147

Bhadra, S., & Kundu, A. (2016). Introducing eco friendly corporate system: A green approach. *International Journal of Green Computing, 7*(1), 1–24. doi:10.4018/IJGC.2016010101

Cao, F., Zhu, M. M., & Wu, C. Q. (2015). Green cloud computing with efficient resource allocation approach. In X. Liu & Y. Li (Eds.), *Green services engineering, optimization, and modeling in the technological age* (pp. 116–148). Hershey, PA: IGI Global. doi:10.4018/978-1-4666-8447-8.ch005

Cecere, G., Corrocher, N., Gossart, C., & Ozman, M. (2014). Technological pervasiveness and variety of innovators in green ICT: A patent-based analysis. *Research Policy, 43*(10), 1827–1839. doi:10.1016/j.respol.2014.06.004

Chen, H., Zhu, X., Guo, H., Zhu, J., Qin, X., & Wu, J. (2015). Towards energy-efficient scheduling for real-time tasks under uncertain cloud computing environment. *Journal of Systems and Software, 99*, 20–35. doi:10.1016/j.jss.2014.08.065

Chen, X., Li, J., & Susilo, W. (2012). Efficient fair conditional payments for outsourcing computations. *IEEE Transactions on Information Forensics and Security, 7*(6), 1687–1694. doi:10.1109/TIFS.2012.2210880

Chitra, S. (2011). Adopting green ICT in business. In B. Unhelkar (Ed.), *Handbook of research on green ICT: Technology, business and social perspectives* (pp. 643–651). Hershey, PA: IGI Global. doi:10.4018/978-1-61692-834-6.ch047

Curtis, D., & Lingarchani, A. (2011). Green ICT system architecture frameworks. In B. Unhelkar (Ed.), *Handbook of research on green ICT: Technology, business and social perspectives* (pp. 446–458). Hershey, PA: IGI Global. doi:10.4018/978-1-61692-834-6.ch032

Dastjerdi, A. V., Tabatabaei, S. G. H., & Buyya, R. (2012). A dependency-aware ontology-based approach for deploying service level agreement monitoring services in cloud. *Software, Practice & Experience, 42*(4), 501–518. doi:10.1002/spe.1104

Deshmukh, A. A., Jothish, M., & Chandrasekaran, K. (2015). Green routing algorithm for wired networks. *International Journal of Green Computing, 6*(2), 16–29. doi:10.4018/IJGC.2015070102

Deshpande, Y., & Unhelkar, B. (2011). Information systems for a green organisation. In B. Unhelkar (Ed.), *Handbook of research on green ICT: Technology, business and social perspectives* (pp. 116–130). Hershey, PA: IGI Global. doi:10.4018/978-1-61692-834-6.ch008

di Salvo, A. L. A., Agostinho, F., Almeida, C. M. V. B., & Giannetti, B. F. (2017). Can cloud computing be labeled as "green"? Insights under an environmental accounting perspective. *Renewable & Sustainable Energy Reviews*, *69*, 514–526. doi:10.1016/j.rser.2016.11.153

Din, N., Haron, S., & Ahmad, H. (2013). The level of awareness on the green ICT concept and self directed learning among Malaysian Facebook users. *Procedia: Social and Behavioral Sciences*, *85*, 464–473. doi:10.1016/j.sbspro.2013.08.375

Duan, Q., Yan, Y., & Vasilakos, A. V. (2012). A survey on service-oriented network virtualization toward convergence of networking and cloud computing. *IEEE eTransactions on Network and Service Management*, *9*(4), 373–392. doi:10.1109/TNSM.2012.113012.120310

Egbuta, I. C., Thomas, B., & Al-Hasan, S. (2014). The contribution of teleworking towards a green computing environment. In E. Ariwa (Ed.), *Green technology applications for enterprise and academic innovation* (pp. 218–232). Hershey, PA: IGI Global. doi:10.4018/978-1-4666-5166-1.ch014

Gahlawat, M., & Sharma, P. (2016). Green, energy-efficient computing and sustainability issues in cloud. In R. Kannan, R. Rasool, H. Jin, & S. Balasundaram (Eds.), *Managing and processing big data in cloud computing* (pp. 206–217). Hershey, PA: IGI Global. doi:10.4018/978-1-4666-9767-6.ch014

Ganesh, K., & Anbuudayasankar, S. P. (2013). *International and interdisciplinary studies in green computing* (pp. 1–238). Hershey, PA: IGI Global. doi:10.4018/978-1-4666-2646-1

Garg, M., Gupta, S., Goh, M., & Desouza, R. (2010). Sustaining the green information technology movement. In N. Bajgoric (Ed.), *Always-on enterprise information systems for business continuance: Technologies for reliable and scalable operations* (pp. 218–230). Hershey, PA: IGI Global. doi:10.4018/978-1-60566-723-2.ch013

Garg, S. K., & Buyya, R. (2013). An environment for modeling and simulation of message-passing parallel applications for cloud computing. *Software, Practice & Experience*, *43*(11), 1359–1375. doi:10.1002/spe.2156

Gasmelseid, T. M. (2016). On the decision criteria for "greening" information systems. In V. Ponnusamy, N. Zaman, T. Low, & A. Amin (Eds.), *Biologically-inspired energy harvesting through wireless sensor technologies* (pp. 187–200). Hershey, PA: IGI Global. doi:10.4018/978-1-4666-9792-8.ch009

Guan, B., Wu, J., Wang, Y., & Khan, S. U. (2014). CIVSched: A communication-aware inter-VM scheduling technique for decreased network latency between co-located VMs. *IEEE Transactions on Cloud Computing, 2*(3), 320–332. doi:10.1109/TCC.2014.2328582

Guo, W., Gong, J., Jiang, W., Liu, Y., & She, B. (2010). OpenRS-Cloud: A remote sensing image processing platform based on cloud computing environment. *Science China: Technological Sciences, 53*(Suppl. 1), 221–230. doi:10.1007/s11431-010-3234-y

Hernandez, A. A., & Ona, S. E. (2016). Green IT adoption: Lessons from the Philippines business process outsourcing industry. *International Journal of Social Ecology and Sustainable Development, 7*(1), 1–34. doi:10.4018/IJSESD.2016010101

Hu, W., & Kaabouch, N. (2012). *Sustainable ICTs and management systems for green computing* (pp. 1–495). Hershey, PA: IGI Global. doi:10.4018/978-1-4666-1839-8

Huang, D., Yi, L., Song, F., Yang, D., & Zhang, H. (2014). A secure cost-effective migration of enterprise applications to the cloud. *International Journal of Communication Systems, 27*(12), 3996–4013. doi:10.1002/dac.2594

Hutchinson, C., Ward, J., & Castilon, K. (2009). Navigating the next-generation application architecture. *IT Professional, 11*(2), 18–22. doi:10.1109/MITP.2009.33

Isaias, P., Issa, T., Chang, V., & Issa, T. (2015). Outlining the issues of cloud computing and sustainability opportunities and risks in European organizations: A SEM study. *Journal of Electronic Commerce in Organizations, 13*(4), 1–25. doi:10.4018/JECO.2015100101

Issa, T., Tolani, G., Chang, V., & Issa, T. (2015). Awareness of sustainability, green IT, and cloud computing in Indian organisations. In X. Liu & Y. Li (Eds.), *Green services engineering, optimization, and modeling in the technological age* (pp. 269–287). Hershey, PA: IGI Global. doi:10.4018/978-1-4666-8447-8.ch011

Jena, R. K. (2013). Green computing to green business. In P. Ordóñez de Pablos (Ed.), *Green technologies and business practices: An IT approach* (pp. 138–150). Hershey, PA: IGI Global. doi:10.4018/978-1-4666-1972-2.ch007

Jena, R. K., & Dey, D. G. (2013). Green computing: An Indian perspective. In S. Siqueira (Ed.), *Governance, communication, and innovation in a knowledge intensive society* (pp. 40–50). Hershey, PA: IGI Global. doi:10.4018/978-1-4666-4157-0.ch004

Jeyarani, R., Nagaveni, N., Sadasivam, S. K., & Rajarathinam, V. R. (2011). Power aware meta scheduler for adaptive VM provisioning in IaaS cloud. *International Journal of Cloud Applications and Computing, 1*(3), 36–51. doi:10.4018/ijcac.2011070104

Kamani, K., Kathiriya, D., Virparia, P., & Parsania, P. (2011). Digital green ICT: Enabling eco-efficiency and eco-innovation. In B. Unhelkar (Ed.), *Handbook of research on green ICT: Technology, business and social perspectives* (pp. 282–289). Hershey, PA: IGI Global. doi:10.4018/978-1-61692-834-6.ch019

Kantarci, B., Foschini, L., Corradi, A., & Mouftah, H. T. (2015). Design of energy-efficient cloud systems via network and resource virtualization. *International Journal of Network Management, 25*(2), 75–94. doi:10.1002/nem.1838

Kasemsap, K. (2015a). The role of cloud computing adoption in global business. In V. Chang, R. Walters, & G. Wills (Eds.), *Delivery and adoption of cloud computing services in contemporary organizations* (pp. 26–55). Hershey, PA: IGI Global. doi:10.4018/978-1-4666-8210-8.ch002

Kasemsap, K. (2015b). The role of cloud computing in global supply chain. In N. Rao (Ed.), *Enterprise management strategies in the era of cloud computing* (pp. 192–219). Hershey, PA: IGI Global. doi:10.4018/978-1-4666-8339-6.ch009

Kasemsap, K. (2016). Examining the roles of virtual team and information technology in global business. In C. Graham (Ed.), *Strategic management and leadership for systems development in virtual spaces* (pp. 1–21). Hershey, PA: IGI Global. doi:10.4018/978-1-4666-9688-4.ch001

Kasemsap, K. (2017a). Sustainability, environmental sustainability, and sustainable tourism: Advanced issues and implications. In N. Ray (Ed.), *Business infrastructure for sustainability in developing economies* (pp. 1–24). Hershey, PA: IGI Global. doi:10.4018/978-1-5225-2041-2.ch001

Kasemsap, K. (2017b). Environmental management and waste management: Principles and applications. In U. Akkucuk (Ed.), *Ethics and sustainability in global supply chain management* (pp. 26–49). Hershey, PA: IGI Global. doi:10.4018/978-1-5225-2036-8.ch002

Kern, E., Dick, M., Naumann, S., & Hiller, T. (2015). Impacts of software and its engineering on the carbon footprint of ICT. *Environmental Impact Assessment Review, 52*, 53–61. doi:10.1016/j.eiar.2014.07.003

Kesswani, N., & Jain, S. K. (2017). Schematic classification model of green computing approaches. In *Nature-inspired computing: Concepts, methodologies, tools, and applications* (pp. 1643–1650). Hershey, PA: IGI Global. doi:10.4018/978-1-5225-0788-8.ch063

Khan, N., Shah, A., & Nusratullah, K. (2017). Adoption of virtualization in cloud computing: A foundation step towards green computing. In *Nature-inspired computing: Concepts, methodologies, tools, and applications* (pp. 1693–1700). Hershey, PA: IGI Global. doi:10.4018/978-1-5225-0788-8.ch066

Khan, S., Honnutagi, A. R., & Khan, M. S. (2015). Development of a research framework for green IT enablers using interpretive structural modelling. *International Journal of Green Computing, 6*(1), 1–13. doi:10.4018/IJGC.2015010101

Khosravi, A., & Buyya, R. (2017). Energy and carbon footprint-aware management of geo-distributed cloud data centers: A taxonomy, state of the art, and future directions. In N. Kamila (Ed.), *Advancing cloud database systems and capacity planning with dynamic applications* (pp. 27–46). Hershey, PA: IGI Global. doi:10.4018/978-1-5225-2013-9.ch002

Kumar, D., Sahoo, B., & Mandal, T. (2016). Heuristic task consolidation techniques for energy efficient cloud computing. In *Web-based services: Concepts, methodologies, tools, and applications* (pp. 760–782). Hershey, PA: IGI Global. doi:10.4018/978-1-4666-9466-8.ch034

Li, C. (2015). Hybrid cloud service selection strategy: Model and application of campus. *Computer Applications in Engineering Education, 23*(5), 645–657. doi:10.1002/cae.21634

Liu, J., Huang, X., & Liu, J. K. (2015). Secure sharing of personal health records in cloud computing: Ciphertext-policy attribute-based signcryption. *Future Generation Computer Systems, 52*, 67–76. doi:10.1016/j.future.2014.10.014

Maenhaut, P. J., Moens, H., Ongenae, V., & de Turck, F. (2016). Migrating legacy software to the cloud: Approach and verification by means of two medical software use cases. *Software, Practice & Experience, 46*(1), 31–54. doi:10.1002/spe.2320

Mair, J., Huang, Z., & Zhang, H. (2012). Energy-aware scheduling for parallel applications on multicore systems. In N. Kaabouch & W. Hu (Eds.), *Energy-aware systems and networking for sustainable initiatives* (pp. 38–58). Hershey, PA: IGI Global. doi:10.4018/978-1-4666-1842-8.ch003

Mardamutu, K., Ponnusamy, V., & Zaman, N. (2016). Green energy in data centers. In V. Ponnusamy, N. Zaman, T. Low, & A. Amin (Eds.), *Biologically-inspired energy harvesting through wireless sensor technologies* (pp. 234–249). Hershey, PA: IGI Global. doi:10.4018/978-1-4666-9792-8.ch012

McWhorter, R. R., & Delello, J. A. (2016). Green computing through virtual learning environments. In *Professional development and workplace learning: Concepts, methodologies, tools, and applications* (pp. 837–864). Hershey, PA: IGI Global. doi:10.4018/978-1-4666-8632-8.ch047

Menzel, M., Ranjan, R., Wang, L., Khan, S. U., & Chen, J. (2014). CloudGenius: A hybrid decision support method for automating the migration of web application clusters to public clouds. *IEEE Transactions on Cloud Computing, 64*(5), 1336–1348. doi:10.1109/TC.2014.2317188

Moreno, I. S., & Xu, J. (2013). Energy-efficiency in cloud computing environments: Towards energy savings without performance degradation. In S. Aljawarneh (Ed.), *Cloud computing advancements in design, implementation, and technologies* (pp. 18–36). Hershey, PA: IGI Global. doi:10.4018/978-1-4666-1879-4.ch002

Palanivel, K., & Kuppuswami, S. (2017). Green and energy-efficient computing architecture for e-learning. In *Nature-inspired computing: Concepts, methodologies, tools, and applications* (pp. 1668–1692). Hershey, PA: IGI Global. doi:10.4018/978-1-5225-0788-8.ch065

Pattinson, C., Oram, D., & Ross, M. (2013). Sustainability and social responsibility in raising awareness of green issues through developing tertiary academic provision: A case study. In R. Colomo-Palacios (Ed.), *Enhancing the modern organization through information technology professionals: Research, studies, and techniques* (pp. 284–294). Hershey, PA: IGI Global. doi:10.4018/978-1-4666-2648-5.ch020

Philipson, G. (2013). A framework for green computing. In K. Ganesh & S. Anbuudayasankar (Eds.), *International and interdisciplinary studies in green computing* (pp. 12–26). Hershey, PA: IGI Global. doi:10.4018/978-1-4666-2646-1.ch002

Prasad, A., & Rao, S. (2014). A mechanism design approach to resource procurement in cloud computing. *IEEE Transactions on Cloud Computing, 63*(1), 17–30. doi:10.1109/TC.2013.106

Quinton, C., Romero, D., & Duchien, L. (2016). SALOON: A platform for selecting and configuring cloud environments. *Software, Practice & Experience*, *46*(1), 55–78. doi:10.1002/spe.2311

Radu, L. D. (2014). Green ICTs potential in emerging economies. *Procedia Economics and Finance*, *15*, 430–436. doi:10.1016/S2212-5671(14)00473-0

Rahman, N. (2016). Toward achieving environmental sustainability in the computer industry. *International Journal of Green Computing*, *7*(1), 37–54. doi:10.4018/IJGC.2016010103

Raisinghani, M. S., & Idemudia, E. C. (2016). Green information systems for sustainability. In U. Akkucuk (Ed.), *Handbook of research on waste management techniques for sustainability* (pp. 212–226). Hershey, PA: IGI Global. doi:10.4018/978-1-4666-9723-2.ch011

Roodt, S., & de Villiers, C. (2012). Teaching green information technology inside and outside the classroom: An undergraduate case-study in the South African context. *International Journal of Innovation in the Digital Economy*, *3*(3), 60–71. doi:10.4018/jide.2012070106

Ryoo, J., & Choi, Y. (2011). A taxonomy of green information and communication protocols and standards. In B. Unhelkar (Ed.), *Handbook of research on green ICT: Technology, business and social perspectives* (pp. 364–376). Hershey, PA: IGI Global. doi:10.4018/978-1-61692-834-6.ch026

Sabry, N., & Krause, P. (2013). Optimal green virtual machine migration model. *International Journal of Business Data Communications and Networking*, *9*(3), 35–52. doi:10.4018/jbdcn.2013070103

Sanduja, S., Jewell, P., Aron, E., & Pharai, N. (2015). Cloud computing for pharmacometrics: Using AWS, NONMEM, PsN, grid engine, and sonic. *CPT: Pharmacometrics & Systems Pharmacology*, *4*(9), 537–546. PMID:26451333

Sasikala, P. (2013). Architectural strategies for green cloud computing: Environments, infrastructure and resources. In S. Aljawarneh (Ed.), *Cloud computing advancements in design, implementation, and technologies* (pp. 218–242). Hershey, PA: IGI Global. doi:10.4018/978-1-4666-1879-4.ch016

Sean, M., Zhi, L., Subhajyoti, B., Juheng, Z., & Anand, G. (2011). Cloud computing: The business perspective. *Decision Support Systems*, *51*(1), 176–189. doi:10.1016/j.dss.2010.12.006

Shivalkar, P., & Tripathy, B. (2015). Rough set based green cloud computing in emerging markets. In M. Khosrow-Pour (Ed.), *Encyclopedia of information science and technology* (3rd ed., pp. 1078–1087). Hershey, PA: IGI Global. doi:10.4018/978-1-4666-5888-2.ch103

Shojafar, M., Cordeschi, N., & Baccarelli, E. (2016). Resource scheduling for energy-aware reconfigurable Internet data centers. In Q. Hassan (Ed.), *Innovative research and applications in next-generation high performance computing* (pp. 21–46). Hershey, PA: IGI Global. doi:10.4018/978-1-5225-0287-6.ch002

Singh, A., Mishra, N., Ali, S. I., Shukla, N., & Shankar, R. (2015). Cloud computing technology: Reducing carbon footprint in beef supply chain. *International Journal of Production Economics*, *164*, 462–471. doi:10.1016/j.ijpe.2014.09.019

Singh, S., & Gond, S. (2017). Green computing and its impact. In *Nature-inspired computing: Concepts, methodologies, tools, and applications* (pp. 1628–1642). Hershey, PA: IGI Global. doi:10.4018/978-1-5225-0788-8.ch062

Smeitink, M., & Spruit, M. (2013). Maturity for sustainability in IT: Introducing the MITS. *International Journal of Information Technologies and Systems Approach*, *6*(1), 39–56. doi:10.4018/jitsa.2013010103

Son, S., Jung, G., & Jun, S. C. (2013). An SLA-based cloud computing that facilitates resource allocation in the distributed data centers of a cloud provider. *The Journal of Supercomputing*, *64*(2), 606–637. doi:10.1007/s11227-012-0861-z

Song, W., & Xiao, Z. (2013). An Infrastructure-as-a-Service cloud: On-demand resource provisioning. In X. Yang & L. Liu (Eds.), *Principles, methodologies, and service-oriented approaches for cloud computing* (pp. 302–324). Hershey, PA: IGI Global. doi:10.4018/978-1-4666-2854-0.ch013

Thakur, P. K., & Verma, A. (2015). Process batch offloading method for mobile-cloud computing platform. *Journal of Cases on Information Technology*, *17*(3), 1–13. doi:10.4018/JCIT.2015070101

Thongmak, M. (2013). A systematic framework for sustainable ICTs in developing countries. *International Journal of Information Technologies and Systems Approach*, *6*(1), 1–19. doi:10.4018/jitsa.2013010101

Voderhobli, K. (2015). An SNMP based traffic characterisation paradigm for green-aware networks. In V. Chang, R. Walters, & G. Wills (Eds.), *Delivery and adoption of cloud computing services in contemporary organizations* (pp. 340–357). Hershey, PA: IGI Global. doi:10.4018/978-1-4666-8210-8.ch014

Wang, B., Li, H., Liu, X., Li, X., & Li, F. (2014). Preserving identity privacy on multi-owner cloud data during public verification. *Security and Communication Networks*, *7*(11), 2104–2113. doi:10.1002/sec.922

Wang, H., & Huo, D. (2014). Green cloud computing: Site selection of data centers. In S. Srinivasan (Ed.), *Security, trust, and regulatory aspects of cloud computing in business environments* (pp. 202–214). Hershey, PA: IGI Global. doi:10.4018/978-1-4666-5788-5.ch012

Wu, Y., Cegielski, C. G., Hazen, B. T., & Hall, D. J. (2013). Cloud computing in support of supply chain information system infrastructure: Understanding when to go to the cloud. *Journal of Supply Chain Management*, *49*(3), 25–41. doi:10.1111/j.1745-493x.2012.03287.x

Xuan, X. (2012). From cloud computing to cloud manufacturing. *Robotics and Computer-integrated Manufacturing*, *28*(1), 75–86. doi:10.1016/j.rcim.2011.07.002

Yang, M., Kuo, C., & Yeh, Y. (2011). Dynamic rightsizing with quality-controlled algorithms in virtualization environments. *International Journal of Grid and High Performance Computing*, *3*(2), 29–43. doi:10.4018/jghpc.2011040103

Yuvaraj, M. (2015). Green libraries on cloud computing platform. In M. Khosrow-Pour (Ed.), *Encyclopedia of information science and technology* (3rd ed., pp. 3901–3911). Hershey, PA: IGI Global. doi:10.4018/978-1-4666-5888-2.ch384

Zhang, J., Huang, H., & Wang, X. (2016). Resource provision algorithms in cloud computing: A survey. *Journal of Network and Computer Applications*, *64*, 23–42. doi:10.1016/j.jnca.2015.12.018

Zhang, J., & Liang, X. J. (2012). Promoting greenICT in China: A framework based on innovation system approaches. *Telecommunications Policy*, *36*(10/11), 997–1013. doi:10.1016/j.telpol.2012.09.001

Zheng, X., & Cai, Y. (2010). Optimal server allocation and frequency modulation on multi-core based server clusters. *International Journal of Green Computing*, *1*(2), 18–30. doi:10.4018/jgc.2010070102

ADDITIONAL READING

Arnfalk, P., Pilerot, U., Schillander, P., & Grönvall, P. (2016). Green IT in practice: Virtual meetings in Swedish public agencies. *Journal of Cleaner Production, 123*, 101–112. doi:10.1016/j.jclepro.2015.08.063

Barrow, C., & Hatch, T. (2015). Finance in the cloud: Myth or today's reality? *Journal of Corporate Accounting & Finance, 26*(5), 5–13. doi:10.1002/jcaf.22057

Bayramusta, M., & Nasir, V. A. (2016). A fad or future of IT?: A comprehensive literature review on the cloud computing research. *International Journal of Information Management, 36*(4), 635–644. doi:10.1016/j.ijinfomgt.2016.04.006

Byington, J. R., & McGee, J. A. (2014). Data security and the cloud. *Journal of Corporate Accounting & Finance, 25*(5), 41–44. doi:10.1002/jcaf.21971

Debnath, B., Roychoudhuri, R., & Ghosh, S. K. (2016). E-waste management: A potential route to greencomputing. *Procedia Environmental Sciences, 35*, 669–675. doi:10.1016/j.proenv.2016.07.063

Ding, J., Xiong, C., & Liu, H. (2015). Construction of a digital learning environment based on cloud computing. *British Journal of Educational Technology, 46*(6), 1367–1377. doi:10.1111/bjet.12208

Fan, W., Yang, S., & Pei, J. (2014). A novel two-stage model for cloud service trustworthiness evaluation. *Expert Systems: International Journal of Knowledge Engineering and Neural Networks, 31*(2), 136–153. doi:10.1111/exsy.12017

Fujinoki, H. (2015). Designs, analyses, and optimizations for attribute-shuffling obfuscation to protect information from malicious cloud administrators. *Security and Communication Networks, 8*(17), 3045–3066. doi:10.1002/sec.1231

Gai, K., Qiu, M., Zhao, H., Tao, L., & Zong, Z. (2016). Dynamic energy-aware cloudlet-based mobile cloud computing model for greencomputing. *Journal of Network and Computer Applications, 59*, 46–54. doi:10.1016/j.jnca.2015.05.016

Huang, X., & Du, X. (2015). Achieving data privacy on hybrid cloud. *Security and Communication Networks, 8*(18), 3771–3781. doi:10.1002/sec.1298

Ismail, L., & Fardoun, A. (2016). EATS: Energy-aware tasks scheduling in cloud computing systems. *Procedia Computer Science, 83*, 870–877. doi:10.1016/j.procs.2016.04.178

Khan, A. N., Kiah, M. L. M., Ali, M., Madani, S. A., & Shamshirband, S. (2014). BSS: Block-based sharing scheme for secure data storage services in mobile cloud environment. *The Journal of Supercomputing*, *70*(2), 946–976. doi:10.1007/s11227-014-1269-8

Kshetri, N. (2016). Institutional and economic factors affecting the development of the Chinese cloud computing industry and market. *Telecommunications Policy*, *40*(2/3), 116–129. doi:10.1016/j.telpol.2015.07.006

Li, B., Ma, X., Li, J., & Zong, Z. (2014). A fixed point model for rate control and routing in cloud data center networks. *Security and Communication Networks*, *7*(9), 1420–1436. doi:10.1002/sec.878

Lin, C. (2012). A novel green cloud computing framework for improving system efficiency. *Physics Procedia*, *24*, 2326–2333. doi:10.1016/j.phpro.2012.02.345

Masdari, M., ValiKardan, S., Shahi, Z., & Azar, S. I. (2016). Towards workflow scheduling in cloud computing: A comprehensive analysis. *Journal of Network and Computer Applications*, *66*, 64–82. doi:10.1016/j.jnca.2016.01.018

Mouchet, C., Urquhart, N., & Kemmer, R. (2014). Techniques for auditing the ICT carbon footprint of an organisation. *International Journal of Green Computing*, *5*(1), 44–61. doi:10.4018/ijgc.2014010104

Mukherjee, A., & De, D. (2016). Femtolet: A novel fifth generation network device for green mobile cloud computing. *Simulation Modelling Practice and Theory*, *62*, 68–87. doi:10.1016/j.simpat.2016.01.014

Prasad, A., & Green, P. (2015). Governing cloud computing services: Reconsideration of IT governance structures. *International Journal of Accounting Information Systems*, *19*, 45–58. doi:10.1016/j.accinf.2015.11.004

Rajeev, T., & Ashok, S. (2015). Dynamic load-shifting program based on a cloud computing framework to support the integration of renewable energy sources. *Applied Energy*, *146*, 141–149. doi:10.1016/j.apenergy.2015.02.014

Ranjan, R., Buyya, R., Leitner, P., Haller, A., & Tai, S. (2014). A note on software tools and techniques for monitoring and prediction of cloud services. *Software, Practice & Experience*, *44*(7), 771–775. doi:10.1002/spe.2266

Ratten, V. (2015). International consumer attitudes toward cloud computing: A social cognitive theory and technology acceptance model perspective. *Thunderbird International Business Review*, *57*(3), 217–228. doi:10.1002/tie.21692

Rhinesmith, C. (2014). The social shaping of cloud computing: An ethnography of infrastructure in east St. Louis, Illinois. *Proceedings of the American Society for Information Science and Technology*, *51*(1), 1–10. doi:10.1002/meet.2014.14505101060

Schniederjans, D. G., & Hales, D. N. (2016). Cloud computing and its impact on economic and environmental performance: A transaction cost economics perspective. *Decision Support Systems*, *86*, 73–82. doi:10.1016/j.dss.2016.03.009

Sharma, Y., Javadi, B., Si, W., & Sun, D. (2016). Reliability and energy efficiency in cloud computing systems: Survey and taxonomy. *Journal of Network and Computer Applications*, *74*, 66–85. doi:10.1016/j.jnca.2016.08.010

Subirats, J., & Guitart, J. (2015). Assessing and forecasting energy efficiency on cloud computing platforms. *Future Generation Computer Systems*, *45*, 70–94. doi:10.1016/j.future.2014.11.008

Sultan, N. (2014). Servitization of the IT industry: The cloud phenomenon. *Strategic Change*, *23*(5/6), 375–388. doi:10.1002/jsc.1983

Tamegawa, K., Ukai, Y., & Chida, R. (2014). Macroeconomic contribution of the cloud computing system to the Japanese economy. *The Review of Socionetwork Strategies*, *8*(2), 101–117. doi:10.1007/s12626-014-0047-7

Trentesaux, D., Borangiu, T., & Thomas, A. (2016). Emerging ICT concepts for smart, safe and sustainable industrial systems. *Computers in Industry*, *81*, 1–10. doi:10.1016/j.compind.2016.05.001

Xue, H., Inati, S., Sørensen, T. S., Kellman, P., & Hansen, M. S. (2015). Distributed MRI reconstruction using gadgetron-based cloud computing. *Magnetic Resonance in Medicine*, *73*(3), 1015–1025. doi:10.1002/mrm.25213 PMID:24687458

Zhang, C., & Liu, C. (2015). The impact of ICT industry on CO_2 emissions: A regional analysis in China. *Renewable & Sustainable Energy Reviews*, *44*, 12–19. doi:10.1016/j.rser.2014.12.011

Zhang, F., Gao, Z., & Ye, Q. (2015). Construction of cloud platform for personalized information services in digital library based on cloud computing data processing technology. *Automatic Control and Computer Sciences*, *49*(6), 373–379. doi:10.3103/S0146411615060127

KEY TERMS AND DEFINITIONS

Cloud Computing: The delivery of hosted services over the Internet.

Energy Consumption: The amount of energy consumed in a process or system, or by an organization.

Information Systems: The combination of hardware, software, infrastructure, and trained personnel organized to facilitate planning, control, coordination, and decision making in an organization.

Internet: The method of connecting a computer to other computers through dedicated routers and servers.

Green Computing: The environmentally responsible utilization of computers and related resources.

Green ICT: The sustainable practice of using computing and information technology resources more efficiently while maintaining or improving overall performance.

Sustainability: The sustainable issue that products and services should be produced in ways that do not use resources that cannot be replaced and that do not damage the environment.

Technology: The scientific method and material used to achieve the commercial or industrial objective.

Chapter 3

Green Evolutionary–Based Algorithm for Multiple Services Scheduling in Cloud Computing

Amjad Gawanmeh
Khalifa University, UAE

Ahmad Alomari
Ecole de Technologie Superieure, Canada

Alain April
Ecole de Technologie Superieure, Canada

Ali Alwadi
Auckland University of Technology, New Zealand

Sazia Parvin
University of New South Wales, Australia

ABSTRACT

The era of cloud computing allowed the instant scale up of provided services into massive capacities without the need for investing in any new on site infrastructure. Hence, the interest of this type of services has been increased, in particular, by medium scale entities who can afford to completely outsource their data-center and their infrastructure. In addition, large companies may wish to provide support for wide range of load capacities, including peak ones, however, this will require very higher costs in order to build larger data centers internally. Cloud services can provide services for these companies according to their need whether in peak load

DOI: 10.4018/978-1-5225-3038-1.ch003

capacity of low ones. Therefore, resource sharing and provisioning is considered one of the most challenging problems in cloud based services since these services have become more numerous and dynamic. As a result, assigning tasks and services requests into available resources has become a persistent problem in cloud computing, given the large number of variables, and the increasing types of services, demand, and requirement. Scheduling services using a limited number of resources is problem that has been under study since the evolution of cloud computing. However, there are several open areas for improvements due to the large number of optimization variables. In general, the scheduling of services on available resources is considered NP complete. As a result, several heuristic based methods were proposed in order to enhance the efficiency of cloud systems. Since the problem has several optimization parameters, there are still several improvements that can be done in this area. This chapter discusses the formalization of the problem of scheduling multiple tasks by single user and multiple users, and then presents a proposed solution for each individual case. First, an algorithm is presented and evaluated for optimum schedule that allocates a number of subtasks on a given number of resources; the algorithm was shown to be linear vs. number of users. Then, an algorithm is presented to address the problem of multiple users allocations, each, with multiple subtasks. The algorithm was design using the single user allocation algorithm as a selection function. Since, this problem is known to be NP complete, heuristic based methods are usually used in order to provide better solutions. Therefore, a green evolutionary based algorithm is proposed in order to address the problem of resource allocation with large number of users. In addition, the algorithm presents allocation schedule with better utility, while the execution time is linear vs. different parameters. The results obtained in this work show that it overcomes the outcome of one of the most efficient algorithms presented in this regard that was based on game theory. Further, this method works with no restrictions on the problem parameters as opposed to game theory methods that require certain parameters restrictions on cost vector or compaction time matrix. On the other hand, the main limitation of the proposed algorithm is that it is only applicable to the scheduling problem of multiple tasks that has one price vector and one execution time vector. However, scheduling multiple users, each with subtasks that have their own price and execution time vector, is very complex problem and beyond the scope of this work, hence it will be addressed in future work.

INTRODUCTION

Cloud concepts (Furht & Escalante, 2010) are dominating the classical host-based architectures with the concept of elastic computing pattern. This new service-oriented paradigm delivers resources and applications on-demand based on the pay-per-use concept. Several cloud service requirements and QoS are to be maintained in order to provide application users with powerful computing facilities that guarantees robustness, fault tolerance, and execution automation. Hence, there are several challenging problems to be addressed in the use of these cloud based systems—in particular—related to efficiency. In addition, the energy efficiency of ICT based systems has become a major issue with the increasing demand of cloud computing, while large datacenters are being established to host these cloud services, which consume huge amount of energy, and at the same time big efforts are put on reducing the management costs. Since cloud-based services have become very dynamic, resource allocation problem is considered more complex and challenging.

While several qualities of service issues in cloud computing systems have been addressed in the literature, it is believed that green based cloud computing problems have not received as much attention. In particular, when addressing the problem of constrained resource allocation, which is proven to be a difficult problem because of the large number of variable parameters, such as assumptions about the services, tasks, subtasks, and communication between servers. On the other hand, scheduling multiple tasks for multiple users on given number of resources is considered NP complete problem, and therefore, it has been addressed in several research methods. Several proposed solutions in the literature are built on top of several assumptions and simplifications. This is due to the large number of optimization parameters in the problem. As a result, several improvements can still be done in this direction.

This work presents a green computing scheduling method to solve the problem of resource allocation in which cloud services request the usage of resources across a cloud-based network, where the cost of computational service depends on the amount of computation. The proposed method is intended to reduce the computation cost, which in turn presents an energy friendly solution to a complex problem. The contributions in this chapter include providing an algorithm for resource allocation for multiple cloud users who request their services to be executed on multiple cloud servers. Then, the complexity of the method is enhanced by using an evolutionary computing based method. Experimental results show that presented method performs in linear time vs different parameters in the problem.

The rest of this chapter is organized as follows: Section 2 provides a brief review on the state of the art on the subject. Section 3.2 describes the formalization of the single user problems and the proposed solution. Section 4.2 address the problem of multiple users scheduling. Section 5 presents the green evolutionary algorithm to solve scheduling problem in linear time vs different parameters with experimental results. Finally, Section 6 concludes the chapter with future work hints.

REVIEW AND BACKGROUND WORK

There are several detailed reviews about this subject can be found in surveys such as (Sagar, Singh, & Ahmad, 2013), (Khan, 2013), (Anuradha & Sumathi, 2014), (Vinothina, Sridaran, & Ganapathi, 2012), (Manvi & Shyam, 2014). However, it is important to present some related work and discuss improvements over existing methods.

Methods that are based on evolutionary genetic algorithms to solve scheduling problem in cloud computing were presented in several works. The work in (Ge & Wei, 2010) presented a genetic algorithm method for task level scheduling in Hadoop MapReduce, while the work can help finding local optimum solution, the execution of the load-balancing algorithm can take long time to make a decision for task assignments. The work in (Kołodziej, Khan, Wang, & Zomaya, 2015) addressed the independent batch scheduling in computational grid by presenting a genetic based algorithm in order to solve the global minimization problem in grid based energy consumption. The main disadvantage of this work, is that it is based only on two criteria, while fixing several other parameters. A genetic based scheduling algorithm was presented by (Saha, Pal, & Pattnaik, 2016) in order to reduce the waiting time of tasks to be scheduled in a cloud environment, while the work in (Sahu, Singh, & Prakash, 2015) presented a method for resource allocation of grid based systems. Karthik et al. (Kumar, Feng, Nimmagadda, & Lu, 2011) presented a method for resource allocation by using QoS metrics from the performance parameters of different Virtual Machines in cloud infrastructure. The method has the advantage of granting the user the ability to select VMs in order to reduce the associated cost. Ergu et al. (Ergu, Kou, Peng, Shi, & Shi, 2013) proposed a method for resource allocation based on the combination of response time, user preferences, and available resources.

There are certain applications where the waiting time can be critical, however, in general, the main issue in this work is to optimize scheduling for waiting time that will have big impact on system utilization, which might not be favorable for several cloud applications. While the use of evolutionary based algorithms can help solving very large scale problems, it cannot guarantee obtaining the absolute optimum solutions, therefore it can be useful in certain cloud applications, however, it cannot be used to provide baseline solutions for scheduling problems. In fact, evolutionary algorithms may make use of methods that provide absolute optimum solution for small scale problems in order to build on these.

Several computing paradigms were adopted in the development of heuristic based methods for resource allocation in cloud computing. For instance, game theory based approaches have also been proposed in (Teng & Magoulès, 2010). This work considers several criteria in the optimization, such as dynamic allocation, variable resources distribution, different requirement of cloud users and their common information. The main issue with this approach is the requirements of strong assumptions about certain system parameters in order to have Nash equilibrium for the game. A similar approach was proposed in (Velayudham, Gohila, Hariharan, & Ramya Selvi, 2014) to solve the problem of resource allocation in cognitive networks in order to increase resource utilization efficiency. The main drawback of this approach is that it requires dividing the payoff equally between all users of the cognitive network in order to work. Game theory and Nash equilibrium based method was proposed in (Wei, Vasilakos, Zheng, & Xiong, 2010) for finding the optimum schedule of tasks on available resources in cloud system. The method considers the computation cost of the used services as well as the execution time. The proposed method can be applied on multiple users problem with subtasks, however, in order to apply game theoretic method optimally and find a Nash equilibrium, the execution time and the price vectors must be given in sorted order. This restriction limits the method into particular applications.

Fuzzy pattern recognition methods were also used in the literature, for instance, the authors in (Wang & Su, 2015) presented a dynamically hierarchical resource-allocation method that can be used within multiple cloud nodes. The algorithm requires intercommunication between nodes and prior knowledge about several task parameters. The work in (Guo, Yu, Tian, & Yu, 2015) used fuzzy clustering for a workflow task scheduling. The major objective of scheduling is to minimize makespan of the precedence constrained applications. The method can only be applied on resource allocation problems that can be modeled as directed acyclic graphs. The use of fuzzy pattern recognition to solve similar problems were also proposed in (Minarolli & Freisleben, 2013). The authors addressed the problem conflicting goals in dynamic resource allocation for virtual machines in cloud computing to guarantee application performance and to reduce operating costs. This work can be useful in certain applications that have restrictions on specific parameters, such as execution time, or cost, in order to find solutions under these constraints. However, it can be applied in order to optimize the schedule under both parameters simultaneously. Overall, the main problem with fuzzy logic approaches is with the requirement and restrictions imposed on the input space so that the algorithm can provide optimum solution.

Auction-based methods were also applied to the problem, such as the works in (Lin, Lin, & Wei, 2010) and (Chang, Lu, Huang, Lin, & Tzang, 2013) who presented an auction mechanism approach for cloud resource allocation that works well under certain requirement including a specific value for the bandwidth between the use and the cloud server. Users are allocated to the available resources using an auction mechanism based on the available bandwidth of the cloud resource provider. The major issue with this approach is that it did not consider the cost of executing specific tasks on the available servers, but only considered bandwidth, which is only one factor of the cost. Another auction method was proposed by (Lee, Wang, & Niyato, 2015) in order to help cloud providers to decide when and how they will allocate their resources and to which users. While the method can be useful in real time resource allocation, it can give an effective solution where a certain task is to be scheduled instantly. It is not practical when the resources and tasks are known ahead and are required to be scheduled to optimize utilization of the system.

Other approaches that can be considered related, but addressed problem with different context include profit and pricing based methods, such as the work by Walker et al. (Walker, Brisken, & Romney, 2010), Buyya et al. (Buyya, Ranjan, & Calheiros, 2010), and (Xiao, Song, & Chen, 2013). User preferences based scheduling for enhancing QOs was also proposed by Ergu et al. (Ergu, Kou, Peng, Shi, & Shi, 2013), (Mohan & Satyanarayana, 2015) and (Senthilnathan & Kalaiarasan, 2013). The work in (Singh, Dutta, & Singh, 2014) proposed error-based resource allocation in order to maintain the consistency in the priorities of the multiple tasks under scheduling. Agent based method was proposed in (Ejarque, Álvarez, Sirvent, & Badia, 2012) which enables modeling interoperability between available resources and users. These types of methods can be useful in the search for cost-effective solutions for certain QoS requirement. However, solving QoS problem given the number of parameters is multitask scheduling is NP complete problem, therefore to find the absolute optimal schedule in terms of QoS measures is not practical. In order to help in this regard, it is required to solve scheduling problem at small scale first, and find optimum strategy, and then use this strategy to design heuristic based algorithms that can enhance existing scheduling methods.

Considering QoS metrics in scheduling, utility is defined to measure the quality of the schedule. The objective is to improve the utility of scheduling algorithms while at the same time reduce energy consumption in cloud system with resource allocation constrains. Therefore, more practical solutions for scheduling and allocation problem must be presented. This work presents a generic solution for the problem of scheduling multi-users with dependent tasks; each is composed of several subtasks to be scheduled on multiple computational resources. The proposed mechanism is based on utility function trying to find a local optimum solution for the NP-hard problem, and then an evolutionary green computing algorithm is presented with linear time vs different design parameters.

Even though there are several proposed methods to address resource allocation in cloud computing, on the subject, there is still possibility for more improved solutions, because the available cloud-based services are dependent on several QoS factors (Wei, Vasilakos, Zheng, & Xiong, 2010). The main contributions of this work include providing a novel method to find optimum solution to allocate resources on given multiple subtasks to be scheduled on a number of resources with given costs, in addition, providing experimental results to show that given solution runs in linear time vs different design parameters. The method is illustrated on a detailed step by step example that shows how the algorithm evolves in order to reach required solution. Experimental results are conducted with practical number of subtasks and resources. Finally, the proposed method is applicable without any restriction on the cost vector or execution time for resources.

SINGLE-USER RESOURCES SCHEDULING

This section presents the problem description and proposes a solution for resource allocation for a single user where multiple subtasks are to be scheduled using multiple available resources, each has different execution turn over time and price. In the following section, the general case of multiple users will be presented.

Single User Problem Description and Formalization

We provide here the problem description based on previous description in (Wei, Vasilakos, Zheng, & Xiong, 2010) and (Gawanmeh & April, A Novel Algorithm for Optimizing Multiple Services Resource Allocation, 2016). Given a number of k subtasks for a cloud services user that are to be scheduled using existing m computational resources: $\{R_1, R_2, ..., R_m\}$. Each resource, R_j, costs a fixed price p_j, hence forming the price vector $p = \{p_1, p_2, ..., p_m\}$. In addition, each resource R_i requires a specific time, t_i, to execute any subtask forming the execution time vector $t = \{t_1, t_2, ..., t_m\}$.

It is required to assign the given set of subtasks each into a single selected resource R_j in order to minimize the total cost. Cost is defined using the expense and total execution time for completing all given subtasks. The solution for the given scheduling problem is a resulting vector that has k elements, each is a non-negative number represent the subtasks assigned to that particular resource. For instance, is element number i in vector represents the number of subtasks allocated to resource R_i. Therefore, the solution vector v must satisfy $\sum_{i=1}^{m} v_i = k$.

We define the following two vectors as follows: the execution time vector, denoted as $\hat{t}$ and the expense cost vector, denoted as $\hat{e}$. The entry $\hat{t}_i$ of $\hat{t}$ represents the turnaround time it takes for resource R_i to complete v_j subtasks of the task S. The entry $\hat{e}_i$ of $\hat{e}$ vector is the expense user S pays for resource R_i to complete v_j subtasks. These two vectors are defined as follows:

$$\hat{t} = v \times t$$

$$\hat{e} = v \times t \times p$$

Based on these, two values for schedule v are calculated, the first represents the total execution time t_{max}, and the second represents the total expense e_v. The execution time for task S is the maximum execution time of tasks assigned to resources, $t_{max} = max\left\{\hat{t}_i | \hat{t}_i \in \hat{t}\right\}$, where $\hat{t}_i$ denotes the i_{th} element of the vector $\hat{t}$.

The total expense e_v is the summation of all expenses paid to all resources, $e_v = \sum_{i=1}^{m} e_i$

We assign weights for schedule costs as follows, w_t for execution time weight, and w_e for expense weight. Then we can define a benefit value of the expense using the following utility function:

$$u\left(v\right) = \frac{1}{w_t \times t_v + w_e \times e_v}.$$

$$u\left(v\right) = \frac{1}{w_t \times max\left\{\hat{t}_i | \hat{t}_i \in \hat{t}\right\} + w_e \times \sum_{i=1}^{m} e_i}$$

The optimum solution is achieved when u is maximized. An illustrative example is shown below in order to demonstrate the allocation problem. Using five available resources *(R1 – R5), m* = 5, and using the price vector of $p = \left(1.2, 1.5, 2, 1.0, 1.8\right)$, with a single task *(S)* with *k* = 3 subtasks. We assume that the execution time vector for each subtask is given as follows: $t = \left(4, 3.5, 3.2, 2.8, 2.4\right)$. Assume that a schedule $v = \left(1, 0, 1, 0, 1\right)$ is used, then we can calculate the execution time vector $\hat{t}$ and the expense cost vector $\hat{e}$, as follows: $\hat{t} = \left(4, 0, 3.2, 0, 2.4\right)$, and $\hat{e} = \left(4.8, 0, 6.4, 0, 4.32\right)$. From these, we obtain $t_v = 4$, which is the maximum value in $\hat{t}$ and $e_v = 15.52$, which is the summation of all values in $\hat{e}$. Assuming $w_t = 1$ and $w_e = 1$, then

$$u = \frac{1}{t_v + e_v} = 0.0152.$$ Changing v, will result in a different utility, for instance, the schedule $v = \left(1, 1, 0, 1, 0\right)$ will result in a utility $u = 0.0593$.

Optimizing Single User Scheduling

This section presents the proposed algorithm for scheduling a user with multiple subtasks on multiple available resources based on selection function (Gawanmeh, Alomari, & April, Optimizing Resource Allocation Scheduling in Cloud Computing services, 2017). For a problem with k subtasks and m resources, the optimum solution for the optimization problem described above is achieved by finding the allocation vector v that maximizes the utility $u(v)$. At first, the problem is solved by defining a variable t_{max} initialized to 0. A selection function called δ with m elements is defined as follows: $\delta = \left(\delta_1, \delta_2, \ldots, \delta_m \right)$, and then initialized as indicated below:

$$\delta_i = max\left(t_{max}, t_i \times \left(1 + v_i \right) \right) + p_i \times t_i \times \left(1 + v_i \right)$$

The allocation of the given k subtasks is archived through procedure, where in every step, one subtask is assigned to one resource. In every step, we chose allocation resource m that satisfies the following set of conditions: (1) $1 \leq j \leq n$, and (2): $\forall i \bullet 1 \leq i \leq m \Rightarrow \delta_j \leq \delta_i$. This means that we chose δ_j which is minimum in δ. Hence, the current subtask is assigned into resource R_j. The schedule v is updated by incrementing v_j. Accordingly, a new $\hat{t}$, δ, and t_{max} are calculated based on the new vector. This step is repeated until all subtasks are scheduled.

This algorithm has a complexity of worst case *O(nk)*. It can be enhanced into $O\left(n \times log\left(k \right) \right)$ by sorting δ, and then whenever, $'_i$ is calculated, it will be inserted into δ while sorted. Applying the above algorithm on the example explained above will result in $v = \left(0, 0, 0, 2, 1 \right)$, with utility *u = 0.0644*, which is the optimum solution.

Illustrative Examples

Let us consider two examples in order to demonstrate the algorithm above to find an optimum allocation vector. In the first, we assume the price vector is given as $p = \left(1, 1.2, 1.5, 1.8, 2 \right)$, the number of resources m = *5*, number of subtasks is k = *4*, the execution time vector for each subtask using the given resources is given as $t = \left(4, 3.5, 3.2, 2.8, 2.4 \right)$. We start calculating initial values of the selection function using the algorithm above, that leads to $\delta = \left(8, 7.7, 8, 7.84, 7.2 \right)$. In addition, we initiate the allocation vector and tmax as follows: $v = \left(0, 0, 0, 0, 0 \right)$, $t_{max} = 0$. Then we chose m, such that δm is minimum, in this case, $\delta_m = 5$, hence, the first subtask will be scheduled to service R5. This is illustrated in the initial step indicated as λ0 in the example below, where the numbers in bold represent the active ones. Based on this, we update the allocation vector, v, the selection function δ, k, and t_{max} in the next step λ1 as follows: $v = \left(0,0,0,0,1\right)$, $\delta = \left(8, 7.7, 8, 7.84, 14.4\right)$, $k = 3$, and $t_{max} = 2.4$. The algorithm proceeds until all subtasks are processed. Table 1 below shows the steps for executing the algorithm on this example. The final allocation vectors becomes $v = \left(1,1,1,0,1\right)$ with $u_v = 0.459$, for $w_t = 1, w_e = 1$, which is the optimum solution.

In the second example, we will use different parameters as follows: the number of resources *m = 10*, number of subtasks is:

$$k = 15, p = \left(4,8,11,10,9,7,13,16,6,12\right)$$

and

$$t = \left(12,11,5,7,5,8,6,8,11,5\right).$$

Algorithm 1. Subtasks resource allocation algorithm

```
 1:   Procedure SubtasksAllocation( )
 2:   Input: k, m, t, p;
 3:   Output: v ;  schedule vector
 4:   Initialize vectors and variables
 5:      v = {0} , t_max = 0 , j = 0
 6:   Initialize the allocation function δ
 7:      REPEAT
 8:            δ_j = p_j × t_j + t_j
 9:            j = j + 1
10:      UNTIL j == m
11:   Process all elements using allocation function
12:      j = 0
13:      REPEAT
14:            Choose r such that δ_r is minimum
15:            (1) 1 ≤ r and r ≤ n
16:            (2) ∀i·1 ≤ i ∧ i ≤ m ⇒ δ_r ≤ δ_i
17:            v_r = v_r + 1 Allocate current subtask to resource R_r
18:            if(v_r × t_r > t_max)
19:                 t_max = v_r × t_r  Update  t_max
20:                 ∀i·1 ≤ i ∧ i ≤ m  δ_i = max  t_max , t_i × 1 + v_i   + p_i + t_i × 1 + v_i   Update δ
21:            else
22:                 δ_r = max  t_max , t_r × 1 + v_r   + p_r + t_r × 1 + v_r
23:            endif
24:            j = j + 1
25:      UNTIL j == m
```

Table 1. Execution of the algorithm on the above example

λ	v	δ	t_{max}	k	m
λ_0	0, 0, 0, 0, 0	(8.0, 7.7, 8.0, 7.84, **7.2**)	0.0	4	5
λ_1	0, 0, 0, 0, 1	(8.0, **7.7**, 8.0, 7.84, 14.4)	2.4	3	2
λ_2	0, 1, 0, 0, 1	(**8.0**, 15.4, 8.3, 8.54, 14.4)	3.5	2	1
λ_3	1, 1, 0, 0, 1	(16.0, 15.4, **8.8**, 9.04, 14.4)	4.0	1	3
λ_4	1, 1, 1, 0, 1	(16, 15.4, 16, **9.04**, 14.4)	4.0	0	4

Executing the algorithm, as shown in Table 2, leads into the schedule $v = \left(2, 1, 2, 1, 3, 1, 1, 1, 2, 1 \right)$, with $u = 0.00104$ for $w_t = 1, w_e = 1$, which is the optimum solution.

The examples above show that the algorithm is simple to implement and at the same time efficient. In fact, when a more complex problem is considered, such as multiple users with tasks with different price vectors, the problem of finding the optimal solution becomes NP complete. However, using a simple and efficient method to find the optimum schedule for the single user case will solve the fundamental step in several heuristic based methods, such as evolutionary ones, that require initial solutions to the problem as a starting point. In the next subsection, we present performance evaluation for the algorithm.

Performance Evaluation

In this section, we study the performance of the given algorithm for different parameters in the problem. We first show the effect of number of subtasks on the execution time of the algorithm. We did an implementation for the algorithm and executed the scheduling process for variable number of subtasks. In order to conduct experimental results, we first provided an implementation for the algorithm in C++. The implementation model of the algorithm is achieved by setting up the selection function with initial values based on input vectors. Then tasks are processed in an iterative process, where every task is allocated for the best available resource provided by the selection function. The selection function is then modified based on this. Next task is scheduled similarly, until all tasks are processed.

In order to study the efficiency of the algorithms, we conducted simulations by generating resources with different costs and computational power, as well as tasks to be scheduled on these resources. In the first experiment, we set the number of resources to a fixed number of 10^4. Then, we tested the execution time for the algorithm for different values of the number of subtasks $k = i \times 10^4$, where

Table 2. Execution of the algorithm on the second example

λ	v	δ	t_{max}	k	m
λ_0	0, 0, 0, 0, 0, 0, 0, 0, 0, 0	(60, 90, 52, 88, **45**, 88, 84, 112, 70, 91)	0	15	5
λ_1	0, 0, 0, 0, 1, 0, 0, 0, 0, 0	(60, 90, **53**, 88, 90, 88, 84, 112, 70, 91)	5	14	3
λ_2	0, 0, 1, 0, 1, 0, 0, 0, 0, 0	(**60**, 90, 104, 88, 90, 88, 84, 112, 70, 91)	5	13	1
λ_3	1, 0, 1, 0, 1, 0, 0, 0, 0, 0	(120, 93, 108, 92, 92, 89, 90, 117, **72**, 96)	5	12	9
λ_4	1, 0, 1, 0, 1, 0, 0, 0, 1, 0	(120, 93, 108, 92, 92, **89**, 90, 117, 140, 96)	12	11	6
λ_5	1, 0, 1, 0, 1, 1, 0, 0, 1, 0	(120, 93, 108, 92, 92, 176, **90**, 117, 140, 96)	12	10	7
λ_6	1, 0, 1, 0, 1, 1, 1, 0, 1, 0	(120, 93, 108, **92**, **92**, 176, 168, 117, 140, 96)	12	9	4,5
λ_7	1, 0, 1, 1, 1, 1, 1, 0, 1, 0	(120, 93, 108, 176, **92**, 176, 168, 117, 140, 96)	12	8	5
λ_8	1, 0, 1, 1, 2, 1, 1, 0, 1, 0	(120, **93**, 108, 176, 135, 176, 168, 117, 140, 96)	12	7	2
λ_9	1, 1, 1, 1, 2, 1, 1, 0, 1, 0	(120, 180, 108, 176, 135, 176, 168, 117, 140, **96**)	12	6	10
λ_{10}	1, 1, 1, 1, 2, 1, 1, 0, 1, 1	(120, 180, **108**, 176, 135, 176, 168, 117, 140, 182)	12	5	3
λ_{11}	1, 1, 2, 1, 2, 1, 1, 0, 1, 1	(120, 180, 156, 176, 135, 176, 168, **117**, 140, 182)	12	4	8
λ_{12}	1, 1, 2, 1, 2, 1, 1, 1, 1, 1	(**120**, 180, 156, 176, 135, 176, 168, 224, 140, 182)	12	3	1
λ_{13}	2, 1, 2, 1, 2, 1, 1, 1, 1, 1	(180, 186, 168, 184, **144**, 178, 180, 234, **144**, 192)	24	2	5,9
λ_{14}	2, 1, 2, 1, 2, 1, 1, 1, 2, 1	(180, 186, 168, 184, **144**, 178, 180, 234, 210, 192)	24	1	5
λ_{15}	2, 1, 2, 1, 3, 1, 1, 1, 2, 1	(180, 186, 168, 184, 184, 178, 180, 234, 210, 192)	24	0	

$i = \{1, 2, ..., 100\}$. For every experiment, we initiated p and t with random values. The choice of the price values was done randomly as follows:

t[j] = LO+static_cast <float> (rand()) / (static_cast <float>(RAND_MAX/(HI-LO)));

p[j] = LO+static_cast <float> (rand()) / (static_cast <float>(RAND_MAX/(HI-LO)));

where the variable LO and HI represents the ranges for the execution time and the price, and were set to LO =1.0,HI = 15.0 for the time, and LO =1.0,HI = 20.0 for the price. These values were selected based constipation of variance of computational power between different practical cloud resources, and these values and ranges will have no effect on the actual complexity of the algorithm as described above. All simulations are run on MS Windows 7 64−bit system with 8.00 GB of RAM, and Intel(R) Core(TM) i7 − 4770 CPU @3.40GHz. Figure 1 illustrates the execution time in seconds vs the number of subtasks, and it shows linear increment.

Figure 1.

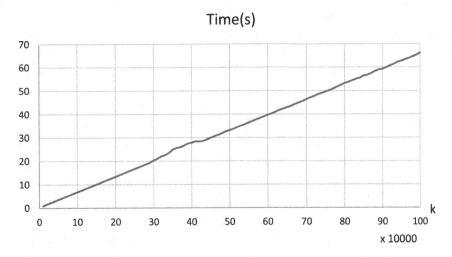

Next, we executed the scheduling process for variable number of resources, while fixing the number of subtasks to $k = 10^4$ subtasks. We initiated p and t with random values similar to above, and then tested the execution time for algorithm for different the following values of subtasks $N = \{4000, 8000, \ldots, 60000\}$. Figure 2 illustrates the execution time in seconds vs the number of resources, and it shows linear increment. Finally, Figure 3 shows the execution time in seconds vs number of subtasks k, and the number of resources simultaneously, which shows shows linear increment vs each for different values, i.e, the execution time is linear vs $k \times n$,

Figure 2.

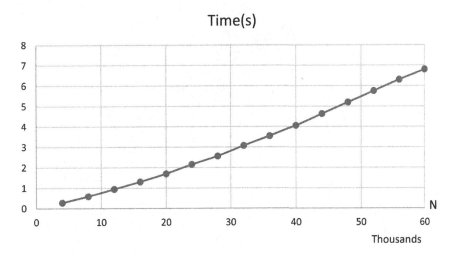

which is consistent with the complexity of *O(kn)*. Finally, in order to test the performance of the algorithm under both number of resources and number of subtasks simultaneously, we repeated the experiment while changing number of subtasks from *1k* up to *20k*, with an increment of *1k*, and the number of resources from *1k* to *15k*, and calculated the execution time of the algorithm. Figure 3 shows the archived results illustrated as linear behavior.

The results achieved in this work solve the intended problem and provide an algorithm with linear execution time. In addition, this work is fundamental in order to provide an efficient method to define selection function, which can be used in finding heuristic based solutions for the NP complete problem of scheduling multiple tasks for multiple users. In fact, the problem of allocating multiple users, each with multiple tasks, on given number of resources is an open one. Several methods have been proposed to provide solutions, however, the presented methods can still be further enhanced if proper optimizing algorithms can be used. In particular, ones that can present optimum solutions for special cases, such as the one presented here. Hence, this algorithm is intended to define a selection function that can serve as heuristic for scheduling multiple users problem.

Figure 3.

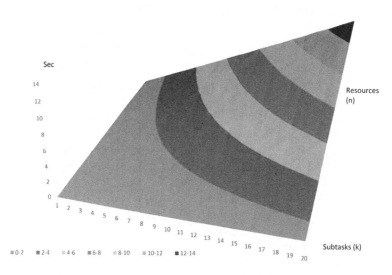

*For a more accurate representation see the electronic version.

MULTIPLE USERS RESOURCE ALLOCATION

Problem Description and Formalization

In this section, we present the model for the problem with multiple users sharing the same number of resources as described above. Given n users $U = \{u_1, u_2, ..., u_n\}$, who are interested in executing n services, $\{S_1, S_2, ..., S_n\}$, where every service, or task S_i is one single task that is composed of k_i subtasks, that are parallel and dependent subtasks with equal amount of computation. The vector $k = \{k_1, k_2, ..., k_n\}$ represents the number of subtasks for all users. There are m computational resources that are shared by all users, $\{R_1, R_2, ..., R_m\}$ with price vector $p = \{p_1, p_2, ..., p_m\}$. All users who allocate their services to resource R_j will proportionally share the capacity and expense of resource R_j. In addition, each resource R_j requires specific time to execute a subtask for user u_i, forming the execution time vector T_j for every resource. The collection of all vectors $T_1, T_2, ..., T_m$ forms the execution time matrix T of $n \times m$ elements. Since all subtasks of S_i are parallel and dependent, the completion time of task S_i is defined by taking the maximum turnaround time taken by any subtask, $T_{imax} = max\{T_{ij} | T_{ij} \in T_i\}$, where T_{ij} denotes the element of matrix T in row i and column j.

The objective is to assign subtasks for each user to a number of resources such that the the total cost is minimized, where cost represents the expense and execution time for completing tasks for all users. The scheduling problem solution is a non-negative matrix A of n rows and m columns, each element represents the number of subtasks assigned for each resource. The entry A_{ij} is the number of subtasks of the task S_i allocated to resource R_j. The allocation matrix A must satisfy the following constraint:

$$\forall i \cdot i \in \{1, 2, .., n\}, \sum_{j=1}^{m} A_{ij} = K_i$$

where $j = \{1, 2, ..., m\}$. In order to define utility for any given schedule, two matrices are defined from execution time matrix T, schedule A, and price vector p, the first one is the completion time matrix, $\hat{T}$ and the second is the expense matrix $\hat{E}$. The element $\hat{T}_{ij}$ of $\hat{T}$ is the turnaround time it takes for resource R_j to complete A_{ij}

subtasks of the task S_i. The entry $\hat{E}_{ij}$ of matrix $\hat{E}$ is the expense user S_i pays for resource R_j to complete A_{ij} subtasks. These two matrices are defined as follows:

$$\hat{T}_{ij} = \sum_{r=1}^{m} A_{ir} \times T_{ij}$$

$$\hat{E}_{ij} = \frac{\hat{T}_{ij} \times p_j}{\sum_{r=1}^{n} A_{rj}}$$

Based on these two matrices, we calculate two vectors for schedule A, the first vector, t_{max}, is composed of n elements, each element t_{maxi} represents the execution time for task S_i using schedule A, and is defined as the maximum execution time of tasks assigned by user u_i to all resources, $T_{maxi} = \max\left\{ \hat{T}_{ij} | j = \{1, 2, .., m\} \right\}$. The second vector, E_{sum}, is composed of n elements, each element, E_{sumi}, represents the total expense for user S_i, and is defined as the summation of all expenses paid to all resources by user u_i, $E_{sumi} = \sum_{j=1}^{m} \hat{E}_{ij}$. We assign weights for schedule costs as follows, w_t for execution time weight, and w_e for expense weight. Then utility for a user u_i with a given schedule A can be defined as follows:

$$U_i^A = \frac{1}{w_t \times T_{maxi} + w_e \times E_{sumi}}$$

$$U_i^A = \frac{1}{w_t \times \max\left\{ \hat{T}_{ij} | j = \{1, 2, .., m\} \right\} + w_e \times \sum_{j=1}^{m} \hat{E}_{ij}}$$

Then the utility of schedule A can be defined as the summation of all user utilities:

$$U^A = \sum_{i=1}^{n} u_i^A$$

The example below is used in order to illustrate the problem described above for multiple users. The problem described here is adopted from the similar problem presented in (Wei, Vasilakos, Zheng, & Xiong, 2010), however, problem description in that work is based on the following two assumptions: (1) the price vector of all resources $p = (p_1, p_2, ..., p_m)$ must satisfies $p_1 < p_2 < ... < p_m$, and (2) the corresponding execution time of any subtask of an arbitrary task S_i satisfies $T_{i1} > T_{i2} > ... > T_{im}$. It is clear that the above assumption will restrict the method into limited applications. On the other hand, the emthod proosed here can be applied on a problem description with any price vector and execution time matrix, regardless of the order. The illustrative example below is used in order to define the problem and show how utility is calculated, and then will be used to demonstrate the proposed algorithm in the following section. For the price vector $p = (1, 1.2, 1.5, 1.8, 2)$, the number of resources m = 5, number of users $n = 3$, with subtask k = {2, 3, 4}, the execution time vector for each subtask using the given resources is given as $t = (4, 3.5, 3.2, 2.8, 2.4)$. We will assume that the schedule A defined below is to be used:

$$A = \begin{pmatrix} 0 & 0 & 0 & 1 & 1 \\ 0 & 1 & 1 & 1 & 0 \\ 1 & 1 & 1 & 0 & 1 \end{pmatrix}$$

Given the problem information, the execution time matrix T can be obtained as follows:

$$T = \begin{pmatrix} 6.0 & 5.0 & 4.0 & 3.5 & 3.0 \\ 5.0 & 4.2 & 3.6 & 3.0 & 2.8 \\ 4.0 & 3.5 & 3.2 & 2.8 & 2.4 \end{pmatrix}$$

From these two, the matrices $\hat{T}$ and $\hat{E}$ as well as two vectors t_{max} and E_{sum} are obtained as follows:

$$\hat{T} = \begin{pmatrix} 0 & 0 & 0 & 6 & 6 \\ 0 & 8.4 & 7.2 & 6.0 & 0 \\ 4 & 7 & 6.4 & 0 & 4.8 \end{pmatrix}$$

$$\hat{E} = \begin{pmatrix} 0 & 0 & 0 & 6.3 & 6 \\ 0 & 5.04 & 5.4 & 5.4 & 0 \\ 4 & 4.2 & 4.8 & 0 & 4.8 \end{pmatrix}$$

$$T_{max} = \begin{pmatrix} 7 & 8.4 & 7 \end{pmatrix}$$

$$E_{sum} = \begin{pmatrix} 12.3 & 15.84 & 17.8 \end{pmatrix}$$

$$U_i^A = \begin{pmatrix} \dfrac{1}{7 + 12.3} \\ \dfrac{1}{8.4 + 15.84} \\ \dfrac{1}{7 + 17.8} \end{pmatrix}$$

$$U_i^A = \begin{pmatrix} 0.0518135 \\ 0.0412541 \\ 0.0403226 \end{pmatrix}$$

$$U^A = \sum_{i=1}^{n} U_i^A = 0.13339$$

The resulting schedule represents a tradeoff between the price and execution time. Hence, proper schedule optimization method is needed. In the following section, a solution for the multiple user scheduling problem will be proposed based on the single user case described above. The algorithm for the multiuser problem will be based on a carefully designed selection function. This function is built on top of the single user case. The selection function considers the effect of scheduling tasks into resources, and it will be used to identify the best available choice for the allocation of every service.

Optimizing Multiple User Scheduling

This section presents the proposed algorithm for scheduling multiple users allocation on multiple available resources based on selection function (Gawanmeh & April,

A Novel Algorithm for Optimizing Multiple Services Resource Allocation, 2016). Applying the single user algorithm alone does not lead into the optimum solution when generalized into the multiple user case. Obviously, the reason is that any subtask scheduled at a given resource, affects the execution time of that resource for other users. Therefore, we have developed the scheduling algorithm based on two issues: scheduling subtasks as pairs, and using a selection function that takes into account the current optimum choice for the single users scheduling problem and combine it with other facts, such as the number of unscheduled subtasks. In fact, the objective is to find the allocation matrix A the maximizes the utility u^A form a given execution time vector t and price vector p. The problem is described in the literature as NP-Complete, and hence heuristic based solutions can be used to provide the best possible solution. For n users, each has k_i subtasks, where $1 \leq i \leq n$, and m resources, we first create two empty matrices $\hat{T}$ and $\hat{E}$, each of $n \times m$ elements and initialize them to zeros. We also create the two vectors T_{max}, and E_{sum}, each of n elements, and a variable T_E, all initialized to zeros as well. Let Δ be a matrix of $n \times m$ elements, initialized as follows: $\Delta_{ij} = \left(1 + P_j\right) \times T_{ij}$.

Next, we define a vector, V of m elements initialized to zero, represents the total number of subtasks assigned to every resource. At any time during the scheduling process, $V_j = \sum_{i=1}^{n} A_{ij}$ and $T_E = \sum_{j=1}^{m} E_{sum_j}$

Finally, we define the selection function, Θ as a vector of n elements as follows: $\Theta_i = 0.01 \times k_i + \dfrac{1}{\Delta_{ir}}$. This selection function takes into account the number of unscheduled subtasks as well as the weight of the current schedule. The value Δ_{ir} is minimum value in row i in the matrix Δ. Subtasks are allocated for users based on the selection function Θ. The process starts with selecting two users, α and β, and two resources, γ for task α, and σ for task β, that leads to best single user utility using the single user optimization algorithm described above, where the following conditions are satisfied:

$$1 \leq \alpha, \beta \leq n \tag{1}$$

$$1 \leq \gamma, \sigma \leq m \tag{2}$$

$$k_\alpha > 0, k_\beta > 0 \tag{3}$$

$$\forall i \cdot i > 0, i \leq n \Rightarrow \Theta_\alpha \leq \Theta_i \tag{4}$$

$$\forall i \cdot i > 0, i \leq n, i \neq \alpha, \Rightarrow \Theta_\beta \leq \Theta_i \tag{5}$$

$$\forall i \cdot i > 0, i \leq n \Rightarrow \Delta_{\alpha\gamma} \leq \Theta_{i\gamma} \tag{6}$$

$$\forall i \cdot i > 0, i \leq n \Rightarrow \Delta_{\beta\sigma} \leq \Theta_{i\sigma} \tag{7}$$

Hence, two subtasks with minimum values in Δ are to be scheduled for two users. In fact, the assignment of the two subtasks are chosen simultaneously for a valid reason, when a single subtask is assigned the allocation matrix will be modified, and hence the local utility matrix Δ will be modified. After several considerations, it was found that selecting a single subtask and assigning it to the best available entry Δij leads to bad schedule, due to the effect of every single subtask scheduled on the final commutation time (maximum time) for every user. We then update the list of parameters in two steps, each for one assignment. All of the variables A, $\hat{T}$, Δ, T_{max}, E_{sum}, V, and T_E are updated by scheduling one subtask for user α on resource [3] and one subtask user β on resource σ, as follows:

$$A_{\alpha\gamma} += 1, A_{\beta\sigma} += 1$$

$$V_\gamma += 1, V_\sigma += 1$$

$$\hat{T}_{\alpha\gamma} = \hat{T}_{\alpha\gamma} + p_\gamma \times T_{\alpha\gamma}$$

$$\hat{T}_{\beta\sigma} = \hat{T}_{\beta\sigma} + p_\sigma \times T_{\beta\sigma}$$

$$T_{max\alpha} = max\left(T_{max\alpha}, \hat{T}_{\alpha\gamma}\right)$$

$$T_{max\beta} = max\left(T_{max\beta}, \hat{T}_{\beta\sigma}\right)$$

$$E_{sum\alpha} = E_{sum\alpha} + p_{\gamma} \times T_{\alpha\gamma}$$

$$E_{sum\beta} = E_{sum\beta} + p_{\sigma} \times T_{\beta\sigma}$$

$$T_E = T_E + p_{\gamma} \times T_{\alpha\gamma} + p_{\sigma} \times T_{\beta\sigma}$$

$$\Delta_{ij} = T_E + p_i \times T_{ij} + \sum_{r=1}^{n} max((V_r + 1) \times T_{ir}, T_{max_r})$$

The single user algorithm described in Section 2 is used in order to modify the values in the matrix Δ. Subtasks for user β are assigned for service σ based on this. Then, two tasks are selected using the function Θ. Similarly, two schedules are assigned, one for each task, using the selection function Θ. The best combination from these pairs is selected. The process is repeated until all tasks are scheduled. In case, there is only one task left with one or more subtasks, then direct assignment using the function Θ is conducted until all subtasks are processed. The outcome depends on the selection function, i.e., the order on which the users are selected for scheduling and the resources their subtasks are allocated to. Hence, we intend to test the algorithm for more than one selection function. Algorithm 2 shows the step by step description of the process and is illustrated on a detailed example in the next Section. In addition, the algorithm is tested with two different selection functions, and in both it outperforms evolutionary and game theory based algorithms.

Illustrative Example

The method is applied on the multiple users schedule example that was discussed in Section 3. The algorithm is applied step by step in order to find an allocation matrix that represents an optimum schedule. The same conditions and initializations are assumed as in the example in the previous section. For the execution of the algorithm, we select $\alpha =3, \beta = 2$ based on the values provided by the selection function. Then we choose two entries in Δ with minimum values: $\gamma = 5$ and $\sigma = 4$. The combination $\left(\gamma, \sigma\right) = \left(5, 4\right)$ is selected as schedule. Hence, a subtask for user

Algorithm 2. Multiple user resource allocation algorithm

```
1:   Procedure Allocation( )
2:   Input: k, n, m, T, p;
3:   Output: A ;  schedule matrix
4:   Initialize vectors and variables
5:   A = {0} , T̂ = {0} , T_max = {0} , V = {0} , E_sum = {0} , T_E = 0 , i = 0
6:   Initialize the allocation function vector Δ
7:       REPEAT
8:           j = 0,  i = i + 1
9:           REPEAT
10:              Δ_ij = p_j × T_ij + T_ij
11:              j = j + 1
12:          UNTIL j == m
13:      UNTIL i == n
14:      REPEAT
15:          Choose α, β using selection function Θ
16:          Choose γ and σ such that Δ_αγ and Δ_βσ are minimum and γ ≠ σ
17:          Schedule subtask for user u_α at Resource R_γ
18:          Schedule subtask for user u_β at Resource R_σ
19:          Updates all schedule parameters for this assignment A_αγ = A_αγ +1,  A_βσ = A_βσ +1,
20:      UNTIL at most one task has unscheduled subtasks
21:      Choose α such that k_α > 0
22:      REPEAT
23:          Choose γ such that is minimum
             Schedule subtask for user u_α at Resource R_γ
24:          Updates all schedule parameters for this assignment
25:          k_α = k_α - 1
26:      UNTIL k_α == 0
27:      RETURN A_l
```

u_3 shall be scheduled to service R_5, followed by a subtask of user u_2 to service R_4. Based on this, the allocation matrix, A, is updated with these schedules in the next step. This is illustrated in the initial step indicated as λ_0 in Table 3, where the numbers in bold represent the active ones.

In the next step, indicated as λ_1, k_3 and k_2 are decremented, leading to $k = \{2, 2, 3\}$. All variables are updated and new selection function values are calculated, which will lead to the following assignment: $\alpha = 3, \beta = 2, \gamma = 2, \sigma = 3$. Hence, subtask for user u_3 is assigned to R_2, and for user u_2 is assigned to R_3, which will appear in A in the next step λ_2, then $k = \{2, 1, 2\}$, and the selection functions gives $\alpha = 3, \beta = 1, \gamma = 1, and \ \sigma = 5$. Hence, subtask of u_3 is assigned to R_1, and subtask of u_1 is assigned to R_5. The step λ_3 leads to $k = \{1, 1, 1\}$, $\alpha = 3, \beta = 2, \gamma = 2, and \ \sigma = 4$. Hence, subtask of u_3 is assigned to R_2 and subtask of u_2 is assigned to R_4. In step λ_4, $k = \{1, 0, 0\}$, therefore only user u_1

Table 3. Execution of the multiple user algorithm on the given example for multiple users

λ	A	Δ	k	θ	α, Υ_α	β, Υ_β
λ_0	0 0 0 0 0 0 0 0 0 0 0 0 0 0 0	12.0 11.0 10.0 9.8 9.0 10.0 9.2 9.0 8.4 8.4 8.0 7.7 8.0 7.8 7.2	2 3 4	0.131 0.149 0.179	3,5	2,4
λ_1	0 0 0 0 0 0 0 0 0 0 0 0 0 0 0	27.6 26.6 25.6 31.9 30.0 22.6 21.8 21.6 24.0 26.2 21.2 20.9 21.2 26.8 22.8	2 2 3	0.059 0.066 0.078	3,2	2,3
λ_2	0 0 0 0 0 0 0 0 0 0 0 0 0 0 0	38.9 46.4 44.5 42.6 40.2 33.3 40.2 35.9 34.7 35.8 31.4 34.6 38.2 36.4 33.0	2 1 2	0.046 0:040 0.052	3,1	1,5
λ_3	0 0 0 0 0 0 0 0 0 0 0 0 0 0 0	59.4 56.4 55.8 53.9 55.6 58.8 56.2 53.2 52.0 60.0 51.4 50.6 54.2 52.4 54.4	1 1 1	0.028 0.029 0.030	3,2	2,4
λ_4	0 0 0 0 0 0 0 0 0 0 0 0 0 0 0	71.4 76.9 67.6 72.2 67.6 68.4 73.5 65.0 66.8 69.6 63.4 66.1 64.4 67.8 66.4	1 0 0	0.025 0.015 0.016	1,3	
λ_5	0 0 0 0 0 0 0 0 0 0 0 0 0 0 0		0 0 0			

has subtasks, and as a result, the selection function for $\alpha = 1$ will result in $\gamma = 3$, hence, the last subtask for user u_1 is assigned to R_3. The resulting schedule, shown below, has the utility of $U^A = 0.134$. This result shows better utility than game theory method using Nash equilibrium (Wei, Vasilakos, Zheng, & Xiong, 2010). In addition, there is no restriction on the input vectors, as opposed to the aforementioned method.

$$A = \begin{pmatrix} 0 & 0 & 1 & 0 & 1 \\ 0 & 0 & 1 & 2 & 0 \\ 1 & 2 & 0 & 0 & 1 \end{pmatrix}$$

Performance Evaluation

The proposed method is evaluated vs. different parameters; we built a model for the cloud services problem and conducted simulation. First, we run the example presented in (Wei, Vasilakos, Zheng, & Xiong, 2010) and the algorithm resulted in a solution with the allocation matrix A shown above, which has a utility $U^A = 0.134$. The obtained utility value shows a significant enhancement over previous results. This is due to the fact that the selection function influences the outcome for the algorithm, therefore, we executed the proposed method with a different selection function defined as $\Theta_i = \dfrac{1}{1+k_i} + \dfrac{1}{\Delta_{ir}}$. This resulted in a new schedule A given below with a utility of $U^A = 0.1416$. This value shows a better utility of 5.7% over the outcome of game theory method.

$$A = \begin{pmatrix} 0 & 0 & 0 & 0 & 2 \\ 0 & 0 & 1 & 2 & 0 \\ 2 & 2 & 0 & 0 & 0 \end{pmatrix}$$

We run the algorithm for several design parameters, including number of users, number of computational resources, and number subtasks. Figure 4 shows the execution time of the algorithm vs number of users, where number of computational resources is fixed at $m = 20$, and number of subtasks is fixed at $K = 100$. It is obvious that execution time is a function of $O\left(n^2\right)$. In the next section, we will try to present a green evolutionary computing based method, in order to enhance the complexity into linear, while at the same time produce allocation with better utility.

Figure 5 shows execution time vs number of computational resources, while number of users and number of subtasks are fixed at n = 20, K = 100. Similarly, Figure 6 shows execution time vs number of subtasks while number of users and

Figure 4.

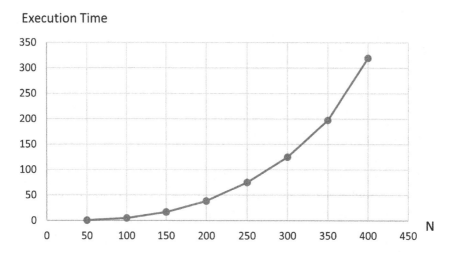

Figure 5.

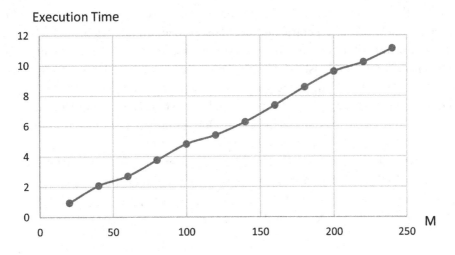

Figure 6.

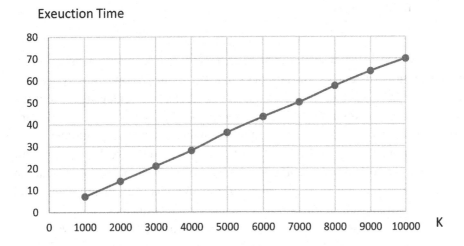

number of computational resources are fixed at n = 20, and m = 20. It is obvious from both figures that the algorithm runs in, linear time vs both parameters.

GREEN EVOLUTIONARY BASED ALGORITHM

A combination of selection function based method and evolutionary based computing is used in order to propose a green evolutionary based algorithm for resource allocation. The algorithm starts with similar steps as Algorithm 3 above. However, instead of generating one solution, we generate a number of solutions, called population W, which will be used by the evolutionary algorithm. In order to generate one solution in population W, we let a specific number of users schedule all of their subtasks using the selection function method defined above while assuming that the remaining users have scheduled their subtasks randomly. Once, the whole population of solations is generated, we follow a simple evolutionary based method in order to combine two solutions into a new solution. If this new solution shows enhancement in terms of utility, it replaces an existing solution with lowest utility. The algorithm proceeds by repeating the process specific number of generations.

The algorithm was run on the same example presented in (Wei, Vasilakos, Zheng, & Xiong, 2010) and the resulting solution shows an allocation matrix A, shown below, with utility $U^A = 0.1437$, which is 6.0% better than the result obtained using game theory with Nash equilibrium.

$$A = \begin{pmatrix} 0\ 0\ 1\ 1\ 0 \\ 0\ 0\ 0\ 0\ 3 \\ 2\ 2\ 0\ 0\ 0 \end{pmatrix}$$

We executed the green evolutionary based algorithm vs number of users, number of computational resources, and number subtasks. Figure 7 shows the execution time of the algorithm vs. number of users, where number of computational resources is fixed at m = 20, and number of subtasks is fixed at $K = 100$. Similarly, Figure 8 shows execution time vs number of computational resources, while number of users and number of subtasks are fixed at $n = 20, K = 100$, and Figure 9 shows execution time vs number of subtasks while number of users and number of computational resources are fixed at n = 20, and $m = 20$. It is obvious from the obtained results that the algorithm runs in linear time vs each one of parameters.

Finally, if both n and m are combined, then the algorithm shall run in $O(nm)$. This is to be investigated further in the future work. In terms of resources the algorithm has $O(nm)$ memory requirements in all different scenarios.

SUMMARY AND FUTURE WORK

Cloud computing systems are getting more complex and demanding due to the increasing demand and requirements for cloud based services. As a result, efficient resource allocation algorithms are required in order to optimize the resources allocation problem, which in turn will result in maximizing profit as well as providing

Figure 7.

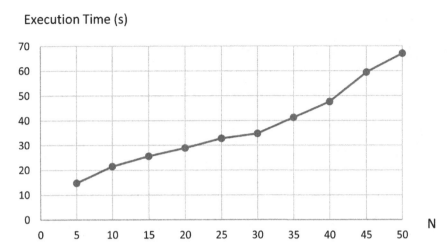

Figure 8.

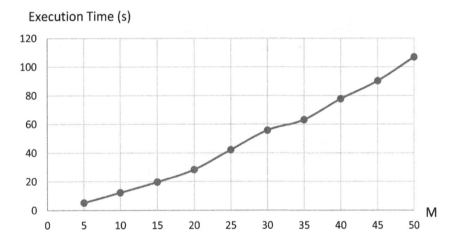

green energy efficient methods. In this chapter, the problem of scheduling multiple services for multiple users on available resources was discussed. Then an optimum algorithm was first proposed in order to solve the simple case of single user with multiple subtasks. While this problem is not practical in the real world, the objective was to use it in order to design a selection function based on metrics obtained from the single user problem and then propose a solution for the multiple user problem. However, since this problem is NP complete, heuristic based methods are needed in order to enface the performance and increase the measured utility of the schedule.

Figure 9.

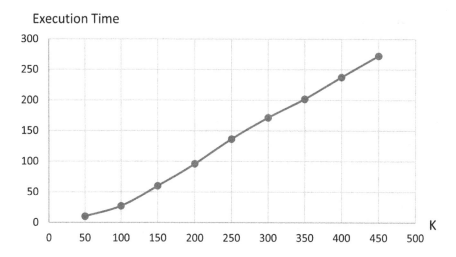

Execution Time

Algorithm 3. Green evolutionary allocation algorithm

1:   Procedure GreenAllocation( )
2:   Input: k, n, m, N; N is the number of iterations to repeat solution evolution
3:   Output: A ; schedule matrix
4:   Initialize population of solutions and counter
5:   $W = \{0\}$, $i = 0$
6:     REPEAT
7:       $i = i + 1$
8:       $W = W \cup \text{GenerateSol( )}$
9:     UNTIL $i == W$
10: $i = 0$
11:     REPEAT
12:       Choose two solutions from W : A_1 and A_2
13:       Create empty solution: A_r
14:       Assign schedule for every user in A_r from A_1 or A_2 randomly.
15:       Choose r such that A_r is minimum in W : $\forall A \cdot A \in W \Rightarrow U^A \leq U^A$
16:       if $U^A \leq U^A$ then $A_r = A_r$
17:       $i = i + 1$
18:     UNTIL $i == N$
19:   Choose r such that A_r is maximum in W : $\forall A \cdot A \in W \Rightarrow U^A \geq U^A$
20:   RETURN A_r
21:   Procedure GenerateSol( )
22:   Create temporary solution matrix A_t
23:   $A_t = \{0\}$, $i = 0$
24:   Allocate all users randomly for schedule A_t
25:   Choose r randomly such that $1 \leq r$ and $r \leq n$
26:   Clear all schedule assignments for user u_r
27:   Calculate all schedule parameters
28:   REPEAT
29:     Choose j such that Δ_{rj} is minimum in Δ .
30:     Schedule subtask for user u_r at resource R_j
31:     Updates all schedule parameters by assigning subtask for user r to service R_j
32:     $i = i + 1$
33:   UNTIL $i == k_r$
34:   RETURN A_t

Hence, a green evolutionary based algorithm for resource allocation of multiple users with multiple tasks is proposed.

The proposed solution is provided by introducing a selection function based on subtasks completion time and task costs. Then, the proposed solution is further enhanced using an evolutionary based method. The experimental results show that the proposed method runs in linear time vs different design parameters. The method presented in this work can be used for scheduling problems without imposing constraints on the vectors that represent the execution time and price, as opposed to game theoretic methods that can reach Nash equilibrium only if this condition is satisfied. In addition, the proposed method outputs schedule with better utility as opposed to other existing methods as illustrated on the example above. The main limitation of the proposed algorithm is that it is only applicable to the scheduling problem of multiple tasks that has one price vector and one execution time vector. However, when scheduling multiple users, each with subtasks that have their own price and execution time vector, then the problem becomes NP complete and this method cannot be used. Next, it is intended to extend the selection function based algorithm with another level of selection that depends on users and the number of their subtasks, and in addition show that the evolutionary algorithm runs in fact in $O(nm)$.

REFERENCES

Anuradha, V. P., & Sumathi, D. (2014). A survey on resource allocation strategies in cloud computing. In *Proceedings of the International Conference on Information Communication and Embedded Systems*, (pp. 1-7). doi:10.1109/ICICES.2014.7033931

Buyya, R., Ranjan, R., & Calheiros, R. N. (2010). Intercloud: Utility-oriented federation of cloud computing environments for scaling of application services. In Algorithms and architectures for parallel processing (pp. 13-31). Springer.

Chang, H.-Y., Lu, H.-C., Huang, Y.-H., Lin, Y.-W., & Tzang, Y.-J. (2013). Novel auction mechanism with factor distribution rule for cloud resource allocation. *The Computer Journal*.

Ejarque, J., Álvarez, J., Sirvent, R., & Badia, R. M. (2012). Resource Allocation for Cloud Computing: A Semantic Approach. In *Open Source Cloud Computing Systems: Practices and Paradigms: Practices and Paradigms*.

Ergu, D., Kou, G., Peng, Y., Shi, Y., & Shi, Y. (2013). The analytic hierarchy process: Task scheduling and resource allocation in cloud computing environment. *The Journal of Supercomputing, 64*(3), 835–848. doi:10.1007/s11227-011-0625-1

Furht, B., & Escalante, A. (2010). *Handbook of Cloud Computing*. Springer. doi:10.1007/978-1-4419-6524-0

Gawanmeh, A., Alomari, A., & April, A. (2017). Optimizing Resource Allocation Scheduling in Cloud Computing services. *Journal of Theoretical and Applied Information Technology, 95*, 31–39.

Gawanmeh, A., & April, A. (2016). A Novel Algorithm for Optimizing Multiple Services Resource Allocation. *International Journal of Advanced Computer Science and Applications, 7*(6), 428–434. doi:10.14569/IJACSA.2016.070655

Ge, Y., & Wei, G. (2010). Ga-based task scheduler for the cloud computing systems. In *Proceedings of the International Conference on Web Information Systems and Mining* (Vol. 2, pp. 181-186). doi:10.1109/WISM.2010.87

Guo, F., Yu, L., Tian, S., & Yu, J. (2015). A workflow task scheduling algorithm based on the resources fuzzy clustering in cloud computing environment. *International Journal of Communication Systems, 28*(6), 1053–1067. doi:10.1002/dac.2743

Khan, S. (2013). A survey on scheduling based resource allocation in cloud computing. *International Journal For Technological Research In Engineering*.

Kołodziej, J., Khan, S. U., Wang, L., & Zomaya, A. Y. (2015). Energy efficient genetic-based schedulers in computational grids. *Concurrency and Computation, 27*(4), 809–829. doi:10.1002/cpe.2839

Kumar, K., Feng, J., Nimmagadda, Y., & Lu, Y.-H. (2011). Resource allocation for real-time tasks using cloud computing. In *Proceedings of the International Conference on Computer Communications and Networks*, (pp. 1-7). doi:10.1109/ICCCN.2011.6006077

Lee, C., Wang, P., & Niyato, D. (2015). A real-time group auction system for efficient allocation of cloud internet applications. *IEEE Transactions on Services Computing, 8*(2), 251–268. doi:10.1109/TSC.2013.24

Lin, W.-Y., Lin, G.-Y., & Wei, H.-Y. (2010). Dynamic auction mechanism for cloud resource allocation. In *Proceedings of the International Conference on Cluster, Cloud and Grid Computing* (pp. 591-592). doi:10.1109/CCGRID.2010.92

Manvi, S. S., & Shyam, G. K. (2014). Resource management for Infrastructure as a Service (IaaS) in cloud computing: A survey. *Journal of Network and Computer Applications*, *41*, 424–440. doi:10.1016/j.jnca.2013.10.004

Minarolli, D., & Freisleben, B. (2013). Virtual Machine Resource Allocation in Cloud Computing via Multi-Agent Fuzzy Control. In *Proceedings of the Int. Conference on Cloud and Green Computing* (pp. 188-194). doi:10.1109/CGC.2013.35

Mohan, V. M., & Satyanarayana, K. V. (2015). Efficient task scheduling strategy towards qos aware optimal resource utilization in cloud computing. *Journal of Theoretical \& Applied Information Technology, 80*.

Sagar, M. S., Singh, B., & Ahmad, W. (2013). Study on Cloud Computing Resource Allocation Strategies. *International Journal of Advance Research and Innovation*, *1*, 107–114.

Saha, S., Pal, S., & Pattnaik, P. K. (2016). A Novel Scheduling Algorithm for Cloud Computing Environment. In *Computational Intelligence in Data Mining* (Vol. 1, pp. 387–398). Springer. doi:10.1007/978-81-322-2734-2_39

Sahu, D. P., Singh, K., & Prakash, S. (2015). Resource Allocation and Provisioning in Computational Mobile Grid. *International Journal of Applied Evolutionary Computation*, *6*(2), 1–24. doi:10.4018/ijaec.2015040101

Senthilnathan, P., & Kalaiarasan, C. (2013). A joint design of routing and resource allocation using qos monitoring agent in mobile ad-hoc networks. *Journal of Theoretical & Applied Information Technology, 55*.

Singh, A., Dutta, K., & Singh, A. (2014). Resource Allocation in Cloud Computing Environment using AHP Technique. *International Journal of Cloud Applications and Computing*, *4*(1), 33–44. doi:10.4018/ijcac.2014010103

Teng, F., & Magoulès, F. (2010). A new game theoretical resource allocation algorithm for cloud computing. In *Advances in Grid and Pervasive Computing* (pp. 321–330). Springer. doi:10.1007/978-3-642-13067-0_35

Velayudham, A., Gohila, G., Hariharan, B., & Ramya Selvi, M. (2014). A Novel Coalition Game Theory Based Resource Allocation And Selfish Attack Avoidance In Cognitive Radio Ad-hoc Networks. *Journal of Theoretical \& Applied Information Technology, 64*.

Vinothina, V., Sridaran, R., & Ganapathi, P. (2012). A survey on resource allocation strategies in cloud computing. *International Journal of Advanced Computer Science and Applications*, *3*, 97–104. doi:10.14569/IJACSA.2012.030616

Walker, E., Brisken, W., & Romney, J. (2010). To lease or not to lease from storage clouds. *Computer*, *43*(4), 44–50. doi:10.1109/MC.2010.115

Wang, Z., & Su, X. (2015). Dynamically hierarchical resource-allocation algorithm in cloud computing environment. *The Journal of Supercomputing*.

Wei, G., Vasilakos, A. V., Zheng, Y., & Xiong, N. (2010). A game-theoretic method of fair resource allocation for cloud computing services. *The Journal of Supercomputing*, *54*(2), 252–269. doi:10.1007/s11227-009-0318-1

Xiao, Z., Song, W., & Chen, Q. (2013). Dynamic resource allocation using virtual machines for cloud computing environment. *IEEE Transactions on Parallel and Distributed Systems*, *24*(6), 1107–1117. doi:10.1109/TPDS.2012.283

Chapter 4
Current State Survey and Future Opportunities for Trust and Security in Green Cloud Computing

Amine Haouari
Mohammed V University, Morocco

Zbakh Mostapha
Mohammed V University, Morocco

Samadi Yassir
Mohammed V University, Morocco

ABSTRACT

In this paper, the authors present a state of art survey of cloud computing, highlighting its architectural principles, implementation as well as research directions in this increasingly important domain. They cover the different security issues that has emanated due to the nature of the service delivery models of a cloud computing system. Furthermore, in this survey the researchers highlight the concept of trust in digital environment as well as the use of containers like Docker, the block chain principle, artificial intelligence, last findings in the field of cryptography and other new concepts used in the domain of security and privacy related to cloud computing environments. They provide in the end an overview of the metrics which are mandatory in order to have a green flavor of cloud computing and the strategies that are currently used.

DOI: 10.4018/978-1-5225-3038-1.ch004

INTRODUCTION

Cloud computing is an emerging as a model which support the "everything-as-a-service" (XaaS) (Baran, 2008). Virtualized physical resources, virtualized infrastructure, as well as virtualized middleware platforms and business applications are being provided and consumed as services in the Cloud (Lenk, Klems, Nimis, Tai, & Sandholm, 2009). Cloud computing started its base in the mid of 2007 and is growing rapidly till date (Rizwana & Sasikumar, 2012). It has many features that make users want to switch to the cloud computing environment. The manufacturer provides relevant hardware, software and service according to the need that users put forward (Shuai, Shufen, Chen, & Huo, 2010). With the rapid development of the Internet, user's requirement is realized through the Internet. In fact, cloud computing is an extend of grid computing, distributed computing, and parallel computing. Its foreground is to provide secure, quick and convenient data storage (Shuai, Shufen, Chen, & Huo, 2010). Many forecasting agencies have said that cloud computing is large and it's only going to grow exponentially. IDC said that in the next year's spending on IT cloud services would increase a lot and would reach several billions of dollars. Another agency said that cloud computing would go to $500 billion as an industry by 2020.

One of the quotes way spread across actually was "There is no reason anyone would want a computer in their home" from Ken Olson who in 1977 who was a president chairman and founder of Dec big business mainframe computer company that was later bought by Compact which was later bought by HP. Back then there was those big mainframe computers and everyone could access them. Over the years and the evolution of the desktop computer everyone had a computer in their home, every person who works in a company has a desktop computer on his desk. Fortunately, things have started to come back around with the growth of server based computing which is similar to mainframe in the concept that computing is happening actually in the datacenter and you really just viewing the screen. Back in the mainframe it was just text that we would see in the screen but today of course there are those nice GUI environments. Some people called this server based computing "the cloud". Marketers throw the term cloud around left and right and that's what created so much confusion. So back to the quote, actually today everyone can use a thin client device and can access the computers that's running in the cloud. But then the question is what exactly is cloud computing?

According to VMware, "Cloud computing is an approach to computing that leverages the efficient pooling of on-demand, self-managed, virtual infrastructure". In other words, IT doesn't have to be as involved. IT provides the virtual infrastructure and the resources that virtual infrastructure can expand or it can contract when it's not needed and this provides us and the company many benefits. So, cloud computing abstracts the business services from the underlying complex IT infrastructure. The think is that the infrastructure today, the servers, storage, network, all those pieces of complex IT infrastructure that IT people struggle to put together to make useful for the business are becoming easy to manage with virtualization which is able to pull all that together and then this pool of resources can be consumed on demand just like utility which gives the business what they need when they need it. As said before cloud computing allows to save both time as well as money. Eli Lilly, which is one of the largest customers of AWS, reputedly, for instance has been benefiting from the ability to bring up new servers fairly quickly. Earlier they reported that it used to take seven and a half weeks for them to deploy a new server. This would involve them setting the specs for the server, then actually purchasing it, and then going through the purchasing process, the server comes in and they set it up and install the necessary operating system and software, and all of this takes took several weeks. Now they can rig up a new server in around 3 minutes, and a 64-node Linux cluster in 5 minutes while it was taking months earlier. This of course saves them time; it also saves them money, because they can save the costs that they might have otherwise had to pay the sysadmins (Gupta, 2016).

Another issue which is important also that also should be analyzed is the importance of green cloud computing. So as known the main room in a datacenter is of course the server's room. It doesn't look very different from the front or from the back; they're just regular machines. But where does the power come from to those servers and switches? To answer this, a lot of the power comes from offsite, such as hydroelectric power or coal power, which is the main source of power today for datacenters. Some of them have solar panels which provide for some small fraction of the datacenter's power usage. In many cases for instance, solar panels might be used to power the lights inside the datacenter. However, there is a couple of important metrics that are used to measure the efficiency of the datacenters in terms of water usage and power usage. These are known as water usage efficiency, or WUE, and power usage efficiency, or PUE. The water usage efficiency is essentially the annual water usage divided by IT equipment energy in liter per kilowatt hour. A lower number here is good, which means the use of less water per energy. PUE is total facility power divided by IT equipment power. Again here, a lower number is good because essentially this means the use of a larger percentage incoming power for powering the servers, routers and switches. For instance, Google has one of the lowest PUEs in the world which is about 1.11.

But once again, this brings back the question of what exactly is a cloud for technical folks who want to understand the deep, detailed aspects of cloud computing. How to secure it? What is the best way to stay green efficient and have a secure environment? What the latest discovery on this area? The authors will go underneath the hood and look at the distributed systems concepts, and the distributed algorithms, and the distributed techniques that underlie today's cloud computing technologies. They dig deep into the new concept and technologies used in the area of security and privacy within cloud computing environment.

CLOUD COMPUTING PRESENT SITUATION AND APPLICATION

Cloud Computing Overview

Nowadays cloud computing is the latest and greatest thing, and being that, marketers for lots of big companies are all using cloud computing terms in their marketing campaigns to make them seem impressive so that they can get clients and get customers. The problem is that most people don't really understand what cloud computing is. Cloud computing is an overall design and philosophy concept and it's much more sophisticated and yet much simpler than people give it credit for.

The basic concept is that with cloud computing there is a separation of the applications from the operating systems, from the hardware that runs everything. So what does it mean? Well, back in the day if you have and email service for your company, it meant that you had sever hardware sitting somewhere in your company. So, you had a server with CPU, RAM, server OS, hard drive and power supply and all that. So, you had the server hardware and you installed Windows NT 4.0 back in the day. Then on top of Windows NT 4.0 OS you installed Microsoft exchange server. So now in order to provide email services to all the people's in your company you had Microsoft exchange server installed on Microsoft NT4 server OS installed on the server hardware. All that was a bundle. The problem with this is that exchange server is now dependent on everything bellow it. So, if there is a problem in the operating system, if the OS get a virus, if a hard drive gets clogged up with too much information, if there is an error etc., your exchange server which means your email service all come to a halt. You no longer get your email services because the OS has failed for whatever reason. Again, just like that with the server hardware, if the CPU stops, if the CPU burns out or the hard drive fails or the power supply fails etc., that of course shuts down the operating system and then no more email server and email server services for all people on the network. So, in the old days, email services or whatever network services were reliant on everything below them. So, there was the service in the application installed on OS which in turn is installed on the hardware. If the hardware fails then the services went down. If the OS failed, then here also the service went down.

Well back then, the idea of cloud computing and virtual computing appeared which consist to disconnect the application, the OS and the hardware from themselves. What virtual computing turn the OS like a container which is then running on hardware. So now if something fails then the instance of that OS automatically migrate to another piece of hardware or another server system and keep going. So, with redundancy for example using virtualization, what can happen is you can have for example 3 physical servers lined up. So you have 3 servers with CPU, RAM and hard drive, etc. You install the virtualization software onto all three of those servers. If everything is running properly and suddenly the power supply of the first server fails. Well through virtualization what will happen is that the OS automatically transfers user's connections to the next server in this little cluster and everything keeps running. So, this is what we meant by separating the applications from the OS from the hardware.

At first glance, Clouds appear to be a mixture of Grids and clusters. Nonetheless, this is not the case. Clouds are clearly data centers with "virtualized" nodes through hypervisor technologies such as VMs, dynamically "provisioned" on demand as a personalized resource collection to meet a specific service-level agreement (SLA).

Although users talk about 'the cloud', cloud computing comes in several different forms, each of which has its own specific strengths and weaknesses – both from business and a security perspective (Guy, 2016).

- **Public Cloud:** The public cloud is what most people think of when they refer to the cloud. It refers to computing facilities and Cloud storage that are accessed remotely, thereby enabling organizations and individuals to outsource services and avoid purchasing servers and infrastructure themselves.
- **Private Cloud:** A private cloud is a model of cloud computing in which the cloud is located behind a corporate firewall.
- **Hybrid Cloud:** As the name suggests, this is a mixture of public and private clouds that allows companies to access the best of both type of cloud.

The abundance of different forms of cloud is also complicated, from a security perspective, by the different service models available, each of which again has its own issues. Bellow a non-exhaustive list of available and daily used available cloud models (Guy, 2016):

- **Infrastructure as a Service (IaaS):** IaaS providers offer their customers computers or virtual machines, typically located in data centers, for remote use. Customers can install their own operating systems and software on them and use them as they would a local machine by connecting over the internet. The advantage is that the user does not have to purchase hardware, or often even concern themselves with upgrades or security patches. These responsibilities are taken on by the provider.

- **Software as a Service (SaaS):** Users have access to software and databases that are run and maintained by cloud providers. These services are purchased by subscription or pay-per-use. Purchase and maintenance of the infrastructure required to host the software services is taken on by the provider, meaning that customers do not need to install or run the software itself.
- **Platform as a Service (PaaS):** With PaaS, customers purchase an entire computing platform, which may comprise an operating system, programming language and its execution environment, a database, web server and so on, so they don't have to purchase and maintain the hardware and software that would otherwise be required for such a platform. Depending on the platform and service model, resources may be scaled automatically.

An Architectural Map to Cloud Computing Present Landscape

The notion of cloud computing has evolved from being a rising technology to a dominant one going beyond simple storage. As digital enterprises continue to require agile solutions for their workforce and customers, the expansion in cloud technologies has demonstrated beneficial from cost reduction, to speed and access.

In January 2017, RightScale conducted its annual survey of the Cloud. The survey questioned technical professionals across a broad cross-section of organizations about their adoption of cloud infrastructure. 1,002 respondents participated ranging from technical executives to managers and practitioners and represent organizations of varying sizes across many industries. Their answers provide a comprehensive perspective on the state of the cloud today (RightScale State of the cloud survey, 2017).

RightScale analyzed and segmented companies based on their levels of cloud endorsement. It identifies four distinct levels of cloud maturity which are:

- **Cloud Watchers:** Are organizations that are developing cloud strategies and aim but have not yet expanded data or applications into the cloud.
- **Cloud Beginners:** Are new to cloud computing. They want to gain experience with cloud in order to determine future projects.
- **Cloud Explorers:** Have multiple projects or applications already deployed in the cloud. Cloud Explorers are focused on expanding and developing their use of cloud resources.
- **Cloud Focused:** Businesses are heavily using cloud infrastructure and are looking to optimize cloud operations as well as cloud costs.

Table 1. Respondents Demographics (Statistics form RightScale 2017 State of the Cloud Report)

	Respondents Level
Architect	26%
Dir/Mgr	23%
Exec	14%
IT/Ops	10%
Dev/QA	8%
DevOps	8%
Other	11%
	Industry Respondents
Tech Services	27%
Software	22%
Other	16%
Financial Services	9%
Telecom	6%
Education	5%
Business Services	5%
Hardware	4%
Healthcare	3%
Media & Publishing	3%
	Regions Respondents
North America	61%
Europe	20%
APAC	14%
Rest of World	5%
	Regions Respondents Role
IT/Ops	39%
Dev	33%
Business	13%
Cloud Architect	15%

DevOps Adoption Spreads in the Enterprise

Referring to Wikipedia definition, DevOps (a clipped compound of "software DEVelopment" and "information technology OPerationS") is a term used to refer to a set of practices that emphasize the collaboration and communication of both software developers and information technology (IT) professionals while automating the process of software delivery and infrastructure changes. It aims at establishing a culture and environment where building, testing, and releasing software can happen rapidly, frequently, and more reliably (Pierre, 2017). So what is the relation between DevOps and Cloud Computing? It's simple. Computing, whether inside your firewall or purchased from a service provider, is essential to success with DevOps. The virtual platform needs to be as fluid as the application, and deployment from development to production needs to be automatic in order to meet the demanding delivery requirements. In other words, with DevOps instead of doing development on one machine and deployment somewhere else, the machine becomes part of the application. It can't be done without virtualization. When infrastructure scales up and down as the application needs it in order to get better reliability and performance. The Puppet Labs survey found that DevOps practitioners spend 33 percent more time on infrastructure issues. Since DevOps is the higher order, end-to-end concept, we can consider cloud at least in the context of this discussion, to be a subordinate enabler of DevOps.

The march toward DevOps is now widespread, and it has become the default approach for developing cloud-based applications. Overall DevOps adoption increased from 74 to 78 percent this year with enterprise adoption reaching 84 percent (RightScale State of the cloud survey, 2017).

Containers: A Disruptive Force in Cloud Computing

At the moment, containers are generally a major topic in the IT world, and security in particular. The world's top technology enterprises, including Google, Microsoft and Facebook, all use them. Despite the fact that it's still in its early days, containers are seeing increasing use in the production environments. Containers guarantee a, easy-to-deploy, streamlined and secure method of implementing specific infrastructure requirements and they also offer a substitute to virtual machines. Containerization is an OS-level virtualization technique for deploying and running distributed applications without launching an entire VM for each application. Rather, we have multiple isolated systems called containers running on a single control host and access a

Table 2. DevOps adoption (RightScale State of the cloud survey, 2017)

	Adopting DevOps	**Not Adopting**	**Don't Know**
2016	74%	16%	10%
2017	78%	15%	7%

single kernel. Because containers share the same OS kernel as the host, containers can be more adequate than VMs, which require separate OS instances. Containers hold the components necessary to run the desired software, such as environment variables, files and libraries. The host OS also hold down the container's access to physical resources -- such as CPU and memory -- so a single container cannot exhaust all of a host's physical resources.

As part of embracing DevOps processes, enterprises often choose to put into practice new tools that allow them to automate and standardize deployment and configuration of servers and applications. These tools include configuration management gizmos (such as Ansible, Chef and Puppet) and, more recently, container technologies, such as Docker, and container scheduling and orchestration tools such as Swarm, Kubernetes and Mesosphere. The rapid rise in the use of containers put Docker on the top DevOps tools. Overall Docker adoption grows up to 35 percent, taking the lead over Chef and Puppet at 28 percent each.

In 2017, there has been a significant rise in the percentage of companies that are adopting DevOps, going up from 21 percent to 30 percent. Among enterprises, Docker use is even higher (40 percent) with an additional 30 percent that are planning to use Docker.

Widespread Cloud Platforms Vendors

There are many cloud computing vendors. Cloud computing enterprises come in all sizes and shapes. All large software vendors either have offerings in cloud space or in the process of launching one. Moreover, there are many startups that

Figure 1. Virtualization architecture vs containers architecture

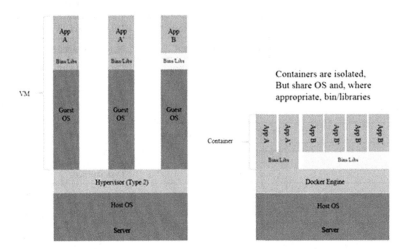

Table 3. Respondents using DevOps tools (CSO Online survey, 2016)

	Use today	Plan to use
Docker	35%	32%
Chef	28%	17%
Puppet	28%	16%
Ansible	21%	15%
Kubernetes	14%	22%
Salt	9%	11%
Docket Swarm	7%	16%
Mesophere	5%	12%
Rancher	3%	8%
Docker Tutum	2%	10%

Table 4. Infrastructure as a service providers (Lenk, Klems, Nimis, Tai, & Sandholm, 2009)

Organization	Service or Tool	Description
Amazon	Elastic Compute Cloud (EC2)	Virtual servers
	Dynamo	Key-value storage system
	Simple Storage Service (S3)	Storage buckets
	SimpleDB	Database-as-a-Service
	CloudFront	Content Delivery
	SQS	Queueing services
AppNexus	AppNexus Cloud	Virtual servers
Bluelock	Bluelock Virtual Cloud Computing	Virtual servers
	Bluelock Virtual Recovery	Disaster Recovery
Emulab	Emulab Network Testbed	Network testbed
ENKI	ENKI Virtual Private Data Centers	On-demand virtual data center resources
EU Reservoir project	Open Nebula	Open source virtual infrastructure engine
FlexiScale	FlexiScale Cloud Computing	Virtual servers
GoGrid	Cloud Hosting	Virtual servers
	Cloud Storage	Disk storage
Google	Google Big Table	Distributed storage system
	Google File System	Distributed file system

continued on following page

Table 4. Continued

Organization	Service or Tool	Description
HP	iLO	Lights out management
	Tycoon	Market-based system for managing compute resources in clusters
Joyent	Accelerator	Virtual servers
	Connector	Pre-configured virtual servers
	BingoDisk	Disk storage
Nirvanix	Nirvanix Storage Delivery Network	Disk storage
OpenFlow	OpenFlow	Network simulation
Rackspace	Mosso Cloud Sites	Pre-configured virtual servers
	Mosso Cloud Storage	Disk storage
	Mosso Cloud Servers	Virtual servers
Skytap	Skytap Virtual Lab	Virtual IT lab environment
Terremark	Infinistructure	Virtual servers
The Globus Alliance	Nimbus	Open source toolkit to turn a cluster into an IaaS cloud.
UCSB	EUCALYPTUS	Open source implementation of Amazons EC2
10gen	Mongo DB	Database for cloud storage
	Babble Application Server	Web application server for cloud deployments

Table 5. Platform-as-a service providers (Lenk, Klems, Nimis, Tai, & Sandholm, 2009)

Organization	Service or Tool	Description
Akamai	EdgePlatform	Content, Site, Application Delivery
Facebook	Facebook Platform	Development tools and execution environment for social networking applications
Google	App Engine	Scalable runtime environment for Python Web applications
Microsoft	Azure	Development environment and runtime for Microsoft applications
	Live Mesh	Platform to sync, share and access a wide range of devices with Microsoft operating systems
NetSuite	SuiteFlex	Toolkit to customize NetSuite online business applications
Salesforce	Force.com	Build and deliver on-demand business applications
Sun	Caroline	Horizontally scalable platform for the development and deployment of Internet services.
Zoho	Zoho Creator	Toolkit to build and deliver on demand business applications

Table 6. Software-as-a service providers (Lenk, Klems, Nimis, Tai, & Sandholm, 2009)

Organization	Service or tool	Description
Google	Google Docs	Online office suite
	Google Maps API	The Google Maps API lets developers embed Google Maps in their own web pages with JavaScript.
	OpenSocial	A common API for social applications across multiple websites.
OpenID Foundation	OpenID	Distributed system to allow users to have a single digital identity across the Internet.
Microsoft	Office Live	Online office suite
Salesforce	Salesforce.com	Customer Relationship Management

have interesting products in cloud space. Bellow some of the main players in the marketplace and their products:

Cloud Computing Applications and Advantages

Prior to cloud computing, if you owned or ran a business, you would need to develop and maintain an expensive IT infrastructure for the effective operation of your business. This included buying servers for capital expenditures of between 3,000$ to 20,000$ each, hiring skilled IT staff for approximately 100,000$ per year each and setting aside valuable business space for server room that required special security and precise cooling systems. Additionally, capital expenses for operating systems and application software would be required. Traditional IT often develop over time into large data centers and server farms that consume a huge portion of your capital budget. Despite off all of these expenditures, this would not have been an efficient IT system. In building this infrastructure, much valuable business time would be reallocated. Your IT infrastructure would provide little flexibility. Scalability would require added capital expenses. Because this, IT infrastructure would need to be built to accommodate time periods of peak need, there would be much waste during normal times, or during periods when business is slow. Also, because maintaining an IT infrastructure often requires the share of your IT resources, the focus of your IT department and often other critical staff would be allocated away from mission critical priorities that would better serve your customers,

With cloud computing, someone else will be responsible for your IT needs while your company focuses on meeting your customers' needs proactively. With cloud computing your company will never again need to focus your valuable time, attention and expenditures on buying servers, buying and upgrading software licenses, IT maintenance and expensive IT personnel. The cloud can insure:

Figure 2. Benefits of cloud computing

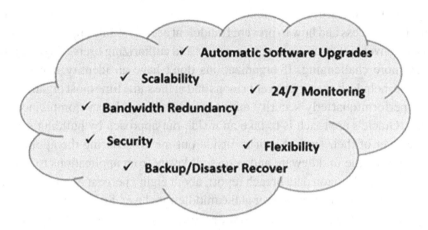

Cloud Computing Challenges, Concerns and Risks

As information applications move further away from our IT organizations that's imply the loss of control and visibility. While most cloud providers focused on performance and scale they've neglected the data security governance and application security controls that should be maintained to reduce risks and satisfy regulatory requirements.

Most of generations cloud highlighted the loss of visibility control that can happen when the applications and data move off-premise. An oracle application user group of IT professionals found that 82% were concerned about data privacy and 40% were worried about the backend integration challenges and silos created by the cloud. A follow-up study by the Ponemon Institute found that 54% of IT professionals who adopted a cloud solution were worried about a security breach happening because of a risk at a cloud provider site

The top five cloud security concerns come from a CSO online survey of security officer's and found that the top five concerns were all related to mobile data access,

Figure 3. Challenges and risks when adopting cloud computing (Cloud at the Crossroads: OAUG Survey on Application Delivery Strategies, 2014)

regulatory compliance and identity management. Most cloud applications will be deployed to provide access to mobile users who are on the go. The top concern is how users get access and how to prevent fraudulent access. While applications in the cloud are convenient, provisioning user access and authorizing users to applications is much more challenging. If organizations don't have an identity management strategy the helpdesk costs can be enormous and at the same time most organizations have to perform quarterly security audits to address regulatory compliance. For example, Oracle's approach is to take an inside-out approach by building security in every layer of their stack. Security inside-out means securing the applications and data within the middleware and across all layers from applications to storage. According to the Verizon data breach report, about eighty percent of breach records implicate a web server or app server at the middleware layer. So by building identity management directly into the middleware layer oracle reduced security risk for applications deployed in the cloud to help organizations to address the new enterprise imperative. Instead of taking a reactive approach IT organizations need to focus on the risks. The risks against the applications, the middleware and databases. It cost 10 times more to remediate a breach than prevented. But ultimately security rely helps unlock the opportunity. With every new cloud initiative, application security and data security are prerequisite.

Despite an increased focus on cloud cost management, only few enterprises are taking critical actions to optimize cloud costs, such as or selecting lower-cost cloud or regions and shutting down unused workloads and workflows. This represents an opportunity for increased in savings and increased efficiency.

Figure 4. Securing the Cloud

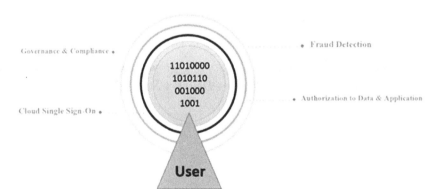

Figure 5. How companies optimize cloud costs (RightScale State of the cloud survey, 2017)

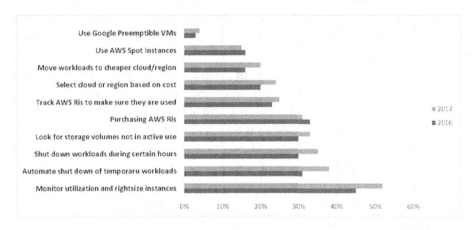

SECURITY AND PRIVACY WITHIN A CLOUD ENVIRONMENT

The Cloud: Is It Our Next Big Hope or Is It a Security Nightmare

IT professionals in general don't trust the cloud for many reasons including losing control, dishonest providers, failing privacy strategies, etc. Nonetheless, the cloud provides a way to address issues such as ubiquitous connected devices and new techniques to defend ourselves against many categories of attacks.

We should redefine security in order to secure our digital assets. We certainly are living in a rapidly changing times. Who had thought just a few years ago that we could today control and secure our homes remotely with our smartphones and computers for just hundred dollars. As security professionals, we certainly know that such systems could be vulnerable. But as the consumers or users that we are, were are expecting the service providers to build the security into their solutions. Taking components that are not secure by nature and turn them into a secure end to end solution. This is a profound shift in responsibility. As the providers of solutions have absolute interest of making that happens, because if not they will expose themselves to liabilities and probably lose their business. In fact the same thing is happening in our business. The cloud is redefining our businesses in a new way that we could not think about it few years ago, and this is just the beginning. As we all know, we are in the internet of thing and artificial intelligence era, digital manufacturing and there are waves of technical innovation that shall come in our way at increasing rapid pace. We see that in our corporate networks. Thus, we moved from mainframe to client server and now to cloud computing which we prefer to call the 'cloud oriented architectures and applications'. This allow our business to interconnect in ways that we couldn't think before and gain agility and competitiveness. There is no a week now that pass by without hearing or reading or maybe receiving such attack ourselves. Every day we learn new attack that happens. The key for us is trying to understand and learn from this attacks.

One of the problems is the points of connection which have exponentially multiplied. If we look back to the attack described above, we understand after that the vendor credentials were compromised which allowed the cyber criminals to go through the procurement system and from there to inject malware into point of sales network and then into the machines and after that very smartly ex-filtrate the data. So, security is becoming a problem of scale.

In corporate network, we are still essentially client-server based which was very useful for us to distribute the computing and information within the company worldwide. But as we said earlier, as we connect more and more systems, the data become much easier to grab. Our security solutions of today which are also client server essentially are not capable for scaling and that explain why we see this exponential increase of data breaches. What we can also learn from these attacks is the fact that the cyber criminals has fantastic century with the cloud and we cannot bring the fight there witch mean we must rethink our security strategies. To do that we should first look externally like the hackers sees us. Then internally and finally identify if they are in.

So first we should look into our perimeters the way hackers do. Now we speak about perimeter-less. The perimeter is everything that is internet facing and it is relevant to our business (browser of the users, browser of our customers, it is the applications that we have on Amazon, etc.). Cyber criminals are very good in scanning continuously almost that perimeters to identify vulnerabilities where they could essentially penetrate our defenses. So how could we use the cloud to essentially identify the vulnerabilities before hacker can exploits them?

If you look to what google did, you will see that they built data centers which can now scan every website on the planet, extract the data so that we can in less than a second find information we are looking for. So, it's not difficult to imagine that we could build an infrastructure in the cloud containing as many scanners as required to continuously look at our perimeter (we should say our extended perimeter because we can have our application in Amazon or Azure for example or furthermore living in an hybrid cloud). Then we will have a long list of vulnerabilities to essentially alert us if for example an FTP server which is normally decommissioned in our perimeter suddenly appears online or that a port who supposed to be closed suddenly become open and turning this solution in an alerting incident response system. We have here uniquely and interesting advantage over the hackers is that because we have this kind of defenses the hackers have to scan very slowly and therefore we can as long we do it continuously identify the vulnerabilities most likely before they can. The second thing we need to do in our perimeter even if we have today firewalls, IDS and IPS which are very good solutions, but we certainly need to do much more and its essentially to analyze traffic coming in and out. And today we have the next generation of firewalls that gave us only awareness. What we need to do now is bringing to the firewalls the end-point awareness as well as the threat awareness. But how can we do that using cloud technology?

If we start by the end-point, today as you know we have this big agent sitting in our end-point doing all the analyzing and computing and this is a model that is no scaling anymore. So, we can think in building agent smaller which in fact would be map the security and identification of this devices continuously. And we can build using the power of the cloud what we could call a cloud 'echo database' of this cloud agents. So, for example, if an end-point connects to a network and leave we will know what the latest status is. When he comes back we only have to analyses in the cloud with all the power that we can throw at it the deltas and then define in real time or real near time if that device becomes suddenly suspicious. Now we can do the same thing with threat-awareness. Now the cloud give us infinite computing power and infinite storage at cost which are extremely low, so we can think of having what we can call a security brain into the cloud where the information passes and we can mix IPS, IDS with threat awareness from other sources and again in real time compute the correlation and passes the information to the firewalls to be always updated with the latest status of what is happening in the cloud.

Now, part of our perimeter are also social networks and we all know that cyber criminals are using them very well for their advantages. They impersonate executives for example, they also using it to delivers malwares to the subscribers in Facebook or Twitter page for example. Today we need to see it like the hackers do so we can take preventive measures.

Finally, the passwords are an important part of the perimeter because this is the first line of attacks. If you read the Verizon 2016 data breach report you will find out that in the 3000 or 4000 data breaches that were investigated 75% of them started with stolen credentials. This is the time to push for 2-factor authentication, which is very similar to the principle in the chip and pin in credit cards. We see today for example Google making a very considered effort to try to bring ubiquity to two-factor authentication.

All what we said before was for the outside of the perimeter. Let's look inside now. We should harden the inside of our networks. Now the shift to cloud is creating a simplification because we can consolidate datacenters, use virtualization, etc... In a mean time till we can build the security in this new infrastructure we need to take certain primordial measures. First thing first is starting with good security 'hygiene' through choosing good passwords, having a good segmentation, reducing access privileges. There is a new tool from SAN institute which is the top 5 controls which allow us the measure the security compliance of our infrastructure and application and there is also the very well-known vulnerability management application which today is not at the level of what should be done because this kind of application are static meaning that they don't scale to the level of distributed systems. So here also we need to rethink vulnerability management in a different way and make it essentially continuous and much more in real time. So again, how could we do that by thinking cloud? If you remember well, we mentioned before. We well use decentralized agents that will gather information in real time and send it to vulnerability management systems using the power of the cloud that give us as much computing power as we need because for security we need real-time and that's the technical challenges we will answer in the chapter IV presenting the different solutions we can use.

Last thing is the case when despite all the measures we've done, the hackers could be insiders or they could found their way to our systems through our defenses layers. These is where IOCs comes in. This is an indicator of compromise which are the new frontier.

IOCs are generated through different sources and methodologies, from sandboxing, forensics, systems agents, from looking at registries and once we have discovered their fingerprint then we can look at detecting if we've been compromised deeper into the enterprise. The challenge today is that is a manual a very difficult process. So, we need community effort essentially to normalizing and standardizing them because if we can do that we can build the detection tools which can scale very cost effectively to the size of our networks. If we look back

Figure 6. IOCs: indicator of compromise

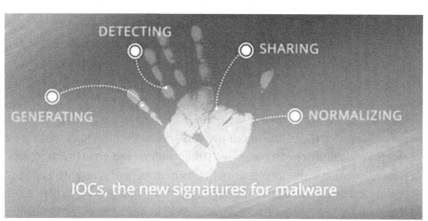

Complete Context of Security Equals Tighter Security Policies

Security best practices dictate that the decisions the enterprises make regarding their ability to report on network activity, their policies and their forensics capacity depend on a context. The context of the website visited, the application in use and the associated payload which are all valuable data points in the effort to protect their network. When the enterprises know exactly which applications are traversing their Internet gateway, operating within the data center or cloud environment, or being used by remote users, then they can apply specific policies to those applications, complete with coordinated threat protection. The knowledge of who the user is, not just their IP address, adds another contextual element that empowers the company to be more granular in their policy assignment. A rich set of highly interactive visualization and log filtering tools provides the context of the application activity, the associated content or threat, who the user is, and on what type of device. Each of these data points by itself paints a partial picture of the network, yet when taken in complete context provides a full view of the potential security risk, allowing them to make more-informed policy decisions. All traffic is continuously classified. As the state changes, the changes are logged for analysis, and the graphical summaries are dynamically updated, displaying the information in an easy-to-use, web-based interface:

- At the Internet gateway, companies can investigate new or unfamiliar applications to quickly see a description of the application, its behavioral characteristics, and who is using it. Additional visibility into URL categories, threats, and data patterns provides a better-rounded picture of network traffic traversing the gateway.
- All files analyzed for unknown malware should be logged on-box with full access to details, including the application used, the user, the file type, target OS and malicious behaviors observed.
- Within the data center, enterprises shall verify all applications under use, and ensure that they are only being used by authorized users. Added visibility into data center activity can confirm that there are no misconfigured applications or rogue uses of SSH or RDP.
- Threat analysis, forensics and hunting workflows are accelerated with threat intelligence service, providing unique contextual threat data.

Proposed Security Solutions

There are considerable research works happening in the field of cloud security. Many groups and organization are implicated in developing security solutions and standards for the cloud. The Cloud Security Alliance (CSA) is assembling solution providers, non-profits and individuals to discuss the current and future best practices for information assurance in the cloud (security best practices for cloud computing, 2009). The authors are listing bellow the latest and greatest solutions (please note that the list below is not ordered)

VPC

Stand on the popular tunneling technologies, a Virtual Private Cloud (VPC) can isolate the virtual networks. Each VPC has an exclusive and unique tunnel ID, and a tunnel ID corresponds to only one VPC. A tunnel encapsulation that pipe a unique tunnel ID is added to each data packet transmitted between the ECS instances within a VPC. Then the data packet is transmitted over the physical network. Because the tunnel IDs for the ECS instances in different VPCs are not the same and they are located on two different routing planes, the communication is impossible between the two tunnels, thus achieving their isolation.

With VPC, computation and workloads are no longer shortened to a fixed site but can be relocated dynamically across multiple geographical sites to improve manageability, performance and fault tolerance. The same way virtual private network

Figure 7. VPC architecture (intl.aliyun.com, 2016)

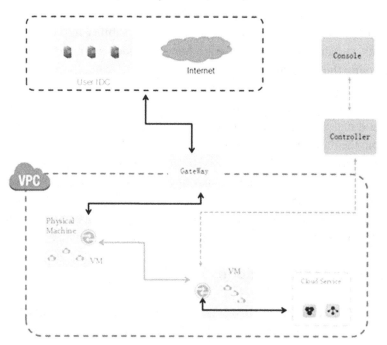

(VPN) provides secure data transfer over the public Internet, a VPC provides secure data transfer between a private enterprise and a public cloud provider, insuring that each customer's data remains isolated from every other customer's data both in transit and inside the cloud provider's network.

TPM

The present computing infrastructure landscape was built with an interoperability and openness which has paid huge dividends in terms of creativity and innovation. But, the same openness is problematic for security. Experience has shown that the access control model of present operating systems is inadequate against many types of attacks particularly in the hands of inexpert users. Trusted computing becomes part of the computing field over the last years. This is because email viruses, spyware, trojans, phishing scams, key-stroke loggers and security flaws are so much a part of the landscape already.

The trusted platform module (TPM) was designed to bridge the gap between a purely software-based security realization and the added protection that hardware realization adds to the security of any system. By achieving all random scheduling algorithm (RSA) private-key cryptographic operations and isolating the RSA private keys within the hardware boundaries, the TPM protects against snooping for keying material contained within a hard drive.

Security Using BLOCKCHAIN Principles

The main idea behind block chain is that there is no centralized authority that is responsible for saying what is true or what is false, rather multiple distributed parties come to consensus, that consensus is entered into the ledger which thereafter can be accessed by anyone in the future. It is computationally infeasible for a single actor (or anything less that majority consensus) to go back and modify history. What about using block chain to secure our transactions in the cloud? In principle, such as system can be easily envisioned. Everything, that happens to data, whether transport, processing or storage of data is entered into the block chain. Afterwards what happened to data, who accessed the data, where it went and how that data was governed can be verified by anyone who has access to the block chain. In essence the block chain freezes the compute platform in time and users of the platform can verify that the platform is in the correct state in real-time.

Such a system would give complete traceability, accountability and transparency for the cloud, entities who are either using or administrating the cloud can be held responsible for their actions, regulators get to audit all processes and everyone involved can verify what happened then. Of course, a reasonable question to ask would be whether such as system could be built in reality. Even a modest petabyte cloud easily implies billions of data transactions every second that would need to be entered into the block chain and distributed out to the edge. The implied network, storage and compute requirements would make it impossible to scale. Now here's a thought - imagine if that block chain wasn't just for one cloud - but for all clouds, and all data - every transport, compute and storage of data across all networks in the world. Imagine what such as a system would imply for accountability and transparency for global society. It would transform our society from one that is trust based to one that is truth based, i.e. humans can choose to trust each other, but they can also prove what happened using the block chain. There is many ongoing research to try to incorporate the principle of block chain into the cloud to secure it (Zyskind & al., 2015) (Buyya, Yeo, & Venugopal, 2008)

Machine Learning and AI-Driven Frameworks Shape Cloud Security

2016 introduced selfie drones and self-driven cars. The technology behind these innovations was heavily driven by machine learning (ML) and artificial intelligence (AI). ML and AI usage within cybersecurity is not new. Cybersecurity vendors have been supporting them for threat analysis and big data challenges posed by intelligence threat. But, the pervasive availability of open source AI/ML frameworks and automation simplicity associated with them will redefine the security automation approaches. Today, security automation is about simplifying and speeding up monotonous tasks associated with cybersecurity policy definition and enforcement in the cloud environment. Very Soon, artificial intelligence and machine learning frameworks will be leveraged for implementing predictive security postures across public, private and SaaS cloud infrastructures. We are already seeing early examples that reflect the above approach. Open source projects, such as MineMeld (paloaltonetworks.com, 2017), are modeling our thinking on leveraging externally sourced threat data and using it for self-configuring security policy based on organization-specific needs. In 2017 and beyond, we will see the rise of autonomic approaches to cybersecurity.

Homomorphic Encryption

Homomorphic encryptions permit complex mathematical operations to be performed on encrypted data without compromising the encryption. In mathematics, homomorphic describes the transformation of one data set into another while preserving relationships between elements in both sets. The term is derived from the Greek words for "same structure." Because the data in a homomorphic encryption scheme retains the same structure, identical mathematical operations -- whether they are performed on encrypted or decrypted data -- will yield equivalent results. Homomorphic encryption is expected to play an important part in cloud computing, allowing companies to store encrypted data in a public cloud and take advantage of the cloud provider's analytic services.

Next-Generation Firewall

Major shifts in application usage, user behavior and convoluted network infrastructure create a threat landscape that exposes vulnerabilities in traditional port-based network security. The users want access to an increasing number of applications, operating across a wide range of device types, often with little regard for the business or security risks. Meantime, data center increase, virtualization, network segmentation and mobility initiatives are compelling us to rethink how to enable access to applications and data, while protecting the network from a new, more sophisticated class of advanced threats that evade traditional security mechanisms. Based on the Asia Pacific Application Usage and Threat Report from Palo Alto Networks, findings expose the fact that application vulnerability exploits target high-value business applications. As threats and attackers innovate as quickly as virtualization has, it is important to ensure that modern security controls are developed and placed into our virtualized data centers. Thus, the Next-Generation Firewall inspects all traffic - inclusive of applications, threats and content – and ties it to the user, regardless of location or device type. The application, content and user become integral components of the enterprise security policy. The result is the ability to align security with the key business initiatives of the enterprise. Below an example of the Palo Alto network's Next-Generation Security Platform which can reduce response times to incidents, discover unknown threats, and streamline security network deployment.

Intrusion Defense Systems (IDS) / Intrusion Prevention Systems (IPS)

Intrusion detection systems are a hardware or software system that continuously monitors the events occurring in a computer system or network, analyzing them for malicious activities or policy violations. Good analogy is to compare IDS with a protocol analyzer. A protocol analyzer is a tool that a network engineer uses to look deep into the network and see what is happening, in sometimes excruciating detail. An IDS is a "protocol analyzer" for the security engineer. The IDS looks deep into the network and sees what is happening from the security point of view. The main intrusion detection techniques are:

Figure 8. Palo Alto Networks Next-Generation Security Platform

- Signature Detection (SD)
- Anomaly Detection (AD)
- Soft Computing based detection

GREEN CLOUD COMPUTING

Explaining Green Computing

Green computing is the new 'kid' on the IT block. Shutting down idle PCs, virtualization and virtual meetings are all difficult to culturally embrace. However, with rising of energy prices increased environmental regulation. IT managers certainly being presented with the data centers energy bill. No business can afford to ignore the environmental of computing application. Today we can't live without PCs, so let's learn to live with them in a way that makes them friendlier to the environment. Currently computers consume far too much electricity and generate to much a waste to be considered an eco-friendly solution by today's standards. Before going to green computing, we have to think how green computing came.

In 1992, the U.S. Environmental Protection Agency launched "Energy Star", a labeling program designed to promote and recognize energy efficiency in monitors, climate control equipment's, etc. So, the term GREEN COMPUTING was coined shortly after star began. In other words, green computing is the environmentally responsible and eco-friendly use of computers and their resources. Green computing focuses on reducing the environmental impact of industrial process and innovative technologies caused by the Earth's growing population. It is the environmentally responsible of computers and related resources. Such practices include the implementation of energy efficient central processing units that is CPUs, servers, resource consumption and proper disposal of electronic based. GC goals is to design better computer systems. Means their processing is better and consume less amount of energy

Information and communication technology accounts for about two percent of global carbon dioxide (ICT = 2% of C02) emissions and it is roughly the same as aviation. At current electricity prices, most computer hardware also costs more to 1 over its lifetime but it does to purchase (Energy costs already exceed hardware costs) in the first place. Computing manufacture additionally has a significant environmental impact (one pc is made from 1.8 tons of chemicals). It takes about 1.8 tons of chemical, fossil fuels and water to produce a typical desktop computer. Many materials currently used in building pcs are also hazardous and difficult to recycle. It's therefore not surprising but the most recent green peace guide to greener electronics does not give any computer manufacturer a satisfactory green ranking.

Energy Reduction

The electricity used by computers can be reduced by turning off idle pcs, using lower power hardware, server virtualization, hardware as a service, and energy-efficient coding research. Research suggests that in the US and UK over 20 billion kilowatts of electricity is wasted each year due to business pcs being left on overnight. This also results in over 15 million tons of needless CO2 emissions. In addition to turning off idle pcs, lower-power hardware is now also available. Indeed, processes such as Intel's Atom™ can allow a pc to consume around 30 watts compared to the 100 to 200 watts used by many desktop computers.

Using a laptop also results in significant energy savings. Corporate data centers can save power through server virtualization. This is where many small underutilized physical servers are replaced with virtual services. Leading the way with virtualization is IBM with its project BIG GREEN. This is currently consolidating 2900 servers on 230 mainframes to achieve 80% energy saving. Smaller companies can achieve virtualization benefits through hardware as a service. This is where they purchase their computer processing requirements from an online facility such as Amazon Elastic Compute cloud. Once again this results in an optimal use of shared computing resources.

Finally, Electricity usage can be reduced through energy efficient coding. This saves power by writing software designed as quickly and efficiently as possible. Today a great deal of software is highly inefficient with many gadgets and gizmos that slow things down and waste a lot of power. Indeed it has been estimated that energy efficient coding could reduce the energy consumption of computers by up to thirty percent.

Part of the Solution

When it comes to being green, computing may be both part of the problem and part of the solution. Indeed Intel recently argued that the microprocessor can become the most energy efficient and mission reducing device ever created. This is because computers can be used to increase business efficiency, to enable dematerialization and to reduce the need for people to travel. Computers can improve business efficiency by neighboring organizations and economies to scale in more energy and resource effective ways (for example through better logistics coordination, empty low can be avoided, transportation reduced and energy saved). Intel argues that computing has already saved more natural resources than it has consumed. Computers development also permit resource saving through dematerialization. This is where physical products are replaced with digital downloads and web-based information services. Computer technology also can assist with travel reduction by enabling people to telework and so avoid a daily commute. Video conference and other online communications tools can also to curtail longer distance travel with some companies have already replaced the travel department with meetings departments to facilitate virtual gatherings. With the improvements in the technology the next stage is the provision of environmental friendly and energy efficient solutions.

FUTURE RESEARCH DIRECTIONS

In summary, cloud computing is definitely a type of computing paradigm that will continue for a long time to come. The future seems to be limited only by the imaginations of innovators. Full automation and application of scalability rules to control services in a holistic manner are granted for future developments on top Clouds infrastructure. More elements helping to reduce services' time to market and provide further support for application design, development, debugging, versioning, updating, etc. are still very much needed. Specific benchmarks for the scaling potential of applications on the Cloud are also to be developed. Generally speaking, the scaling applications in the Cloud will face some challenges, detecting code parallelism, distributing application components in clusters and service operations in cores will remain subject to massive research in future. The classification of the extensive literature in the domains of cloud computing, green computing, and green ICT will provide the potential opportunities for future research. Sustainability is the business strategy that drives the long-term corporate growth and profitability by mandating the inclusion of environmental and social issues in the business model (Kasemsap, 2017). An examination of linkages among cloud computing, green computing, green ICT, sustainability, environmental sustainability, environmental management, and CSR would seem to be viable for future research efforts.

CONCLUSION

As described in this chapter, there are extreme advantages in using a cloud-based system, there are yet many practical problems which have to be solved. Cloud computing is a disruptive technology with profound implications not only for Internet services but also for the IT sector as a whole. Still, several outstanding issues exist, particularly related to service-level agreements (SLA), security and privacy, and power efficiency. As described, currently security has lot of loose ends which scares away a lot of potential users. Until a proper security module is not in place, potential users will not be able to leverage the advantages of this technology. The authors discussed through this chapter what should be done to have a green secure flavor in a computing environment. As cloud computing becomes more widespread, the energy consumption of the network and computing resources that underpin the cloud will grow. This is happening at a time when there is increasing attention being paid to the need to manage energy consumption across the entire information and communications technology (ICT) sector. Every element in the cloud should be analyzed at the macro and micro level and an integrated solution must be designed and deployed in the cloud to attract and enthrall the potential consumers. Until then, cloud environment will remain cloudy.

REFERENCES

Baran, D. (n. d.). Cloud computing basics. *Webguild.org*. Retrieved November 11, 2016 from http://www.webguild.org/2008/07/cloud-computing-basics.php

Brandon, G. (n. d.). Ultimate Guide and List of Cloud Computing Security Companies, Vendors, Services, Issues and Solutions. Secure your Cloud. Cloudnewsdaily.com. Retrieved January 15, 2017 from http://cloudnewsdaily.com/cloud-security/

Cloud Security Alliance (CSA). (n. d.). *Security best practices for cloud computing*. Retrieved February 05, 2017 from https://cloudsecurityalliance.org/

CSO. (n. d.). *CSO Online survey*. Retrieved January 5, 2017 from https://eforms. cso.ie/

Gupta, I. (n. d.). *Cloud Computing Concepts*. Retrieved February 02, 2017 from https://www.coursera.org/learn/cloud-computing

InformationWeek Report. (2014). *Return of the Silos*. Retrieved December 10, 2017 from http://www.oracle.com/us/products/ondemand/collateral/cloud-executive-strategy-1559197.pdf

InformationWeek Report. (n. d.). *Cloud at the Crossroads: OAUG Survey on Application Delivery Strategies*. Retrieved January 13, 2017 from http://www.ebizroundtable.com/CORE/Presentations/2014 _Summer/On_Ramp_to_the_Clouds-APS_and_OMCS.pdf

Intl.aliyun. (n. d.)Error! Hyperlink reference not valid.. *VPC/ECS*. Retrieved December 17, 2016 from intl.aliyun.com: https://intl.aliyun.com/help/doc-detail/34221.html

Kasemsap, K. (2017). Advocating sustainable supply chain management and sustainability in global supply chain. In M. Khan, M. Hussain, & M. Ajmal (Eds.), *Green supply chain management for sustainable business practice* (pp. 234–271). Hershey, PA: IGI Global. doi:10.4018/978-1-5225-0635-5.ch009

Lenk, A., Klems, M., Nimis, J., Tai, S., & Sandholm, T. (2009). What's inside the Cloud? An architectural map of the Cloud landscape. In *Proceedings of the 2009 ICSE Workshop on Software Engineering Challenges of Cloud Computing CLOUD '09* (pp. 23–31). IEEE Computer Society, Washington, DC, USA. doi:10.1109/CLOUD.2009.5071529

paloaltonetworks. *Secure the network*. Retrieved January 02, 2017 from https://www.paloaltonetworks.com/products/secure-the-network/subscriptions/minemeld

Ponemon. (2017). *Ponemon Survey 2017*. Retrieved December 14, 2017 from https://www.ponemon.org/

RightScale. (n. d.). *RightScale State of the cloud survey*. Retrieved February 04, 2017. Retrieved from http://www.rightscale.com/

Shaikh, R. & Sasikumar, M. (2012). *Security Issues in Cloud Computing: A survey*. *International Journal of Computer Applications, 44*(19), pp. 4–10.

Shuai, Z., Shufen, Z., Chen, X., & Huo, X. (2010). Cloud Computing Research and Development Trend. In *Proceedings of the Second International Conference on Future Networks ICFN '10* (pp. 93–97).

Vriens, P. (n. d.). *What could be a valid definition of DevOps?* Retrieved October 15, 2016, from https://devops.stackexchange.com

Zhang, Q., Cheng, L., & Boutaba, R. (2010). Cloud computing: state-of-the-art and research challenges. *Journal of Internet Services and Applications*, *1*(1), 7–18.

Zyskind, G., & Nathan, O. (2015). Decentralizing privacy: Using block chain to protect personal data. In *Proceedings of the Security and Privacy Workshops (SPW)* (pp. 180–184).

ADDITIONAL READING

Arnfalk, P., Pilerot, U., Schillander, P., & Grönvall, P. (2016). Green IT in practice: Virtual meetings in Swedish public agencies. *Journal of Cleaner Production*, *123*, 101–112. doi:10.1016/j.jclepro.2015.08.063

Bayramusta, M., & Nasir, V. A. (2016). A fad or future of IT?: A comprehensive literature review on the cloud computing research. *International Journal of Information Management*, *36*(4), 635–644. doi:10.1016/j.ijinfomgt.2016.04.006

Botta, A., de Donato, W., Persico, V., & Pescapé, A. (2016). Integration of Cloud computing and Internet of Things: A survey. *Future Generation Computer Systems*, *56*, 684–700. doi:10.1016/j.future.2015.09.021

Byington, J. R., & McGee, J. A. (2014). Data security and the cloud. *Journal of Corporate Accounting & Finance*, *25*(5), 41–44. doi:10.1002/jcaf.21971

Debnath, B., Roychoudhuri, R., & Ghosh, S. K. (2016). E-waste management: A potential route to green computing. *Procedia Environmental Sciences*, *35*, 669–675. doi:10.1016/j.proenv.2016.07.063

Fan, W., Yang, S., & Pei, J. (2014). A novel two-stage model for cloud service trustworthiness evaluation. *Expert Systems: International Journal of Knowledge Engineering and Neural Networks*, *31*(2), 136–153. doi:10.1111/exsy.12017

Fernandes, D. A. B., Soares, L. F. B., Gomes, J. V., Freire, M. M., & Inácio, P. R. M. (2014). Security issues in cloud environments: A survey. *International Journal of Information Security*, *13*(2), 113–170. doi:10.1007/s10207-013-0208-7

Fujinoki, H. (2015). Designs, analyses, and optimizations for attribute-shuffling obfuscation to protect information from malicious cloud administrators. *Security and Communication Networks*, *8*(17), 3045–3066. doi:10.1002/sec.1231

Khan, A. N., Kiah, M. L. M., Ali, M., Madani, S. A., & Shamshirband, S. (2014). BSS: Block-based sharing scheme for secure data storage services in mobile cloud environment. *The Journal of Supercomputing*, *70*(2), 946–976. doi:10.1007/s11227-014-1269-8

Kshetri, N. (2016). Institutional and economic factors affecting the development of the Chinese cloud computing industry and market. *Telecommunications Policy*, *40*(2/3), 116–129. doi:10.1016/j.telpol.2015.07.006

Lee, T.-H., Wen, C.-H., Chang, L.-H., Chiang, H.-S., & Hsieh, M.-C. (2014). A Lightweight Intrusion Detection Scheme Based on Energy Consumption Analysis in 6LowPAN. In Advanced Technologies, Embedded and Multimedia for Human-centric Computing, LNEE (Vol. 260, pp. 1205–1213).

Subirats, J., & Guitart, J. (2015). Assessing and forecasting energy efficiency on cloud computing platforms. *Future Generation Computer Systems*, *45*, 70–94. doi:10.1016/j.future.2014.11.008

Zhang, F., Gao, Z., & Ye, Q. (2015). Construction of cloud platform for personalized information services in digital library based on cloud computing data processing technology. *Automatic Control and Computer Sciences*, *49*(6), 373–379. doi:10.3103/S0146411615060127

KEY TERMS AND DEFINITIONS

Anomaly: Misbehavior detected in the network with is different from normal traffic.

Constrained Devices: A device that has limited processing and storage capabilities, and that often runs on batteries.

Datacenter: A data center is a facility used to house computer systems and associated components, such as telecommunications and storage systems.

Energy Consumption: The amount of energy consumed in a process or system, or by an organization.

Green ICT: The sustainable practice of using computing and information technology resources more efficiently while maintaining or improving overall performance.

GUI: Graphical user interface.

Intrusion: Intrusion could be any type of attack or anomalous activity happening on the network.

PUE: Power usage effectiveness.

Sustainability: The sustainable issue that products and services should be produced in ways that do not use resources that cannot be replaced and that do not damage the environment.

WUE: Water usage effectiveness.

Chapter 5
Green Cloud Computing

Indira K.
Thiagarajar College of Engineering, India

Thangavel M.
Thiagarajar College of Engineering, India

ABSTRACT

Cloud computing is a highly scalable and cost-effective infrastructure for running HPC, enterprise and Web applications. However, the growing demand of Cloud infrastructure has drastically increased the energy consumption of data centers, which has become a critical issue. High energy consumption not only translates to high operational cost, which reduces the profit margin of Cloud providers, but also leads to high carbon emissions which is not environmentally friendly. Hence, energy-efficient solutions are required to minimize the impact of Cloud computing on the environment. Thus, in this chapter, we discuss various elements of Green Clouds which contribute to the total energy consumption. The chapter also explains the role of Green Cloud Performance metrics and Green Cloud Architecture.

INTRODUCTION

With the growth of high speed networks over the last decades, there is an alarming rise in its usage comprised of thousands of concurrent e-commerce transactions and millions of Web queries a day. This ever-increasing demand is handled through large-scale datacenters, which consolidate hundreds and thousands of servers with other infrastructure such as cooling, storage and network systems. Many internet companies such as Google, Amazon, eBay, and Yahoo are operating such huge datacenters around the world. The commercialization of these developments is

DOI: 10.4018/978-1-5225-3038-1.ch005

defined currently as Cloud computing, where computing is delivered as utility on a pay-as-you-go basis. Traditionally, business organizations used to invest huge amount of capital and time in acquisition and maintenance of computational resources. The emergence of Cloud computing is rapidly changing this ownership-based approach to subscription-oriented approach by providing access to scalable infrastructure and services on-demand. Users can store, access, and share any amount of information in Cloud. That is, small or medium enterprises/organizations do not have to worry about purchasing, configuring, administering, and maintaining their own computing infrastructure. They can focus on sharpening their core competencies by exploiting a number of Cloud computing benefits such as on-demand computing resources, faster and cheaper software development capabilities at low cost. Moreover, Cloud computing also offers enormous amount of compute power to organizations which require processing of tremendous amount of data generated almost every day. For instance, financial companies have to maintain each day dynamic information about their hundreds of clients, and genomics research has to manage huge volumes of gene sequencing data. Therefore, many companies not only view Clouds as a useful on-demand service, but also a potential market opportunity. According to IDC (International Data Corporation) report [1], the global IT Cloud services spending is estimated to increase from $16 billion in 2008 to $42 billion in 2012, representing a compound annual growth rate (CAGR) of 27%. Attracted by this growth prospects, Web-based companies (Amazon, eBay, Salesforce.com), hardware vendors (HP, IBM, Cisco), telecom providers (AT&T, Verizon), software firms (EMC/VMware, Oracle/Sun, Microsoft) and others are all investing huge amount of capital in establishing Cloud datacenters. According to Google's earnings reports, the company has spent $1.9 billion US on datacenters in 2006, and $2.4 billion US in 2007.

Figure 1. Cloud and environmental sustainability

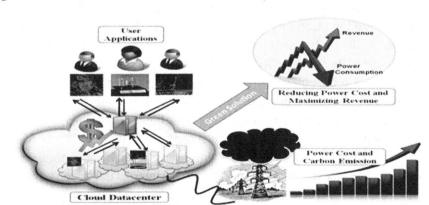

Clouds are essentially virtualized datacenters and applications offered as services on a subscription basis as shown in Figure 1. They require high energy usage for its operation. Today, a typical datacenter with 1000 racks need 10 Megawatt of power to operate, which results in higher operational cost. Thus, for a datacenter, the energy cost is a significant component of its operating and up-front costs. In addition, in April 2007, Gartner estimated that the Information and Communication Technologies (ICT) industry generates about 2% of the total global CO_2 emissions, which is equal to the aviation industry. According to a report published by the European Union, a decrease in emission volume of 15%–30% is required before year 2020 to keep the global temperature increase below 2 ^{0}C. Thus, energy consumption and carbon emission by Cloud infrastructures has become a key environmental concern. Some studies show that Cloud computing can actually make traditional datacenters more energy efficient by using technologies such as resource virtualization and workload consolidation. The traditional data centres running Web applications are often provisioned to handle sporadic peak loads, which can result in low resource utilization and wastage of energy. Cloud datacenter, on the other hand, can reduce the energy consumed through server consolidation, whereby different workloads can share the same physical host using virtualization and unused servers can be switched off. A recent research by Accenture shows that moving business applications to Cloud can reduce carbon footprint of organizations. According to the report, small businesses saw the most dramatic reduction in emissions – up to 90 percent while using Cloud resources. Large corporations can save at least 30-60 percent in carbon emissions using Cloud applications, and mid-size businesses can save 60-90 percent. Contrary to the above opinion, some studies, for example Greenpeace [6], observe that the Cloud phenomenon may aggravate the problem of carbon emissions and global warming. The reason given is that the collective demand for computing resources is expected to further increase dramatically in the next few years. Even the most efficiently built datacenter with the highest utilization rates will only mitigate, rather than eliminate, harmful CO_2 emissions. The reason given is that Cloud providers are more interested in electricity cost reduction rather than carbon emission. The data collected by the study is presented in Table 1 below. Clearly, none of the cloud datacenter in the table can be called as green.

In summary, Cloud computing, being an emerging technology also raises significant questions about its environmental sustainability. While financial benefits of Cloud computing have been analyzed widely in the literature, the energy efficiency of Cloud computing as a whole has not been analyzed. Through the use of large shared virtualized datacenters Cloud computing can offer large energy savings. However, Cloud services can also further increase the internet traffic and its growing information database which could decrease such energy savings. Thus, this chapter explores the environmental sustainability of Cloud computing by analyzing various

Table 1. Comparison of significant cloud datacenter

CloudData centers	Location	Estimated power Usage Effectiveness	% of Dirty Energy Generation	% of Renewable Electricity
Google	Lenoir	1.21	50.5% Coal	3.8%
			38.7% Nuclear	
Apple	Apple, NC		50.5% Coal	3.8%
			38.7% Nuclear	
Microsoft	Chicago, IL	1.22	72.8% Coal	1.1%
			22.3% Nuclear	
Yahoo	La Vista, NE	1.16	73.1% Coal	7%
			14.6% Nuclear	

technologies and mechanism that support this goal. Our analysis is important for users and organization that are looking at Cloud computing as a solution for their administrative, infrastructural and management problems. Finally, we also propose and recommend a Green Cloud framework for reducing its carbon footprint in wholesome manner without sacrificing the quality of service (performance, responsiveness and availability) offered by the multiple Cloud providers.

Cloud Computing and Energy Usage Model: A Typical Example

In this section, through a typical Cloud usage scenario we will analyze various elements of Clouds and their energy efficiency. Figure 5 shows an end user accessing Cloud services such as SaaS, PaaS, or IaaS over Internet. User data pass from his own device through an Internet service provider's router, which in turn connects to a Gateway router within a Cloud datacenter. Within datacenters, data goes through a local area network and are processed on virtual machines, hosting Cloud services, which may access storage servers. Each of these computing and network devices that are directly accessed to serve Cloud users contribute to energy consumption. In addition, within a Cloud datacenter, there are many other devices, such as cooling and electrical devices, that consume power. These devices even though do not directly help in providing Cloud service, are the major contributors to the power consumption of a Cloud datacenter. In the following section, we discuss in detail the energy consumption of these devices and applications.

Figure 2. Cloud usage model

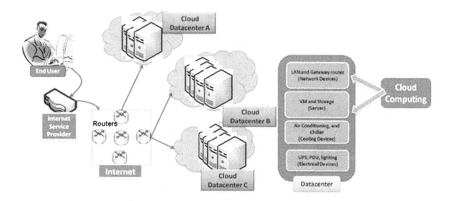

User/Cloud Software Applications

The first factor that contributes to energy consumption is the way software applications are designed and implemented. The Cloud computing can be used for running applications owned by individual user or offered by the Cloud provider using SaaS. In both cases, the energy consumption depends on the application itself. If application is long running with high CPU and memory requirements then its execution will result in high energy consumption. Thus, energy consumption will be directly proportional to the application's profile. The allocation of resources based on the maximum level of CPU and memory usage will result in much higher energy consumption than actually required. The energy inefficiency in execution of an application emanates from inaccurate design and implementation. The application inefficiencies, such as suboptimal algorithms and inefficient usage of shared resources causing contention lead to higher CPU usage and, therefore, higher energy consumption. However, factors such as energy efficiency are not considered during the design of an application in most of the application domains other than for example embedded devices such as mobile phone.

Cloud Software Stack for SaaS, PaaS, IaaS Level

The Cloud software stack leads to an extra overhead in execution of end user applications. For instance, it is well known that a physical server has higher performance efficiency than a virtual machine and IaaS providers offer generally access to a virtual machine to its end users. In addition, the management process in the form of accounting and monitoring requires some CPU power. Being profit oriented, service providers regularly have to adhere to Service Level Agreements

(SLA) with their clients. These SLAs may take the form of time commitment for a task to be completed. Thus, Cloud provider for meeting certain level of service quality availability, provision extra resources than generally required. For instance, to avoid failure, fast recovery and reduction in response time, providers have to maintain several storage replicas across many datacenters. Since workflow in Web applications require several sites to give better response time to its end user, their data is replicated on many servers across the world. Therefore, it is important to explore the relationships among Cloud components and the tradeoffs between QoS and energy consumption.

Network Devices

The network system is another area of concern which consumes a non-negligible fraction of the total power consumption. The ICT energy consumption estimates just for Vodafone Group radio access network was nearly 3 TWh in 2006. In Cloud computing, since resources are accessed through Internet, both applications and data are needed to be transferred to the compute node. Therefore, it requires much more data communication bandwidth between user's PC to the Cloud resources than require the application execution requirements. In some cases, if data is really large, then it may turn out to be cheaper and more carbon emission efficient to send the data by mail than to transfer through Internet.

In Cloud computing, the user data travels through many devices before it reaches a datacenter. In general, the user computer is connected to Ethernet switch of his/her ISP where traffic is aggregated. The BNG (Broadband Network Gateway) network performs traffic management and authentication functions on the packets received by Ethernet switches. These BNG routers connect to other Internet routers through provider's edge routers. The core network is further comprised of many large routers. Each of these devices consumes power according to the traffic volume. According to the study conducted by Tucker, public Cloud is estimated to consume about 2.7 J/b in transmission and switching in comparison to 0.46J/b for a private Cloud. They found out that power consumption in transport represents a significant proportion of the total power consumption for Cloud storage services at medium and high usage rates. Even typical network usage can result in three to four times more energy consumption in public Cloud storage than one's own storage infrastructure. Therefore, with the growth of Cloud computing usage, it is expected that energy efficiency of switches and routers will play a very significant role in what since they need to provide capacity of hundreds of terabits of bandwidth.

In the network infrastructure, the energy consumption depends especially on the power efficiency and awareness of wired network, namely the network equipment or system design, topology design, and network protocol design. Most of the energy in network devices is wasted because they are designed to handle worst case scenario. Therefore, the energy consumption of these devices remains almost the same during both peak time and idle state. Many improvements are required to get high energy efficiency in these devices. For example, during low utilization periods, Ethernet links can be turned off and packets can be routed around them. Further energy savings are possible at the hardware level of the routers through appropriate selection and optimization of the layout of various internal router components (i.e. buffers, links, etc.).

Datacenter

The Cloud datacenters are quite different from traditional hosting facilities. A cloud datacenter could comprise of many hundreds or thousands of networked computers with their corresponding

storage and networking subsystems, power distribution and conditioning equipment, and cooling infrastructures. Due to large number of equipment, datacenters can consume massive energy consumption and emit large amount of carbon. According to 2007 report on computing datacenters by US Environmental Protection Agency (EPA), the datacenters in US consumed about 1.5% of total energy, which costs about $4.5 billon. This high usage also translates to very high carbon emissions which was estimated to be about 80-116 Metric Megatons each year. Table 2 lists equipment typically used in datacenters with their contribution to energy consumption. It can be clearly observed that servers and storage systems are not the only infrastructure that consumes energy in the datacenter. In reality, the cooling equipment consume equivalent amount of energy as the IT systems themselves. Ranganathan suggests that for every dollar spent on electricity costs in large-scale datacenters another dollar is spent on cooling.

Further energy consumption occurs due to lighting, loss in the power distribution, and other electrical equipment such as UPS. In other words, the majority of power usage within a datacenter is used for other purposes than actual IT services. Thus, to achieve the maximum efficiency in power consumption and CO_2 emissions, each of these devices need to be designed and used efficiently while ensuring that their carbon footprint is reduced. A key factor in achieving the reduction in power consumption of a datacenter is to calculate how much energy is consumed in cooling and other overheads.

Standard metrics are emerging such as Power Usage Effectiveness (PUE) which can be used to benchmark how much energy is being usefully deployed versus how much is spent on overhead. The PUE of a datacenter is defined as the ratio of the total power consumption of a facility (data or switching center) to the total power consumption of IT equipment (servers, storage, routers, etc.). PUE varies from

Table 2. Percent of power consumption by each datacenter device

Cooling device (Chiller, Computer Room Air Conditioning (CRAC))	33%+9%
IT Equipment	30%
Electrical Equipment (UPS, Power Distribution Units (PDUs), lighting)	28%

datacenters depending on the place where datacenter is located and devices used in its construction. Research from the Lawrence Berkley National Labs shows that 22 datacenters measured in 2008 have PUE Values in the range 1.3 to 3.0. PUE of datacenter can be useful in measuring power efficiency of datacenters and thus provide a motivation to improve its efficiency.

Features of Clouds Enabling Green Computing

Even though there is a great concern in the community that Cloud computing can result in higher energy usage by the datacenters, the Cloud computing has a green lining. There are several technologies and concepts employed by Cloud providers to achieve better utilization and efficiency than traditional computing. Therefore, comparatively lower carbon emission is expected in Cloud computing due to highly energy efficient infrastructure and reduction in the IT infrastructure itself by multi-tenancy. The key driver technology for energy efficient Clouds is "Virtualization," which allows significant improvement in energy efficiency of Cloud providers

by leveraging the economies of scale associated with large number of organizations sharing the same infrastructure. Virtualization is the process of presenting a logical grouping or subset of computing resources so that they can be accessed in ways that give benefits over the original configuration. By consolidation of underutilized servers in the form of multiple virtual machines sharing same physical server at higher utilization, companies can gain high savings in the form of space, management, and energy. According to Accenture Report, there are following four key factors that have enabled the Cloud computing to lower energy usage and carbon emissions from ICT. Due to these Cloud features, organizations can reduce carbon emissions by at least 30% per user by moving their applications to the Cloud. These savings are driven by the high efficiency of large scale Cloud data centers.

Dynamic Provisioning

In traditional setting, datacenters and private infrastructure used to be maintained to fulfill worst case demand. Thus, IT companies end up deploying far more infrastructure than needed. There are various reasons for such over-provisioning:

a) it is very difficult to predict the demand at a time; this is particularly true for Web applications and b) to guarantee availability of services and to maintain certain level of service quality to end users. One example of a Web service facing these problems is a Website for the Australian Open Tennis Championship. The Australian Open Website each year receives a significant spike in traffic during the tournament period. The increase in traffic can amount to over 100 times its typical volume (22 million visits in a couple of weeks). To handle such peak load during short period in a year, running hundreds of servers throughout the year is not really energy efficient. Thus, the infrastructure provisioned with a conservative approach results in unutilized resources. Such scenarios can be readily managed by Cloud infrastructure. The virtual machines in a Cloud infrastructure can be live migrated to another host in case user application requires more resources. Cloud providers monitor and predict the demand and thus allocate resources according to demand. Those applications that require less number of resources can be consolidated on the same server. Thus, datacenters always maintain the active servers according to current demand, which results in low energy consumption than the conservative approach of over-provisioning.

Multi-Tenancy:

Using multi-tenancy approach, Cloud computing infrastructure reduces overall energy usage and associated carbon emissions. The SaaS providers serve multiple companies on same infrastructure and software. This approach is obviously more energy efficient than multiple copies of software installed on different infrastructure. Furthermore, businesses have highly variable demand patterns in general, and hence multi-tenancy on the same server allows the flattening of the overall peak demand which can minimize the need for extra infrastructure. The smaller fluctuation in demand results in better prediction and results in greater energy savings.

Server Utilization

In general, on-premise infrastructure run with very low utilization, sometimes it goes down up to 5 to 10 percent of average utilization. Using virtualization technologies, multiple applications can be hosted and executed on the same server in isolation, thus lead to utilization levels up to 70%. Thus, it dramatically reduces the number of active servers. Even though high utilization of servers results in more power consumption, server running at higher utilization can process more workload with similar power usage.

Datacenter Efficiency

As already discussed, the power efficiency of datacenters has major impact on the total energy usage of Cloud computing. By using the most energy efficient technologies, Cloud providers can significantly improve the PUE of their datacenters. Today's state-of-the-art datacenter designs for large Cloud service providers can achieve PUE levels as low as 1.1 to 1.2, which is about 40% more power efficiency than the traditional datacenters. The server design in the form of modular containers, water or air based cooling, or advanced power management through power supply optimization, are all approaches that have significantly improved PUE in datacenters. In addition, Cloud computing allows services to be moved between multiple datacenter which are running with better PUE values. This is achieved by using high speed network, virtualized services and measurement, and monitoring and accounting of datacenter.

Towards Energy Efficiency of Cloud Computing: State-of-the-Art

Applications

SaaS model has changed the way applications and software are distributed and used. More and more companies are switching to SaaS Clouds to minimize their IT cost. Thus, it has become very important to address the energy efficiency at application level itself. However, this layer has received very little attraction since many applications are already on use and most of the new applications are mostly upgraded version of or developed using previously implemented tools. Some of the efforts in this direction are for MPI applications, which are designed to run directly on physical machines. Thus, their performance on virtual machine is still undefined.

Various power efficient techniques for software designs are proposed in the literature but these are mostly for embedded devices. In the development of commercial and enterprise applications which are designed for PC environment, generally energy efficiency is neglected. Mayo et al. presented in their study that even simple tasks such as listening to music can consume significantly different amounts of energy on a variety of heterogeneous devices. As these tasks have the same purpose on each device, the results show that the implementation of the task and the system upon which it is performed can have a dramatic impact on efficiency. Therefore, to achieve energy efficiency at application level, SaaS providers should pay attention in deploying software on right kind of infrastructure which can execute the software most efficiently. This necessitates the research and analysis of trade-off between performance and energy consumption due to execution of software on multiple platforms and hardware. In addition, the energy consumption at the compiler level and code level should be considered by software developers in the design of their future application implementations using various energy-efficient techniques proposed in the literature.

Cloud Software Stack: Virtualization and Provisioning

In the Cloud stack, most works in the literature address the challenges at the IaaS provider level where research focus is on scheduling and resource management to reduce the amount of active resources executing the workload of user applications. The consolidation of VMs, VM migration, scheduling, demand projection, heat management and temperature-aware allocation, and load balancing are used as basic techniques for minimizing power consumption. As discussed in previous section, virtualization plays an important role in these techniques due to its several features such as consolidation, live migration, and performance isolation. Abdelsalam et al. proposed a power efficient technique to improve the management of Cloud computing environments. They formulated the management problem in the form of an optimization model aiming at minimization of the total energy consumption of the Cloud, taking SLAs into account. The current issue of under-utilization and over-provisioning of servers was highlighted by Ranganathan et al. They present a peak power budget management solution to avoid excessive over-provisioning considering DVS and memory/disk scaling. There are several other research works which focus on minimizing the over provisioning using consolidation of virtualized server. Majority of these works use monitoring and estimation of resource utilization by applications based on the arrival rate of requests. However, due to multiple levels of abstractions, it is really hard to maintain deployment data of each virtual machine within a Cloud datacenter. Thus, various indirect load estimation techniques are used for consolidation of VMs. Although above consolidation methods can reduce the overall number of resources used to serve user applications, the migration and relocation of VMs for matching application demand can impact the QoS service requirements of the user. Since Cloud providers need to satisfy a certain level of service, some work focused on minimizing the energy consumption while reducing the number of SLA violations. One of the first works that dealt with performance and energy trade-off was by Chase et al. who introduced MUSE, an economy-based system of resource allocation. They proposed a bidding system to deliver the required performance level and switching off unused servers. Kephart et al. addressed the coordination of multiple autonomic managers for power/performance tradeoffs using a utility function approach in a non-virtualized environment. Song et al. proposed an adaptive and dynamic scheme for efficient sharing of a server by adjusting resources (specifically, CPU and memory) between virtual machines. At the operating system level, Nathuji et al. proposed a power management system called VirtualPower integrating the power management and virtualization technologies. VirtualPower allows the isolated and independent operation of virtual machine to reduce the energy consumption. The soft states are intercepted by Xen hypervisor and are mapped to changes in the underlying hardware such as CPU frequency scaling according to the virtual power management rules. In addition; there are works on improving the energy efficiency of storage systems. Kaushik et al. presented an energy conserving self-adaptive Commodity Green Cloud storage called Lightning. The Lightning file system divides the Storage servers into Cold and Hot logical zones using data classification. These servers are then switched to inactive states for energy saving. Verma et al proposed an optimization for storage virtualization called Sample-Replicate-Consoidate Mapping (SRCMAP) which enables the energy proportionality for dynamic I/O workloads by consolidating the cumulative workload on a subset of physical volumes proportional to the I/O workload intensity. Gurumurthi et al. proposed intra-disk parallelism on high capacity drives to improve disk bandwidth without increasing power consumption. Soror et al. [34] addressed the problem of optimizing the performance of database management systems by controlling the configurations of the virtual machines in which they run. Since power is dissipated in Cloud datacenter due to heat generated by the servers, several works also have been proposed for dynamic scheduling of VMs and applications which take into account the thermal states or the heat dissipation in a data centre. The consideration of thermal factor in scheduling also improves the reliability of underline infrastructure. Tang et al. formulated the problem using a mathematical model for maximizing the cooling efficiency of a data center. Heath et al. proposed emulation tools for investigating the thermal implications of power management. Ramos et al. proposed a software prediction infrastructure called C-Oracle that makes online predictions for data center thermal management based on load redistribution and DVS. Moore et al. proposed a method for automatic reconfiguration of thermal load management system taking into account thermal behavior for improving cooling efficiency and power consumption. They also propose thermal management solutions focusing on scheduling workloads considering temperature-aware workload placement. Bash et al. propose a workload placement policy for a datacenter that allocate resources in the areas which are easier to cool resulting in cooling power savings. Raghavendra et al. propose a framework which coordinates and unifies five individual power management solutions (consisting of HW/SW mechanisms).

Datacenter Level: Cooling, Hardware, Network, and Storage

The rising energy costs, cost savings and a desire to get more out of existing investments are making today's Cloud providers to adopt best practices to make datacenters operation green. To build energy efficient datacenter, several best practices has been proposed to improve efficiency of each device from electrical systems to processor level. First level is the smart construction of the datacenter and choosing of its location. There are two major factors in that one is energy supply and other is energy efficiency of equipments. Hence, the datacenters are being constructed in such a way that electricity can be generated using renewable sources such as sun and wind. Currently the datacenter location is decided based on their geographical features; climate, fiber-optic connectivity and access to a plentiful supply of affordable energy. Since main concern of Cloud providers is business, energy source is also seen mostly in terms of cost not carbon emissions. Another area of concern within a datacenter is its cooling system that contributes to almost 1/3 of total energy consumption. Some research studies have shown that uneven temperature within datacenter can also lead significant decline in reliability of IT systems.

In datacenter cooling, two types of approaches are used: air and water based cooling systems. In both approaches, it is necessary that they directly cool the hot equipment rather than entire room cooling systems, and in-server, in-rack, and in-row cooling by companies such as SprayCool. Other than that, the outside temperature/ climate can have direct impact on the energy requirement of cooling system. Some systems have been constructed where external cool air is used to remove heat from the datacenter. Another level at which datacenter's power efficiency is addressed is on the deployment of new power efficient servers and processors. Low energy processors can reduce the power usage of IT systems in a great degree. Many new energy efficient server models are available currently in market from vendors such as AMD, Intel, and others; each of them offering good performance/watt system. This server architecture enables slowing down CPU clock speeds (clock gating), or powering off parts of the chips (power gating), if they are idle. Further enhancement in energy saving and increasing computing per watt can be achieved by using multi-core processors. For instance, Sun's multicore chips, each 32-thread Niagara chip, UltraSPARC 1, consumes about 60 watts, while the two Niagara chips have 64 threads and run at about 80 watts. However, the exploitation of such power efficiency of multi-core system requires software which can run on multi-CPU environment. Here, virtualization technologies play an important role. Similarly, consolidation of storage system helps to further reduce the energy requirements of IT Systems. For example, Storage Area Networks (SAN) allow building of an efficient storage network that consolidates all storage. The use of energy efficient disks such as tiered storage (Solid-State, SATA, SAS) allows better energy efficiency.

The power supply unit is another infrastructure which needs to be designed in an energy efficient manner. Their task is to feed the server resources with power by converting the high-voltage alternating current (AC) from the power grid to a low-voltage direct current (DC) which most of the electric circuits (e.g. computers) require. These circuits inside Power Supply Unit (PSU) inevitably lose some energy in the form of heat, which is dissipated by additional fans inside PSU. The energy efficiency of a PSU mainly depends on its load, number of circuits and other conditions (e.g. temperature). Hence, a PSU which is labeled to be 80% efficient is not necessarily that efficient for all power loads. For example, low power loads tend to be the most energy inefficient ones. Thus, a PSU can be just 60% efficient at 20% of power load. Some studies have found that PSUs are one of the most inefficient components in today's data centers as many servers are still shipped with low quality 60 to 70 percent efficient power supplies. One possible solution offered is to replace all PSUs by ENERGY STAR certified ones. This certificate is given to PSUs which guarantee a minimum 80% efficiency at any power load.

Monitoring/Metering

It is said that you cannot improve what you do not measure. It is essential to construct power models that allow the system to know the energy consumed by a particular device, and how it can be reduced. To measure the unified efficiency of a datacenter and improve its' performance per-watt, the Green Grid has proposed two specific metrics known as the Power Usage Effectiveness (PUE) and Datacenter Infrastructure Efficiency (DciE).

- PUE = Total Facility Power/IT Equipment Power
- DciE = 1/PUE = IT Equipment Power/Total Facility Power x 100%

Here, the Total Facility Power is defined as the power measured at the utility meter that is dedicated solely to the datacenter power. The IT Equipment Power is defined as the power consumed in the management, processing, and storage or routing of data within the datacenter.

PUE and DCIE are most common metrics designed to compare the efficiency of datacenters. There are many systems in the marketplace for such measurements. For instance, Sun[SM] Eco Services measure at a higher level rather than attempting to measure each individual device's power consumption. For measuring and modeling the power usage of storage system, Researchers from IBM have proposed a scalable, enterprise storage modeling framework called STAMP. It side steps the need for detailed traces by using interval performance statistics and a power table for each disk model. STAMP takes into account controller caching and algorithms, including protection schemes, and adjusts the workload accordingly. To measure the power consumed by a server (e.g. PowerEdge R610) the Intelligent Platform Management Interface (IPMI) is proposed. This framework provides a uniform way to access the power-monitoring sensors available on recent servers. This interface being independent of the operating system can be accessed despite of operating system failures and without the need of the servers to be powered on (i.e. connection to the power grid is enough). Further, intelligent power distribution units (PDUs), traditional power meters (e.g. Watts Up Pro power meter) and ACPI enabled power supplies can be used to measure the power consumption of the whole server.

Network Infrastructure

As discussed previously, at network level, the energy efficiency is achieved either at the node level (i.e. network interface card) or at the infrastructure level (i.e. switches and routers). The energy efficiency issues in networking is usually referred to as "green networking", which relates to embedding energy-awareness in the design, in the devices and in the protocols of networks. There are four classes of solutions offered in literature, namely resource consolidation, virtualization, selective connectedness, and proportional computing. Resource consolidation helps in regrouping the under-utilized devices to reduce the global consumption. Similar to consolidation, selective connectedness of devices consists of distributed mechanisms which allow the single pieces of equipment to go idle for some time, as transparently as possible from the rest of the networked devices. The difference between resource consolidation and selective connectedness is that the consolidation applies to resources that are shared within the network infrastructure while selective connectedness allows turning off unused resources at the edge of the network. Virtualization as discussed before allows more than one service to operate on the same piece of hardware, thus improving the hardware utilization. Proportional computing can be applied to a system as a whole, to network protocols, as well as to individual devices and components. Dynamic Voltage Scaling and Adaptive Link Rate are typical examples of proportional computing. Dynamic Voltage Scaling reduces the energy state of the CPU as a function of a system load, while Adaptive Link Rate applies a similar concept to network interfaces, reducing their capacity, and thus their consumption, as a function of the link load. The survey by Bianzino et al. gives more details about the work in the area of Green networking.

Green Cloud Architecture

From the above study of current efforts in making Cloud computing energy efficient, it shows that even though researchers have made various components of Cloud efficient in terms of power

and performance, still they lack a unified picture. Most of efforts for sustainability of Cloud computing have missed the network contribution. If the file sizes are quite large, network will become a major contributor to energy consumption; thus, it will be greener to run application locally than in Clouds. Furthermore, many works focused on just particular component of Cloud computing while neglecting effect of other, which may not result in overall energy efficiency. For example, VM consolidation may reduce number of active servers but it will put excessive load on few servers where heat distribution can become a major issue. Some other works just focus on redistribution of workload to support energy efficient cooling without considering the effect of virtualization. In addition, Cloud providers, being profit oriented, are looking for solutions which can reduce the power consumption and thus, carbon emission without hurting their market. Therefore, we provide a unified solution to enable Green Cloud computing. We propose a Green Cloud framework, which takes into account these goals of provider while curbing the energy consumption of Clouds. The high-level view of the green Cloud architecture is given in Figure 3. The goal of this architecture is to make Cloud green from both user and provider's perspective. In the Green Cloud architecture, users submit their Cloud service requests through a new middleware Green Broker that manages the selection of the greenest Cloud provider to serve the user's request. A user service request can be of three types i.e., software, platform or infrastructure. The Cloud providers can register their services in the form of green offers to a public directory which is accessed by Green Broker. The green offers consist of green services, pricing and time when it should be accessed for least carbon emission. Green Broker gets the current status of energy parameters for using various Cloud services from Carbon Emission Directory. The Carbon Emission Directory maintains all the data related to energy efficiency of Cloud service. This data may include PUE and cooling efficiency of Cloud datacenter which is providing the service, the network cost and carbon emission rate of electricity, Green Broker calculates the carbon emission of all the Cloud providers who are offering the requested Cloud service. Then, it selects the set of services that will result in least carbon emission and buy these services on behalf users. The Green Cloud framework is designed such that it keeps track of overall energy usage of serving a user request. It relies on two main components, Carbon Emission Directory and Green Cloud offers, which keep track of energy efficiency of each Cloud provider and also give incentive to Cloud providers to make their service "Green". From user side, the Green Broker plays a crucial role in monitoring and selecting the Cloud services based on the user QoS requirements, and ensuring minimum carbon emission. for serving a user. In general, a user can use Cloud to access any of these three types of services (SaaS, PaaS, and IaaS), and therefore process of serving them should also be energy efficient. In other words, from the Cloud provider side, each Cloud layer needs to be "Green" conscious.

Figure 3. Green cloud architecture

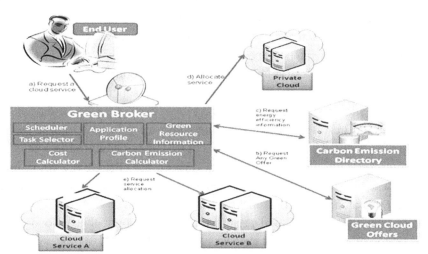

SaaS Level

Since SaaS providers mainly offer software installed on their own datacenters or resources from IaaS providers, the SaaS providers need to model and measure energy efficiency of their software design, implementation, and deployment. For serving users, the SaaS provider chooses the datacenters which are not only energy efficient but also near to users. The minimum number of replicas of user's confidential data should be maintained using energy-efficient storage.

PaaS Level

PaaS providers offer in general the platform services for application development. The platform facilitates the development of applications which ensures system wide energy efficiency. This can be done by inclusion of various energy profiling tools such as JouleSort. It is a software energy efficiency benchmark that measures the energy required to perform an external sort. In addition, platforms itself can be designed to have various code level optimizations which can cooperate with underlying complier in energy efficient execution of applications. Other than application development, Cloud platforms also allow the deployment of user applications on Hybrid Cloud. In this case, to achieve maximum energy efficiency, the platforms profile the application and decide which portion of application or data should be processed in house and in Cloud.

IaaS Level

Providers in this layer plays most crucial role in the success of whole Green Architecture since IaaS level not only offer independent infrastructure services but also support other services offered by Clouds. They use latest technologies for IT and cooling systems to have most energy efficient infrastructure. By using virtualization and consolidation, the energy consumption is further reduced by switching-off unutilized server. Various energy meters and sensors are installed to calculate the current energy efficiency of each IaaS providers and their sites. This information is advertised regularly by Cloud providers in Carbon Emission Directory. Various green scheduling and resource provisioning policies will ensure minimum energy usage. In addition, the Cloud provider designs various green offers and pricing schemes for providing incentive to users to use their services during off-peak or maximum energy-efficiency hours.

Case Study: IaaS Provider

In this section, we describe a case study example to illustrate the working of the proposed Green Architecture in order to highlight the importance of considering the unifying picture to reduce the energy and carbon emissions by Cloud infrastructure. The case study focuses on IaaS service providers. Our experimental platform consists of multiple Cloud providers who offer computational resources to execute user's HPC applications. A user request consists of application, its estimated length in time and number of resources required. These applications are submitted to the Green broker who acts as an interface to the Cloud infrastructure and schedules applications on behalf of users as shown in Figure 7. The Green Broker interprets and analyzes the service requirements of a submitted application and decides where to execute it. As discussed, Green Broker's main objective is to schedule applications such that the CO_2 emissions are reduced and the profit is increased, while the Quality of Service (QoS) requirements of the applications are met. As Cloud data centers are located in different geographical regions, they have different CO_2 emission rates and energy costs depending on regional constraints. Each datacenter is responsible for updating this information to Carbon Emission Directory for facilitating the energy-efficient scheduling. The list of energy related parameters is given in Figure 4

In order to validate our framework and to prove that it achieves better efficiency in terms of carbon emission, we have studied five policies (Green and profit-oriented) employed for scheduling by Green Broker.

Figure 4. Carbon emission related parameter of a datacenter

Parameter	Notation
Carbon emission rate (kg/kWh)	$r_i^{CO_2}$
Average COP	COP_i
Electricity price ($/kWh)	p_i^c
Data transfer price ($/GB) for up-load/download	p_i^{DT}
CPU power	$P_i = \beta_i + \alpha_i f^3$
CPU frequency range	$[f_i^{min}, f_i^{max}]$
Time slots (start time, end time, number of CPUs)	(t_s, t_e, n)

1. Greedy Minimum Carbon Emission (GMCE): In this policy, user applications are assigned to Cloud providers in greedy manner based on their carbon emission.

2. Minimum Carbon Emission (MCE-MCE): This is a double greedy policy where applications are assigned to the Cloud providers with minimum Carbon emission due to their datacenter location and Carbon emission due to application execution.

3. Greedy Maximum Profit (GMP): In this policy, user applications are assigned in greedy manner to a provider who execute the application fastest and get maximum profit.

4. Maximum Profit - Maximum Profit (MP-MP): This is double greedy policy considering profit made by Cloud providers and application finishes by its deadline.

5. Minimizing Carbon Emission and Maximizing Profit (MCE-MP): In this policy, the broker tries to schedule the applications to those providers which results in minimization of total carbon emission and maximization of profit.

Above GMCE, MCE-MCE and MCE-MP are "Green" policies while MP-MP and GMP are profit-oriented policies. A more extensive detail on modeling of energy efficiency of a Cloud datacenter, experimental data and results is available in previous work. Here, we present some important results to illustrate the validity of our presented framework.

Figure 5 shows the course of experiments conducted with varying user's urgency for executing his application and job arrival rate. The metrics of total carbon emission and total profit are us since the resource provider needs to know the collective loss in carbon emission and gain in profit across all datacenters. From these results three main inferences can be made.

- Green policies reduce the carbon emission by almost 20% in comparison to profit based policies. This observation emphasizes the inclusion of overall carbon efficiency of all the Cloud providers in scheduling decisions.
- With the increase in user's urgency to execute the application, the gain in carbon emission reduces almost linearly. This clearly shows how important is

Figure 5. Carbon emission and profit of provider using green cloud framework

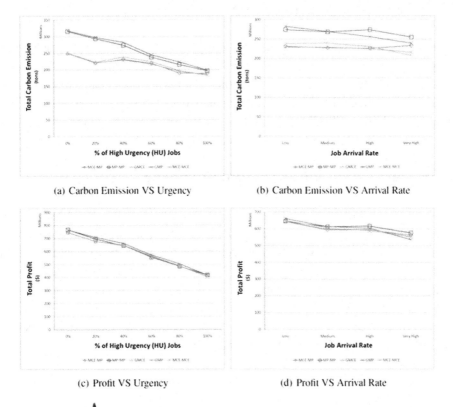

(a) Carbon Emission VS Urgency   (b) Carbon Emission VS Arrival Rate

(c) Profit VS Urgency   (d) Profit VS Arrival Rate

the role of user in making Cloud computing in general "Green". If users are more patient and schedule the applications when the datacenters are running at higher energy efficiency, more energy and carbon gain can be made. Thus, in our framework, we introduce the need of Green Cloud Offers from providers.

- The green policies also have minimal effect on the provider's profit. This clearly shows that by using energy efficient solutions such as Green Cloud Framework both Cloud providers and users can benefit.

METRICS USED FOR MEASURING POWER CONSUMPTION IN DATA CENTERS.

(TDE) Thermal Design Power

It is the measurement of maximum amount of power required by cooling of computer system to dissipate. It is the maximum amount of power which a computer chip can take when running a real application.

(PUE) Power Usage Effectiveness

It is used for comparison of energy used by computing application and infrastructure Equipment and the energy wasted in overhead. The PUE can be described as the ratio of overall electricity consumed by the facility of a data center to the overall electricity consumed by IT equipment's (network peripherals, servers, storage, routers, etc.). Value of PUE depends on the location of datacenters and construction done for that Datacenter. Thus, it is different for all datacenters.

(DCiE) Data center Infrastructure Efficiency

It is the reciprocal of PUE. PUE and DCiE are most commonly used metrics that were designed for the comparison of efficiency of datacenters. IT Equipment Power can be described as the power that data center has taken for the management of IT equipment's, processing of IT equipment's and storing the data in disk drives or routing the data within the datacenter. Total Facility Power is IT equipment power plus power needed by uninterrupted power supply (UPS), generators (needed to provide power in case of power failure), batteries, cooling system components such as chillers, CRACs, DX air handler pumps, units, and cooling towers.

(CPE) Compute Power Efficiency

It is a measure of the computing efficiency of a datacenter. As each watt consumed by server or cluster did not draw fruitful work all the time, some facilities consumed power even in an idle state and some consumed power for computing. Although 100% of facility capacity will never be used, we still want maximum output from the datacenter based on electrical power.

REFERENCES

Allenotor, D., & Thulasiram, R. K. (2008). Grid resources pricing: A novel financial option based quality of service-profit quasi-static equilibrium model. In *Proceedings of the 8th ACM/IEEE International Conference on Grid Computing*, Tsukuba, Japan. doi:10.1109/GRID.2008.4662785

Avanzi, R. M., Savas, E., & Tillich, S. (2005). Energy-efficient software implementation of long integer modular arithmetic. In *Proceedings of 7th Workshop on Cryptographic Hardware and Embedded Systems*, Edinburg, Scotland.

Baliga, J., Ayre, R., Hinton, K., & Tucker, R. S. (2010). Green Cloud computing: Balancing energy in processing, storage and transport. *Proceedings of the IEEE*, *99*(1), 149–167.

Beloglazov, A., Buyya, R., Lee, Y. C., & Zomaya, A. (2011). A taxonomy and survey of energy-efficient data centers and cloud computing systems. In M. Zelkowitz (Ed.), *Advances in Computers*. Amsterdam: Elsevier.

Bianchini, R., & Rajamony, R. (2004). Power and energy management for server systems. *Computer*, *37*(11), 68–74.

Buyya, R., Yeo, C. S., & Venugopal, S. (2008). Market-oriented Cloud computing: Vision, hype, and reality for delivering it services as computing utilities. In *Proceedings of the 10th IEEE International Conference on High Performance Computing and Communications*. doi:10.1109/HPCC.2008.172

Chabarek, J., Sommers, J., Barford, P., Estan, C., Tsiang, D., & Wright, S. (2008). Power Awareness in Network Design and Routing. In *Proceedings of 27th IEEE INFOCOM*. doi:10.1109/INFOCOM.2008.93

Chase, J. S., Anderson, D. C., Thakar, P. N., Vahdat, A. M., & Doyle, R. P. (2001). Managing energy and server resources in hosting centers. In *Proceedings of 18th ACM Symposium on Operating Systems Principles (SOSP '01)*, Banff, Canada. doi:10.1145/502034.502045

Freeh, V. W., Pan, F., Kappiah, N., Lowenthal, D. K., & Springer, R. (2005). Exploring the energy-time trade-off in MPI programs on a power-scalable cluster. In *Proceedings of the 19th IEEE International Parallel and Distributed Processing Symposium*, CA, USA doi:10.1109/IPDPS.2005.214

Gleeson, E. (2009). Computing industry set for a shocking change. *Moneyweek.com*. Retrieved January 10, 2010 from http://www.moneyweek.com/investment-advice/computing-industry-set-for-ashocking-change-43226.aspx

Gurumurthi, S., Stan, M.R., & Sankar, S. (2009). Using intra-disk parallelism to build energy-efficient storage systems. *IEEE Micro*, *29*(1), 50-61.

Kaushik, R. T., Cherkasova, L., Campbell, R., & Nahrstedt, K. 2010. Lightning: selfadaptive, energy-conserving, multi-zoned, commodity green Cloud storage system. In *Proceedings of the 19th ACM International Symposium on High Performance Distributed computing (HPDC '10)*. New York, NY, USA: ACM. doi:10.1145/1851476.1851523

Mayo, R. N., & Ranganathan, P. (2005). Energy consumption in mobile devices: Why future systems need requirements-aware energy scale-down. In *Proceedings of 3rd International Workshop on Power-Aware Computer Systems*, San Diego, CA, USA doi:10.1007/978-3-540-28641-7_3

Mell, P., & Grance, T. (2009). *The NIST Definition of Cloud computing*. National Institute of Standards and Technology.

Ranganathan, P. (2010). Recipe for efficiency: principles of power-aware computing. Communication, 53(4), 60–67.

Smith, J., & Nair, R. (2003). *Virtual Machines: Versatile Platforms for Systems and Processes*. Los Altos, CA: Morgan Kaufmann.

Chapter 6
Detection of Worms Over Cloud Environment: A Literature Survey

Thangavel M.
Thiagarajar College of Engineering, India

Jeyapriya B.
Thiagarajar College of Engineering, India

Suriya K. S.
Thiagarajar College of Engineering, India

ABSTRACT

In recent years, computer worms are the remarkable difficulties found in the distributed computing. The location of worms turns out to be more unpredictable since they are changing quickly and much more refined. The difficulties in gathering worm's payload were recognized for identifying and gathering worm's payloads and the honey pot which is high-intelligent to gather the payload of zero-day polymorphic heterogeneous and homogeneous stages in distributed computing. The Signature-based discovery of worms strategies work with a low false-positive rate. We propose an irregularity based interruption location instrument for the cloud which specifically benefits from the virtualization advancements all in all. Our proposed abnormality location framework is detached from spreading computer worm contamination and it can recognize new computer worms. Utilizing our methodology, a spreading computer worm can be distinguished on the spreading conduct itself without getting to or straightforwardly affecting running virtual machines of the cloud.

DOI: 10.4018/978-1-5225-3038-1.ch006

INTRODUCTION

The usage of IT assets is offered by distributed computing, for example, figuring the force and capacity as an administration through a system on the interest. The organization can spare the buy of the own server farm or by the livelihood of own IT authority. This is conceivable by virtualization innovations. The cloud comprises of a system of equipment hubs in which every hub can run a few virtualized OS in parallel utilizing a virtual machine screen called as hypervisor. A unified cloud chief will outlines and screen the assets of all the associated equipment hubs and figure out which hub offers free assets to begin another virtual machine when required. These virtual machines contain extra programming parts or asked for information alongside working framework. VMs are available in a huge number of numbers in distributed computing systems. Such systems are suspected to get assaulted from the aggressors and malware programs; the cloud supplier needs to guarantee the security in their cloud networks. Computer worms that mischief cloud systems are thought to be exceptionally risky. Worms can perform vindictive action, for example, taking the data, dispatch flooding attacks, etc. Worms attempt to shroud themself or make them imperceptible to the extent that this would be possible to taint numerous more has. On the other side the cloud suppliers attempt to minimize worm's life and spreading in their cloud systems. There are different diverse for distributed computing. At the more often than not arrangement of dynamic remote administrations is joined in distributed computing. Fig: specialized purpose of cloud in which we work. The cloud system has been separated into front end and the back end. In the frontend cloud administration programming is introduced, this will screen the asset which is in the back end, and it is additionally associated with the outside system, e.g.: Internet. In the front end the client will make a solicitation with the assistance of web interface, the client will characterize which sort of virtual machine they need to begin in the back end. The characterized virtual machine can contain the working framework which has chooses before and asked for programming extra. The back end is the center part of the cloud. It comprises of numerous equipment hubs in which each has introduced hypervisor programming. With the assistance of this hypervisor programming, VM can be propelled in parallel on a solitary equipment hub. At that point the administration segment interfaces the association from the outside client to begin VM in the back end.

Huge development of the interest in the computational outsourcing has lead the way to make huge scale distributed computing server farms. The association offers their computational needs to the cloud server farms as opposed to causing high cost of acquiring IT base and managing every one of the overhauls, upkeep of both programming and the equipment. In the distributed computing server farms the virtualization innovation to permit the production of numerous virtual machine

Figure 1. The distributed computing front end and back end

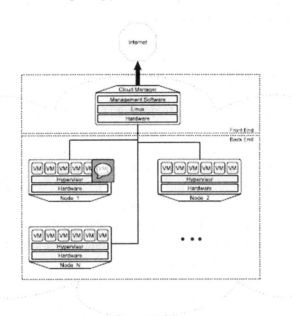

occurrences on the physical server which is single and various virtual systems are made on a solitary physical system. The distributed computing system contains thousands of virtual machine those systems are suspected to get assaulted from the assailants and some sort of malware project, so to avoid them the cloud suppliers needs to find a way to guarantee the security inside their system. Computer worms are the most perilous malware program which makes hurt our cloud network. Worms will perform some vindictive exercises, for example, dispatching surge attack, steal data against server, etc. The aggressor composes the worms program as imperceptible as far as might be feasible. On the other side the cloud supplier will attempt to minimize worm's life and spread in their cloud system. Virtualization programming, for example, VMware, Xen and KVM, every one of the parts in the genuine physical system can be virtualized and the spreading of worms and this will minimize by secluding the activity of each virtual system from other system. On the off chance that VM is available in the same physical server the activity is disconnected and their virtual interface will transmit movement over the basic NIC. The VM which is available outside of the virtual system can't infuse or sniff the movement into the system. Still now VM are suspected to be under assaults from worms which is running in the same virtual system Distinguishing and gathering the payload of worms are the most noteworthy procedures in safeguarding against worms which are obscure. The payload gathered are utilized to create worms signature and to learn about their malevolent exercises.

CLOUD COMPUTING

Distributed computing alludes to both applications conveyed as administrations over the web and the equipment and frameworks programming in the server farms that give those administration (Armbrust, 2010), they characterized the administrations as programming as an administration (SaaS). The server farm equipment and programming is the thing that has been resolved as a cloud. The scientists likewise specified two classes of cloud; the first being people in general cloud which is accessible to the overall population and the second one which is the private cloud that is operable for an organization. Figure-2 represents the parts of the clients or administration suppliers for the distributed computing. Programming establishment, applications, administrations, upkeep and brought together control over rendition into cloud are the obligation of administration suppliers. These applications or administrations on the mists can be used through web programs and web administrations by utilizing the web.

Figure 2. Clients and suppliers of cloud

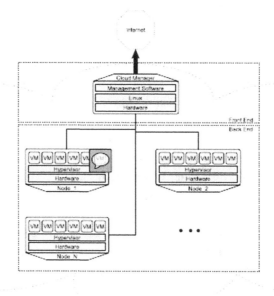

Adjusted from Cloud processing is characterized as the equipment and programming benefits in a general sense reserved in web servers, and cloud associated on the web (Aymerich, 2008). A computer, PDA or some other gadget is vital for the client to get to administrations into cloud by means of a program and a web association whenever anyplace. The clients are supplied with the administrations and information they require by administration suppliers. Administration of video organizers, web mail, photograph and different administrations are supplied by distributed computing. Cloud has been characterized as an appropriated registering worldview which is a scattered processing model (Foster, 2008), directed by limits of scale comprising of virtuality, stockpiling, stages and administrations which are gotten to and exchanged on interest over the Internet to clients. Cloud engineering can be characterized into four layers; applications, stage, bound together asset and fabric. The application layer comprises of the applications which would work in Cloud. The stage layer expands a gathering of exceptionally planned apparatuses and administrations to a dissemination stage as on account of a web facilitating area. Bound together layer comprises of assets which have been remote or wrapped as a rule by virtualization, for example, a sound documenting framework and database. Equipment assets, for example, stockpiling, system and registering assets are contained in the fabric layer.

RELATED WORKS

In the previous couple of years there is a quick development of utilizing VMI for the interruption recognition. In the conventional methodologiess the devices are introduced in VMs which are helpless against assault by the assailant Over the most recent years, numerous methodologies have proposed to inspect the VM from the outside to enhance and abstain from joining.

The irregularity based interruption recognition instrument, which abused virtual machine thoughtfulness which is utilized to gather a rundown of the running procedures or modules of the running virtual machines. All the gathered data are accumulated and investigated by an incorporated peculiarity indicator which is available in the single virtual machine. Any obscure procedure that happens on an expanding number in the virtual machines is thought to be computer worm. The proposed strategy is to gather data about innocuous procedures which is obscure.

The conveyed system of recognition operators is to organize location crosswise over entire cloud system. Every specialist is conveyed in the virtual machine screen (VMM) in the physical cloud server. By utilizing VMI, operators will gather data of the running VMs on servers they have a place with. Specialists will screen VM circle picture, system action, and the condition of VM memory. Operators will share data to decide dangers that crosscut the physical servers. This methodology will decrease the heap of the system joins by dispersing the identification of worms. Observing all running VMs in the cloud server farms will expands the expense of cooling and working these server farms, which will diminish the pay benefit and its additionally assets expending process.

The arrangement of side effects distinguished is to demonstrate the likelihood of malignant activities. A Forensic virtual machine (FVM) is utilized for every indication, characterized to search for this manifestation running in VMs. Measurable virtual machine use VMI to assess running VMs from outside. In the event that any indication is found in any of the VM, different Forensics virtual machine are coordinated to examine this VM for different manifestations. Gathered data is sent to a brought together module to dissect them and to take further activities.

There is high-connection honey pot screen, which is utilized to reviews memory of the running virtual machine on Xen by utilizing the open source crime scene investigation instrument Volatility.

COMPUTER WORMS

A worm is a self-repeating malware program which is proliferated in the system without or with human intercession. Worms will send their duplicate to casualty machine and pick up the control of that machine. After that they will execute the remote system to the casualty machine to execute. Worms will pick up control by infusing the pernicious code into the project and this will contaminate the control stream of the system and result in defiling the information.

The worms can be recognized by two techniques, they are irregularity based and signature based location. The oddity based discovery utilizes the learning of considering what an ordinary conduct to distinguish computer worms is. Inconsistency recognition will help in the discovery of new and obscure computer worms. This will lessen the system speed by checking every one of the bundles furthermore the computer execution by observing every one of the exercises. Signature based location will recognize the computer worms from the other system by contrasting them and the mark of the known computer worms

WORM ATTACKS DEFINITION

A worm is a hurtful code that can meddle with the frameworks and the applications and has the ability to transform their essential codes which causes those frameworks and applications to alter and consequently can't be utilized for standard operation (McGraw, 2000). A worm has been characterized as a standout amongst the most disturbing sorts of malevolent codes and infringes tremendous volumes of web applications by means of programming codes (Marhusin, 2012).

A gatecrasher, amid a cloud assault, will try to actualize into the cloud framework and it requires the foe to shape its own particular throne administration application (SaaS or PaaS) or VM to the cloud framework and after that endeavor to put himself(attacker) as a cloud client. On the off chance that fruitful, the cloud framework will, as is normally done, deflect the true-blue client notification to the pointed administration application in addition to the gatecrasher's code is expert (Jensen, 2009).

In distributed computing (Kanaker, 2014) showed an illustration on how a worm assault works and determined its activities by receiving dynamic investigation. The result of this has been shown that the worm erased a record in "C" catalog, C:Windows\System32\Worm64.dll which will be used by the worm to disregard cloud server consequently annihilating documents, registry and information spared in the server.

IDENTIFICATION OF WORM ATTACKS IN CLOUD ENVIRONMENT

Remote servers and web are used for saving information and application in distributed computing environment. Clients can utilize administrations applications through cloud (Ren, 2009) unfortunately distributed computing is at danger from the aggressors including assaults from intruders. Security dangers and worm infusion assaults are not kidding issues of distributed computing (Qaisar, 2012; Zunnurhain, 2010). A worm assault in the cloud is the place the worm barges in and turns into a legitimate administration operation along these lines making cloud administrations unscrupulous. Worm assaults are perplexing and can adjust information essentially which results in a gridlock this will urges the client to hold up until the assaults are performed effectively. The worm works in the cloud operations and gets rights and portion to control all cloud environments.

A portion of the arrangements were considered to address this specific issue. Most importantly, when a client gets to a record in the cloud, the cloud supplier instantly structures client's picture in a Virtual Machine in the picture document arrangement of cloud. Furthermore, it was suggested that a more elevated amount of honesty be presented on the grounds that it is to a great degree trying for an interloper to enter in the Iaas level. It was likewise upheld utilizing File Allocation Table method (FAT).

(Zunnurhain,2010) proposed a higher command of security in the equipment level, since it is essentially burdensome for an assailant to enter the IaaS level and trying for an interloper to encroach in the IaaS level. This system screens shouldn't something be said about the applications that the client is going to work. It can likewise be confirmed that it has been used and executed beforehand from the client's machine to decide legitimacy and respectability. Likewise, they utilize hypervisor strategy for booking all occasions yet preceding that the supplier verifies the trustworthiness of the case from the FAT Table of the client's VM. The other heading is to store the OS kind of the client when they open a record. Before dispatching an occurrence in a cloud, it studies the OS sort from which the case was asked for taking into account the OS kind of the client. For the cloud supplier, these arrangements require a long-time frame to handle. Amid a worm infusion assault an assailant will endeavor to build up an individual noxious administration into the cloud structure to pollute administration, VM or application. The client will then demand the malevolent administration, feeling that it is a lawful administration, and the pernicious code will be embedded into the framework. Regularly, the aggressor transfers an infection program and scatters it on cloud structure. At the point when clients utilize the noxious administration, the cloud barrages the infection over the web to the customer, consequently tainting the customer's machine supported a counter-measure to cure this issue, for example, finding out the genuineness for getting messages and putting away the first picture demand and contrasting it and the hash esteem by utilizing the hash capacity. This arrangement is not idiot proof on the grounds that the aggressor can frame a honest to goodness hash quality to handle cloud framework and hence they were not able enough distinguish worm and stay away from the assault in distributed computing environment.

Another review location methodology was proposed in light of Portable Executable (PE) position record connections (Liu, 2010). Utilizing a Hadoop stage a framework was actualized including map decreasing occupations for disseminated figuring and information stockpiling, three computers and utilized 18 worms. Review recognition was utilized and allows the recognizable proof of worms from matured data when host or clients enter related documents. At the point when a danger is analyzed it then structures PE logs group records in every computer where the logs hold data about all new PE documents. Should any changes be distinguished in PE it is then easy to catch worm to review identification of worm assaults. The log arranges a logging system which gathers document data and later the logs will be charged to the cloud server where record indexing forms every log and connection indexing and guide diminishment. The document indexing points of interest what PE records are in presence and in which computer. The connection indexing demonstrates which computer holds an authoritative contact with PE documents. In guide lessening, the record indexing and connection indexing structure one list to review strategy for identifying worm assaults by distributed computing. This framework delivers an expanded divulgence rate (94%) together with a diminished false positive rate when contrasted with past studies. The methods for worm detection are given in Table 1 *(Kanaker, 2015)*.

HYPERVISOR BASED INTERRUPTION IDENTIFICATION FRAMEWORKS

Hypervisor based interruption identification framework (HPIDS) is on a very basic level an interruption recognition framework intended for hypervisors and is a gathering to work VMs. HIDS licenses clients to screen and assess interchanges in the middle of hypervisor and VM, in the middle of VMs and inside of the bounds the hypervisor based virtual system (Modi, 2013). One of the ideal models of hypervisor based interruption identification framework is VM introspection based IDS (Garfinkel, 2003). A pool of virtualized computer assets and to oversee different VMs and hypervisors is characterized as distributed computing. Hypervisor based IDS in distributed computing is one of the huge strategies to identify interruption in a virtual situation (Modi, 2013). The obstacles of this strategy are absence of experience by clients. (Garfinkel, 2003) proposed virtual machine contemplation based IDS (VMI IDS) engineering which acknowledge equipment cases, occasions and programming conditions of host. The obligation of VM is equipment virtualization furthermore indicates perception and intervention properties.

Table 1. Methods used to detect worms and challenges for improvement

Title	Method Used For Worm Detection	Challenges For Improvement
Cloud computing network security threats and countermeasure.	-check the authenticity for received messages. -store the original image file using the hash function.	-Attacker can create a legitimate hash value to deal with the cloud system.
Security attacks and solution in cloud.	-using file allocation table techniques. -utilize the hypervisor method. -storing the OS type of the user.	-process time for the cloud provider is high.
Retrospective detection of malware attacks by cloud computing	-Portable Executable (PE) format file relationships. -May reduce job. -Hadoop platform. -File indexing. -File-relation index.	-These methods are only effective on Hadoop platform. -Some worms can generate different log file each time so cannot be detected easily. -Process time is high due to a large number of files. -Detection method based on behavior only.

VM interface is utilized for VMI IDS to associate with VMM; VMI IDS to take VM state data, perception particular occasions and controlling VMs. Synopsis of different Intrusion Detection Systems (IDS) are appeared in Table-2 (Kanaker, 2015).

DETECTION OF MALWARE

Signature Based Detection

Signature based detection method involves using patterns extricated from numerous malwares to authenticate them. A signature like a fingerprint is a unique characteristic

Table 2. Intrusion detection technique, features and challenges

Ids Technique Signature Detection Method	Features This Include	Challenges
Signature Detection	-A unique features for each of the file. -An efficient solution to detect the unknown worms. -worm attacks	-requires high amount of man power and it takes time to extract unique signature of each worms. -With this method alone the detection of worm is not sufficient. -unable to detect the unknown attacks.
Detecting the behavior	-It has the capability to detect different types of malware	-It causes false alarm and its very hard to detect the malware
IDS Genetic algorithm	-helps to choose best features for detection.	-used in particular mode rather than general
Artificial neural network based IDS	-Multiple invisible layers in ANN increase performance of classification. -this will classify unstructured network packet efficiently.	-For training there is a need of huge number of samples. -Has minimum elasticity. -It takes more time at training stages.
Fuzzy Logic based on IDS	-supply best elasticity to some uncertain problems. -used for quantitative features.	-precision decision is lower than ANN
HIDS	-determine intrusion by observation host's file system, system calls or networks. -No further hardware needed events	-It can observe attacks only on host where it is deployed. -Needed to be installed in each machine such as host machine, hypervisor or VM
Hypervisor based IDS	-This will allow the user to observe and analyze the connection between hypervisor, VM and within hypervisor based Virtual machine.	-shortage of experience -New and difficult to understand

for individual files but the drawback with this method is that significant manpower and time is required to extract unique signatures. It is insufficient to use this method solely for the detection of malware. It would be an obstacle to encounter malwares which mutate their codes in individual infections such as polymorphic and metamorphic. According to suggested a detection system to expose intruders and attacks in a cloud computing environment based on the signature method. This system investigates network traffic and checks for skeptical activity. It has the ability to take steps against barbed traffic such as, impeding the user IP address from entering the network. By utilizing the intrusion detection system, it exposes unknown signatures founded on seeking for definitive signatures of known threats. A signature based intrusion detection system monitors packets on the network and compares them with a database of signatures from acknowledged malicious threats. They deploy intrusion detection system sensors for cloud users who require an intrusion detection system to expose attacks on their services and to be aware if the used services or hosts are attacking other victims. The cloud provider can use VMM functions to monitor virtual machines. (Truelove, 2010) The Conferred an anti-malware system called Split Screen which is based on signature-based parameters. This system executes an extra screening stage prior to the signature matching in their system. Screening steps are used to filter non-infected files and identify malware signatures that are not of interest. The files can then be scanned using only the necessary signatures. Split Screen was implemented as an extension of ClamAV and was proven that scanning throughput is improved using signature sets using half the memory. (Martinez, 2010) presented a model to detect malware on cloud computing integrating intrusion ontology representation using signature methods. Multiple engine services which follow a set of defined parameters and standards for web service technologies are used in this model and also, founded on analysis with precise applications residing on the client who can enhance their performance, if they are moved to the network, where instead of running complicated software on every host, it gives each process a light to enter the system files and then it sends them to the network. The multiple engine analyze the network and then decide whether or not they are executed according to the report of threat delivered. This model is a multi-engine based file analysis service which is deployed in the cloud computing, via a group of protocols and standards for web services. It is used to identify the files with malicious codes through the remote analysis by multiple engines. The result offers the contingency of expanding the rate of the assertion characterization of harmful files. An efficient solution for detecting known or variations of attack is signature based detection but is unable to detect unknown attacks or variation of known attacks.

Behavior Based Detection

Behavior based malware detection technique scrutinizes program behavior to decide whether it is corrupt. It has the ability to expose various types of malware based on signature techniques but this method is very difficult to detect thereby possibly causing a false alarm as the technique observes what an executable file does. Various samples of malware can be identified by a single behavior.

This (Dolgikh, 2013) proposed a novel approach to monitor the execution status of user application programs and detects auspicious processes in cloud servers using behavioral method. They combined the hypervisor to monitor all OS level system calls in all VMs in cloud computing environment. Two phases were used in this approach, which is the learning stage and the detection stage to search for the malware in the cloud. During the training

Phase, they intercepted and analyzed a stream of system calls for a sufficient time period to cover the majority of normal system operations. While in detection phase, they observed the stream of system calls and detected any deviation from the previously defined model of normal behavior. Malware performs benign functionalities unpredictable with normal manners, which is instrumental for attack detection. The detection of the suspicious processes in cloud by monitoring system calls of processes running in each virtual machine. The proposed behavioral modeling scheme aims at addressing the software-oriented threats in categories. This (Wagener, 2008) proposed a flexible and automated approach to pull out malware activities by observing all the system function calls performed in a virtualized execution environment. Similarities and distances between malware behaviors are computed. It will allow classifying malware behaviors. The main features of this approach reside in coupling a sequence alignment method to compute similarities and leverage the Hellinger distance to calculate related distances. The classification process proposed by this work is using a phylogenetic tree. However, this technique has a limitation due to the wrongly classified malware behavior. A framework was implemented for improving behavior based analysis of malware (Martignoni, 2009). The framework only improves the capabilities of existing dynamic behavior based detectors such as TTAnalyze, Panorama and CWSandbox and is not the malware detector. The framework was founded on cloud computing environment by examining a piece of malware on behalf of multiple end users in concert. Cloud can detect anonymous attacks at different strata by behavior detection techniques. In cloud, huge numbers of incidents like (system level or network level) develop making it arduous to observe or domination them using behavior detection technique. There are numerous techniques utilized to enhance detection precision and efficiency of signature based detection and behavior based detection, such as Genetic Algorithm (GA), Artificial Neural Network (ANN), Fuzzy Logic, etc.

INTRUSION DETECTION SYSTEM (IDS) IN CLOUD COMPUTING

Genetic Algorithm (GA) Based Ids

Genetic algorithms (GAs) (Dhanalakshmi, 2008) are used to choose network features or to decide optimal parameters which can be used in other mechanisms to generate useful solutions to optimization and improve accuracy of IDS. This (Lu, 2004) presented Genetic Programming (GP) for detecting novel attacks on networks and four genetic operators; namely reproduction, mutation, crossover, and dropping condition and are used to evolve new rules from network features. However, these new rules take more time to generate. The proposed a method (Dhanalakshmi, 2008) to detect misuse and anomaly by combining genetic algorithms and fuzzy techniques. The Fuzzy is used to include quantitative parameters in intrusion detection, whereas genetic algorithm is used to find best fit parameters of introduced numerical fuzzy function. Information theory and GA based approach is used to detect abnormal behavior (Xiao, 2005). It determines a small number of network features closely linked with network attacks based on mutual information between network features and type of intrusion. This approach only considers discrete features. Genetic algorithm is a family of computational models based on principles of evolution and natural selection, and is primarily used for finding optimal solutions to a specific problem (Li, 2004). According to the process (Pohlheim, 2003) of a genetic algorithm starts with a randomly generated population, evolves through selection, recombination (crossover), mutation. Finally, the best individual (chromosome) is selected as the final result once the optimization criterion is met. Figure 2 shows the structure of a simple genetic algorithm in a cloud computing environment, a selection of Optimization parameters (network features) will increase the precision of underlying IDS for intrusion detection. For that reason, Genetic Algorithm (GA) based IDS can be used in Cloud. Figure 3-Structure of a simple genetic algorithm (Li, 2004) has defined genetic algorithm as a programming mechanism, which mimics biological development as a problem-solving approach. The genetic algorithms are advocates the survival of the fittest among the population. Therefore, a solution obtained by applying genetic algorithms to any problem, consists of only those optimal candidate solutions which are said to satisfy a predefined fitness value (EidHebba, 2011, Srinivasa, 2012). Based on previous work of genetic algorithms, the researchers' contribution in this paper will be use genetic algorithms to develop a model that effectively detects worm attacks and avoids worms from further propagation in cloud computing environment. Moreover, this research also aims to identify and evaluate various strategies of worm attacks, which vital prior designing and developing a robust model to track the worm attacks. Genetic Algorithms will be utilized to research the most advantageous solution to detect worm attack in cloud computing more efficiently because GAs are easy to modify, provide a wider solution space, possess tremendous capabilities for parallel processing, easily discoverable global minima, do not need prior knowledge of the problem space, least affected by the discontinuities in the problem space and reliable enough not to become trapped in local minima. The implementation of genetic algorithms offers many advantages to intrusion detection systems which are: Genetic algorithms work with populations of solutions rather than a distinct solution. This makes them suitable for behavior based intrusion detection, where the behavior attributes may exhibit varying values.

1. Genetic algorithms are capable of working in multiple directions simultaneously. This makes them beneficial for analyzing the huge volumes of multi-dimensional data to be processed by an intrusion detection system.
2. Genetic algorithms are highly re trainable. Therefore, using genetic algorithms for intrusion detection will add to the adaptability of the system.

Artificial Nueral Network (ANN) Based Ids

Role of ANNs (Han, 2006) for intrusion detection is to be capable of generalizing information from incomplete information and to be able to distribute information as being normal or intrusive. Types of ANN used in IDS are as follows (Ibrahim 2010): Multi-Layer Perceptron (MLP), Multi-Layer Feed Forward (MLFF) Neural Nets (NN) and Back Propagation (BP). MLP based IDS were presented by (Moradi, 2004), they showed that inclusion of more invisible layers increase the detection

Figure 3. Structure of a simple genetic algorithm (Li, 2004)

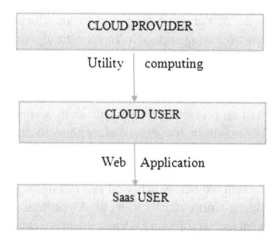

precision of IDS. For misuse detection in network suggested a three-layer neural network (Cannady, 2010). The feature vector used in was composed of nine network features (Protocol ID, Source Port, Destination Port, Source IP Address, Destination IP Address, ICMP Type, ICMP Code, Raw Data Length, and Raw Data). However, the intrusion detection precision is significantly low. An efficient and effective solution of unstructured network data is ANN based IDS. The intrusion detection precision of this approach is based on number of invisible layers and training stage of ANN. Needs more training and more time for effective learning of ANN. Only use ANN based IDS cannot be an effective solution to detect intrusions for cloud as it requires a fast intrusion detection technique. The proposed approach for cloud environment using ANN based anomaly detection technique, which demands more training samples as well as more extra time for detecting intrusions effectively.

Fuzzy Logic Based Ids

Fuzzy logic (Han, 2006) can be used to handle inaccurate description of intrusions. It supplies some elasticity to the uncertain problem of intrusion detection. Fuzzy association rules presented in (Su, 2009) are utilized to detect network intrusion in real time. There are two rule groups produced which are mined online from training data. Features for comparison are taken from network packet header. This approach is used for large scale attacks such as DoS/DDoS. (Tillapart, 2002) proposed Fuzzy IDS (FIDS) for network intrusions like SYN and UDP floods, Ping of Death, Email Bomb, FTP/Telnet password guessing and port scanning. The Evolving fuzzy neural network. (EFuNN) is introduced in (Chavan, 2004) for reducing training time of ANN. It uses mixture of unsupervised and supervised learning. The experimental results shown point out that using reduced number of inputs EFuNN has better classification accuracy for IDS than only using ANN. The approaches cannot be used in real time for detecting network intrusions as the training time is significant. To reduce training time of, fuzzy logic with ANN can be used for fast detection of unknown attacks in Cloud.

Host Based Interruption Discovery Frameworks (HIDS)

A host-based interruption discovery framework (HIDS) is an interruption identification framework which watches and investigations the data gathered from a particular host machine, the data, for example, system occasions, framework calls and record framework. HIDS can watch any change happening in this data and gives the reports presence of assault (Modi, 2013). With distributed computing, HIDS can be running in VM or hypervisor and host machine to recognize meddling conduct through observing and breaking down log record, client login data, security get to and control approaches. If there should arise an occurrence of introducing HDIS on VM it ought to be observed by Cloud client while introducing HDIS on Hypervisor, Cloud supplier ought to screen it. (Vieira, 2010) The Proposed HIDS based engineering for Cloud registering environment. In this engineering, every hub of cloud contains IDS which gives cooperation among administration offered, IDS administration and capacity administration. The occasion examiner takes information from various assets like framework logs. In light of the information got from occasion examiner, the IDS administration is utilized for recognizing interruption by utilizing learning based method or conduct based system. Conduct based method is utilized to recognize obscure assaults though the learning based system is utilized to distinguish known assaults. The impediment of this methodology is that it can't recognize any insider interruptions which are running on VMs.

OUTLINE AND IMPLEMENTATION

The point of the proposed methodology is identifying and gathering payloads of zero-day dynamic polymorphic worms in homogeneous and heterogeneous distributed computing stages without damaging the client security.

In the proposed methodology, worms' spreading is constrained by detaching activity of each virtual system from the movement of different systems by utilizing virtual switches as a part of XenServer or in VMware vCenter Server.

Figure 4. Demonstrates the seclusion between two virtual systems utilizing virtual conveyed switches as a part of VMware vCenter Server (Shahin, 2014)

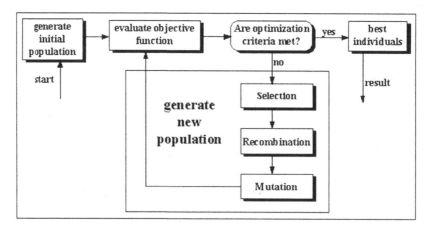

Each virtual system contains two virtual servers, which fit in with the same circulated port gathering. A circulated virtual switch has been made with one appropriated port gathering for each virtual system. Virtual servers are situated in ESXi has. Despite the fact that, VM1 and VM3 are situated at the same physical server and there traffics are transmitted over the same hidden NIC, they can't sniff or infuse movement into each other in light of the fact that each of them has a place with various conveyed port gathering and distinctive circulated switch

This proposed approach architecture. Self-examination controller makes virtual machine assessors from virtual machine monitors' templates. Self-thought controller doles out an arrangement of virtual systems to each VM examiner. By recovering a rundown of virtual conveyed switch from vCenter server database Introspection controller recognizes current virtual systems

VM investigator will makes the honey pot VMs from honey pot formats. Each of the honey pot layouts contains a subset of programming from the most well-known programming which has been conveyed in distributed computing system. There will

Figure 5. Shows the distinguish and to gather polymorphic worms in the network (Shahin, 2014)

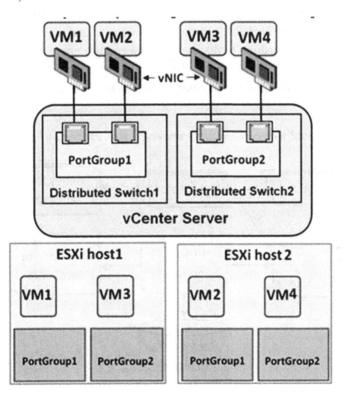

be an allotment present and each of the dividing minimizes the span of honey pots and permits each of the honey pot to catch a particular sort of worms which is identified with this subset of programming. VM investigator will associates each of the honey pot with one virtual system by adding honey pot to the port gathering (Figure 3). VM assessor will make and associates honey pots consecutively to abstain from devouring countless resources. If any of the virtual system is tainted by dynamic worms, the worms will find the honey pot and defile it. After a considerable measure of time, VM reviewer will detaches the honey pot from the virtual system and afterward it will interface it with another occurrence of the honey pot, which is made from the same honey pot format (Fig. These two honey pots shape a two-fold honey pot. By this strategy it diminishes false positive and false negative on the grounds that just dynamic worms can find and contaminate the new honey pot.

Honey pot layout is composed in a way that it will take a depiction of the running VM intermittently and consequently. VM controller will investigates the memory previews of running honey pots utilizing Volatility, it is the acclaimed criminological apparatuses. By Using this Volatility, VM investigator can pick up a parcels and bunches of data about the running VMs. For instance, VM examiner can list the running procedures, the already ended procedures, concealed procedures, and the stacked DLLs for the running procedures. Every one of these rundowns which are recorded are spared in an isolated content document and utilized as info to the Checker segment. The Checker contrasts these rundowns and already spared records gathered from typical rushing to distinguish abnormality procedures or modules.

Honey pot Virtual Machine format has been composed with the free and non-steady hard plate. This element will permit VMware running Virtual Machine to

Figure 6. Honeypot2 was created and connected with Honeypot1 (Shahin, 2014)

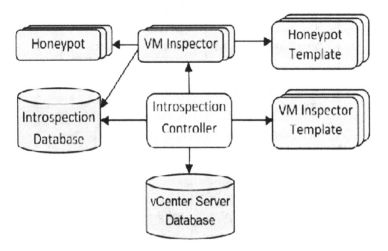

spare it to any altered squares to an isolated log record .VM auditor utilizes Virtual Disk API capacities with log and VMDK documents to recover the rundown of the circle parts that have been changed and to recover the rundown of documents that have been created, modified, or deleted. Using depictions, VM reviewer restores honey pots plate information and virtual machine state to the first information and state in turn way. This rebuilding permits worms running in honey pots to re-defile honey pots again on the off chance that they check their presence in the objective machine before sending their code. VM controller stores every single gathered data in the reflection database to be utilized as a part without bounds by mark generators. After a significant number of cycles, VM reviewer stops the circle, demolishes honey pots, and makes another honey pot to investigate the following virtual system.

Open Problem and Approach

In the year 2003, the worm named "Blaster" tainted a great many 2003 frameworks by remotely misusing a computer bug in the Windows 2000, XP and Windows Server. Every single contaminated framework was running a procedure called "msblast.exe" which began together with the working framework at boot time. The spreading conduct of the "Blaster" computer worm turned into an irritating and gigantic unreasonable scourge.

Toward the beginning of November 2008, the "Conficker" computer worm contaminated up to 15 million Windows frameworks by misusing a remote NetBIOS bug. It infuses a haphazardly named dynamic connection library (DLL) into the genuine "svchost.exe" Windows process and tries to shroud its nearness along these lines. Adaptation An of the "Conficker" computer worm was particularly centered around the contamination of different frameworks that were associated inside of an interior system which created quick spreading inside of associations. Conficker B incorporated a savage power assault component to recover neighborhood passwords and form C even incorporated a P2P convention for its own particular Distribution.

In the year 2010, the "Stuxnet" computer worm proclaims the new period of spreading pernicious programming. This computer worm plans to control mechanical control frameworks, yet it is additionally conveyed on Windows frameworks from 2000 to 7 utilizing different misusing techniques. The event of the "Stuxnet" computer worm has at the end of the day demonstrated that the risks of spreading pernicious programming are far from over.

These computer worms constitute just a few samples of computer worms which brought about tremendous monetary harm in the most recent years. The danger of spreading computer worms is not over: the past demonstrated that constantly new worms emerge, regardless of the arrangement of new methods for identification and reduction. Infection recognition programming or interruption identification programming can be introduced on frameworks, yet this product can likewise be controlled by pernicious procedures or even deactivated from the clients themselves by mix-up. Up to this point, control of quick spreading worms is an open issue to which no delightful countermeasure is known. Not at all like customary system subnets, on which one working framework was introduced on every equipment hub associated specifically to the system, today's organizing segments are virtualized, i.e. different frameworks keep running in parallel on one equipment hub, oversaw by a hypervisor programming part from which the frameworks are totally disconnected. In such virtual figuring situations, worms can in any case spread through customary methods. By using the current virtualization foundation, more valuable data of every single running virtual machine can be gotten from the outside in a uninvolved way. Virtual machine thoughtfulness (VMI) permits to get data on running virtual machines through the hypervisor layer without the need to specifically get to the machines. This data can contain a rundown of the present running procedures of the working framework, current stacked modules or even a picture of the entire irregular access memory (RAM). There are exible libraries accessible that give virtual machine thoughtfulness without obliging changes to the hypervisor

In light of this innovation, interruption identification frameworks (IDS) can be produced which screen virtualized frameworks all things considered. This design has the advantage that this sort of interruption discovery frameworks cannot be controlled or even recognized by malignant programming running on the tainted virtual machine, in light of the fact that the IDS code is out of range and along these lines in a totally isolated programming environment.

The virtual base of the cloud system offers an exquisite approach to distinguish an irresistible spread without assistant worm marks. In a virtualized system, data can be gotten from every running virtual machine through VMI. A solitary brought together observing programming part can get this data of all running virtual machines and decipher the present status of the system.

Along these lines, IDS can be fabricated taking into account abnormalities distinguished in the entire virtualized distributed computing system. To exhibit the practicality of this methodology, we constructed a unified oddity finder which gathers data utilizing VMI of all running virtual machines in the cloud back-end. Our methodology offers quick discovery of pernicious spreading conduct due to the unified dynamic perspective on the cloud system. Utilizing our methodology, spreading noxious procedures can be identified in light of their spreading conduct in the back-end system itself, even without having past learning about the risk like marks.

After the identification of a computer worm, a mark can be created and further utilized as a part of a system movement based IDS like "Grunt" to boycott the danger at the doors of the system.

TECHINCAL APPROACH

To understand the proposed thought, we first need to characterize what we consider a peculiarity in the distributed computing system. By our definition, a peculiarity is a gathering of more than one seeming single irregularities. Specifically, we distinguish two distinctive irregularities that can show up in a working framework in our virtual distributed computing system. An irregularity emerges on the off chance that one or a greater amount of the accompanying occasions are recognized on a running virtual machine in the cloud utilizing VMI or hypervisor data when all is said in done:

1. A new process is begun which is not in a rundown of known or regular procedures.
2. A new module is stacked which is not in a rundown of known or regular modules.

In this setting, the execution of a "known" procedure or module is not remarkable and understood. Interestingly, an "obscure" procedure or module can be a procedure or module which is not extremely well known or which execution is exceptionally bizarre. Obviously, one can characterize more mind-boggling occasion that bring about irregularities, which may incorporate, for instance, strange high cordial activity of a virtual machine or consistent high CPU execution. There are numerous approaches to characterize triggers for irregularities in the distributed computing system. In this paper, we restrain our irregularity to the two recorded occasions above.

Single irregularities are not indisputable; notwithstanding, if a constant circulation or expanding of the very same irregularity in the cloud back-end system can be found, one can gather an inconsistency. We characterize that an abnormality happens when in progressive sweeps of running virtual machines utilizing VMI at predefined time interims T a constant enduring increment of an irregularity in the cloud back-end system surpasses a predefined limit L.

These perceptions permit to identify computer worms in a roundabout way through their spreading conduct. These computer worms are obscure procedures or modules even themselves or they utilize other unordinary procedures or modules amid their vindictive work on the working framework.

For instance, the accompanying steps recognize a progressing risk with the assistance of watched running procedures on virtual machines in the cloud back-end system:

1. Recover a rundown of running procedures of a haphazardly picked virtual machine utilizing VMI as a part of the cloud back-end system.

2. Discover forms which are not in a rundown of known or regular procedures and add these data incidentally to a rundown of obscure procedures.

3. After a bigger number of outputs, distinguish a potential spreading process, described by the way that this irregularity happens on an expanding number of virtual machines.

4. In the event that the event of this distinguished procedure surpasses the estimation of a predefined limit L, make restorative move (e.g. disconnect tainted virtual machines from the back-end system for further examinations).

5. Interestingly, if the event of this procedure diminishes and comes to not the estimation of as far as possible L, add its data to the rundown of known procedures and proceed. For this situation, it is expected that the procedure is not a computer worm, but rather an occasion happening in parallel, for example, e.g. an all the while dispatched redesign on various virtual machines.

A calculation taking after these strides is not just ready to recognize a spreading process in the cloud back-end system; it additionally enhances itself by learning data about obscure innocuous procedures. This can be useful to recognize the spread of malignant programming and consistent redesigns, which can have qualities of a computer worm on the off chance that they are introduced on virtual machines all the while from the Internet.

Utilizing these proposed steps, a computer worm can be recognized just by its spreading conduct itself. Along these lines, no earlier learning about the computer worm is vital, for example, a mark. This methodology is profiting from the virtualization advances of the cloud all in all by latently watching the running virtual machines with the assistance of VMI and it is likewise profiting by a conceptual brought together view on all system hubs of the whole cloud back-end system. New and obscure computer worms can be identified and the activated irregularity may prompt further more dynamic countermeasures.

ASSESSMENT

Presently, we come back to the already recorded difficulties in area 2 to demonstrate that the proposed approach beat these difficulties.

Polymorphic Worms

the proposed approach gathers polymorphic worm payload utilizing two-fold honey pot, and intermittently restores honey pots to the first state (before sullying) to gather worms that check in the event that they are running in the objective machine before sending their code.

Customer Protection

To abstain from damaging the clients' security, the proposed approach does not assess the clients' VMs specifically. The proposed approach utilizes honey pots to permit existing worms (assuming any) to taint them and review the contaminated honey pots as opposed to investigating the clients' VMs.

Worms Spreading

Honey pots are made from clean VMs' layouts and every is associated with stand out virtual system to abstain from exchanging worms between virtual systems. All examination devices are running outside the assessed honey pots (in hypervisor layer). Accordingly, worms can't distinguish or sully them.

Out-Box Examination

In the proposed approach, VMs reviewers investigate honey pots from the outside by assessing depictions. Accordingly, worms can't control or recognize them.

Homogeneous and Heterogeneous Stages

The proposed approach utilizes diverse VMs' format for honey pots to accomplish varieties between virtual systems. Each VM format is intended to catch a classification of worms that are intended to utilize vulnerabilities in its product.

Cloud Processing Administration Methods

In the proposed approach, VMs auditors associate honey pots with virtual systems by adding them to the port gatherings in virtual conveyed switches, which permits honey pots to continue associated with virtual systems regardless of the possibility that they are moved between hosts.

Scalability

Thoughtfulness controller makes and decimates VM investigators in view of the quantity of the running virtual systems to take after the developing and the contracting of the distributed computing data centers.

Computational Assets

The proposed approach does not review all running virtual machines. Each VM overseer utilizes one honey pot for each virtual system and examines virtual systems consecutively to minimize computer assets utilized amid investigation process. To quicken the reflection, all made VM monitors running simultaneously. The proposed approach decreased the time required to dissect document framework by breaking down log and REDO records that contain just altered divisions as opposed to examining entire VM circle picture. For Example, in our execution, we made four honey pot VM layouts with the particulars appeared. Figure 5- demonstrates the measure of REDO (log) documents made amid running VMs from these layouts. As appeared in Figure 5, the span of REDO document is not similar with the measure of the VM circle picture and we can lessen its size by diminishing the association time before restoring the first information. For instance, in honey pot VM format for Windows Xp proficient, we dissect the log documents (around 40 megabyte) rather than examining VM plate picture with 5 GB.

Test Implementation

Our test execution utilizes a basic setup. We concentrated just on checking running procedures; in like manner we got a present procedure rundown of running virtual machines toward the back hubs. The usage comprises of a brought together cloud system administration segment including a "Spreading Process Monitor" part running on Linux. The cloud chief comprises of scripts which can exchange virtual machine pictures to associated hubs, dispatch, stop and obliterate them.

Each associated hub utilizes the Xen hypervisor and appropriately each associated hub incorporates a managerial virtual machine which is brought in Xen "Space 0" ("dom0"). This authoritative virtual machine can give data about the CPU use or the system movement of the running virtual visitor machines ("domU") on the same equipment hub. For the usage, the "dom0" virtual machine also utilizes the XenAccess2 VMI library bundle to recover a rundown of the present running procedures on each virtual visitor machine on this equipment hub.

This is finished with the assistance of direct memory access technics and beforehand characterized information about the structure of the RAM subject to the picked Operating framework. Figure 2 shows the strategy of virtual machine thoughtfulness on a solitary equipment hub in the cloud back-end system. (Source: http://code. google.com/p/xenaccess/) During the runtime, the "Spreading Process Monitor" gathers the procedure arrangements of arbitrarily picked virtual visitor machines on various equipment hubs in the system. Ceaselessly gathering and contrasting these rundowns offers the open door with recognize spreading irregularities which expand their appearance on other virtual visitor machines in the cloud back-end system. This strategy is outlined in Figure 3. As countermeasures, confining or solidifying contaminated virtual machines are conceivable and this can be additionally controlled by the unified cloud administrator. The system movement of all virtual visitor machines is steered through a scaffold, which is arranged in the regulatory \dom0" virtual machine. The present system Activity of every visitor machine can be effectively checked, examined furthermore blocked utilizing host-based system sifting programming in further strides after an abnormality. Recovering the procedure arrangements of virtual visitor machines of the back-end organize and subdivide this gathered data in arrangements of known and obscure procedures. Along these lines, activity of contaminated virtual machines can be separated or sifted, so that tainted virtual machines can be kept from contaminating other uninfected virtual machines inside the inner cloud back-end system. This is a straightforward yet powerful way to deal with get the continuous spreading risk under control and to get more opportunity for nitty gritty examinations.

CONCLUSION

Distributed computing is changing the IT world and presents gigantic and incredible enhancements. Still, cloud establishments are powerless against great open issues, for example, quick spreading computer worms. Customary location techniques, normally in view of a mark, are not ready to bring this issue under control, in light of the fact that the measure of new happening computer worms is relentlessly developing. Peculiarity identification methodologies are more powerful than mark based location techniques; however they require significant data from the system. The cloud offers new chances to screen the system without straightforwardly impacting or getting to single virtual machines utilizing virtual machine thoughtfulness. Along these lines, this can be utilized to have a dynamic perspective on the whole framework and to translate the condition of the system with the assistance of a concentrated locator to distinguish malevolent spreading irregularities. In this paper, we demonstrated that it is conceivable to utilize highlights offered by virtual machine reflection to identify and to contain the spreading of computer worms. Our discovery strategy depends on peculiarities and works by watching the spreading conduct of suspicious irregularities in the virtualized cloud back-end system. We advanced this recognition technique utilizing an arrangement of various reproductions and we examined the affected of various parameters and a countermeasure.

In this paper, we have distinguished difficulties confronting current methodologies amid gathering polymorphic computer worms in distributed computing. A high-intuitive twofold honey pot has been proposed to address the recognized difficulties.

The proposed approach reviews VMs from outside to identify concealed procedures and to keep away from discovery by worms. Clients' protection has been preserved by maintaining a strategic distance from specifically reviewing their VMs. Utilized computer assets have been lessened by assessing cloud server farms by virtual system rather than by VM. The proposed approach continues following VMs regardless of the possibility that there are areas changed after some time. In our future work, we plan to explore how to diminish the season of investigating VM memory and how to lessen the quantity of honey pots required to examine virtual systems. Moreover, we plan to extend our way to deal with assess system movement alongside memory and document framework.

Distributed computing is a quick developing innovation all-inclusive and offers numerous preferences, for example, diminished costs, dynamic virtualized assets, enormous information stockpiling and improved efficiency. In the meantime, distributed computing has different security dangers and dangers. Worm assaults in cloud are a creating risk and seen as one of the essential dangers in digital world. It is a standout amongst the most hazardous sorts of pernicious codes that can infringe into cloud arrangement and endeavor to obliterate a noxious administration, application or VM. Research foresees a contemporary strategy to recognize worm assaults in distributed computing by utilizing hereditary calculation which is at last more profitable. For future work, hereditary calculation will be coordinated to distinguish worm's assault all the more effectively in distributed computing environment.

REFERENCES

Armbrust, M., Fox, A., Griffith, R., Joseph, A., Katz, R., Konwinski, A., & Zaharia, M. et al. (2010, April). A view of cloud computing. *Communications of the ACM*, *53*(4), 50–58. doi:10.1145/1721654.1721672

Aymerich, F. M., Fenu, G., & Surcis, S. (2008, August). An approach to a Cloud Computing network. In Proceedings of the First International Conference on the Applications of Digital Information and Web Technologies ICADIWT '08 (pp. 113-118). doi:10.1109/ICADIWT.2008.4664329

Bobor, V. (2006). Efficient Intrusion Detection System Architecture Based on Neural Networks and Genetic Algorithms.

Cannady, J. (2010). Artificial Neural Networks for Misuse Detection. In *Proceedings of the National Information Systems Security Conference*.

Chavan, S., Shah, K., Dave, N., & Mukherjee, S. (2004). Adaptive neuro-fuzzy intrusion detection systems. In Proceedings of the IEEE international conference on information technology: coding and computing (ITCC'04) (pp. 70-74). doi:10.1109/ITCC.2004.1286428

Dhanalakshmi Y & Ramesh Babu I (2008). Intrusion Detection Using Data Mining Along Fuzzy Logic and Genetic Algorithms. *International Journal of Computer Science and Network Security, 8*(2).

Dolgikh, A., Birnbaum, Z., Chen, Y., & Skormin, V. (2013). Behavioral Modeling for Suspicious Process Detection in Cloud Computing Environments. In Proceedings of the 2013 IEEE 14th International Conference on In Mobile Data Management (MDM) (Vol. 2, pp. 177-181). doi:10.1109/MDM.2013.90

Eid, H.F., Darwish, A., Hassanien, A., & Tai-Hoon, K. (2011). Intelligent Hybrid Anomaly Network Intrusion Detection System. In Communication and Networking (pp. 209-218).

Eid, H.F., Darwish, A., Hassanien, A., & Tai-Hoon, K. (2011). Intelligent Hybrid Anomaly Network Intrusion Detection System. In Communication and networking (pp. 209-218).

Foster, I., Zhao, Y., Raicu, I., & Lu, S. (2008). Cloud Computing and Grid Computing 360-Degree Compared. In *Proceedings of the Grid Computing Environments Workshop GCE '08*. doi:10.1109/GCE.2008.4738445

Garfinkel, T., & Rosenblum, M. (2003). A Virtual Machine Introspection Based Architecture for Intrusion Detection. In *Proceedings of Network and Distributed Systems Security Symposium* (pp. 191-206).

Han, J., & Kamber, M. (2006). *Data Mining Concepts and Techniques* (2nd ed.). Morgan Kaufmann Publishers.

Ibrahim, L. (2010). Anomaly network intrusion detection system based on distributed time-delay neural network. *Journal of Engineering Science and Technology, 5*(4), 457-471.

Jensen, M., Schwenk, Gruschka N. & Iacono L. (2009). On Technical Security Issues in Cloud Computing. In *Proceedings of the IEEE International Conference on Cloud Computing*. doi:10.1109/CLOUD.2009.60

Kanaker, H., Saudi, M., & Marhusin, M. (2014). Detecting Worm Attacks in Cloud Computing Environment: Proof of Concept. In *Proceedings of the IEEE 5th Control and System Graduate Research Colloquium (ICSGRC)* (pp. 253-256).

Kanaker, H. M., Saudi, M. M., & Marhusin, M. F. (2015, February). A systematic analysis on worm detection in cloud based systems. *Journal of Engineering and Applied Sciences (Asian Research Publishing Network)*, *10*(2).

Li, W. (2004, January). Using genetic algorithm for network intrusion detection. *Proceedings of the United States Department of Energy Cyber Security Group*.

Li, W. (2004). Using genetic algorithm for network intrusion detection. In *Proceedings of the United States Department of Energy Cyber Security Group*.

Liu, T., & Chen, Y. (2010). Retrospective Detection of Malware Attacks by Cloud Computing. In *Proceedings of the International Conference on Cyber-Enabled Distributed Computing and Knowledge Discovery* (pp. 510-517). doi:10.1109/CyberC.2010.99

Lu, W., & Traore, I. (2004). Detecting new forms of network intrusion using genetic programming. In *Proceedings of the Conference on Evolutionary Computation* (pp. 475-494). doi:10.1111/j.0824-7935.2004.00247.x

Marhusin, M.F. (2012). Improving the Effectiveness of Behaviour-based Malware Detection [doctoral dissertation]. UNSW, Canberra. Retrieved from http://www. unsworks.unsw.edu.au/primo_library/libweb/action/dlDisplay.do?vid=UNSWOR KS&docId=unsworks_10868. 2012.

Martignoni, L., Paleari, R., & Bruschi, D. (2009, December 14-18). A framework for behavior-based malware analysis in the cloud. In *Proceedings of the 5th International Conference (ICISS)* (pp. 1-15). doi:10.1007/978-3-642-10772-6_14

Martinez, C., Echeverri, G., & Sanz, A. (2010, November). Malware Detection based on Cloud Computing integrating Intrusion Ontology representation. In *Proceedings of the 2010 IEEE Latin-American Conference on Communications (LATINCOM)*. doi:10.1109/LATINCOM.2010.5641013

McGraw, G., & Morrisett, G. (2000). Attacking Malicious Code. *IEEE Software*, *17*(5), 33-41.

Modi, C., Patel, D., Patel, H., Borisaniya, B., Patel, A., & Rajarajan, M. (2013). A survey of intrusion detection techniques. Cloud, 36(1), 42–57.

Moradi, M., & Zulkernine, M. (2004). A Neural Network Based System for Intrusion Detection and Classification of Attacks. In *Proceedings of the 2004 IEEE International Conference on Advances in Intelligent Systems Theory and Applications*.

Pohlheim, H. (2003). Genetic and Evolutionary Algorithms: Principles, Methods and Algorithms. Retrieve from http://www.pg.gda.pl/~mkwies/dyd/geadocu/algindex.html

Qaisar, S., & Khawaja, K. (2012). *Cloud Computing: Network/Security Threats and Countermeasures. Interdisciplinary Journal of Contemporary Research*, *3*(9), 1323–1329.

Ren, K., & Lou, W. (2009). Ensuring Data Storage Security in Cloud Computing. Retrieved From http://www.ece.iit.edu/~ubisec/IWQoS09.pdf

Shahin, A. A. (2014). Polymorphic Worms Collection in Cloud Computing. *International Journal of Soft Computing, Mathematics and Control*.

Srinivasa, K. (2012). *Application of Genetic Algorithms for Detecting Anomaly in Network Intrusion Detection Systems. In CCSIT 2012* (pp. 582–591). doi:10.1007/978-3-642-27299-8_61

Su, M., Yu, G., & Lin, C. (2009). A real-time network intrusion detection system for large-scale attacks based on an incremental mining approach. *Computers & Security*, *28*(5), 301–309. doi:10.1016/j.cose.2008.12.001

Tillapart, P., Thumthawatworn, T., & Santiprabhob, P. (2002). Fuzzy intrusion detection system. *AU JT*, *6*(2), 109–114.

Truelove, J., & Brumley, D. (2010). Split Screen: Enabling Efficient, Distributed Malware Detection. In *Proceedings of School of Computer science at Research Showcase @ CMU Conference*.

Vieira, C., & Schulter, A. (2010). Intrusion detection techniques in grid and cloud computing environment. *IT Professional*, *12*(4), 38-43.

Wagener, G., State, R., & Dulaunoy, A. (2008). Malware behaviour analysis. *Journal of Virology*, *4*(4), 279-287.

Xiao, T., Qu, G., Hariri, S., & Yousif, M. 2005. An Efficient Network Intrusion Detection Method Based on Information Theory and Genetic Algorithm. In *Proceedings of the 24 th IEEE International Performance Computing and Communications Conference (IPCCC)*, Phoenix, AZ, USA.

Zunnurhain K & Vrbsky S (2010). Security Attacks and Solutions in Clouds. In *Proceedings of the Service Aggregated Linked Sequential Activities (SALSAHPC)*.

Chapter 7
Data Integrity in Mobile Cloud Computing

Abhishek Majumder
Tripura University, India

Samir Nath
Tripura University, India

Avijit Das
Tripura University, India

ABSTRACT

With the help of cloud computing Mobile Cloud Computing (MCC) overcomes the limitations of a mobile device such as security, performance and environment. But, security of the data stored in the cloud is a very challenging issue. Since the cloud cannot be fully trusted, data stored in the cloud is not fully secured. Integrity of the stored data is very important for the data owner. Therefore, it is a big problem to maintain the integrity of the data stored in the cloud environment. This chapter discusses existing schemes for data integrity in the mobile cloud environment. In this chapter a scheme has been proposed for enhancing data integrity in Mobile Cloud Environment. To make integrity checking fast the size of the data file is used. It has also been shown that how fast the integrity loss can be detected if the file size is considered. Finally, the proposed scheme is compared with some of the existing scheme.

DOI: 10.4018/978-1-5225-3038-1.ch007

INTRODUCTION

The data storage and processing has been shifted to the centralized and powerful systems located inside the cloud from the mobile devices because of the platform provided by the Mobile cloud computing (MCC). MCC (Dinh, 2013, Chetan et al., 2010; Gupta et al., 2012; Mane et al., 2013) offers an infrastructure where data processing and storage is performed outside the mobile device. By this way, the services of MCC can be provided not only to the smart phone users but also to much wide range of mobile users. An example of MCC is shown in Figure 1.

In MCC Mobile Client gets relived from the burden of computation and storage because most of their data files are put into the cloud. But it gives rise to some new problems and challenges. The owners of the data are often worried about the integrity of the data stored in the cloud because, when the data is stored, owners do not have full control over the data. The cloud cannot be fully trusted; therefore, the data stored in the cloud is not fully secured. CSP can be dishonest and can disclose or manipulate the stored information. This kind of activities will not be acceptable to data owner. Mishaps such as tempering and information disclosure can take place with the data while residing in the cloud. So, data confidentiality and security is very important for the owner. If data is altered by any unauthorized person, the integrity of the data gets severely damaged. Therefore, for the clients it is very vital to guarantee that their data is correctly maintained and stored in the cloud. So, maintaining the integrity of the user data is a challenging issue in mobile cloud environment.

Figure 1. Mobile cloud computing architecture

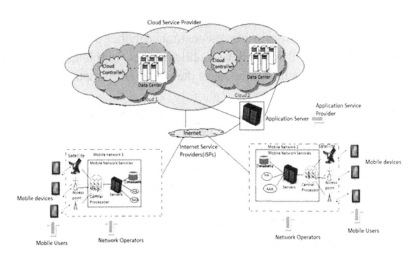

The main objective of this chapter is to design a mechanism to ensure the data integrity as well as the confidentiality of the user's data stored in cloud in MCC environment. In this scheme the objective is to make the data secret not just from the cloud service provider (CSP) but also from trusted third party (TPA). Secondly, to build a simple and efficient mechanism through which the resource constrained mobile device can also be benefited by offloading most of the tasks like encryption, decryption and integrity verification tasks to the TPA.

MOBILE CLOUD COMPUTING

In today's world, handheld devices such as, smart phone, tablet PCs have emerged as an integral part of human life as they are very convenient and effective tools for communication at any place and at any time. The users have the expectation that all the information should be accessible at their fingertips anytime anywhere. But, compared to conventional processing devices such as PCs and laptops mobile devices have lack of resources (e.g. bandwidth, storage and battery life).

For overcoming the limitations of handheld devices, a new technology named mobile cloud computing has emerged which combines both cloud computing and mobile computing. The concept of mobile has been introduced not much after the launch of cloud computing in mid-2007. Since mobile cloud computing reduces the cost for development and running of mobile applications, it has attracted the attention of large number of industrialist (Soyata et al., 2013).

Advantages of Mobile Cloud Computing

- **Extending Battery Lifetime:** Intensive computations and complicated processing are moved from resource-constrained mobile devices to resourceful servers of the cloud. It will relieve mobile devices from long execution time of the processes. This in turn, reduces the power consumption and increases battery life of mobile device.
- **Improving Data Storage Capacity and Processing Power:** Limited storage capacity is a deficiency of the mobile devices. MCC has been developed to enable the mobile devices for storing and retrieving large amount of data to and from the cloud using the wireless media. Few of the existing services are: ShoZu, Flickr, Image Exchange, Amazon Simple Storage Service (Amazon S3).
- **Improving Reliability:** The reliability of the stored data and application in the cloud is more because the content is stored and backed up on multiple

systems. This will reduce the chances of data or application loss if mobile device crashes or is lost.

Application

- **Mobile Commerce (M-Commerce):** It provides a business model for commerce utilizing mobile devices.
- **Mobile Learning:** Conventional applications of m-learning have disadvantages in terms of (a) High device and network cost. (b) Limited resources for education. (c) Low network transmission rate. For solving these limitations cloud-based m-learning applications have been developed. For example, the applications offer users much enhanced services with respect to longer battery life, higher processing speed and much enriched services in terms of data using a cloud having high processing ability and huge storage capacity.
- **Mobile Healthcare:** For reducing limitation of conventional medical treatment, MCC can be applied. Resources (e.g. patient healthcare records) can be accessed very fast and easily using mobile healthcare (m-healthcare). Healthcare centers and hospitals can access many on-demand services instead of maintaining a standalone application in its local server.
- **Mobile GAMING:** For service providers, a lucrative market to obtain large revenue is Mobile game (m-game). The game engine is completely offloaded by M-game form the mobile device to the cloud servers. The screen interface on the device is used by the user to interact. The energy of the mobile device is saved through offloading of multimedia. So, the game playing time of mobile device increases.

Table 1.

Application Classes	Type	Examples
Mobile Shopping	B2B (Business to Business) B2C (Business to Customer)	Using a mobile device order or locate specific products.
Mobile Advertising	B2C	Based on user's current location sending of custom made advertisement.
Mobile Financial application	B2B, B2C	Mobile-user fees, brokerage firms, banks.

Issues

Though mobile devices have very limited computation capacity but the cloud has very large storage capacity and computation ability. Therefore, implementation of cloud computing for mobile is very challenging (Alizadeh et al., 2013; Qi et al., 2012). Some of the issues with mobile cloud computing are:

- **Limited Resources:** Since the mobile devices have limited resources, using cloud computing in mobile device is very challenging. Some of the limited resources are: low quality display, limited battery and limited computing power.
- **Network Related Issues:** The processing of data is carried out in the cloud through the network. Therefore, the issues related to network such as heterogeneity, availability and bandwidth create challenge in MCC.
- **Security:** Large number of security issues is faced by the mobile device since data is stored in the cloud. For addressing this issue many mechanisms have been developed. But, still there are lot of challenges related to the security of the stored data. Moreover privacy of the user is also a challenging issue. The use of Global Positioning System (GPS) in the handheld device reveals the position of the user.

SECURITY IN MOBILE CLOUD COMPUTING

The primary concerns of mobile cloud computing security (Khan et.al., 2013; Chaturvedi et al., 2011; Garg et al., 2013; Huang et al., 2011; Ruebsamen et al., 2012, Zissis et al., 2012):

- **Security of Data/Files:** One of the important concerns of mobile cloud computing is to secure the data stored by the mobile users in the cloud. The data/file stored in the cloud is very vulnerable to the threats. An unauthorized person may access and change the stored data. Therefore, maintenance of the security of the stored data/file is very essential since the data may be confidential as well as important for the user.
- **Security of Mobile Applications:** The services are provided by application model to the mobile users by using cloud resources. Therefore, it is very important to secure the mobile application and application model. The capacity of the mobile device is increased by the use of mobile application model.

Data Integrity

Protecting data from unauthorized fabrication, modification and deletion is known as data integrity (Khaba et al., 2013; Khatri et al., 2012). Mobile users' data storage capacity is increased by uploading the files in the cloud. But the mobile device loses physical control over the stored data. So, a mechanism should be there for ensuring the correctness of user's uploaded data. Through integrity verification, the correctness of the uploaded files can be verified.

Different Security Threats

User's data residing in the cloud may face different security threats. Some of the attacks are discussed through Table 2.

RELATED WORK

To solve the problem of data integrity in mobile cloud computing many schemes has been proposed. In this section, some of the existing schemes have been discussed.

Energy Efficient Framework for Integrity Verification

Using the concept of trusted computing and incremental cryptography, Itani et al. (December, 2010) proposed an energy efficient framework for handheld devices to ensure the integrity of the mobile users' data/files stored on the cloud server. There are three main entities in the system design: mobile client, cloud service provider, and trusted third party. The storage services offered by the cloud service provider are used by the mobile user. Efficient management, allocation and operation of the resources are the responsibility of the cloud service provider. Installation of

Table 2. The different security threats in MCC

Name of the Attack	Description
Identity Spoofing	In this attack a person impersonate as someone who is the owner of the data.
Viruses and worms	These are very known attacks. These are the codes whish degrade the performance of any application.
Repudiation	When a person refused after sending a message that he did not send it.
Tampering	When any unauthorized person does some changes in other user's data.
Information disclosure	The secure information of owner is disclosed to any unauthorized user.

tamperproof coprocessors on the remote cloud is the responsibility of the trusted third party. Multiple registered mobile clients are associated with each coprocessor. The Secret Key (SK) is distributed with associated mobile clients by the coprocessor. On behalf of the mobile client, the coprocessor generates a message authentication code. Figure 2 shows the interaction among different entities:

The processes of uploading, insertion of block, deletion of block and verification for integrity of files in the MCC are discussed by the authors. To upload a file in the cloud server, the mobile client creates an incremental Message Authentication Code (MAC_f) using SK.

$$MAC_f = \sum_{i=1}^{k} HMAC\left(F_i, SK\right) \tag{1}$$

where, MAC_f is the sum of increment message authentication codes, Fi represents the ith part of the file and k is the total logical partition of file. MAC_f is stored on local storage by the mobile client. The files are uploaded on the cloud server.

Insertion, deletion and updation operations on the uploaded file(s) are performed by the mobile client at any time. For insertion or deletion of the block at jth position of a file, the mobile client sends request to a cloud server for the file. The file is transferred to the trusted coprocessor and the mobile client by the cloud server. MAC_{cop} is reconstructed by the trusted coprocessor and sent to the mobile client.

Figure 2. Interaction among the mobile client, CSP and trusted processor

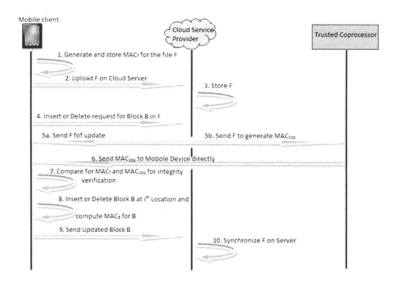

MAC_{cop} as well as the file is received by the mobile client from trusted coprocessor and cloud server respectively. The mobile client compares the stored MAC_f with MAC_{cop} for integrity verification. If he values of recalculated and received MACs are same, the integrity of the file is confirmed. When the integrity of the file is verified, the block at j^{th} location of the file is inserted or deleted by the mobile client. Then the value of MAC_f is recalculated using SK, old MAC_f and inserted or deleted blocks. For reducing communication overhead, only the location information and the updated block are sent to the cloud server to synchronize storage. The integrity of the files stored in the cloud storage can be verified by the mobile client. The process for integrity verification is initiated by the mobile client through sending of a request to the cloud server. After receiving the request the files are transferred from the cloud servers to the trusted coprocessor. The incremental authentication code for each message is computed by coprocessor and sent to the mobile client. To verify the integrity, the stored MAC_f and received MAC_{cop} needs to be compared by the mobile client.

Encryption Based Scheme (EnS)

The encryption based scheme is proposed by Ren et al. (2011). In this scheme, integrity checking as well as file encryption is carried out by Mobile Device (MD) itself. Three major entities or operators of MCC scenarios are:

1. **Mobile Device (MD):** MDs are the devices capable of wireless communication, storage and computing. Some examples of MDs are: wireless sensor node, tablet PC, smart phone etc.
2. **Cloud Server (CS):** CS generally offers computing and storage services to the clients. This scheme considers storage service only. This service can further be divided into two categories: back-end CS and portal CS. MD directly accesses the back-end CS. On the other hand, portal CS accesses the back-end CS.
3. **User (U):** MD is manipulated by the user. There may be multiple users who desire to access the same data or file in CS. Data or file is the operated object both are denoted as F. A file is downloaded (uploaded) from (into) CS.

Uploading Process

The process for uploading is given as follows:

1. MD prompts to ask U to input a password before the file F is uploaded. The password is denoted by PWD.

Figure 3. Entities in mobile cloud computing

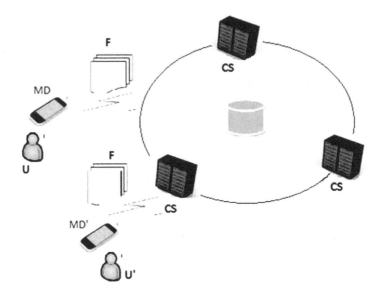

2.   MD creates integrity key IK = H(FN || PWD||FS) and encryption key EK= H(PWD||FN || FS), where H(.) is hash function, FS is the file size and H(.) and FN is the file name.

3.   F is encrypted by MD with EK as F′ = ENC(F, EK), where symmetric key encryption function is denoted by ENC(.,.).

4.   File integrity authentication code is generated by MD. It is denoted as MAC = {H(F, IK)}.

5.   MD sends {F′ || H(FN) ||MAC} to portal CS.

6.   MD stores T = ⟨FN⟩ locally and deletes EK and IK.

Downloading Process

The downloading process is as follows:

1.   Let MD desires to fetch F with the name FN. Then H(FN) is sent to CS by MD. CS searches in ⟨F′,H(FN),MAC⟩. Then it sends back {F′ ||MAC} that matches H(FN) to MD.

2.   U is asked to input corresponding PWD for the FN. This process is prompted by MD.

3.   MD creates integrity key IK = H(FN || PWD ||FS) and encryption key EK= H(PWD ||FN || FS), where FS is the size of F′, which has |F′ |=|F |= FS .

4.   MD decrypts out F = DEC(F′,EK), and checks whether MAC = H(F, IK) is held, where, DEC(.,.) is the symmetric key decryption function.

5.   If the values of calculated and received MACs are same, the integrity of the file is confirmed.

Provable Data Possession Scheme

The scheme is proposed by Yang et al. (2011). In this scheme, there are three main entities in the system model:

1.   **Mobile End-User:** The mobile end-user contains a Trusted Platform Model (TPM) chip. It stores data files into the cloud and expects to get trusted storage validation.

2.   **Trusted Third Party Auditor (TPA):** TPA is credible to the clients. In this scheme, it performs authentication tasks as well as encryption.

3.   **Cloud Storage Service Provider (CSP):** CSP provides storage services to the clients. The storage capacity of the CSP is very large. Proof of data possession can also be provided by the CSP when needed.

In case of mobile clients, the device's ability of computation and storage is very limited. But, mobile device can user TPM chip for producing and storing secret key. The TPA is located between the gateway of the IP network services and the mobile

Figure 4. System structure model

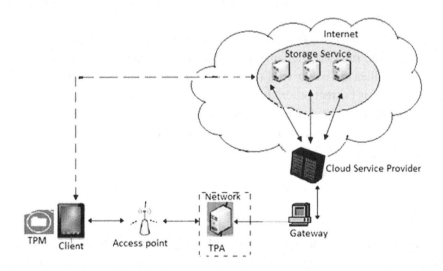

access point. The TPA is required to have limited storage space and high computing ability. The memory is used to only store a small part of information of the client and current session message. To provide services, the connection between TPA and the client should be secure. Using internet, the CSP provides redundant and high-capacity storage services. Generally, the CSP is malicious as well as unsafe entity. Which means, for some financial interests, the user's original data can be read, deleted or tempered. The proof of data possession can also be forged. There, encrypted files should be sent to the CSP. The scheme assumes that all the parties communicate through authenticated, reliable and secure channels.

Following functions are performed in this scheme:

- **KenGen(1k) → (pk,sk):** An initial secure parameter 1k is taken by this algorithm. It returns the private key sk and the public key pk. In this scheme, the keys are generated by the end-user and maintained in TPM chip.
- **Encapek(F) → F':** This algorithm is used by the TPA for encrypting the raw file F using the seal key ek and encoding it with erasure codes. the sealed file F' is returned.
- **SigGen_Clientsk (F') → Sigsk (H(R)):** End user runs this algorithm. The hash value of the root of the Merkle hash tree (MHT) is taken as input. The end user's signature is outputted as metadata.
- **SigGen_TPA(F') → Φ:** TPA runs this algorithm. Each of the data blocks {mi} of the sealed file F' is taken as input. The signature collection $\Phi = \{ \sigma_i \}$ on {mi} is outputted.
- **GenProof (chal,F', Sigsk(H(R)), Φ) → (P):** Storage server runs this algorithm. It takes the signature set Φ, the metadata signature, the stored file F' and the verification challenge message"chal" generated by TPA as input and returns the possession proof P.
- **Verify(P, chal)→ {TRUE|FALSE}:** Using the proof P returned from the server, the random challenge chal and some metadata of the end-user, the TPA verifies the integrity of the data file. If the output is TRUE, the integrity of the file is correct otherwise, integrity of the data is incorrect.
- **Decapdk(F')→F:** A request is sent by the end user to extract a file F. The corresponding sealed file F' is retrieved by the TPA. The the file F' is decoded and decrypted with the decryption key (dk) to get F. After that F is sent to end-user.

Setup

In this phase it is assumed that the remote identification with the TPA is completed by the TPM which resides in the end-user. A trusted communication channel is also set up.

- At first Diffie-Hellman key exchange is completed. After that, the TPA and the client share a symmetric key $g^{\alpha\beta}$.
- The original file F is encrypted using the key. The file is then sent to the TPA.
- On receiving the original file F from the client, the pair of asymmetric keys (ek, dk) are created by invoking KenGen(*), where (dk) is for decrypting the file and (ek) for encrypting the file.
- Using Encap$_{ek}$(F), the file is encrypted by TPA. Then it is divided into small blocks and encoded with erasure codes.
- H(R) is then calculated by TPA.
- After encrypting H(R) and dk with the shared key $g^{\alpha\beta}$, the TPA sends them to the client.
- The client signs H(R) using Singen_Client$_{sk}$(F'). Then it sends the signature of H(R) back to the TPA.
- The signature collection of each blocks of F' is calculated by the TPA using SinGen_TPA(F'). Then {Sigsk (H(R)), F', Φ} is sent to the cloud storage servers.

Integrity Verification

Following steps are executed for integrity verification:

- A verification challenge is sent from the TPA or the client to the cloud storage service provider (CSP).
- Based on the challenge, the proof of verification is computed by CSP. Then the CSP sends the proof of verification to the TPA.
- The TPA sends the result to the client after verification of the proof.

TPA generates the challenge message "chal". c random numbers are chosen in the set [1, N] by the TPA for constituting a sequence subset I . For each i∈I, the TPA chooses a random element vi∈Zp. The number i and the corresponding vi compose the challenge message sent to CSP. The CSP uses GenProof(chal, F, Sigsk (H(R)), Φ) for creating the proof after receiving the "chal". It contains the corresponding hash value H(mi) of the data blocks {mi} for every i∈I. In addition to that it also contains information Ωi to rebuild the root H(R) of the MHT.

File Retrieval

Before retrieving the file, through Diffie-Hellman key exchange protocol the TPA and the client negotiates to form a symmetric session key (Ks).

- After encrypting the decryption key (dk) using Ks, the client sends it to the TPA. Then the CSP is requested by TPA to extract the file F'.
- F' is sent to the TPA by the CSP.
- For getting the raw file F the TPA runs Decap$_{dk}$(F'). Then it sends F to the end-user using the secure communication channel.

Efficient and Secure Data Storage Operations for MCC

Based on Attribute Based Data Storage (ABDS) system and Privacy Preserving Cipher text Policy Attribute Based Encryption (PP-CP-ABE) Zhou et al. (October, 2012) developed a scheme for secure and efficient data storage operations. Encryption and decryption operations can be securely outsourced by lightweight mobile devices to the CSP using PP-CP-ABE.

Following entities are there in this scheme:

- **Data Owner (DO):** A sensor or wireless mobile device can be a DO. Storage service of the cloud is used by the DO.
- **Trust Authority (TA):** The responsibility of cryptographic key distribution lies on TA. It is very trusted.
- **Encryption Service Provider (ESP):** Without the knowledge of actual encryption key, ESP performs encryption of data owner's file.
- **Decryption Service Provider (DSP):** Decryption service is offered to the data owner by DSP. But it does not have any information about actual content.
- **Storage Service Provider (SSP):** Storage services are provided by the client by SSP. The ESP encrypts the file before uploading it on the cloud. Figure 5 shows the system model of the scheme.

Setup and Key Generation Phase

- **A Bilinear Map E:** G0×G0→G1 of prime order p having generator g is chosen by trusted authority to set up PP-CP-ABE. The public parameters are:

PK={G0, g, h=gβ, f=g1/β, e(g, g)α}.

where, α, β are randomly selected α, β∈ Zp. Master Key MK = (β, gα) is only known to TA.

Private Key (SK)= { D = g(α+r)/β ; for all j∈S: Dj=gr × H(j)ri; Dj=grj}.

Figure 5. System architecture

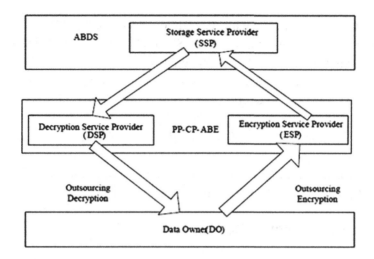

where, r∈ ZP and rj ∈ZP are randomly selected for each attribute j ∈S. SK is sent to Data Owner by TA using a secure channel.

Encryption Phase

For outsourcing encryption, a policy tree T=TESP ∧ TDO is defined by DO, Where, TESP and TDO are two sub trees and ∧ is logical AND operator. The data access policy controlled by DO is denoted by TDO. On the other hand, data access policy controlled by ESP is denoted by TESP.

- **ESP Produces Cipher Text:** CTESP = { y∈YESP: Cy = gqy(0), C'y= H(att(y))qy(0)}.

where, YESP is set of leaf nodes in TESP.

- DO computes CTDO = {y∈Y2: Cy = gqy(0), Cy= H(att(y))qy(0)}, Ĉ = M e(g, g)αs and C = hs, where the message is denoted by M. DO sends {CTDO, C, Ĉ } to ESP.

when ESP receives message from DO, it generates Cipher Text CT={T = TESP ^ TDO; Ĉ = M e(g, g)αs; C = hs ; y ∈ YESP U YDO: Cy = gqy(0), C'y= H(att(y)) qy(0)} and sends CT to SSP.

Decryption Phase

Following steps are carried out when decryption phase is executed:

At first, a private key is built by DO as SKblind= { Dt=gt(α+r)/β,$\forall$ j$\in$S: Dj = gr . H(j)rj,Dj=grj}. where, t$\in$ZP and Dt= gt(α+r) /β.

DO checks if the access policy tree is satisfied by its attributes. If no, DO sends request to SSP for the encrypted file else it sends SKblind to DSP.

- Now, SSP sends CT= { T; C = hs ; $\forall$ y $\in$ Y1 U Y2: Cy = gqy(0), Cy= H(att(y))qy(0)} where, CT' is subset of CT.
- When DSP receives SKblind and CT, decryption of the encrypted file is carried out and sent to DO. After that, DO can obtain the original message M.

A Framework for Secure Data Service in MCC

A secure data service has been proposed by Jia et al. (April, 2011) to outsource security and data to cloud in trusted mode. Through the secure data service the mobile users can share as well as move data into the cloud without disclosing any information. The proposed network model has three main entities: (a) cloud service provider, (b) data owner, and (c) data sharer. The network model is shown in Figure 6.

The files are shared by the data owner. Access is also granted by the DO. For data storage and retrieval both data owner and data sharer utilize the cloud storage service.

For achieving secure data service, identity base encryption and proxy re-encryption schemes are used. In proxy re-encryption scheme, the cipher text encrypted using A's public key is converted into another cipher text using B's public key by a semi trusted proxy. The bilinear mapping is used in identity based encryption scheme. A bilinear map can be defined as:

$$e: G_1 \times G_1 \rightarrow G_T \tag{2}$$

The bilinear map with the properties of non-degeneracy, computability and bilinearity is represeinted in Eq. (2). The G_1 and G_T are the multiplicative cyclic groups with prime order q and g is the generator of the G_1. The scheme uses two independent hash functions: H_1 and H_2.

$$H1: \{0, 1\}^* \rightarrow G1, H2: GT \rightarrow G1 \tag{3}$$

There are six phases in this scheme:

Figure 6. Proposed framework's network model

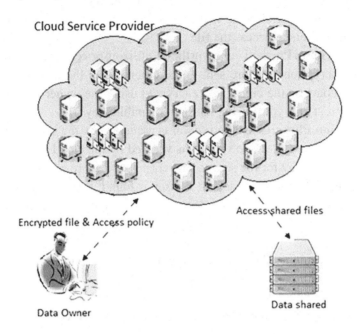

1. **Setup Phase:** During this phase, system parameters (G_1, G_T, g, g^s) as well as system Master Key (MK) is generated, where s $\in Z_q$ is randomly selected. The information about MK is by the authority only. The system parameters are public and disseminated among mobile users.

2. 2. **Key Generation Phase:** For obtaining SK mobile users need to register in the system. SK is computed based on H_1 and mobile users' identity using MK. Eq. 4 shows the computation of SK_{ID}.

$$SK_{ID} = H_1(ID)^{MK}, \text{ where } ID \in \{0, 1\}^* \tag{4}$$

3. 3. **Encryption Phase:** The file is divided into n chunks by the Mobile user. m_i represents each chunk. m_i is encrypted under owner identity (ID_{owner}) as a public key. The encryption under identity is known as identity based encryption.

$$EF = (g^r, m_i \cdot e(g^s, H_1(ID_{owner})^r)) \text{ where } 1 \leq i \leq n \tag{5}$$

Here, r $\in Z_q$ is selected randomly. The Encrypted File (EF) is then uploaded on the cloud server.

4. **Re-Encryption Key Generation Phase:** Re-encryption keys are generated by the mobile user after EF is uploaded. These keys are generated to enable authorized users to access the file.

5. **Re-Encryption Phase:** To encrypt the EF utilizing proxy re-encryption scheme, the re-encryption keys are sent to the cloud. Then the proxy re-encryption scheme converts the cipher text encrypted using the owner's public key into a cipher text encrypted using the sharer's public key.

6. **Decryption Phase:** The cloud server is requested by the sharer for obtaining the re-encrypted file. The validity is verified by the cloud after checking the re-encryption key for the sharer. The corresponding re-encrypted file is sent to the sharer by the cloud server, if a key is found. Because of the cipher text transformation, the file can be decrypted by the sharer without involving the data owner.

The scheme provides data privacy as well as access control. It has minimized the cost incurred for communication and updation of access policy.

Framework for Secure Storage Services in MCC

For ensuring the integrity and security of the mobile users' file stored in cloud server Hsueh et al. (June, 2011) proposed a scheme for smart phones. For authenticating the owner of the uploaded file the scheme has introduces an authentication mechanism. There are three modules in the framework: mobile device, cloud service provider, certification authority and telecommunication module. The interaction between different modules is shown in Figure 7.

Cloud service is utilized by mobile device. To authenticate the mobile user certification authority is responsible. The password and related information is generated and kept by the telecommunication module for using cloud service. It has been assumed that the Session Key (SK), Public Key (PK) and Secret Key (SK) are distributed securely among certification authority, telecommunication module and mobile devices. Using certification authority, a mobile user needs to register in the telecommunication module for using the cloud services. After successful registration, a Password (PWD) is issued for mobile device by the telecommunication module. The PWD is used by the mobile device for using cloud resources. The registration request can be represented as:

$$MD \rightarrow CA: E_{PK_T} E (MU, Num, TK)$$

$$U_N, S_{SK_{MU}} (H (MU, Num)), H(MU, Num) \tag{6}$$

Figure 7. Framework for secure storage

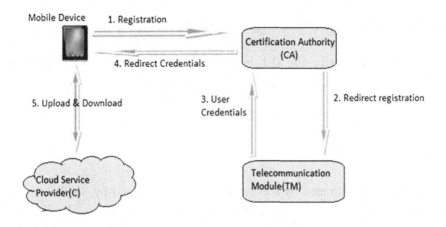

where, H represents a standard hash function, U_N is randomly generated number for the proof of identity, Num is the mobile user's number, MU represents the mobile user's name, TK represents the combination of the Num and PWD, $S_{SK\ MU}$ produces a signature for the mobile user using a cryptographic function on the passed value and SK of the mobile device and $E_{PK\ TM}$ represents encryption with the PK of telecommunication module. When the certification authority receives the message from the mobile device, using the received signature it validates the message authenticity. Following message is sent by the certification authority to the telecommunication module if the message is received from a valid user.

$$CA \rightarrow TM: E_{PK\ TM}\ (MU, Num, TK)$$

$$U_N, S_{SK\ CA}\ (H\ (MU, Num)) \tag{7}$$

Using S_{SKCA} the certification authority is authenticated by the telecommunication module. When the certification authority is authenticated successfully, the mobile user gets registered in the telecommunication module. The information of the mobile user is stored in the local database of telecommunication module. In the future, this stored information can be used for verification. The telecommunication module has the responsibility of generating PWD for the mobile user to access the resources. The mobile user's information is encrypted by telecommunication module using the mobile device's PK. This is done to securely deliver PWD to the mobile device. Again, TK is used to encrypt PWD again so that only authorized mobile user can decrypt the password. The encrypted information is forwarded to the mobile device by the telecommunication module through the certification authority.

$$TM \rightarrow CA: E_{PK\,MU}\,(MU, Num, U_N, ETK\,(PWD))$$

$$CA \rightarrow MD: E_{PK\,MU}\,(MU, Num, U_N, ETK\,(PWD)) \tag{8}$$

The file is encrypted using SEK by the mobile device. Then it is uploaded in the cloud along with S_{SKMU}, MU and PWD.

$$MD \rightarrow C: PWD, MU, ESEK\,(Data)$$

$$S_{SK\,MU}\,(H\,(MU \parallel SV \parallel ESEK\,(Data))) \tag{9}$$

where secret value created by the mobile device is denoted by SV. It is assumed that telecommunication module, cloud and mobile device know SV. The mobile device sends H(MU ∥ SV), MU and PWD to the cloud for downloading a file. Using SV and MU the hash value is regenerated by the cloud. The signature received is compared with the newly computed hash value to authenticate the mobile device's request. The cloud sends the signature as well as the encrypted file to the mobile device after authentication is successful.

$$C \rightarrow MD: E_{SEK}\,(Data), H\,(E_{SEK}\,(Data) \parallel SV) \tag{10}$$

The signature is verified by the mobile device. Then the file is decrypted using SEK. A secure file sharing mechanism is also introduced in this scheme. The mechanism is used to share the file between two users, A and B. The user B needs to inform A about PWD_B, Num_B and MU_B for accessing the file if it wants to share some file with A. On the basis of a signature stored with the encrypted file, the owner of the file can be authenticated by A when it is received from B. Through sharing mechanism, A can know B's secret information. The secret information of B can be used by A for impersonating B in future.

PROPOSED SCHEME

Limited processing power, storage and battery life are the primary limitations of mobile devices. For benefiting resource constrained mobile devices MCC has been introduced. Offloading more tasks to the cloud for saving the processing power and battery life is the main objective of MCC.

Offloading is carried out in this scheme to minimize the burden of the. In this scheme, all the encryption, decryption and integrity verification has been moved to a remote third party called third party auditor, which will perform all this on behalf of the mobile and will minimize the burden of the mobile device.

All the schemes already discussed above which uses the third-party auditor for the purpose of encryption and decryption as well as integrity checking of user's data, assumes that TPA is fully trusted one and the cloud service provider is untrusted. But as the TPA is also a third party and beyond the reach of owner of the data, so there is a chance that TPA can be curious about the user's data and can be dishonest also (Gupta et al., 2013). So, though TPA is trusted one, but we cannot consider it fully trusted.

So, if the TPA becomes dishonest, then what should be the way that can protect the user's data? For addressing this problem, a technique has been proposed in this section.

In this scheme the main objective is to make the whole data secret not only to the CSP, but also to the TPA. By user-side encryption this can be achieved. The mobile device (MD) will encrypt the file with password (PW) which will be provided by the user (U), and will send this encrypted data to the TPA through a secure channel. While receiving the data, MD will decrypt the data/file with the same PW. The only thing is that, the mobile device has to do the work encryption/decryption at the client side. As only the mobile device is the only one which is fully trusted, so it will be beneficial for us i.e. client side encryption/decryption. Nowadays, mobile phones are coming with high configurations according to their CPU, RAM and large battery life. So, it is possible for the mobile device to do this task easily.

After receiving the encrypted data, TPA will a perform encryption, decryption and integrity verification tasks over the data before uploading it to the cloud.

Secondly for integrity verification of user's data, in this scheme the size of the file has been considered. The idea behind considering the file size is that; If the data being changed or damaged or any unauthorized person does something with the intention to destroy the data (tempering), then the size of the data changes. Any deletion, modification, updation of the data affects the file size. So, this simple change can be a factor to check the integrity of data which have been proposed in this scheme.

Entities

In the proposed scheme three entities are used:

1. **Mobile Device (MD):** User utilizes the services offered by cloud through this. It performs encryption and decryption over user data through PW. It is a trusted one.

2.   **Third Party Auditor (TPA)**: Performs encryption, decryption and integrity verification over user data. Though it trusted one, but in this scheme, it is considered as semi trusted.

3.   **Cloud Service Provider (CSP):** Provides storage services to clients. It is responsible for operating, managing and allocating cloud resources. It is untrusted one.

Process

Data owner uses the mobile device to access the cloud. He/she then uses the mobile devices to store /retrieved files from the cloud. It has been assumed that the user has already completed the authentication tasks with the CSP. Whole process divided into two parts:

1.   Uploading process
2.   Downloading process

Uploading Process

The different steps during the uploading process has been described below:
   Steps:

1.   Mobile device first encrypts file with the password provided by the user. MD sends the encrypted file to the TPA.
2.   TPA calculates the size of the received file.
3.   TPA than calculates the hashes of the received file. This hash values will be used for integrity checking. Any changes in the data will change the hash value of the same file.
4.   TPA then encrypts the file and sends the encrypted file to the CSP.

Downloading Process

The different steps during the downloading process have been described below:
   Steps:

1.   User first requests for the intended file through TPA to the CSP.
2.   CSP sends the file to the TPA.
3.   TPA decrypts the file.
4.   For integrity verification TPA performs the following tasks:

    a.   TPA first calculates the size of the received file. If the file size is matched with the previously stored one

        i.   TPA calculates the hash of the received file and matches it with the stored one.

        ii.   If it matches then data integrity is maintained.

        iii.   Else then data integrity is not maintained

    b.   Else

        i.   Integrity of the file has been lost.

5.   After verification TPA sends the data to MD if its integrity is not lost.

6.   MD decrypts the file with the same password as provided by the user.

IMPLEMENTATION

For performance evaluation, the proposed scheme has been implemented through Java socket programming. The experiment has been carried out in the Computer Science & Engineering laboratory of Tripura University. Three PCs connected through LAN are considered in this experiment. One PC is marked as client and other two as TPA and cloud storage respectively. For simplicity, only the string type data has been taken as user data to implement the scheme. The string name has also been considered to be unique. The data is stored on the cloud with respect to the string name. In case of retrieval of data, the same name is used. A swing interface

Figure 8. Remote data integrity through third party auditor

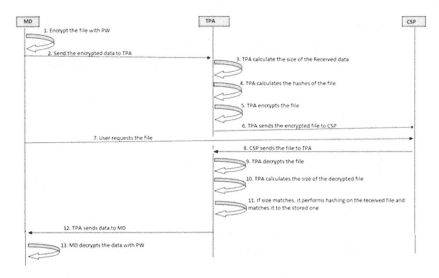

at the client side has been designed through which the client store and retrieves his data stored on the cloud.

For the client side, there is two processes:

1. **Data Store:** The user stores data with respect to a name.
2. **Data Retrieve:** The user requests his data to the cloud by the name.

The configuration of PCs is given as: Processor: Core i5 (2.6 GHz), Hard disk: 260 GB, RAM: 2GB (DDR 3), OS: Windows 7.

Following tables are used by different entities:

- **TTP Table:** TTP maintains a table for every user's data. TTP maintains a database of the fields which is necessary for the purpose of integrity checking of the data. The entities of the table are:
  ○ Name Size MD Key
  ○ Where,
  ○ Name is the unique name given to the data.
  ○ Size is the length of the data (String data).
  ○ MD is the message digest of the data and used an MD5 algorithm to generate the message digest of the user's data.
  ○ Key is the unique key used by the TTP to encrypt/decrypt the data. The TTP uses the key to encrypt the data before sending the data to the cloud and the same key to decrypt while retrieval.
- **Cloud Service Provider Table:** CSP also maintains a table to store the user data. The entities of the table are:
  ○ Name Data
  ○ Where,
  ○ Name is the unique name given to the data.
  ○ Data is the actual data of the user which is in encrypted from.

Figure 9. Simple scenario of the implementation

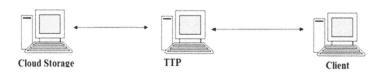

Cloud Storage   TTP   Client

RESULT AND COMPARISON

In the propose scheme there are two cases for the purpose of data checking, one is through the size of the data and another is the message digest of the data. Here for the string type of data the length of the message has been considered as size and for message digest the MD5 algorithm has been used which generates unique message digest for every unique data.

The data stored on the cloud is in encrypted from. Though the data is in encrypted from the data is not safe. The attacker can access the data and can do the following with the intension to modify, delete the data. If the attacker does the following, then there may be two cases:

1. The attacker can temper the data by deleting. The whole data or a part of the data.
2. The attacker can modify the data.

The solutions of two cases have been discussed.

Case 1

Suppose the data is "University" with the name UNIV. Table 3 shows the TPA table.
Table 4 shows the Cloud.

Here the attacker can modify the data by deleting the whole data or some of the characters of the data as seen Table 5.

If the attacker does so, the size of the data changes. Then the size will not match with the previously stored one and this will result an error that means the integrity

Table 3.

Name	Size	MD	Key
UNIV	21	ef03714edac9a27853b66cfcc21657b7	Key

Table 4.

Name	Data
UNIV	&Y|⌐ ¶♫E┼↑E8♀‼┐ ◀Y/⌐

Table 5.

Name	Data
UNIV	&Y|⌐¶8♀‼⌐ ◀Y/⌐

of the data has been lost. There is no need to run the MD5 algorithm to check the integrity of the message. The TPA then sends a message confirming that the integrity of the message has been lost.

Case 2

The attacker is somehow able to modify the data by maintaining the data size (see Table 6).

The characters of the above table have been replaced/modified like that: & -> A, 8 -> 9, Y -> Z

Though the size of the data remains same but the message digest of the data will not match with the previously stored one and it will result as an error and a message will be sent to the client confirming that the integrity of the message has been lost.

Time Comparison

In this scheme for the purpose of integrity verification at first the data/file size is considered. Then the message digest is considered. The size of any file is computed by the operating system automatically when it is created and any change in the file

Table 6.

Name	Data
UNIV	&Y|⌐¶♫E┼↑E8♀‼⌐ ◀Y/⌐

Table 7.

Name	Data
UINV	AY|⌐¶♫E┼↑E9♀‼⌐ ◀Z/⌐

also changes the file size. So, in the proposed scheme file size is calculated and stored in the database for the purpose of integrity verification.

Let the original file F and size of the file is S1. S1 is stored on the TPA's database. Let the file size is modified to F' and the size becomes S2.

Here, for integrity verification TPA simply calculates the S2 and matches it to S1. If S1≠S2 then integrity of the file is lost.

On the other hand, calculating message digest of any file is a complex process and it takes more time compared to calculating the file size. Any message digest algorithm goes through several rounds of interaction and so forth consumes more time. So, if we consider that time to generate the message digest of any file F is t1 and to calculate the length of the file is t2, then always t1>t2.

For example, time to calculate the MD5 of the data "My name is Avijit Das" is 71820664 ns (approx). But time to calculate the size (length) of the data "My name is Avijit Das" is 9938 ns (approx). That means, t1>t2.

Secondly, like the existing schemes, the proposed scheme also checks the integrity of the message considering message digest to counter the case when the file size remains same after modification.

Comparison

1. In energy efficient frame work for integrity verification, discussed in the related work section, it can be observed that the mobile device generates the MAC code of the data/file during uploading of the data to the cloud as well as during the downloading process. MAC code is stored in the local database of the mobile device. The burden on the mobile device is increased. Therefore, the mobile device needs to perform lots of task on the client's side (MAC code generation).

For retrieving the file a request is sent to the CSP. In response, the CSP sends one copy of file/data to the mobile client and the other to the trusted coprocessor (TC). The file's MAC code is then generated by TC. The MAC code is sent from the TC to the client. The client compares the previously stored MAC with the newly received MAC. In this way, also the burden of the mobile phone increases because it has to do all the integrity verification tasks.

But in this scheme instead of sending data twice to the mobile client and TC, the data is sent to the TPA first and then to the client after verification. The TPA does all the encryption, decryption and integrity verification tasks on behalf of the mobile device. This way it relieves the mobile device from the burden of all computations.

2.   In Encryption based scheme, it has seen that all the encryption, decryption as well as the integrity verification tasks are performed by the mobile device. The cloud simply stores the data and there is no third party in between. This way the burden of the mobile device increases.

But in proposed scheme offloads all of the tasks to the third party which is in between the client and CSP. The third party does all the encryption, decryption as well as integrity verification tasks while uploading and downloading the data from the cloud and thus relieves the mobile device from the burden of computations.

3.   The proposed scheme performs encryption as well as decryption with the help of a password (user given) at the mobile side considering that the TPA can also be dishonest some time and can lick the data also. Nowadays, the mobile phones are coming with much high configuration (smart phones, tablets, etc.). So, the task can be easily done at the client side for better security of the data.

CONCLUSION AND FUTURE WORK

MCC allows the user to get benefitted by the services offered by the cloud. Through MCC user of the mobile device can access his/her data stored on the cloud at anytime, anywhere if there is an internet connection. Users of the cloud are not aware of the physical location of their data on the cloud. As a result data security is the major concern of the cloud consumers. Customer do not want to lose their private information or do not want any change on their data without their permission as a result of malicious insiders in the cloud. So data integrity is the most important issue related to security risks of cloud as well as MCC. Data stored on the cloud may suffer from any damage occurring during transition from cloud to mobile, while residing on the cloud etc. So it is very essential to ensure the integrity i.e. correctness of the data. In this chapter a scheme has been proposed to solve the problem of data security specially data integrity. The proposed scheme has been implemented and its performance has been analyzed. The proposed scheme has been compared with some of the existing schemes. The future work remains as improvement of the scheme in more realistic way and to analyze the performance of the proposed scheme in a large network.

REFERENCES

Alizadeh, M., Hassan, W. H., Behboodian, N., & Karamizadeh, S. (2013). A brief review of mobile cloud computing opportunities. *Research Notes in Information Science, 12*, 155–160.

Chaturvedi, M., Malik, S., Aggarwal, P., & Bahl, S. (2011). Privacy & Security of Mobile Cloud Computing. *Ansal University Sector, 55*.

Chetan, S., Kumar, G., Dinesh, K., Mathew, K., & Abhimanyu, M. A. (2010). Cloud computing for mobile world. Retrieved from chetan.ueuo.com

Dinh, H. T., Lee, C., Niyato, D., & Wang, P. (2013). A survey of mobile cloud computing: architecture, applications, and approaches. *Wireless communications and mobile computing, 13*(18), 1587-1611.

Garg, P., & Sharma, V. (2013). Secure data storage in mobile cloud computing. *International Journal of Scientific & Engineering Research, 4*(4), 1154–1159.

Gupta, P., & Gupta, S. (2012). Mobile cloud computing: The future of cloud. *International Journal of Advanced Research in Electrical. Electronics and Instrumentation Engineering, 1*(3), 134–145.

Gupta, V., & Rajput, I. (2013). Enhanced data security in cloud computing with third party auditor. *International Journal of Advanced Research in Computer Science & Software Engineering, 3*(2), 341–345.

Hsueh, S. C., Lin, J. Y., & Lin, M. Y. (2011, June). Secure cloud storage for convenient data archive of smart phones. In *Proceedings of IEEE 15th International Symposium on Consumer Electronics (ISCE)*. (pp. 156-161). doi:10.1109/ISCE.2011.5973804

Huang, D., Zhou, Z., Xu, L., Xing, T., & Zhong, Y. (2011, April). Secure data processing framework for mobile cloud computing. In *Proceedings of IEEE Conference on Computer Communications Workshops (INFOCOM WKSHPS)*. (pp. 614-618). doi:10.1109/INFCOMW.2011.5928886

Itani, W., Kayssi, A., & Chehab, A. (2010, December). Energy-efficient incremental integrity for securing storage in mobile cloud computing. In *Proceedings of International Conference on Energy Aware Computing (ICEAC)* (pp. 1-2). doi:10.1109/ICEAC.2010.5702296

Jia, W., Zhu, H., Cao, Z., Wei, L., & Lin, X. (2011, April). SDSM: a secure data service mechanism in mobile cloud computing. In *Proceedings of IEEE Conference on Computer Communications Workshops (INFOCOM WKSHPS)* (pp. 1060-1065).

Khaba, M. V., & Santhanalakshmi, M. (2013). Remote Data Integrity Checking in Cloud Computing. *International Journal on Recent and Innovation Trends in Computing and Communication, 1*(6), 553–557.

Khan, A. N., Kiah, M. M., Khan, S. U., & Madani, S. A. (2013). Towards secure mobile cloud computing: A survey. *Future Generation Computer Systems, 29*(5), 1278–1299. doi:10.1016/j.future.2012.08.003

Khatri, T. S., & Jethava, G. B. (2012, November). Survey on data Integrity Approaches used in the Cloud Computing. *International Journal of Engineering Research and Technology, 1*(9), 1–6.

Mane, Y. D., & Devadkar, K. K. (2013). Protection concern in mobile cloud computing–a survey. *IOSR Journal of Computer Engineering, 3*, 39-44.

Qi, H., & Gani, A. (2012, May). Research on mobile cloud computing: Review, trend and perspectives. In *Proceedings of Second International Conference on Digital Information and Communication Technology and it's Applications (DICTAP)* (pp. 195-202).

Ren, W., Yu, L., Gao, R., & Xiong, F. (2011). Lightweight and compromise resilient storage outsourcing with distributed secure accessibility in mobile cloud computing. *Tsinghua Science and Technology, 16*(5), 520–528. doi:10.1016/S1007-0214(11)70070-0

Ruebsamen, T., & Reich, C. (2012). Enhancing mobile device security by security level integration in a cloud proxy. In *Proceedings of Third International Conference on Cloud Computing, GRIDs and Virtualization* (pp. 159-168).

Soyata, T., Ba, H., Heinzelman, W., Kwon, M., & Shi, J. (2013). Accelerating mobile cloud computing: A survey. In *Communication Infrastructures for Cloud Computing* (pp. 175-197). Hershey, PA: IGI Global.

Yang, J., Wang, H., Wang, J., Tan, C., & Yu, D. (2011). Provable data possession of resource-constrained mobile devices in cloud computing. *JNW, 6*(7), 1033–1040. doi:10.4304/jnw.6.7.1033-1040

Zhou, Z., & Huang, D. (2012, October). Efficient and secure data storage operations for mobile cloud computing. In *Proceedings of 8th international conference and 2012 workshop on systems virtualiztion management (svm), Network and service management (cnsm)* (pp. 37-45).

Zissis, D., & Lekkas, D. (2012). Addressing cloud computing security issues. *Future Generation Computer Systems, 28*(3), 583–592. doi:10.1016/j.future.2010.12.006

ADDITIONAL READING

Ali, M. (2009, December). Green cloud on the horizon. In *Proceedings of the IEEE International Conference on Cloud Computing* (pp. 451-459).

Buyya, R., Yeo, C. S., Venugopal, S., Broberg, J., & Brandic, I. (2009). Cloud computing and emerging IT platforms: Vision, hype, and reality for delivering computing as the 5th utility. *Future Generation Computer Systems, 25*(6), 599–616. doi:10.1016/j.future.2008.12.001

Cai-dong, G. et al.. (2010, November). The investigation of cloud-computing-based image mining mechanism in mobile communication WEB on Android. In *Proceedings of the 9th International Conference on Grid and Cooperative Computing (GCC)* (pp. 408-411). doi:10.1109/GCC.2010.85

Chen, Y. J., & Wang, L. C. (2011, September). A security framework of group location-based mobile applications in cloud computing. In *Proceedings of 40th International Conference on Parallel Processing Workshops* (pp. 184-190). doi:10.1109/ICPPW.2011.6

Chow, R., Jakobsson, M., Masuoka, R., Molina, J., Niu, Y., Shi, E., & Song, Z. (2010, October). Authentication in the clouds: a framework and its application to mobile users. In *Proceedings of the 2010 ACM workshop on Cloud computing security workshop* (pp. 1-6). doi:10.1145/1866835.1866837

Cuervo, E., Balasubramanian, A., Cho, D. K., Wolman, A., Saroiu, S., Chandra, R., & Bahl, P. (2010, June). MAUI: making smartphones last longer with code offload. In *Proceedings of the 8th International Conference on Mobile Systems, Applications, and Services* (pp. 49-62). doi:10.1145/1814433.1814441

Davis, J. W. (1993, May). Power benchmark strategy for systems employing power management. In *Proceedings of the International Symposium on Electronics and the Environment* (pp. 117-119). doi:10.1109/ISEE.1993.302825

Di Fabbrizio, G., Okken, T., & Wilpon, J. G. (2009, November). A speech mashup framework for multimodal mobile services. In *Proceedings of the 2009 International Conference on Multimodal Interfaces* (pp. 71-78). doi:10.1145/1647314.1647329

Dong, Y., Zhu, H., Peng, J., Wang, F., Mesnier, M. P., Wang, D., & Chan, S. C. (2011). RFS: A network file system for mobile devices and the cloud. *Operating Systems Review, 45*(1), 101–111. doi:10.1145/1945023.1945036

Doukas, C., Pliakas, T., & Maglogiannis, I. (2010, August). Mobile healthcare information management utilizing Cloud Computing and Android OS. In *Proceedings of Annual International Conference of the IEEE on Engineering in Medicine and Biology Society (EMBC)* (pp. 1037-1040).

Gao, H. Q., & Zhai, Y. J. (2010, October). System design of cloud computing based on mobile learning. In *Proceedings of 3rd International Symposium on Knowledge Acquisition and Modeling* (pp. 239-242).

Garcia, A., & Kalva, H. (2011, January). Cloud transcoding for mobile video content delivery. In *Proceedings of International Conference on Consumer Electronics (ICCE)* (pp. 379-380). doi:10.1109/ICCE.2011.5722637

Hoang, D. B., & Chen, L. (2010, December). Mobile cloud for assistive healthcare (MoCAsH). In *Proceedings of IEEE Asia-Pacific Services Computing Conference (APSCC)* (pp. 325-332).

Huang, D., Zhang, X., Kang, M., & Luo, J. (2010, June). MobiCloud: building secure cloud framework for mobile computing and communication. In *Proceedings of Fifth IEEE International Symposium on Service Oriented System Engineering (SOSE)* (pp. 27-34). doi:10.1109/SOSE.2010.20

Huerta-Canepa, G., & Lee, D. (2010, June). A virtual cloud computing provider for mobile devices. In *Proceedings of the 1st ACM Workshop on Mobile Cloud Computing & Services: Social Networks and Beyond*. doi:10.1145/1810931.1810937

Jin, X., & Kwok, Y. K. (2010, December). Cloud assisted P2P media streaming for bandwidth constrained mobile subscribers. In *Proceedings of 16th International Conference on Parallel and Distributed Systems (ICPADS)* (pp. 800-805).

Keahey, K., Tsugawa, M., Matsunaga, A., & Fortes, J. (2009). Sky Computing. *IEEE Internet Computing*, *13*(5), 43–51. doi:10.1109/MIC.2009.94

Koukoumidis, E., Lymberopoulos, D., Strauss, K., Liu, J., & Burger, D. (2011, March). Pocket cloudlets. In *Proceedings of the 16th International Conference on Architectural Support for Programming Languages and Operating Systems (ASPLOS)* (pp. 171-184).

Lagerspetz, E., & Tarkoma, S. (2010, March). Cloud-assisted mobile desktop search. In *Proceedings of 8th IEEE International Conference on Pervasive Computing and Communications Workshops (PERCOM Workshops)* (pp. 826-828).

Li, L., Li, X., Youxia, S., & Wen, L. (2010, October). Research on mobile multimedia broadcasting service integration based on cloud computing. In *Proceedings of International Conference on Multimedia Technology* (pp. 1-4). doi:10.1109/ICMULT.2010.5630979

Li, Y. C., Liao, I. J., Cheng, H. P., & Lee, W. T. (2010, December). A cloud computing framework of free view point real-time monitor system working on mobile devices. In *Proceedings of International Symposium on Intelligent Signal Processing and Communication Systems (ISPACS)* (pp. 1-4).

Liu, L., Moulic, R., & Shea, D. (2010, November). Cloud service portal for mobile device management. In *Proceedings of 7th International Conference on e-Business Engineering (ICEBE)* (pp. 474-478). doi:10.1109/ICEBE.2010.102

Nkosi, M. T., & Mekuria, F. (2010, November). Cloud computing for enhanced mobile health applications. In *Proceedings of IEEE Second International Conference on Cloud Computing Technology and Science (CloudCom)* (pp. 629-633). doi:10.1109/CloudCom.2010.31

Oberheide, J., Cooke, E., & Jahanian, F. (2007, August). Rethinking Antivirus: Executable Analysis in the Network Cloud. In *Proceedings of the 2nd USENIX workshop on Hot topics in security (HOTSEC)*.

Oberheide, J., Cooke, E., & Jahanian, F. (2008, July). CloudAV: N-Version Antivirus in the Network Cloud. In *Proceedings of the USENIX Security Symposium* (pp. 91-106).

Papakos, P., Capra, L., & Rosenblum, D. S. (2010, November). Volare: context-aware adaptive cloud service discovery for mobile systems. In *Proceedings of the 9th International Workshop on Adaptive and Reflective Middleware* (pp. 32-38). doi:10.1145/1891701.1891706

Rahman, M., & Mir, F. A. M. (2005, November). Fourth Generation (4G) mobile networks-features, technologies & issues. In *Proceedings of 6th IEE International Conference on 3G and Beyond* (pp. 1-5).

Samimi, F. A., McKinley, P. K., & Sadjadi, S. M. (2006). Mobile service clouds: A self-managing infrastructure for autonomic mobile computing services. In *Proceedings of the 2nd International Workshop on Self-Managed Networks, Systems, and Services* (pp. 130-141).

Satyanarayanan, M. (1996, May). Fundamental challenges in mobile computing. In *Proceedings of the fifteenth annual ACM symposium on Principles of distributed computing* (pp. 1-7). doi:10.1145/248052.248053

Stoer, M., & Wagner, F. (1997). A simple min-cut algorithm. *Journal of the ACM, 44*(4), 585–591. doi:10.1145/263867.263872

Subashini, S., & Kavitha, V. (2011). A survey on security issues in service delivery models of cloud computing. *Journal of Network and Computer Applications, 34*(1), 1–11. doi:10.1016/j.jnca.2010.07.006

Tang, W. T., Hu, C. M., & Hsu, C. Y. (2010, October). A mobile phone based homecare management system on the cloud. In *Proceedings of 3rd International Conference on Biomedical Engineering and Informatics (BMEI)* (pp. 2442-2445). doi:10.1109/BMEI.2010.5639917

Wang, S., & Dey, S. (2010, December). Rendering adaptation to address communication and computation constraints in cloud mobile gaming. In *Proceedings of Global Telecommunications Conference (GLOBECOM)* (pp. 1-6). doi:10.1109/GLOCOM.2010.5684144

Wang, S., & Wang, X. S. (2010, May). In-device spatial cloaking for mobile user privacy assisted by the cloud. In *Proceedings of Eleventh International Conference on Mobile Data Management (MDM)* (pp. 381-386). doi:10.1109/MDM.2010.82

Yang, X., Pan, T., & Shen, J. (2010, July). On 3G mobile e-commerce platform based on cloud computing. In *Proceedings of 3rd IEEE International Conference on Ubi-media Computing (U-Media), 2010* (pp. 198-201).

Ye, Z., Chen, X., & Li, Z. (2010, October). Video based mobile location search with large set of SIFT points in cloud. In *Proceedings of the 2010 ACM Multimedia Workshop on Mobile Cloud Media Computing.* (pp. 25-30). doi:10.1145/1877953.1877962

Zhao, W., Sun, Y., & Dai, L. (2010, August). Improving computer basis teaching through mobile communication and cloud computing technology. In *Proceedings of 3rd International Conference on Advanced Computer Theory and Engineering* (pp. V1-452-V1-454).

Zhenyu, W., Chunhong, Z., Yang, J., & Hao, W. (2010, August). Towards cloud and terminal collaborative mobile social network service. In *Proceedings of IEEE Second International Conference on Social Computing (SocialCom)* (pp. 623-629). doi:10.1109/SocialCom.2010.97

KEY TERMS AND DEFINITIONS

Certification Authority: Certification authority provides digital certificate. This digital certificate certifies the ownership of the public to a particular subject. This certificate allows others to rely on the signature of the subject done by using his private key. A certification authority is trusted by subject or the owner of the public key and the party which rely on the certificate.

Cloud Computing: It is the facility through which computing services such as software, networking, database and Storage are delivered to the users through the internet. Companies which are providing the services to the clients are known as cloud service provider. The users are charged by the cloud service providers based on the usage.

Cloud Service Provider: It is an organization that offers cloud computing based solutions and services to the customers. The services it can provide may be rented and maintained by the service provider. The services may be computation hardware, platform for hosting website or application software. Since cloud is scalable and cost effective the services of the cloud isare becoming increasingly desirable.

Data Security: The technique through which unauthorized access to websites, databases and computer gets prevented is known as data security. It also protects the data from corruption. It is very necessary for any organization of any size. It is a critical issue in case of cloud computing.

Mobile Device: It is a hand held device designed to be extremely portable. Using the services of the cloud, the users can perform large set of tasks through these hand held device.

Third Party Auditor: The primary role of Third Party Auditor (TPA) is to check periodically whether the CSP is complying to or deceiving from the service layer agreement. TPA can also perform the integrity check of the data stored in the cloud on demand of the user. It is an entity which acts on behalf of the client.

Chapter 8
Cloud Computing Technology for Green Enterprises

Prachi Chaturvedi
Madhav Institute of Technology and Science, India

ABSTRACT

Computing technology acting a very vital role in our day to day activities. Later the associated high volume of energy consumption has become a major concern every economically and environmentally. Green computing is associate rising application in computing effectively that leads to very important greenhouse gas reduction. In toughened computing has become an important half that has got to be thought of seriously by ordered generation data and communication technology designers. Green computing is to use computer and connected resources in atmosphere, friendly ways in which. Such practices embrace the implementation of energy-efficient central method unit (CPU), servers and peripheral any as finding innovative ways in which of reducing resource consumption and proper disposal of electronic waste. Many IT manufacturers and vendors endlessly invest in designing energy economical computing devices, reducing the use of dangerous material, and galvanizing the recyclability of digital devices and printing papers.

INTRODUCTION

The field of "green technology" encompasses a broad range of subjects — from new energy-generation techniques to the study of advanced materials to be used in our daily life. Green technology focuses on reducing the environmental impact of industrial processes and innovative technologies caused by the Earth's growing

DOI: 10.4018/978-1-5225-3038-1.ch008

population. It has taken upon itself the goal to provide society's needs in ways that do not damage the natural resources. This means creating fully recyclable products, reducing pollution, proposing different technologies in numerous fields, and making a middle of economic activity around technologies that profit the atmosphere. The massive quantity of computing factory-made worldwide contains a direct impact on atmosphere problems, and scientist's area unit conducting varied studies so as to scale back the negative impact of computing technology on our natural resources. A central purpose of analysis is testing and applying different non-hazardous materials within the products producing method.

HISTORY OF GREEN COMPUTING

In 1992, the U.S. Environmental Protection Agency launched Energy Star, a voluntary labeling program that is meant to push and acknowledge energy potency in monitors, climate management instrumentation, and different technologies. This resulted within the widespread adoption of sleep mode among shopper physics. The term "green computing" was in all probability coined shortly when the Energy Star program began; For a computer disposal, it's necessary to grasp everything there's to grasp so as to be concerned inexperienced computing. Basically, the full Green side took place quite an few years back once the news that the atmosphere wasn't a natural resources extremely move and other people started realizing that that they had to try and do their half to guard the atmosphere. Basically, the economical use of com putters and computing is what Green computing all is concerning. The triple bottom line is what's necessary once it involves something Green and therefore the same goes for Green Computing. This considers social responsibility, economic viability and therefore the impact on the atmosphere. Several businesses imply target a bottom line, instead of an Green triple bottom line, of economic viability once it involves computers. The thought is to create the full method encompassing computers friendlier to the atmosphere, economy, and society. This suggests makers produce computers in an exceedingly manner that reflects the triple bottom line completely. Once computers area unit sold-out businesses or individuals use them in an exceedingly Green manner by reducing power usage and doing away with them properly or utilization them. The thought is to create computers from getting down finishing a Green product.

BACKGROUND

Governments Go Green

Many governments worldwide have initiated energy-management programs, like Energy Star, a global commonplace for energy economical equipment that was created by thus Environmental Protection Agency in 1992 and has currently been adopted by many different countries. Energy Star reduces the number of energy consumed by a product by mechanically change it into ——sleep mode once not in use or reducing the number of power employed by a product once in ——standby mode. Amazing, standby——leaking, the electricity consumed by appliances once they area unit changed, will represent the maximum amount as 12% of a typical household's electricity consumption. In Australia, standby power may be a primary issue for the country's increased greenhouse emission emissions — quite five megatons (CO_2 equivalent) annually.

Green Computing

Green computing is that the study and follow of exploitation computing resources expeditiously. The goals area unit like green chemistry; that's cut back the utilization of unsafe materials, maximizes energy potency throughout the product's period, and promotes recyclability or bio-degradability of defunct merchandise and manufacturing plant waste. Taking into thought the popular use of knowledge technology business, it's to guide a revolution of types by turning Green during a manner no business has ever done before. Its price action that this Green technology should not be on the subject of sound bites to impress activists however concrete action and structure policy. Opportunities belongs Green technology like never before in history and organizations area unit seeing it as the simplest way to form new profit centers whereas making an attempt to assist the environmental cause.

In the arrange towards Green IT ought to embody new electronic merchandise and services with optimum potency and every one attainable choices towards energy savings. Modern IT systems rely on an advanced mixture of folks, networks and hardware; in and of it, a green computing initiative should be general in nature, and address progressively subtle issues. Components of like answer might comprise things like user satisfaction, management restructuring, restrictive compliance, disposal of electronic waste, work, virtualization of server resources, energy use, skinny shopper solutions, and come on investment (ROI). As twenty first century belongs to computers, gizmos and electronic things, energy problems can get a significant ring within the returning days, because the oral presentation on carbon emission, heating and temperature change gets hotter.

Taking into thought the popular use of knowledge technology business, it's to guide a revolution of types by turning green during a manner no business has ever done before (Info-tech, 2009; (Depavath Harinath, 2008). Green Computing is that the term accustomed denote economical use of resources in computing. This term typically relates to the utilization of computing resources in conjunction with minimizing environmental impact, maximizing economic viability and making certain social duties. Green Computing is extremely a lot of associated with different similar movements like reducing the utilization of environmentally unsafe materials like CFCs, promoting the utilization of utile materials, minimizing use of non-biodegradable elements, and inspiring use of property resources. One among the spin-offs of Green Computing is EPEAT or Electronic merchandise Environmental Assessment Tool. EPEAT merchandise serves to extend the potency and lifetime of computing merchandise. Moreover, these merchandise area unit designed to reduce energy expenditures, minimize maintenance activities throughout the lifetime of the merchandise and permit the re-use or usage of some materials.

The first manifestation of the Green Computing movement was the launch of the ENERGY STAR program back in 1992 and ENERGY STAR served as a sort of voluntary label awarded to computing merchandise that succeeded in minimizing use of energy whereas maximizing potency, so ENERGY STAR has been applied to products like monitors, TV sets and temperature management devices like refrigerators, air conditioners, and similar things. One of the primary results of Green Computing is that the Sleep mode perform of PC monitors that place a consumer's equipment on standby mode once a pre-set amount of your time passes once user activity isn't detected because the idea activity isn't detected because the idea developed, Green Computing began to cover skinny shopper solutions, energy accounting, virtualization practices, and E-Waste.

Green Computing Practices

Some common Green Computing practices embody turning off the monitor once it's not in use or exploitation a lot of energy economical monitors like LCDs rather than ancient CRT monitors, volunteer computing or file sharing practices, virtualization of servers, exploitation a lot of energy economical and fewer droning cooling systems (like exploitation liquid cooling systems rather than the traditional heat sinks and fans), temperature maintenance and regulation to scale back thermal shock wear and tear to pc components, and increased on-line security measures through the utilization of firewalls, anti-spyware and anti-virus programs to scale back the increasing quantity of E-Waste on the web and on different networks.

WHY GREEN COMPUTING?

In a world wherever business is transacted 24/7 across each potential channel obtainable, corporations ought to collect, store, track and analyze huge volumes of knowledge—everything from click stream data and event logs to mobile decision records and a lot of however this all comes with a price to each businesses and also the surroundings. Knowledge warehouses and also the sprawling knowledge centers that house them dissipate an enormous quantity of power, each to run legions of servers and to cool down them simply however much? A large sixty one billion kilowatt-hours of electricity, at associate degree calculable value of $4.5B annually (Info-tech, 2009). The IT business has begun to deal with energy consumption within the knowledge center through a range of approaches as well as the employment of a lot of economical cooling systems, virtualization, blade servers and cargo area networks (SANs). However a elementary challenge remains. As knowledge volumes explode, ancient, appliance central knowledge reposting approaches will solely still throw a lot of hardware at the matter. This can quickly negate any inexperienced gains seen through higher cooling or a lot of tightly packed servers. (Info-tech, 2009) to reduce their hardware footprint, organizations conjointly ought to shrink their "data footprint" by addressing what quantity server area and resources their info analysis needs within the initial place.

A mix of latest info technologies expressly designed for analysis of huge quantities of knowledge and reasonable, resource-efficient, open-source software system will facilitate organizations economize and become greener (Info-tech, 2009).

Organizations (Figure 1) will do therefore within the following 3 key areas: reduced knowledge footprint, reduced reading resources, and reduced in progress management and maintenance (Info-tech, 2009). This technology is useful as it:

- Scale back energy consumption of computing resources throughout peak operation Save energy.
- Throughout idle operation Use eco-friendly sources of energy.
- Scale back harmful effects of computing resources.
- Scale back computing wastes

Figure 1. Green computing design

Global warming and also the drawback of minimizing environmental impact from fossil-fuel emissions have raised to the highest of worldwide public policy agenda. As a result, businesses and customers alike have begun to embrace environmentally property merchandise that provide low-carbon solutions that may not solely scale back their international gas (GHG) emissions, however will do therefore by a lot of economical energy consumption and lower prices. Sensible readying of a lot of economical computing resources, beginning with Green PCs, has become a key focus for several businesses and customers trying to scale back their own energy consumption and carbon footprint. this is often fueled by a rise publicly awareness of the consequences of global climate change, recognition by businesses and customers that reducing energy usage will save prices and by government regulation covering everything from energy potency to power management and reduction of dangerous materials to e-waste disposal.

EXISTING WORKS IN GREEN COMPUTING

Today all manufactures corporations try to determine such knowledge center that area unit low cost and use low energy/power. In America in 1992 introduced an energy star program. Its main aim was given awarded to those computing merchandise that use minimum energy and provides most potency in its operating. In Energy star program were enclosed such product as laptop monitor, TV sets, white goods, Air conditioning and other physical science devices of these merchandise could also be friendly Green computing (Depavath Harinath, 2008).

EPEAT (Electronic merchandise Environmental Assessment Tool) check the product's normal. All products that area unit registered area unit higher to guard human health and these items will be simply upgraded and recycled. This merchandise has reduced the proportion of lead, mercury and metallic element. These merchandise area unit a lot of efficient in energy and scale back the environmental impact.

IBM additionally has additionally contributed these problems. IBM has helped the purchasers to buy the merchandise consistent with green computing. Consistent with the analysis of the IBM in 1990, He saved 4.6 billion KWh of electricity and additionally prevented 3 million metric tons of greenhouse gas emission.

Google is making an attempt to determine its knowledge Centre building on Oregon's river to faucet electricity power. Microsoft Company is additionally making an attempt to determine its knowledge Centre building close to Washington for electricity power money services company (HSBC) is making ready its building of information Centre close to Niagara Falls for cooling and low energy consumption. In knowledge centre the servers evolve an outsized quantity of warmth therefore for his or her cooling company establishes totally air-con equipment's. The lot of powerful instrumentation of servers and so a lot of cooling needed from warming and secure operating accurately. Consistent with the report of employee scientists Jonathan Koomey of Lawrence Berkeley National Laboratory and AMD that was free in 2005 to chill and power the servers one.2% of total USA electricity is needed. In 2010 consistent with Gartner the 2000 world companies can pay a lot of energy on knowledge centers on servers than hardware's of the computers. Kumar says that energy prices is currently 100% of the common IT budget of the planet can increase five hundredth in next few years. The percentage of greenhouse gas is increasing terribly quickly. The annual rise of the greenhouse gas in air is given in graph,

The graph shows that annual emission of greenhouse gas in past years, the black, blue and brown lines show the

rise of greenhouse gas owing to cool, fossil fuel and oil severally and therefore the line shows the whole emission of greenhouse gas including all such factors that additionally includes physical science.

If we tend to see the energy consumption throughout the particular use of the merchandise and through the standby mode, we tend to observe that in the standby mode the energy consumption quantitative relation is a lot of. e.g. Ink jet printer use twelve watts during use whereas printing and take five watts throughout idle state. Table 1 shows the facts and figure clearly.

Different physical science merchandise use completely different energy consumption. during this table it's seen that if we tend to switch off the merchandise

Figure 2. Annual rise of greenhouse gas in air
(Taruna, 2014)

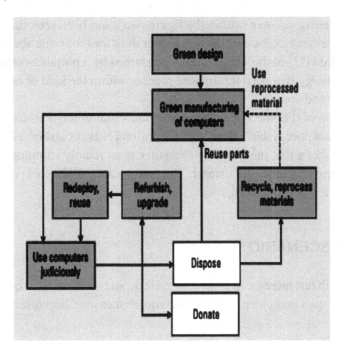

Table 1. The annual power wastage and price

Appliance	Hours per Day	Watt When on	Annual Cost of Use	Watt on Stand by	Annual Cost on Standby	% Wasted
TV	2	75	$ 7.12	14	$ 14.61	67%
VCR	1	15	$0.07	8	$9.07	99%
Computer	2	60	$5.69	13	$13.57	70%
Micro wave	25	1700	$20.17	24	$27.05	57%
Battery Charger	6	12	$ 3.41	10	$3.79	53%
Total cost			$ 49.36		$ 104.50	

(Priya Rana (2010))

once victimization, we will save an outsized quantity of energy which might be utilized different functions. By this way, we will decrease our budget annually and supply higher setting to the planet. Intel printed a report regarding green computing within which they showed that elements of laptop use energy especially monitor or show consumes an outsized quantity of energy.

If we tend to turn off of the portable computer once it's idle state. we will save energy and cash. The PC architecture try to line up such style within which show unit consume less energy/power. within the figure two it has been seen that in portable computer all elements consume energy however show unit consume abundant energy that is one third (1/3) of the whole energy consumed by a portable computer. Most a part of the energy is wasted throughout process within the kind of heat that is the loss of energy and sources.

In the on top of (Figure 3) it's cleared that show unit of the portable computer is intense abundant energy that's thirty third of the total energy consumed by a portable computer. It's been that the portable computer is incredibly stunning however its battery charging efficiency isn't smart. The performance of the CPU depends upon the battery of the portable computer.

PRESENT SCENARIO

These days with fast increase in technology, electronic merchandise square measure used for brief span and older merchandise square measure drop often. One reason

Figure 3. Power Consumption of average lap high
(Willium & Curtis, 2008)

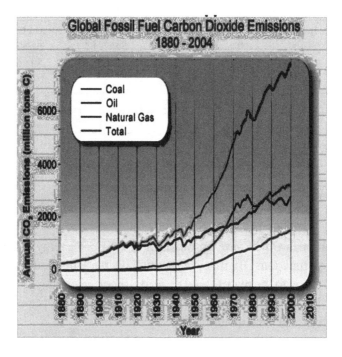

is replacement is way cheaper than repairing of electronic gadgets. in keeping with North American nation environmental protection agency several electronic products that don't seem to be in used i.e. regarding 3/4th in quantity were thrown away either drop in waste, unused, aggressive land i.e. Landfills or destroy by burning or exported to completely different countries like Asian countries.

If drop in unused lands, then the virulent chemicals made by this electronic product either unleash within the atmosphere or get combine into soil and water. In European countries measures are taken to forestall such style of electronic waste disposing. By burning chemicals like lead, mercury, cadmium-ashes square measure combining in air that is such a lot harmful that it unwell impact organic phenomenon. As, whereas burning PVC plastic that is gift in creating laptop and in several physical science elements produces dioxins and frame that once more is dangerous.

Another methodology followed by developing countries currently is to export their e-waste to developing countries usage that is happening over this electronic waste may be a smart factor, however a lot of that the unsatisfactory purpose is that the method the raw materials from this merchandise square measure processed and handled, which might hurt the employees World Health Organization square measure handling this merchandise whereas usage moreover as is harmful to surroundings.

The distinction between the usage method in developed and developing countries is that, in developed countries like Europeans elements, a number of the e-waste like plastics don't seem to be reprocessed to evade brominates furans and dioxins being discharged, whereas in developing countries there's no such steps condemned usage. During a survey of 2005, eighteen Europeans seaports were inspected and it's found that regarding 475 of e-waste was tried to export lawlessly. this is often conjointly a serious concern that violation of law of nations are happening to urge eliminate e-waste to such associate degree extent that in UK alone a minimum of twenty 3,000 metric tons was lawlessly shipped to Republic of India, continent and China (Taruna, 2014). In this method, in North American nation conjointly it's found that 50-80% of the waste ought to be used for usage in their country.

It is lawlessly exported, China tried to solved this major drawback by prohibition the import of e-waste, however these laws don't seems to be operating as still tones of e-waste is foreign lawlessly (Figure 4). A best example is GUIYA of GWANGDONG province, Republic of India conjointly facing this e-waste trade drawback. Several scrap yards may be seen in metropolis, Mumbai, Bangalore, Firozabad, Meerut, were thousands of employees square measure leading perished life as a result of they're thinking to earn for these days discarding the thought that what is going to happen to them tomorrow.

If they still board between dangerous chemicals. Now, why developed countries square measuring selling, exportation their e-waste in developing countries, answer is that the low value of usage. To recycle a glass of monitor in North American nation

Figure 4. Landfills due improper disposal of computers

it'll value ten times a lot of then in any developing countries, and why developing countries square measure mercantilism these e-waste answer is –recycling of this e-waste will extract substance like copper, nickel, iron, gold, silicon-by mercantilism these metals scraps recyclers will create cash.

It is cheaper to own the arduous labor of pull apart and melting down items done place aspect the country although which means the useless scraps and alternative dangerous materials can litter that space (Wikibooks, 2002). And in developing countries in contrast to developed countries laws, are in abdicate. individuals square measure taking job in their scrap yards as a result of it offers them tight wages to measure and infrequently kids square measure seizing their jobs, that square measure terribly dangerous for his or her health. Surroundings in developed countries is paying a lot of specialize in priority over the profit drawing specially in business and economy, and innovation in own hometown than social control of laws. It's not higher to ship developed countries electronic waste to alternative countries for disposal rather than- proper strategies ought to be created to recycle most element utilized in producing and usage of minimum dangerous chemicals and last although to dispose their e-waste, disposal should be complete 100% eco-friendly method.

It will be higher to use completely different chemical composition for brand new discovery in order that single chemical won't reside in atmosphere in abundance, as a result of the abundance presence of specific component will cause major dangerous effects.

One way that EU has adopted, that is kind of spectacular conjointly is- once producing associate degree instrumentality, manufacturer is accountable financially or physically for his or her instrumentality, until their survivability- that arises a competitive encouragement for corporations to set up greener merchandise (Wikibooks, 2002).

The strategies, operations that China, Republic of India and Islamic Republic of Pakistan has adopted- that's the e-waste usage and discarding square measure extraordinarily polluting and is extremely unhealthy for humans. Examples as well as open burning of plastic waste, exposure of virulent solders, stream selling of acids, and widespread general selling.

In developing countries stakeholders customers square measure probing for smart facility however cheaper product. In keeping with Basel Action Network administrator Jim Pockett- once associate degree electronic waste is taken for recycler, eightieth of that material is loaded in instrumentality ship, aiming to countries like Republic of India, China, Pakistan, wherever the worst happens to that (Wikibooks, 2002).

In developing countries stakeholders /customers square measure probing for heaper smart facility profitable product, once a budget word comes means that comprising with the weather utilized in the manufacture of product, as star merchandise square measure very little expensive however a lot of surroundings friendly ;this a good drawback as in developing countries versus developed countries price of currencies encompasses a large distinction that also plays a key role in selecting the merchandise, moreover as makes a good gap within the non-public sector businesses.

POLICIES IN DEVELOPED COUNTRIES

Many government programs round the world nowadays centered on environmental property, are exploring technology initiatives for reducing greenhouse gases. As an example, the ministry of science, technology and innovation, of Denmark's efforts for Green IT institution and another example is from the ministry of economy, trade and business of Japan- that established Green IT initiative, which give a robust model of Green innovation policy.

The two organizations people example USA Department of Energy (DOE) and therefore USA Environmental Protection Agency (EPA) has also initiated within the field of Green ICT. Technology is also necessary to in also necessary to Green innovation however strategic public policy is crucial. To encourage clean energy projects, the USA administrations has dedicated $71 billion US to scrub energy funding with a supplementary people $20 billion for loan assurance and tax input (Araya, 2010).

The temperature change at (2008) sets a wrongfully binding objective for diminish kingdom greenhouse gas emission by eightieth from 1990 levels by 2050 (Porritt, 2010).

In Australian Government's ICT property set up 2010-15 Tony Chan pointed plans and actions for the agencies to reduce their unharnessed (Chan, 2010).

The ROHS (Restriction of the utilization of bound venturesome Substances in Electrical and Electronic equipment) laws (directive 2004/95/EC), operative since thirteen February 2003, is marked because the initial law within the world that limits the utilization (2004/95/EC), operative since thirteen February 2003, is marked because the initial law within the world that limits the utilization of venturesome substances in electrical and equipment.

Six nephrotoxic substances are constricted: lead, mercury, cadmium, hexavalent atomic number 24, poly brominates biphenyls (PVV) and poly brominates diphenyl ethers (PEDS). For metallic elements, the most worth that is been set is 0.01%, that is Associate in Nursing exception case and for others it's been thought about the worth shouldn't exceed 0.1%.

The WEEE (Waste Electrical and electronic equipment) legislation (directive 2002/96/EC) has conjointly are available in force on thirteen February 2003.This regulation is regarding assortment, utilization and return of electronic merchandise. It's supported take back system wherever the used product will be came back by the shoppers that are freed from price and also the authority is given to the assembly team for managing e-waste properly (Hanne, 2011). Green grid pool may be a tremendous initiative. It is a world association of corporations devoted to developing and endorses standards, measuring methodology, processes and new technologies that lead to energy potency in information centers (The Green Grid, 2010).

POLICIES IN DEVELOPING COUNTRIES

In Kobenhavn summit, Republic of India has committed to reduce IT emission by 20-25% as compared to the 2005 emission levels. For Green Republic of India, Government of Republic of India, ministry of environment and forest (2011) has conjointly initiated few steps beneath National Action set up on Climate Change (NAPCC). They need projected tentative action set up for implementation of Green Republic of India mission throughout 2011 to 2012 (Kavita Suryawanshi, 2012).

To control Associate in nursing increasing downside in Africa, Safaricom has initiated Associate in nursing e-waste theme in African nation, in conjunction with African nation. In Africa, most of the utilization is finished on a straightforward go, casual, free basis typically in wild ungoverned dumpsites or landfills. The problem is that the majority African countries don't however have policies in situ to support the established of e-waste plants. Republic of Zambia alone has regarding ten million mobile users, the estimation is given by the Republic of Zambia info and Communication Technology Authority (ZICTA) that is that the regulator of states medium sector. Most of the countries are counterfeit devices from China that simply last many months and are disposal of carelessly. AS compared to different regions the usage of electrical Associate in nursing equipment isn't to it extent high however still it's increasing in an unpleasant part (Malakata, 2014).

MAIN PROBLEM AND ISSUES

As we all know that these days the most issue is that the manufactures are making ready such devices that are however additional economical and correct however they use additional energy and evolve terribly toxics, dangerous gases and chemicals. Several physical science firms particularly in pc use lead, mercury, metal and different toxics chemicals. It's been calculated that in producing of computers will four to eight pounds of lead alone.

According to a replacement analysis it's calculable that computers and different physical science devices form up two-fifth of all lead in land-fills on the planet. Thanks to this reason pollution is increasing terribly quickly. Information center servers use fifty times additional the energy per sq. ft. as in workplace. Information centers are the most energy consumption sources. In a survey in America energy consumed by information center in USA and every one over the globe are going to be doubled in next few years.

DISTINCTIVE FEATURES OF A GREEN COMPUTER

Green pc options facilitate in crucial whether or not the pc users obtain is actually green or not. Most computer makers have introduced a series of green PCs, however don't investigate the subsequent options to establish however green their computers are.

- **Low Use of Risky Elements:** Plenty of risky substances are utilized in the assembly of a pc starting from the additional deadly ones like metal, lead, chromium, and mercury to the comparatively less risky ones like flame retardants, pesticides, and chlorinated plastics. A Green PC parts ought to ideally be fully freed from these deadly substances; so IEEE environmental performance criteria needs the makers of green computers to expressly declare the share composition of those substances on the merchandise. As for the less risky substances, the main focus is on reduction of their use, since their elimination might not be fully doable.

- Energy potency is one among the options of Green Computers that pleases not solely the environmental enthusiasts however conjointly the budget-conscious purchaser. Each Green PC can have associate energy star rating on that, and therefore the additional the celebrities the additional energy economical the pare going to be. Some Green computers are accessible with the choice of running them on renewable energy like solar power that the makers can provide with all the desired accessories.

  - **Recycled Materials Used for Manufacturing:** A really Green PC can have most of its parts, particularly the plastic ones, made from recycled materials. So, the makers are needed to declare of recycled material utilized in the assembly of the PC and it ought to be with minimum thresholds at 10 percent. However, it's additional environmentally friendly to decide on a PC designed with quite twenty-five % of recycled material. Ideally, computer circuit boards are the sole things which will not contain recycled material.

  - **Finish of Life Recovery:** The Green computers are designed in such how that at the tip of their life their parts is simply reused, disassembled, or recycled. A minimum of sixty fifth of the components of the pc ought to be useful or reusable. Apparently, a number of the higher brands of Green computers guarantee a minimum of ninetieth reusable or useful components. Also, the components that are risky ought to be marked consequently for straight forward identification and skilled handling.

  - **Use of Renewable and Bio-Based Materials:** Another of the necessary inexperienced pc feature is that the accumulated use of renewable or bio-based materials. once more a minimum of 10% of such materials ought to be utilized in the production of the Green PC parts, and therefore the same should be declared.

  - **Longer Life:** Green computers are available standard and upgradeable styles with the thought of extending their life cycle. The makers are needed to produce a minimum of three years warrant or guarantee, and that they should conjointly ensure that the replacement components are going to be created accessible to all or any patron's up to a minimum of 5 years and this is often definitely an honest reason to shop for a Green PC.

  - **Finish of Life Take-Back Facility:** Each Green PC comes with a take back policy, whereby the manufacturer provisions to require back the pc at the tip of its life and provide the customer a replacement purchase at a competitive worth. Hence, it's obligatory to verify the complete of Green PC in shopping for or taking back.

○ **Manufacturer's Certification:** Before decide on a selected complete of inexperienced computers, should make sure that its manufacturer has ISO-14001 certification, that is that the clean minimum for a manufacturer to qualify as environmental policy compliant.

○ **Packaging Material:** More the question of the fabric utilized in useful packages too necessary. Therefore, checking the packaging material details is essential to check that the fabric used is totally non-toxic and a minimum of ninetieth of it's useful. It'll be even higher if the packaging is formed of recycled material.

○ **EPEAT Ratings:** Before creating the ultimate call of the acquisition slightly of analysis on WWW.epeat.net, wherever all Green computers and laptops are allotted a rating and. Clearly tell however green the pc is and with this the buyer can notice careful reports on however every of those computers score on the various environmental criteria.

WORK IN GREEN COMPUTING

Today computers play important role in our lives. Computers are the wealth of data of internet. It's in no time in communication and to share alternative peoples. These are its smart qualities however it takes plenty of energy to form, package, and store and move knowledge from one place to alternative once technology changes then the computer are drop during lowland. It's a significant downside and it produces pollution. Once Manufacturer Company prepares computers, then these use lead, cadmium, mercury and alternative cytotoxic materials. It's been calculable that four to 8 pound of lead alone is employed during a single pc. Computers and alternative physics create (2/5) of all lead in lowland, because of this reason it's realizing that Green PC ought to introduce. Within the starting in computers it had been given attention their speed, worth and price. However currently it's tried that these devices use less and less energy. Currently such material is developed that is a lot of green and cytotoxic material is exchange by them. It has been guessed that carbonic acid gas emission, heating and climate changes are becoming hotter to hotter. It is calculable that out $250 billion power per annum is spent within which V-day of that power is spent on computing. Faster processor use a lot of energy and slower or inefficient processor may additionally use double power that is that the wastage of energy in style of heat that produce pollution in the environment. The waste heat conjointly causes reliability issues in central processing unit because it might crash because of abundant temperature. Equally he facility offer that are used in PC are inefficient. It has been calculable that these are forty seventh of total offers. However currently power offer technology has been changed, as a result of it's accepted that each one components of pc rely upon power offer. That the economical and low energy consumption is introduced. Currently eightieth offer are a lot of economical. Software package that manage power are also facilitate the PC to sleep or log of or hibernate once computer isn't in use.

GREEN COMPUTING, PROBLEMS AND ADVANTAGES

1. In engineering virtualization is an incredibly vital effective tool. It's value effective, Green energy and efficient computing. During this tool the most servers is split into multiple virtual machines that facilitate the server to run completely different applications. By exploitation this system corporations will enhance their server utilization rates.

2. The businesses ought to manufacture such processors that use low energy. Intel, Sun and Advance small Devices (AMD) are currently attempting to manufacture such processor. Sun has designed multicore processors that are terribly economical regarding fuel.

3. In computers power choice setting is additionally useful, within which sleep mode is active, once the system isn't working. It's an honest follow. These features are often set through PC's control board. It takes PC's in standby mode and switch off the monitor, once laptop is in idle mode.

4. It's conjointly determined that flat monitor use less energy than electron beam tube (CRT) monitor. Liquid display (LCD) uses terribly low energy than typical monitor.

5. Disk drives take less power than alternative physical components of PC. Currently solid state drives as flash memory or DRAM is accustomed store knowledge. They take less energy as a result of they need no moving half, so the energy consumption could also be reduced as compared to the disk.

6. We must always use print paper only if we'd like. We will browse soft copy. If we wish textual matter (print copy), we ought to use such variety of printers that have the capability to print the paper each aspect. It reduces paper consumption and energy consumption. Recycled used ink in powder type and toner of the printer are often used again.

7. Screen savers are active once system is in idle state, if we have a tendency to permit the monitor to travel to standby mode throughout idle state of the PC. It'll conjointly decrease energy consumption.

8. PC manufacturer ought to design such a variety of pcs which might be battery-powered from non-typical sources of energy like Sun energy, air energy, pedaling a motorbike, turning a hand crank etc.

9. In pc some devices also are vital. Video card, graphic card, 3D performance software package take a really great amount of energy. If we have a tendency to use older video card, these cards use very little power. In these cards, there is not a heat sink or fan. Green Computing will facilitate United States of America to secure and safe place for United States of America within the world. If every person attempts to save the atmosphere, then our mother earth can healthy and happy for survival. Here are given some advantages of Green computing, it helps United States of America to scale back the quantity of pollution in air or close. It saves the facility consumption and reduces the quantity of warmth that evolved the merchandise. It conjointly reduces the pressure on paper trade that could be a main issue. Renewable resources are inspired to use once more Green Computing facilitate to market the effective utilization of natural resources. It conjointly promotes United States of America to avoid such merchandise that destroys green computing.

Figure 5. Green computing

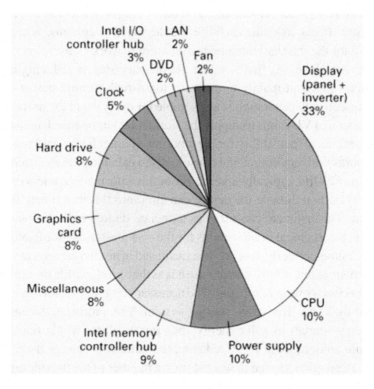

AN EXAMPLE OF VIA TECHNOLOGIES GREEN COMPUTING

VIA Technologies, a Taiwanese company that manufactures motherboard chipsets, CPUs, and alternative element, introduced its initiative for "green computing" in 2001. With this green vision, the corporate has been that specialize in power potency throughout the look and producing process of its merchandise. Its environmentally friendly merchandise area unit factory-made employing a vary of fresh computing ways, and also the company is endeavor to coach markets on the advantages of green computing for the sake of the setting, additionally as productivity and overall user expertise.

Carbon-Free Computing

One of the VIA Technologies' concepts is to scale back the "carbon footprint" of users — the number of greenhouse gases created, measured in units of dioxide (CO_2). Greenhouse gases naturally blanket the planet and area unit answerable for its additional or less stable temperature. A rise within the concentration of the most greenhouse gases – dioxide, methane, inhalation general anesthetic, concentration of the most greenhouse gases — dioxide, methane, inhalation general anesthetic, and fluorocarbons — is believed to be answerable for Earth's increasing temperature, that could lead on to severe floods and droughts, rising ocean levels, and alternative environmental effects, touching each life and the world's economy. When the 1997 city Protocol for the international organization Framework Convention on Climate amendment, the globe has finally taken the primary step in reducing emissions. The emissions area unit mainly a results of fossil-fuel-burning power plants. (In the us, such electricity generation is answerable for thirty-eight PC of the country's dioxide emissions.) VIA aims to supply the world's 1st laptop merchandise certified carbon free, taking responsibility for the amounts of greenhouse gas they emit. The corporate works with environmental consultants to calculate the electricity used by the device over its life, typically 3 years. From this information, one will conclude what quantity carbon dioxide the device can emit into the atmosphere throughout its operation. This estimate can serve as associate degree indicator, and also the company can pay regional organizations for the – sequestering, or offsetting, of the emissions. Counteractive dioxide are often achieved in numerous ways in which, one way is to plant trees that absorb greenhouse gas as they grow, within the region within which the processors were purchased. The necessary quantity of trees per processor is described by VIA's Tree Mark scoring system. VIA promotes the employment of such energy sources as solar energy, thus power plants would not go to bum the maximum amount fossil fuels, reducing the number of energy used. Wetlands conjointly offer a good service in sequestering a number of the dioxide emitted into the atmosphere through they create up solely four to PC of the Earth's terra firma, wetlands area unit capable of interesting twenty-five PC of the atmospheric dioxide. VIA is functioning closely with organizations answerable for protective wetlands and alternative natural habitats, et al United Nations agency support intensive use programs for ICT equipment. The numbers paid to those organizations are described by a proportion of the carbon free product's worth. Carbon-emissions management has been key issues for several corporations United Nations agency have expressed a firm commitment to property. Dingle could be a ideal of an organization with an inexperienced image, known for its free worldwide product-recycling program. Dell's Plant a Tree on behalf of me project permits customers to offset their carbon emission by paying an additional $2 to $4, counting on the merchandise purchased. AMD, a world chip manufacturer, is additionally operating toward reducing energy consumption in its merchandise, reducing on unsafe waste and reducing its eco-impact. The company's use of silicon-on-insulator (SOI) technology in its producing, and strained semiconductor capping films on transistors (known as dual stress liner technology), have contributed to reduced power consumption in its merchandise.

Solar Computing

Amid the international race toward alternative-energy sources, VIA is setting its eyes on the sun, and also the company's star Computing initiative could be a vital a part of its green-computing comes. For that purpose, VIA partnered with Motech Industries, one among the most important producers of star cells worldwide. Solar cells match VIA's power economical semiconductor, platform, and system technologies and alter the corporate to develop totally solar powered devices that area unit nonpolluting silent, and extremely reliable. star cells need little or no maintenance throughout their life, and once initial installation price area unit lined, they supply energy at just about no price. Worldwide production of solar cells has raised chop-chop over the previous couple of years; and as additional governments begin to acknowledge the advantages of solar energy, and also the development of electrical phenomenon technologies goes on, costs are expected to still decline. As a part expected to still decline. As a part of VIA's ——pc-1 initiative, the corporate established the first-ever solar-powered cyber civic center within the Pacific, powered entirely by star technology.

Quiet Computing

A central goal of VIA's green-computing initiative is that the development of energy-efficient platforms for low-power, small-form issue (SFF) computing devices. In 2005, the corporate introduced the VIA C7-M and VIA C7 processors that have a most power consumption of a pair of 0W at 2.0GHz and a median power consumption of 1W. These energy-efficient processors turn out over fourfold less carbon throughout their operation and may be expeditiously embedded in solar-powered devices. VIA isn't the sole company to handle environmental concerns: Intel, the world's largest semiconductor maker, disclosed eco-friendly merchandise at a recent conference in London. The company uses virtualization computer code, a method that allows Intel to mix many physical systems into a virtual machine that runs on one, powerful base system, so considerably reducing power consumption. Earlier this year, Intel joined Google, Microsoft, and alternative corporations within the launch of the Climate Savers Computing Initiative that commits businesses to fulfill the Environmental Protection Agency's Energy Star tips for energy-efficient devices. Kevin Fisher, Intel's EU standards director, says that whereas the corporate is devoted to its green-computing plans, it's vital to not blame the IT business alone for carbon emissions worldwide. He argues that the business conjointly helps in saving vast amounts of power thanks to the web, enabling, as an example, on-line looking and asking. Worldwide, standby power is calculable to account for the maximum amount as one PC of worldwide greenhouse emissions. Most of the energy utilized by merchandise on standby doesn't result any helpful perform. A small amount are often required for maintaining memory or an enclosed clock, remote-control activation, or alternative features; however most standby power is wasted energy. Energy Star–enabled merchandise minimizes this waste.

STEPS TO GREEN COMPUTING

1. Develop a property inexperienced computing set up. See the business leaders the weather that ought to be factored into such a concept, as well as structure policies and checklists. Such a concept ought to embrace utilization policies, recommendations for disposal of used instrumentation, government pointers and proposals for buying proposals for buying green PC instrumentation. Green Computing best practices and policies ought to cowl power usage, reduction of paper Consumption, in addition as recommendations for brand spanking new instrumentation and utilization recent machines. Organizational policies ought to embrace communication and implementation.

2. Recycle Discard used or unwanted equipment in a very convenient and environmentally accountable manner. Computers have poison metals and pollutants that may emit harmful emissions into the setting. ne'er discard computers in a very lowland. Recycle them instead through manufacturer programs like HP's Planet Partners utilization service or utilization facilities in your community. Or give still-working computers to a non-profit agency.

3. Create environmentally sound purchase choices. Purchase Electronic Product Environmental Assessment Tool registered product. EPEAT could be a procurance tool promoted by the non-profit-making in experienced physical science Council to:

    a. Facilitate institutional purchaser's measure, compare and choose desktop computers, notebooks and monitors supported environmental attributes.

    b. Give a transparent, consistent set of performance criteria for the planning of product.

    c. Acknowledge manufacturer efforts to scale back the environmental impact of product by reducing or eliminating environmentally sensitive materials, planning for longevity and reducing packaging materials.

4. Scale back Paper Consumption. There square measure several simple, obvious ways that to scale back paper consumption: email, electronic archiving, and use the ——track changes feature in electronic documents, instead of separate corrections on paper. after you do print out documents, make certain to use either side of the paper, recycle frequently, use smaller fonts and margins, and by selection print needed pages.

5. Conserve energy close up your pc after you understand you won't use it for associate degree extended amount of your time. Activate power management options throughout shorter periods of inactivity. Power management permits monitors and computers to enter low-power states once sitting idle. By merely striking the keyboard or moving the mouse, the pc or monitors awakens from its low power sleep mode in seconds. Power management techniques will save energy and facilitate shield the setting.

SUSTAINING THE LONGER TERM

- The greatest challenges for businesses making an attempt to be eco-responsible square measure very understanding what that basically means that, and then creating changes that square measure property over time, whereas adding business worth.

- Another challenge is leveling the requirements of assorted stakeholders United Nations agency every have completely differently ideas of what changes ought to be created. Some environment non- governmental organizations would really like sure flame retardants far from electronic product, whereas the fireplace safety community thinks. About removing or dynamical flame retardants in physical science. One drawback is that the substitute replacements square measure fairly new, they need not been essentially assessed with identical rigor applied to the first materials.

221

SOLUTIONS TO BE ADOPTED

As E-waste square measure originating day by day in developed countries and even turning into issues for everybody, thus currently it's time to scale back the impact of e-waste and to require a necessary steps towards Green Computing to create our surroundings clean and free from all this sort of nephrotoxic chemicals. One amongst the solutions concerning this be in and of itself the countries particularly focusing towards the developing countries should ought to undergo the policies strictly or to adopt this policy seriously that the govt. are secure.

The developing countries should conjointly avoid into take a waste from the developed countries at low cost. Victimization them for producing of another product that price them low cost as doing so. Another resolution may be with the contribution of voters in addition because the manufacturers/producers. The voters or customers may contribute towards this by creating their desirable option to buy those electronic products which might be recycled or it may be use and conjointly those that contains a less nephrotoxic chemicals.

In academic institutes create Green IT subject a required one instead of associate degree nonobligatory one, in order that new ideas may be developed by students, supported green IT and there upon on innovation during this field that would create product a lot of cheaper and fewer venturesome and may have the skills to draw in a lot of customers than traditional product. By introducing in academic establishments is that the solely thanks to invite a lot of project and ideas. Awards, scholarships ought to be created to extend a lot of and a lot of contribution during this field. Awareness among public is needed however what if cheaper healthy product square measure launched in market positively individuals can get drawn to get them. Like on each health venturesome product warning is come back same approach on electronic gadgets it ought to be written weather it's green product or not. Government ought to charge further tax on those corporation that aren't following Green ICT rules as well as not manufacturing green ICT product.

CONCLUSION

Green computing represents a accountable thanks to address the problem of worldwide warming. By adopting green computing practices, business leaders will contribute completely to setting stewardship—and shield the environment whereas conjointly reducing energy and paper prices.

REFERENCES

Araya, D. (2010). ICTs and the Green Economy.

Chan, T. (2010). Inside the Australian Govt. ICT sustainability plan 2010-2015.

Depavath, H. (2008). Emerging trends in Green IT.

Hanne, F. Z. (2011). Green IT: Why Developing Countries Should Care. *International Journal of Computer Science Issues*, 8(4).

Info-tech. (2009). Green IT: Why Mid-Size Companies Are Investing Now.

Malakata M. (2014). Safari.com to tackle Kenya's growing e-waste problem.

Porritt, J. (2010). Green IT a global benchmark".

Rana, P. (2010). Green Computing Saves Green. *International Journal of Advanced Computer and Mathematical Sciences*, 1(1), 45–51.

Suryawanshi, K. (2012). Green ICT implementation at Professional Education Institutions.

Taruna, S. (2014). Green Computing in Developed and Developing Countries.

The Green Grid. (2010). About the green grid. Retrieved from http:/www.the greengrid.org/about-thegreen-grid

Wikibooks. (2002). The computer revolution/computers and environment/disposal/recycling. Retrieved from http://en.wikibooks.org/wiki/The_Computer_Revolution/Computers_and_Environment/Disposal/Recycling

Williams, J., & Curtis, L. (2008). Green: The new computing coat of arms? *IT Professional Magazine*, 10(1), 12.

Chapter 9
Big Data Processing on Cloud Computing Using Hadoop Mapreduce and Apache Spark

Yassir Samadi
Mohammed V University, Morocco

Mostapha Zbakh
Mohammed V University, Morocco

Amine Haouari
Mohammed V University, Morocco

ABSTRACT

Size of the data used by enterprises has been growing at exponential rates since last few years; handling such huge data from various sources is a challenge for Businesses. In addition, Big Data becomes one of the major areas of research for Cloud Service providers due to a large amount of data produced every day, and the inefficiency of traditional algorithms and technologies to handle these large amounts of data. In order to resolve the aforementioned problems and to meet the increasing demand for high-speed and data-intensive computing, several solutions have been developed by researches and developers. Among these solutions, there are Cloud Computing tools such as Hadoop MapReduce and Apache Spark, which work on the principles of parallel computing. This chapter focuses on how big data processing challenges can be handled by using Cloud Computing frameworks and the importance of using Cloud Computing by businesses

DOI: 10.4018/978-1-5225-3038-1.ch009

INTRODUCTION

Cloud Computing and Big Data induce a major transformation in the digital use by all economic sectors companies. Related issues link the activity and job creation within the digital actors, and enable user companies to generate competitiveness gains. Nowadays, the enterprises and organizations are producing and storing data on large scale every day and the rate is dynamic by nature, mainly in the web and online social networks applications, such as Facebook, Twitter, and YouTube, to name a few. The quantitative explosion of digital data has forced researchers and developers to find new ways of seeing and analyzing the world. This is to discover new orders of magnitude concerning acquisition, searching, sharing, storage, analysis and presentation of the data. The main concern of Big Data (Gandomi & Haider, 2015) is storing a tremendous amount of information on a numerical basis that becomes difficult to process with conventional database management tools. Big data is not just data, it is also a set of technologies, architecture, tools and procedures allowing an organization to quickly capture, process and analyze large quantities of heterogeneous data, and extract relevant information at an affordable cost. The main challenges of data-intensive computing are analyzing and processing exponentially growing data volumes for different purposes in a minimum delay. Also, new algorithms which can scale to search and process massive amounts of data should be developed. Several solutions are available to deal with the requirements of Big Data. Among the proposed solutions, there are Cloud Computing tools such as Hadoop MapReduce and Apache Spark.

Hadoop Mapreduce is a framework that has mainly been used to store and analyze a large amount of data. Hadoop was designed for batch processing providing scalability and fault tolerance but not fast performance (Apache Hadoop, 2017). It enables applications to run in thousands of nodes with petabytes of data. Hadoop Mapreduce responds to the large amount of data by splitting up the data elements and assigns each element in a given cluster node for analysis. It follows a similar strategy for computing by breaking jobs into a number of smaller tasks that will be executed in nodes of the cluster. However, Hadoop's performance is not suitable for real-time applications (SAP Business By Design, 2017) because it writes and reads data from and to an external storage system, e.g., a distributed file system. This generates additional overheads due to data replication and input/output operations on a physical disk, which can increase the application's execution time. To solve this problem, Matei Zaharia has proposed a new framework called Spark (Zaharia, Chowdhury, Michael, & Shenker, 2010). Spark minimizes these data transfers from and to disk by using effectively the main memory and performing in-memory computations. Also, Spark is designed to cover a wide range of workloads such as batch applications, iterative algorithms, interactive queries and streaming.

Cloud Computing affirms the ability to scale computing resources as needed without a large upfront investment in infrastructure and with affordable cost. Therefore, Cloud Computing facilitates movement towards Big Data, linked to the need for greater computing capacity and storage of data flow from the increased use of new digital technologies. Consequently, Companies should continue to manage an exponential increase in the volume of generated data (structured, semi-structured or unstructured) and analyze as soon as possible to try to extract value. Cloud Computing and Big Data represent a rapidly developing field, providing many opportunities for value creation.

This chapter focuses first on integration of Big Data frameworks on Cloud Computing environment and the reason that enterprises should migrate their applications to the cloud. The chapter is organized as follows: Section II gives an overview of Cloud Computing and its architecture. Section III provides comprehensive review of Big Data and its classification. Section IV describes the relationship between Cloud Computing and Big Data. In section V, the authors focus on the current researches targeting the issues and challenges of Big Data storage and management for analytics. Section VI outlines the two Cloud computational frameworks Hadoop Mapreduce and Apache Spark. Section VII discusses the main advantages and benefits of Big Data processing in Cloud Computing for business. Section VIII provides a survey of some of the dominant solutions for Big Data related to Cloud Computing. Finally, authors draw the conclusion.

CLOUD COMPUTING BACKGROUND

Defining Cloud Computing

Cloud Computing can be defined as an emerging computing technology that uses the internet and central remote servers to the delivery of on-demand resources and services over the internet. It refers to the storage and access to data via the internet rather than via the hard disk of a computer. Cloud Computing allows consumers and businesses to use applications without installation and access their personal files at any computer with internet access (Borko, 2010).

The emergence of Cloud Computing has made a tremendous impact on the Information Technology (IT) industry over the past few years. Cloud Service providers are solely responsible for the management of infrastructure, constituted by several physical hardware and software (Sugam, 2016). They aim to provide more powerful, cost-efficient and reliable cloud platforms, where business enterprises seek to reshape their business models to gain benefit from this new paradigm. Indeed, Cloud Computing offers several benefits and features for business users and end users that make it attractive to business owners. Some of these benefits include self-service provision, elasticity, and pay-as-you-go. Self-service provision allows cloud consumers to access any on-demand computer resource. The elasticity offers the opportunity to increase or decrease the consumption of resources according to the needs of the enterprise. Finally, pay-as-you-go allows enterprises to pay only for resources consumed. Moreover, Cloud Computing reduces business risks and maintenance expenses by outsourcing the service infrastructure to the Cloud providers, a service provider shifts its business risks (such as hardware failures) to infrastructure providers (Zhang, Cheng, & Boutaba, 2010).

Cloud Services

Cloud Computing can be viewed as a collection of services. NIST (National Institute of Standards and Technology) defines three models of services for Cloud Computing as depicted in Figure 1 (Mell & Grance, 2011).

Software-as-a-Service (SaaS)

The customer is able to use the provider's applications remotely from the cloud, these applications are accessible from various client devices. SaaS gives clients complete freedom from managing and controlling the underlying cloud infrastructure and the entire software stack which enables them to concentrate on using the features of the service to achieve their business objectives. Examples of SaaS providers include Salesforce.com (Salesforce CRM, 2017), Rackspace (Web Hosting by Rackspace Hosting, 2017) and SAP Business ByDesign (SAP Business By Design, 2017).

Figure 1. Cloud Service Models (OPENSTACK FORMATION USER, 2017)

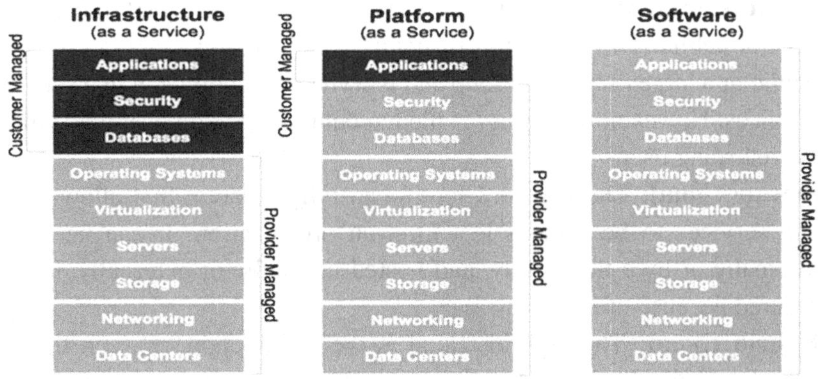

Platform-as-a-Service (PaaS)

The client has the ability to create and deploy on a Cloud PaaS infrastructure its own applications using the provider's languages and tools. PaaS provides a ready-deployed software stack that caters to the development and deployment of custom applications in a Cloud Computing environment. Furthermore, it enables developers to completely focus on application development by eliminating the need for developers to work at the image-level. Examples of PaaS providers include Google App Engine (Google App Engine, 2017), Microsoft Windows Azure (Windows Azure, 2017) and Force.com (Salesforce CRM, 2017).

Infrastructure-as-a-Service (IaaS)

It provides access to fundamental resources such as physical machines, virtual machines, virtual storage, etc. The consumer does not manage or control the underlying Cloud infrastructure but has control over storage, operating systems, and deployed applications (Stavrinides & Karatza, 2015). The consumer can also choose the main features of network equipment such as load sharing, firewalls, etc. Examples of IaaS providers include Amazon EC2 (Amazon Elastic Computing Cloud, 2017), GoGrid (CLoud Computing and Hybrid Infrastructure from GoGrid, 2017) and Flexiscale (Cloud Computing and Hosting, 2017).

Types of Clouds

Cloud Computing can be classified in terms of who owns and manages the cloud. There are four types of Cloud Computing as a common distinction including Public Clouds, Private Clouds, Hybrid Clouds and Community Clouds (Hai, Shadi, Tim, Wei, & Dachuan, 2010).

- **Public Cloud:** It allows systems and services to be easily accessible to general public. The Cloud infrastructure is rendered available to the general public or a large industrial group and is owned by a company that sells Cloud Services. However, the access is hidden behind the valid user credentials for the returning user.
- **Private Cloud:** The Private Cloud is an infrastructure that allows systems and services to be accessible within an organization. It can be managed internally or by a third party, and hosted internally or externally. It is more secured because of its private nature.
- **Hybrid Cloud:** The Hybrid Cloud is the intersection between the Public Cloud and the Private Cloud. Organizations can perform very important

tasks or sensitive applications on the Private Cloud, and use the Public Cloud for tasks requiring scalability of resources. Hybrid Cloud aims to create a unified, automated and scalable environment that leverages Public Cloud infrastructure while maintaining full control over data.

- **Community Cloud:** In a Community Cloud, the infrastructure of the cloud can be shared by several organizations that have similar requirements, thus increasing their scale while sharing the cost.

OVERVIEW OF BIG DATA

Definition

Big Data is the term for a collection of large amount of data that it becomes difficult to process using conventional database management tools or traditional data processing applications (Aarti & Anjali, 2015). Big Data is typically large volume of un-structured (or semi structured) and structured data that gets created from various organized and unorganized applications, activities and channels such as emails, web logs, etc. (Suren, Lambodar, & Santosh, 2015). Big Data (Hurwitz, 2013) is a combination of technologies which include data management that evolved over time. It supports enterprises to process, store, and analyze huge amounts of data at the correct speed and right time to gain the true insights. Big Data is also used in science, for scientific applications such as weather forecasting, molecular modeling, and genetic sequencing. Many of these applications require servers to run with tens of petabytes of storage. Big Data is arriving from multiple sources at an alarming velocity, volume, variety and value as shown in Figure 2.

- **Velocity:** This means how fast the data is being produced and how fast the data needs to be processed to meet the demand.
- **Volume:** Volume defines the amount of data. However, the literature does not specify a threshold. Some evoke a few terabytes while others grow to the petabytes. Data are characterized by Big Data when their processing with conventional databases becomes difficult.
- **Variety:** This means that the category to which Big Data belongs is also a very essential fact that needs to be known by data analysts. The data comes in a disorderly and non-predictable manner and it is structured, semi-structured and unstructured. This variety of data requires companies to use new equipment as well as new methods of collecting and analyzing such data.
- **Value:** Value corresponds to the monetary worth that an enterprise can derive from employing Big Data computing (Aarti & Anjali, 2015).

Figure 2. Properties of Big Data

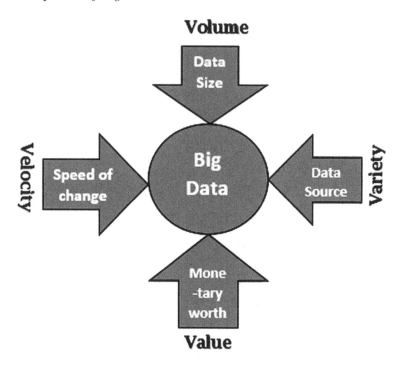

In summary, Big Data is required when the data has a large volume, multiple structures and demands real time processing.

Big Data Classification

It is helpful to look at the characteristics of the Big Data and to know how the data is collected, analyzed, and processed. Broadly, Big Data can be classified based on data sources, content format, data stores, data staging and data analysis. Once the data is classified, it can be matched with the appropriate Big Data pattern. Figure 3 shows a summarized view of the classification of Big Data with its respective classes (Hashem et al., 2015).

- **Data Sources:** Big Data Sources are repositories of large volumes of data. They are the location where the data that is being used comes from, such as web and social media, machine-generated, and human-generated, etc. Identifying all the data sources helps determine the scope from a business perspective. Figure 3 shows the most widely used data sources (Kiranjit & Bhabani, 2016).

Figure 3. Classification of Big Data based on five aspects
(Hashem et al., 2015)

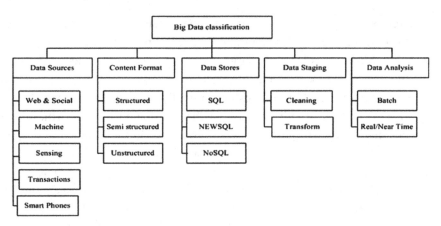

- **Content Format:** There are three types of data that need to be considered, namely structured, unstructured, and semi-structured. Format determines how the data needs to be processed and analyzed. Also, it is key to choosing tools and techniques and defining a solution from a business perspective (Kiranjit & Bhabani, 2016).
- **Data Stores:** Data Stores include enterprise data warehouses, operational databases, and transactional databases, such as SQL and NoSQL. This data can be typically structured or unstructured and can be consumed directly or transformed easily to suit requirements. Such data may or may not be stored in the distributed file system, depending on the context of the situation.
- **Data Staging:** Data Staging services use asynchronous methods for data extraction from compute nodes. Therefore, instead of blocking and waiting for data output to complete, they allow the application to overlap data extraction with its computational actions to reduce I/O overheads on applications' total processing times (Abbasi, Wolf, Eisenhauer, & Klasky, 2010).
- **Data Analysis:** Whether the data is analyzed in real time or batched for later analysis. The tools that consumers choose depend largely on what the purposes are for processing the data in the first place. Batch Processing is usually done on historical data, typically huge historical datasets. Real time processing refers to a type of processing in which the system imports and updates the data and at the same time produces results (Kiranjit & Bhabani, 2016).

RELATIONSHIP BETWEEN CLOUD COMPUTING AND BIG DATA

Big Data refers to large, heterogeneous, and often unstructured digital content that is difficult to process using conventional data management tools and techniques (Talia, 2013). Enterprises have had large volumes of data for decades. These data were mainly processed locally in data warehouses consisting of several structured databases. Gradually, the data sources have broadly diversified, and have become relatively heterogeneous. In addition, they have become mainly located on the internet. Another peculiarity is that this information is produced continuously with a sustained rate. In order to exploit these mines of information and data flows, significant computing capacities are required, often only available in large data centers. Most of the real-world scenario needs long-term storage or real-time analysis, or massive processing operations on the data. Big Data needs large on-demand compute power, distributed storage and high-level resources to deal with the 4V data problem. Cloud seamlessly provides this elastic on-demand compute and unlimited computing resources. Cloud Computing has emerged as a robust technology for complex and massive-scale computations that shifts the burden of maintaining the expensive computing resources and dedicated space from onsite clients to third party dedicated service providers (Sugam, 2016). Big Data uses distributed storage technology based on Cloud Computing rather than local storage attached to a computer or electronic device. Big Data is dependent on Cloud Computing for the flexibility that it provides. Hence, the processing of Big Data tools is facilitated in an adaptable environment to optimize analytical operations. Indeed, the union between Cloud Computing and Big Data becomes a good practice in the management of information systems. The reasons to use Cloud Computing for Big Data technology implementation are hardware cost reduction, processing cost reduction, and ability to test the value of Big Data. The major concerns regarding Cloud Computing are security and loss of control (Purcell, 2014). The use of Cloud Computing in Big Data is shown in Figure 4 (Hashem et al., 2015).

BIG DATA CHALLENGES AND ISSUES

In this section, authors discussed current research targeting the issue of Big Data storage and management for analytics. Thus, more information can be gathered from daily life. The top seven big data drivers are science data, finance data, mobile device data, internet data, sensor data, RFID data and streaming data (Ji, Li, Qiu, Awada, & Li, 2012). Big Data brings many attractive opportunities. At the same time, researches are also facing a lot of challenges (James, Bruce, Gabrielle, & Steve, 2011). When handling Big Data problems, difficulties lie in data storage,

Figure 4. The relationship between Cloud Computing and Big Data (Hashem et al., 2015)

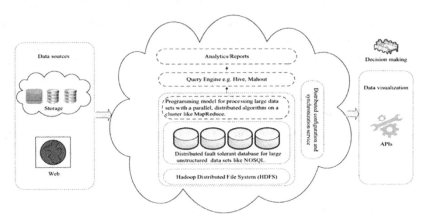

management and analysis. If those challenges cannot be surmounted, Big Data will become a gold ore. However, it will not be beneficial, especially when information exceeds the capability to deal with it (Philip & Chun-Yang, 2014). For marketing and research, many businesses use Big Data, but they may not have the fundamental assets, particularly from a management perspective. Some of the most common issues associated with Big Data includes but not limited to:

- **Big Data Storage and Management**: the quantity of data has exploded each time researchers have invented a new storage medium. Moreover, data is being created by everyone not just, as heretofore, by professionals, such as scientists and journalists (Stephen, Frank, Alberto, & William, 2013). Current disk technology limits are about four terabytes per disk (Stephen, Frank, Alberto, & William, 2013). Hence, they are not able to satisfy the needs of Big Data storage. Furthermore, traditional computer algorithms are not able to effectively store large volumes of information in a way that it can be timely retrieved due to the heterogeneity of the Big Data. Therefore, Big Data management will perhaps be the most difficult problem to address with regard to Big Data due to the increasing volume of the data generated by enterprises and organizations. There is a need to develop a data management ecosystem around these algorithms so that users can manage their data, enforce consistency properties over it and browse to understand their algorithm results (Avita, Mohammad, & Goudar, Big Data: Issues, Challenges, Tools and Good Practices, 2013).
- **Big Data computation and analysis**: in addition to storage, the other top Big Data challenge is analytics. Conventional data analytics applications cannot

well manage Big Data because of the huge volumes of data involved. These data are typically aggregated from multiple sources at different time points, using different technologies. This creates issues of heterogeneity, experimental variations and statistical biases (Fan, Han, & Liu, 2014). The type of analysis to be done on this huge amount of data, which can be unstructured, semi structured or structured requires a large number of advanced skills. To get useful information from large amounts of data, it requires having scalable analysis algorithms and tools to produce timely results. Moreover, the type of analysis needed to be done on the data depends highly on the results to be obtained, i.e. decision making (Avita, Mohammad, & Goudar, 2013).

DEALING WITH BIG DATA

Several traditional solutions have emerged for dealing with Big Data such as Distributed Computing, Parallel Computing, and Grid Computing. However, elastic scalability is important in Big Data which could be supported by Cloud Computing tools which are described in this section. Cloud Computing has several capabilities for handling Big Data challenges which are mentioned in the previous section including storing and computing of Big Data. Cloud computing provides a cluster of resources (storage and computing) that could be added anytime. These features allow cloud computing to become an emerging technology for dealing with Big Data (Mehdi & Mukesh, 2015).

Cloud Computational Frameworks

As mentioned before, one of the biggest challenges of the current Big Data landscape is the inability to process and analyze vast amounts of data in a reasonable time (Jorge, Oneto, & Anguita, 2015). An effective technique for Big Data processing is achieved through using Cloud Computing frameworks (Divyakant, Sudipto, & El Abbadi, 2011). Cloud Computing has intended to access large amounts of computing power by aggregating resources and offering a single system view. It is becoming a powerful architecture to perform large-scale and complex computing. Moreover, it has provided a scalable and cost efficient solution to the Big Data challenges (Ji, Li, Qiu, Awada, & Li, 2012). Conventional solutions generally require large investments (Furuta, Kameda, Fukuda, & Frangopol, 2004) in hardware and software. Instead, Cloud platforms, usually hosted by Cloud providers, such as Google, Amazon, and Microsoft, lease services at affordable prices to people and organizations according to their requirements (Carlyle, Harrell, & Smith, 2010). Furthermore, the rise of Cloud Computing and the growing requirement for processing and storing large volumes of data, resulted in the combination of Cloud Computing and Big Data. The Cloud Computing frameworks that have been discussed in this chapter are Hadoop Mapreduce and Apache Spark.

Hadoop

Hadoop (Lu, 2012) (Apache Hadoop, 2017) is an open source Java framework for distributed applications and intensive data management. It enables applications to work with thousands of nodes and petabytes of data. It was designed to respond to the needs of Big Data, both technically and economically. Hadoop is based on MapReduce programming model, which is developed for batch processing (Mavridis & Karatza, 2017). Hadoop is an Apache project improved and supported by companies such as Cloudera. Large datasets can be processed by using Hadoop across a cluster of servers and applications running on systems with thousands of nodes (Venkata, Sailaja, & Srinivasa, 2014). Hadoop offers great flexibility. Its performance changes almost linearly depending on the number of machines on the cluster. When speaking about Hadoop, the focus is mainly on HDFS (Hadoop Distributed File System) and MapReduce, the two most important components of Hadoop framework. In addition, the term is also used to refer to a set of related programs that are used for distributed processing of large-scale data, such as Hive (APACHE HIVE, 2017), Mahout (What is Apache Mahout?, 2017), Zookeeper (Apache ZooKeeper, 2017). Hadoop Distributed File System is the Hadoop component responsible for storing data in a Hadoop cluster. MapReduce is a programming model designed specifically to read, process and write large volumes of data. Hadoop is the representative of the related technology as shown in Figure 5. Obviously, Hadoop has distributed storage structure. It stores the data in similar devices that are independent from one another.

Hadoop Distributed File System

HDFS (Chitahranjan & Kala, 2013) is a file system designed for storing very large data sets reliably, and for streaming those data sets at high bandwidth to user applications. HDFS is the primary storage system used by Hadoop applications. HDFS (Nagele, 2013) is a file system written in Java, which executes on top of the file system that is used by the host machine. It stores metadata on a dedicated server called the NameNode, and applications data are stored on other servers called DataNodes. As illustrated in Figure 6, the files are separated into blocks of a fixed size and stored at different cluster nodes (HDFS Users Guide, 2017). HDFS is a master-slave architecture. According to this, each cluster consists of a NameNode

Figure 5. Hadoop cluster
(Apache Hadoop, 2017)

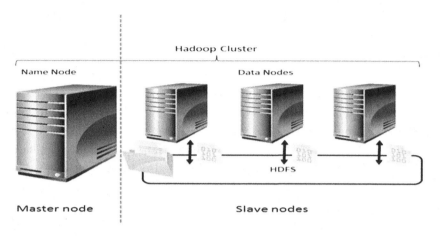

and a set of DataNodes. NameNode is a master server that manages the file system namespace and regulates access to files by the clients. Also, it effectively coordinates the interaction with the distributed DataNodes. The creation of a file in HDFS appears to be a single file, even though it blocks "chunks" of the file into pieces that are stored on individual DataNodes. DataNodes manage the storage attached to the hosting nodes. They also serve clients' requests for reading and writing functions on blocks after the NameNode's requests.

Figure 6. Hadoop Distributed File System architecture
(Hadoop HDFS, 2017)

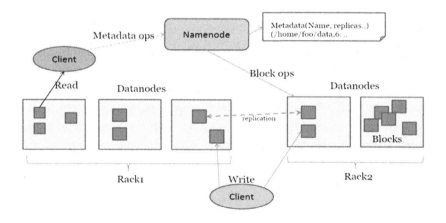

MapReduce

MapReduce is a software programming model introduced by Google. It writes applications that perform parallel processing of large amounts of unstructured and structured data in a reliable and fault-tolerant way across a cluster of thousands of nodes (Ahmed, Ismail, & Hyder, 2014). A MapReduce program consists of the Map phase and the Reduce phase (Dean & Ghemawat, 2008). In Mapreduce, the computation takes a set of input key/value pairs, and produces a set of output key/value pairs. The user of the MapReduce library expresses the computation as two functions: Map and Reduce. The Map phase takes input file and splits it into several Map functions; each Map function runs in parallel. This phase produces the output of intermediate (key, value) pairs. The Reduce phase takes all pairs for a given key and produces a new value for the same key, which is the same output of the MapReduce model (Dean & Ghemawat, 2008). Generally, the input and the output of each Mapreduce task are stored in a file-system. In addition, Mapreduce takes care of scheduling, monitoring and re-executing failed tasks. The MapReduce cluster consists of a master server called JobTracker and a number of slave servers called TaskTrackers. The JobTracker is responsible for assigning tasks and the TaskTracker is responsible for execution. Mapreduce task execution is composed of different steps. When a job comes into the MapReduce, it is split into small pieces of tasks that are run onto multiple DataNodes in a cluster. After that, the JobTracker coordinates the activity by scheduling tasks to run on different DataNodes and assigns subtasks to each TaskTracker (Samadi, Zbakh, & Tadonki, 2016). The TaskTracker executes each task individually and sends the progress report to the JobTracker. Moreover, the TaskTracker periodically sends heartbeat signals to the JobTracker so as to notify it of current state of the system. Thus, the JobTracker keeps track of the overall progress of each job. If the status of the job is changed to successful, the client polls the job and eventually notices that the job is finished. In case of task failure, the JobTracker can reschedule it on a different TaskTracker.

Spark

Apache Spark is an open source cluster-computing project that was created at AMPLabs in UC Berkeley in 2009 by Matei Zaharia and became open source as Apache project in 2010 (Sanjay, Howard, & Shun-Tak, 2003). Spark is a framework for high performance parallel computing designed to efficiently facilitate writing, and to improve the speed of the execution of Big Data applications that re-use data repeatedly (Zaharia, Chowdhury, Michael, & Shenker, 2010), such as supervised machine learning algorithms. It is based on the concept of maintaining data in memory rather than in disk as it is done by other frameworks such as Apache Hadoop that require data reloading and incur considerable latencies. Spark follows Hadoop and can operate independently (with HDFS on its file system), on Hadoop 2 (with YARN) or on Mesos.

Resilient Distributed Dataset

One of the main principles of Spark is the use of Resilient Distributed Datasets (RDD). An RDD (Zaharia, Chowdhury, Michael, & Shenker, 2010) represents a partition of the data that the user will use for his computations. This partition is stored on memory (RAM); thus, avoiding the system to make disk reads whenever data is needed for a computations. Indeed, this is the repeated disk reads that slow Hadoop. RDDs are fault-tolerant. In addition, they offer parallel data structures that allow users to persist explicitly the intermediate data in memory and control their partitioning in order to optimize the location of the data. Spark hides data partitioning by using RDD and distribution that, in turn allowed them to design parallel computational framework with a higher-level programming interface (API).

Spark Ecosystem

The components of Spark ecosystem are getting developed, and several contributions are being made every now and then. Primarily, Spark Ecosystem comprises four principle components that can be manipulated in Java, Scala and Python as shown in Figure 7. These components are built on top of Spark Core Engine (Lightning-fast cluster computing, 2016).

Figure 7. Spark Ecosystem
(Lightning-fast cluster computing, 2016)

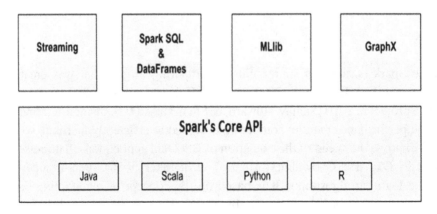

- **Spark SQL:** It can expose Spark data sets via the JDBC API, and can run SQL queries using BI tools and traditional visualization.
- **Spark Streaming:** It can be used for real-time processing of data flow. Spark Streaming leverages the fast scheduling capacity of Spark Core to perform streaming analytics by ingesting data in mini-batches.
- **Spark MLlib:** MLlib is a distributed machine learning framework above Spark, similar to Mahout. MLlib provides multiple types of machine learning algorithms, including classification, regression, clustering, and collaborative filtering. It also supports features such as model evaluation and data import.
- **GraphX:** It is the new API for the treatment of graphs including parallelization. It is similar to other widely used graph processing tools or databases, like Girafe and many other distributed graph databases.

Performance Comparison of Hadoop and Spark

Spark is generally faster than Hadoop by using its in-memory cluster computing that increases the processing speed of an application. Spark helps to run an application in Hadoop cluster up to 100 times faster in memory, and 10 times faster on disk. This is possible by reducing number of read/write operations to disk. Based on previous work of the authors (Samadi, Zbakh, & Tadonki, 2016) that compare the performance of Spark and Hadoop using Hibnech benchmarks, authors have concluded that Spark is more efficient than Hadoop to deal with a huge amount of data in major cases. However, Spark requires higher memory allocation, since it loads the data to be processed into memory and keeps them in caches for a while. So, Spark performance can be affected if the system does not have sufficient memory and could become slower than Hadoop. Therefore, if we do not have abundant memory and the speed is not a demanding requirement, Hadoop will be a better choice. Table 1 summarized the comparison between Hadoop and Spark.

SOLUTIONS FOR BIG DATA RELATED TO CLOUD COMPUTING

The discussion on the relationship between Big Data and Cloud Computing is complemented by reported solutions for Big Data related to Cloud Computing technology. A new category of Big-Data-as-a-Service (BDaaS) solutions is provided by multiple cloud providers such as Hadoop-as-a-Service and Spark-as-a-Service. Therefore, the deployment of Big Data applications on the cloud has many advantages compared to the deployment of these applications on virtual machines. Some of these advantages include rapid deployment and easiness of its integration, lower cost, availability and performance enhancement, etc. So, the deployment of

Table 1. Comparison of Hadoop and Spark

Features	Hadoop Mapreduce	Apache Spark
Language Support	Mostly Java	Supports Java, Scala, python and R
Language Developed	Java	Scala
Processing Speed	Map-Reduce processes data much slower than Spark	Spark processes 100 times faster than MapReduce, because of it is in-memory processing system
Iterative Processing	Does not support iterative processing natively	Spark iterates its data in batches. In Spark, for iterative processing, each iteration has to be scheduled and executed separately
Computation Model	Hadoop adopted batch-oriented model	Spark's core also follows batch model but has adopted micro-batching
Fault tolerance	Hadoop is highly fault tolerant	Spark Streaming recovers lost work and delivers exactly-once semantics out of the box
Cost	Hadoop can run on less expensive hardware as it does not attempt to store everything in memory.	As spark requires a lot of RAM to run in-memory, increasing it in cluster, gradually increases its cost.
Scalability	Hadoop has incredible scalability potential	Spark is also highly scalable
Easy to use	MapReduce developers need to hand code each and every operation	Spark is easy to program as it has tons of high level operators
Security	Hadoop supports Kerberos authentication	Spark only supports authentication via shared secret (password authentication)

Big Data frameworks as cloud services can perform parallel data processing in a distributed environment with affordable cost and reasonable time. In this section, authors provide a survey of some of the dominant Cloud Computing products for Big Data processing.

Amazon EC2

Amazon services include Amazon Elastic Compute Cloud (EC2) and Amazon Simple Storage Service (S3). Amazon EC2 is a web service platform that allows scalable deployment of applications by providing a web interface whereby a user can create virtual machines. The simple interface of Amazon EC2 Web service provides complete control of computing resources (Amazon Elastic Computing Cloud, 2017). Amazon EC2 provides scalable computing capacity in the Amazon Web Services (AWS) cloud. Using Amazon EC2 eliminates companies' needs to invest in hardware up front, so they can develop and deploy applications faster. S3 is an object-based, replicated storage service that supports simple PUT and GET operations on file-like binary object (Juve, et al., 2009). It provides storage through web services interface that can be used at any time, from anywhere on the web (Amazon Elastic Computing Cloud, 2017). S3 is supported by a several computer systems distributed across multiple data centers in the United States and Europe (S3-Europe). Furthermore, it offers low data access latency, infinite data durability, and 99.99% availability (Mayur, Adriana, Matei, & Simson, 2008).

Google App Engine

Google App Engine is a Cloud Computing platform which allows users to run and host their web applications on Google-managed data centers. These applications run across multiple servers and they are easy to build, easy to maintain and easy to scale whenever traffic and data storage needed (Zahariev, 2009). App Engine shares the available resources among multiple applications, but isolates the data and security between each application as well. The role of Google App Engine is to hide the functionality and complexity of Google's servers. The clients' requests are handled by the Load Balancer, which is responsible for distributing loads on the various fault-tolerant clusters. Google App Engine provides more infrastructure than other scalable hosting services such as Microsoft Azure. In addition, it also makes easier to write scalable applications by eliminating some system administration and developmental tasks.

Microsoft Azure Platform

Microsoft Azure, formerly known as Windows Azure, is Microsoft's public Cloud Computing platform. It designed by Microsoft to successfully deploy, and manage applications and services through a global network of data centers. The Microsoft Azure platform is considered as a service, which is an imperative component of a Cloud Computing platform. Microsoft Azure includes a larger set of integrated cloud services that developers and IT professionals use to create, deploy, and manage applications. Among these services, there are SQL Azure Database, SQL Azure Reporting, Content Delivery Network (CDN) and Windows Azure Connect (Zach, Jie, Ming, Arkaitz, & Marty, 2011). The platform also offers an analytics option and a new management function for deployment automation. The main purpose of developing Microsoft Azure is to minimize the overhead associated with the creation, distribution and upgrade of the Web applications. Table 2 summarizes the aforementioned examples of Cloud Computing platforms.

Table 2. Comparison of cloud computing platforms

Features	Cloud Provider		
	Amazon EC2	Google App Engine	Microsoft Azure
Classes of Utility Computing	Infrastructure service	Platform service	Platform service
Service Type	Virtual machine	HTTP(request/response)	Web role Worker role
Language Support	Almost all C/C++, JAVA, PHP…	Python only	.NET languages
Target Applications	General-purpose applications	Traditional web applications with supported framework	General-purpose Windows applications
Storage	RDBMS installed on AMI	DataStore API & GQL (Google Query Language)	ADO.NET Data Svc
Pricing	• $0.10 per CPU core-hour • $0.15 per GB-month of storage • $0.10 - $0.17 per GB outgoing BW • $0.10 per GB incoming BW	• $0.10 - $0.12 per CPU core-hour • $0.15 - $0.18 per GB-month of storage • $0.11 - $0.13 per GB outgoing BW • $0.06 - $0.11 per GB incoming BW	Depends on • Level of services • Resource consumption

MOVING DATA TO THE CLOUD

Cloud Computing has become increasingly popular as mechanism for sharing files, for data collaboration, for backing up or archiving data. But not everything should go to the cloud, and IT execs should consider carefully the strategy behind each cloud investment. Before moving data to the cloud, one has to consider the following factors:

- **Quality of Service Considerations:** One of the less obvious things that IT leaders should keep in mind is what performance and Quality of service should look like. Establish baselines in performance and speed of applications so that you can set in place the best strategy and SLA, and have a way to measure success.
- **Cost Considerations:** Not all cloud-based solutions follow a pay-as-you-use costing structure. First, organizations need to recognize the type of cloud services they are paying for. Infrastructure as a Service (IaaS) does not work in the same way as Software as a Service (Saas), etc.

- **Security Considerations:** It is important for businesses to choose a verified Cloud Service Provider before they surrender control of their intellectual property in order to prevent their companies from being on the wrong side of litigation. Preparation for security concerns should be undertaken at the beginning of any cloud strategy to ensure that the company's data is secure.
- **Reliability Considerations:** Before offloading data management to cloud, enterprises want to ensure that the cloud provides required level of reliability for the data services. Also, keeping a check on the accessibility and availability of cloud services can help enterprises decide the best suitable cloud service provider for their business.

BENEFITS OF CLOUD COMPUTING FOR BUSINESS

Currently, enterprises continue to grow larger and larger, not only in the number of employees, but in the number of departments and type of employees. In cases such as these, Cloud Computing solution can be the answer to all information technology (IT) requirements, providing all of the data storage, services and security that enterprises need, without having to invest in a very expensive local IT infrastructure (Manyikab, et al., 2011). Cloud Computing can be seen as a beneficial tool for businesses for several reasons as shown in Figure 8. Cloud Computing offers many benefits for enterprises to implement Big Data technology. It allows organizations to set up what is essentially a virtual office to give the flexibility of connecting to their business anywhere and anytime. In addition, Cloud Computing enables enterprises to benefit from competitive storage advantages in order to reduce costs and accelerate innovation by improving collaboration with partners and customers. More specifically, Cloud Computing brings three major benefits to businesses to use Cloud Computing for Big Data technology implementation.

- The costs of Data Centers and IT services can be reduced and established in proportion to usage. Depending on the amount of use, the costs will be more or less higher due to the rapid elasticity.
- Expenses and risk-taking for innovation can be greatly reduced through cloud computing. Thus, companies can take riskier bets and test more new ideas. New projects can be supported directly if they grow in scale, or abandoned if they fail. Scalability and elasticity provide companies new opportunities to try out new business ideas and develop them if they are relevant.
- Cloud Computing enables an enterprise to collaborate in a new way with its business partners. By developing shared workspaces within community clouds, employees of multiple companies can work together in a virtual

enterprise network as if they were working for one company. They all participate in the same value creation system, and share their information and computer resources.

The concept of Cloud Computing in business may sound ideal and easy to implement, but it has both positive and negative aspects like all new technology being introduced into a business that already has system and method in place. Thus, it is necessary to examine if these benefits and drawbacks are beneficial or detrimental to businesses when deciding whether or not to implement Cloud Computing (Abdulaziz, 2012).

GOOD BIG DATA PRACTICES

In addition to the Big Data challenges described in Big Data challenges and issues section, there are also some technical challenges such as the difficulty to deal with heterogeneous data and to maintain the quality of data during Big Data processing stage. To deal with these challenges, authors present in this section some good Big Data practices to be followed.

- Data quality needs to be better. Different tasks like filtering, cleansing, conforming, matching, and diagnosing should be applied at the earliest touch points possible.

Figure 8. Reasons for choosing the cloud by businesses
(Jutras, 2011)

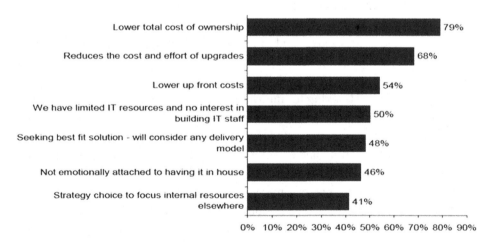

- Maximizing reporting performance by partitioning data to match its likely use and minimizing the number of records per object.
- When deleting large volumes of data, a process that involves deleting one million or more records, use the hard delete option of the Bulk API. Deleting large volumes of data might take significant time due to the complexity of the deletion process.
- Securing the Investment by putting the appropriate policies and tools in place to protect critical customer and corporate data.
- IT leaders and Business leaders should cooperate to produce more business value from the data. Collecting, storing and analyzing data comes at a cost. Business leaders will deal with it but IT leaders have to take care for many things like technological limitations, staff restrictions etc. The decisions taken should be revised to ensure that the enterprise is considering the right data to produce insights (Avita, Mohammad, & Goudar, Big Data: Issues, Challenges, Tools and Good, 2013).

CONCLUSION

This chapter surveys the state-of-the-art of Big Data and Cloud Computing, covering their essential concepts, prominent characteristics, key technologies as well as the issues and challenges of Big Data and solutions by using Cloud computational frameworks Hadoop Mapreduce and Apache Spark. The volume of data generated by modern applications is growing at a tremendous rate. This Big Data is being seen by businesses as a way of obtaining advantage over their competitors in such a way that if one business is able to extract relevant information at an affordable cost from these data, it will be able to get more costumers. Nevertheless, Big Data analytics has many challenges ranging from building storage systems that can accommodate these large datasets to collecting data from geographically distributed sources into storage systems to running several computations on data. To solve the aforementioned problems and to process and analyze this vast amount of data, there are many powerful Cloud Computing tools like Hadoop Mapreduce and Apache Spark, which are mainly used in the context of Big Data. With Cloud Computing as a new way to consume IT services, enterprises can be much more flexible and productive in utilizing dynamically allocated resources to operate.

REFERENCES

Aarti, A. G., & Anjali, D. (2015). Big Data Security Issues and Challenges in Cloud Computing. *Asian Journal of Convergence in Technology*.

Abbasi, H., Wolf, M., Eisenhauer, G., Klasky, S., Schwan, K., & Zheng, F. (2010). Datastager: Scalable data staging services for petascale applications. *Cluster Computing*, *13*(3), 277–290. doi:10.1007/s10586-010-0135-6

Abdulaziz, A. (2012). Cloud Computing for Increased Business Value. *International Journal of Business and Social Science*, *3*(1), 234-239.

Ahmed, H., Ismail, M., & Hyder, M. (2014). Performance Optimization of Hadoop Cluster Using Linux Services. In *Proceedings of the 7th IEEE International Multi Topic Conference: Collaborative and Sustainable Development of Technologies* (pp. 167-172). doi:10.1109/INMIC.2014.7097331

Amazon Elastic Computing Cloud. (2017, January 3). Retrieved from http://www.aws.amazon.com/ec2

Apache Hadoop. (2017, January 20). Retrieved from http://hadoop.apache.org

APACHE HIVE. (2017, February 10). Retrieved from http://hive.apache.org/

Apache Mahout. (2017, February 1). What is Apache Mahout? Retrieved from http://mahout.apache.org

Apache Spark Web site. (2016, December 28). Lightning-fast cluster computing. Retrieved from http://Spark.apache.org/

Apache Wiki. (2017, January 1). Apache Hadoop. Retrieved from http://wiki.apache.org/hadoop/

Apache ZooKeeper. (2017, February 9). Retrieved from http://zookeeper.apache.org/

Avita, K., Mohammad, W., & Goudar, R. H. (2013). Big Data: Issues, Challenges, Tools and Good. In *Proceedings of the International Conference on Contemporary Computing* (pp. 404-409).

Avita, K., Mohammad, W., & Goudar, R. H. (2013). Big Data: Issues, Challenges, Tools and Good Practices. In *Proceedings of Contemporary Computing (IC3)* (pp. 404-409).

Borko, F. (2010). Cloud Computing Fundamentals. In F. Borko & E. Armando (Eds.), *Handbook of Cloud Computing* (pp. 24–40). Boca Raton: Springer.

Carlyle, A. G., Harrell, S. L., & Smith, P. M. (2010). Cost-effective HPC: The community or the cloud? In *Proceedings of the IEEE International Conference on Cloud Computing Technology and Science* (pp. 169–176). doi:10.1109/CloudCom.2010.115

Chitahranjan, K., & Kala, K. A. (2013). A review on hadoop-HDFS infrastructure extensions. In *Proceedings of the IEEE Conference on Information and Communication Technologies* (pp. 132-137).

Cloud Hosting Web. (2017, January 3). CLoud Computing and Hybrid Infrastructure from GoGrid. Retrieved from http://www.gogrid.com

Data hadoop tutorial Web site. (2017, January 30). Hadoop HDFS. Retrieved from https://datahadooptutorial.blogspot.com/2016/11/hadoop-architecture.html

Chen, C. P., & Zhang, C. Y. (2014). Data-intensive applications, challenges, techniques and technologies: A survey on Big Data. *Information Science, 275*, 314–347. doi:10.1016/j.ins.2014.01.015

Ahrens, J., Hendrickson, B., Long, G., Miller, S., Ross, R., & Williams, D. (2011). Data-intensive science in the US DOE: Case studies and future challenges. *Computing in Science & Engineering, 13*(6), 14–24.

Dean, J., & Ghemawat, S. (2008). MapReduce: Simplified Data Processing on Large Cluster. *Communications of the ACM, 51*(1), 107–113. doi:10.1145/1327452.1327492

Divyakant, A., Sudipto, D., & El Abbadi, A. (2011). Big data and cloud computing: current state and future opportunities. In *Proceedings of the International Conference on Extending Database Technology* (pp. 530–533).

Fan, J., Han, F., & Liu, H. (2014). Challenges of Big Data analysis. *National science review, 1*(2), 293-314.

FlexiScale. (2017, January 5). Cloud Computing and Hosting. Retrieved from http://www.flexiscale.com

Furuta, H., Kameda, T., Fukuda, Y., & Frangopol, D. (2004). Life-cycle cost analysis for infrastructure systems: Life cycle cost vs. safety level vs. service life. In *Life-cycle performance of deteriorating structures: Assessment, design and management* (pp. 19–25).

Gandomi, A., & Haider, M. (2015). Beyond the hype: Big data concepts, methods, and analytics. *International Journal of Information Management, 35*(2), 137–144. doi:10.1016/j.ijinfomgt.2014.10.007

Ghemawat, S., Gobioff, H., & Leung, S. T. (2003). The Google file system. In *Proceedings of the 19th Symposium on Operating Systems Principles* (pp. 29-43).

Google. (2017, January 2). Google App Engine. Retrieved from http://code.google.com/appengine

Hadoop HDFS Web site. (2017, February 8). HDFS Users Guide. Retrieved from http://hadoop.apache.org/docs/r2.4.1/hadoop-project-dist/hadoop-hdfs/HdfsUserGuide.html

Hai, J., Shadi, I., Tim, B., Wei, G., & Dachuan, H. (2010). Cloud Types and Services. In F. Borko & E. Armando (Eds.), *Handbook of Cloud Computing* (pp. 356–376). Boca Raton: Springer.

Hashem, I. A., Yaqoob, I., Anuar, N. B., Mokhtar, S., Gani, A., & Khan, S. U. (2015). The rise of big data on cloud computing: Review and open research issues. *Information Systems, 47*, 98–115. doi:10.1016/j.is.2014.07.006

Hill, Z., Li, J., Mao, M., Ruiz-Alvarez, A., & Humphrey, M. (2011). Early observations on the performance of Windows Azure. *Scientific Programming, 19*(2-3), 121-132.

Hurwitz, J. (2013). *Big data for dummies*. Wiley Hoboken.

Inukollu, V. N., Arsi, S., & Ravuri, S. R. (2014). Security issues associated with big data in cloud computing. *International Journal of Network Security & Its Applications, 6*(3), 45-56.

Ji, C., Li, Y., Qiu, W., Awada, U., & Li, K. (2012). Big Data Processing in Cloud Computing Environments. In *Proceedings of the International Symposium on Pervasive Systems, Algorithms and Networks* (pp. 17-23). doi:10.1109/I-SPAN.2012.9

Jorge, L. R., Oneto, L., & Anguita, D. (2015). Big Data Analytics in the Cloud: Spark on Hadoop vs MPI/OpenMP on Beowulf. *Procedia Computer Science, 53*, 121-130.

Jutras, C. (2011). *QAD on demand gives manufacturers the tools they need to become global*. Aberdeen Research Group.

Juve, G. E., Deelman, K. V., Mehta, G., Berriman, B., Berman, B. P., & Maechling, P. (2009). Scientific workflow applications on Amazon EC2. In *Proceedings of the 5th IEEE International Conference on e-Science* (pp. 59-65).

Kiranjit, P., & Bhabani, S. P. (2016). Introduction to Big Data Analysis. In *Techniques and Environments for Big Data Analysis Parallel, Cloud, and Grid Computing* (pp. 11-30).

Lu, L. H. (2012). Assessing MapReduce for Internet Computing: A Comparison of Hadoop and BitDew-MapReduce. In *Proceedings of the 2012 ACM/IEEE 13th International Conference on Grid Computing* (pp. 76-84). IEE Computer Society. doi:10.1109/Grid.2012.31

Manyika, J., Chui, M., Brown, B., Bughin, J., Dobbs, R., Roxburgh, C., & Byers, A. H. (2011). *Big data: The next frontier for innovation, competition, and productivity.* McKinsey Global Institute.

Mavridis, I., & Karatza, H. (2017). Performance evaluation of cloud-based log file analysis with Apache Hadoop and Apache Spark. *Journal of Systems and Software, 125*, 133–151. doi:10.1016/j.jss.2016.11.037

Mehdi, B., & Mukesh, S. (2015). The Role of Cloud Computing Architecture in Big Data. In *Pedrycz* (pp. 275–295). Information Granularity, Big Data, and Computational Intelligence.

Mell, P., & Grance, T. (2011). *The NIST Definition of Cloud.* NIST Spec.

Microsoft. (2017, January 2). Windows Azure. Retrieved from http://www.microsoft.com/azure

Nagele, T. (2013). *MapReduce Framework Performance Comparison.* Radboud University Nijmegen.

Osones. (2017, January 26). Openstack Formation User. Retrieved from https://osones.com/formations/openstack-user.html

Palankar, M. R., Iamnitchi, A., Ripeanu, M., & Garfinkel, S. (2008). Amazon S3 for Science Grids: a Viable Solution? In *Proceedings of ACM International Workshop on Data-aware Distributed Computing* (pp. 55-64).

Purcell, B. M. (2014). Big Data Using Cloud Computing. *Journal of Technology Research*, 1-8.

Rackspace. (2017, February 5). Web Hosting by Rackspace Hosting. Retrieved from http://www.rackspace.com

Salesforce. (2017, January 8). Salesforce CRM. Retrieved from http://www.salesforce.com/platform

Samadi, Y., Zbakh, M., & Tadonki, C. (2016). Comparative study between Hadoop and Spark based on Hibench benchmarks. In *Proceedings of the 2nd International Conference on Cloud Computing Technologies and Applications (CloudTech16)* (pp. 267- 275).

SAP Business By Design. (2017, January 15). Retrieved from www.sap.com/sme/solutions/businessmanagement/businessbydesign/index.epx

Shau, S. K., Jena, L., & Satapathy, S. (2015). Big Data Security issues and challenges in Cloud Computing Environment. *International Journal of Innovations in Engineering and Technology, 6*(2), 297-306.

Stavrinides, G. L., & Karatza, H. D. (2015). A cost-effective and QoS-aware approach to scheduling real-time workflow applications in PaaS and SaaS clouds. In *Proceedings of the 3rd International Conference on Future Internet of Things and Cloud (FiCloud'15)* (pp. 231-239). doi:10.1109/FiCloud.2015.93

Stephen, K., Frank, A., Alberto, J. E., & William, M. (2013). Big Data: Issues and Challenges Moving Forward. In *Proceedings of the 46th Hawaii International Conference on System Sciences* (pp. 995-1004).

Sugam, S. (2016). Expanded cloud plumes hiding Big Data ecosystem. *Future Generation Computer Systems*, 59, 63–92.

Talia, D. (2013). *Toward cloud-based big-data analytics*. IEEE Computer Science.

Zaharia, M., Chowdhury, M., Michael, J., & Shenker, I. (2010). Spark: Cluster Computing with Working Sets. In *Proceedings of the 2nd USENIX conference on Hot topics in cloud computing* (pp. 10-10).

Zahariev, A. (2009). *Google App Engine*. Otaniemi: Helsinki University of Technology.

Zhang, Q., Cheng, L., & Boutaba, R. (2010). Cloud computing: state-of-the-art and research challenges. *Journal of Internet Services and Applications, 1*(1), 7–18.

Chapter 10
Anomaly Detection in Cloud Computing and Internet of Things Environments:
Latest Technologies

Rachid Cherkaoui
Mohammed V University, Morocco

Mostapha Zbakh
Mohammed V University, Morocco

An Braeken
Vrije Universiteit Brussel, Belgium

Abdellah Touhafi
Vrije Universiteit Brussel, Belgium

ABSTRACT

This chapter contains the state of the art of the latest security issues of cloud computing as well as security issues of internet of things (IoT) applications. It discusses the integration of IoT platforms with cloud computing services, security of the hosted data, intrusion and anomaly detection techniques used to detect attacks in virtualized networks. The chapter also discusses some of the lightweight anomaly detection techniques to use in integrated constrained devices' ecosystems with cloud computing environments. This chapter focuses on efficient integration of cloud hosting with IoT applications as well as integration of lightweight intrusion detection systems in the latter environments.

DOI: 10.4018/978-1-5225-3038-1.ch010

INTRODUCTION

Nowadays, cloud computing is a well-known term in scientific and professional domains. It is the main interest of many specialists in information and communication technologies. Foster et al. (2008) define cloud computing as "A large-scale distributed computing paradigm that is driven by economies of scale, in which a pool of abstracted, virtualized, dynamically-scalable, managed computing power, storage, platforms, and services are delivered on demand to external customers over the Internet". Cloud computing as defined by Mell and Grance of NIST (2011) is "…a model for enabling ubiquitous, convenient, on-demand network access to a shared pool of configurable computing resources (e.g., networks, servers, storage, applications, and services) that can be rapidly provisioned and released with minimal management effort or service provider interaction. This cloud model is composed of five essential characteristics, three service models, and four deployment models.", as shown in Figure 1. Cloud computing services are increasingly popular during the last years. These days, everyone uses cloud computing services when consulting an email service, social networks, academic applications, professional software, etc. Indeed, Forbes state that the "Worldwide spending on public cloud services will grow at a 19.4% CAGR from $70B in 2015 to $141B in 2019.". This grow shows the importance of this technology. Actually, cloud computing is very helpful to many fields like Healthcare, E-Commerce, Big data, Education and Research, etc.

Internet of things (IoT) is a new paradigm which interest a very large research community and IT professionals. IoT permits the users to gather data from sensors and many types of devices (mobile phone, phablets, sensors, computers, etc.) and send the data to servers or stations via internet. Figure 2 shows a simple architecture of IoT environments. Because the devices used in the IoT domain are in most cases

Figure 1. The five essential characteristics, three service models, and four deployment models of the cloud model based on definition of cloud computing by NIST

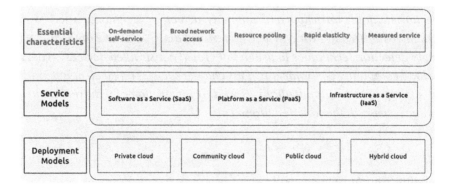

Figure 2. A simple IoT architecture

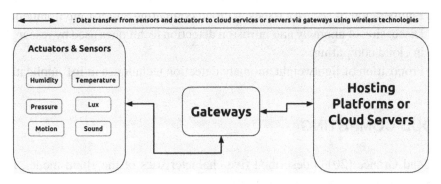

constrained which means they have less RAM and processing capacity, cloud computing is one of the best options for IoT applications when talking about hosting and organization of data. One of the residing issues in these environments is data hacking and compromising. If the data collected from IoT devices is modified without permissions, this could be very dangerous to some applications especially in the healthcare field where we are dealing with patients' data. For this, an intrusion detection and prevention system could be very good candidate for minimizing the risks of compromising and network attacks.

Intrusion detection and prevention is an area that interested many researchers for years. Intrusion detection in a computer network is an important element to the overall security of information systems. Intrusion prevention is even more important for critical systems such as those of the bank. Big Data and Cloud Computing technologies have created several advantages for the research community. Their ability to handle large volumes of data, storing them and extracting useful information from them are just some of the features of the said technologies. Unfortunately, attackers are also using the latest advances of these technologies for non-legitimate purpose, which leads to the growth of the number of specialists and researchers in the field of computer security to make more effort in order to minimize the risk of having their systems attacked. At the end of minimizing intrusions, intrusion detection systems (IDS) are among the most used. However, they are not fully integrated into cloud computing environments. The IDS is a very important component of information systems. The arrival of cloud computing and IoT technologies created a new field of research for the community. Intrusion detection and anomaly detection in integrated cloud computing environments and IoT are among the very interesting new fields of research.

Among the objectives of this chapter are the following:

- Description of cloud computing architectures.

- Description of the characteristics of IoT applications.
- Enumeration of security issues in cloud computing and IoT environments.
- Discussion of anomaly and intrusion detection techniques used by researchers in cloud computing.
- Proposition of lightweight anomaly detection techniques in IoT applications.

CLOUD COMPUTING

Mell and Grance (2011) described five characteristics of the cloud model, three service models and four deployment models.

Cloud Computing Characteristics

Among the characteristics of cloud computing we have the following:

- **On-Demand Self-Service:** Service provided by cloud vendors enabling the clients applications to provide cloud resources whenever they are required.
- **Broad Network Access:** Resources hosted in the cloud that are available online for access by heterogenous thin or thick client platforms (smart phones, tablets, laptops, etc.).
- **Resource Pooling:** A situation in which cloud providers serve multiple clients, customers or tenants with services (multitenancy).
- **Rapid Elasticity:** Capability to provide scalable services to the clients.
- **Measured Service:** The cloud provider measures or monitors the provision of services for effective use of resources or predictive planning.

Service Models

Many cloud service models exist nowadays, the main defined by well-known institutions are as follows:

1. **Software as a Service:** SaaS means the capability to consume the cloud provider's applications using a web browser or program interface. The client has limited user specific application configuration settings.
2. **Platform as a Service:** The cloud provider lets the consumer deploy his own developed platforms or those acquired. The consumer does not control the infrastructure (network, servers, operating systems, etc.), but has control on the configuration setting for deployed platforms.

3. **Infrastructure as a Service:** IaaS offers more control to the consumer to provision processing, storage, networks. The client can deploy his own operating system, control deployed platforms and in some cases, control some network components like firewalls.

4. **XaaS:** Stroud (2016) defines XaaS as anything-as-a-service, for the extensive variety of services and applications emerging for users to access on demand over the Internet as opposed to being utilized via on-premises means. Different XaaS exist: storage as a service, desktop as a service, disaster recovery as a service, Database as a service, etc.

Deployments Models

All cloud computing models use the Pay As You Go (PAYG) method which allow the end users or organization to scale, customize and provision computing resources, including software, storage and development platforms.

1. **Private Cloud:** The cloud infrastructure is provisioned for exclusive use by a single organization comprising multiple consumers (e.g., business units). It may be owned, managed, and operated by the organization, a third party, or some combination of them, and it may exist on or off premises.

2. **Community Cloud:** The cloud infrastructure is provisioned for exclusive use by a specific community of consumers from organizations that have shared concerns (e.g., mission, security requirements, policy, and compliance considerations). It may be owned, managed, and operated by one or more of the organizations in the community, a third party, or some combination of them, and it may exist on or off premises.

3. **Public Cloud:** The cloud infrastructure is provisioned for open use by the general public. It may be owned, managed, and operated by a business, academic, or government organization, or some combination of them. It exists on the premises of the cloud provider.

4. **Hybrid Cloud:** The cloud infrastructure is a composition of two or more distinct cloud infrastructures (private, community, or public) that remain unique entities, but are bound together by standardized or proprietary technology that enables data and application portability (e.g., cloud bursting for load balancing between clouds).

5. **Virtual Private Cloud:** This model is mentioned by less sources in literature, and it consists on using Virtual Private Network (VPN) connectivity to create virtual private or semi-private clouds, resorting to secure pipes supplied by VPN technology and by assigning isolated resources to customers (Fernandes,

D.A.B. et al. (2014)). A VPC is a particular case of a private cloud existing within any other. It allows entities to use cloud services without worrying about operating in shared or public environments.

INTERNET OF THINGS

Colina et al. define IoT as a complex network connecting billions of devices using a multi-technology, multi-protocol and multi-platform infrastructure. The main aim of IoT is to provide an intelligent environment which connect the physical, the digital and the virtual domains. The IoT environment provides more intelligence to many fields like transport, energy, smart cities, assisted living environments, etc. This intelligence resides in the capacity of collecting the data by sensors and analysis of the latter to extract more precise information which will be needed. Van Kranenburg, R. (2008) defines IoT as "...a dynamic global network infrastructure with self-configuring capabilities based on standard and interoperable communication protocols where physical and virtual 'Things' have identities, physical attributes, and virtual personalities and use intelligent interfaces, and are seamlessly integrated into the information network." Cisco (2011) states that the number of connected IoT devices will be increased by 50 billion in 2020. Indeed, many big IT companies like Ericsson predict a high increasing number of the IoT devices in the next years. By using IoT applications, the users will have more control on the situation. Good management of the electricity consumption in a smart house, early detection of heart attack by some monitors connected to the body, detection of lost keys and efficient management of the lights of the streets are just examples of the benefits of using IoT technology. As the number of persons using IoT devices increase, the data generated from the sensors, smartphones, tablets increase. The risks for getting hacked is increasingly important also. For these reasons, some security mechanisms should be integrated in the IoT environment. One of the important tools which will help to secure the network of the IoT ecosystem are intrusion and prevention systems.

INTRUSION AND ANOMALY DETECTION

Intrusion detection and prevention is a very interesting area of research which interested many researchers since many years ago. Besides firewall, an IDS is a tool that can help in the detection of attacks or anomalies happening in the computer network. It uses many techniques like artificial intelligence, neuron networks, etc. There are three types of intrusion detection systems:

- **Host Intrusion Detection System (HIDS):** Generally, it is a software capable of monitoring the host (computer, server, station) or the operating systems used by the host. This software could detect any change on the files like logs. A host-based intrusion detection systems as described by Ou, C.-M. (2012) consists of different agents installed on the system(s) for the aim of detecting intrusions by analyzing system calls, application logs, modifications on the file system and the activities and states of the host.
- **Network Intrusion Detection System (NIDS):** Gascon et al. define the NIDS as solutions that can monitor the network traffic in order to detect attacks on vulnerabilities and services.
- **Hybrid Intrusion Detection System:** This system mixes between techniques used by host based systems and network intrusion detection systems. In general, it is capable of monitoring the state of the network traffic and the state of file systems. For this reason, it uses agents which gather data from different parts either of the operating system and the network.

TECHNIQUES OF ANOMALY AND INTRUSION DETECTION SYSTEMS

Modi, C et al. (2013) Summarized the techniques used by the IDSs and the IPSs in the following:

- Signature based detection identifies intrusions by comparing the captured data with a preconfigured knowledge base. When dealing with known attacks, the detection rate using this technique is very high and the cost of computation is low. The drawback of the technique is the incapability of detection of new or variant attacks. Also, the false alarm rate for unknow attacks is high.
- Anomaly detection is Characterized by the use of statistics on profiles describing the normal state of the traffic (in general IPv4 or IPv6 packets). It has a lower false alarm rate for unknown attacks but it is limited as it needs more time to identify the attacks and the detection accuracy is based on the amount of collected features, profiles or behavior.
- Artificial neural network classifies the network packets with efficiency and especially with multiple hidden layers but requires more time and more samples during the training phase, also this technique is not flexible.
- Fuzzy logic is used when dealing with o lot of features quantitatively, it provides more flexibility to unknown problems. The accuracy rate of the latter is lower than artificial neural networks.

- Association rule detects known attack signatures or relevant attacks but it cannot detect unknown attacks, requiring many databases for scanning in order to generate rules for misuse detection.
- Support vector machine classifies intrusions if the sample data provided is limited. It can handle massive number of features. Its drawback is that it can only classify discrete features, requiring a pre-processing of them.
- Genetic algorithm has better efficiency and is used to select the best features for detection. The disadvantage of the latter resides in complexity and its usage in specific manner not general one.
- Hybrid techniques is a very efficient method which consists of mixing between the precedent cited methods and/or with new techniques. The only issue with this technique is the cost of computation which increases when mixing more than one technique.

Many IDSs and IPSs products exist for production and research purpose. Table 1 enumerates some of these products.

CLOUD COMPUTING SECURITY ISSUES

Cloud computing services suffer from security issues which could lead to service stop. Modi, C. et al. (2013) enumerate some of the security issues of cloud computing. Among the cited issues by the authors are the following:

- **Service Availability:** With the development of technology especially CPU and RAM technologies, attackers can collaborate and launch attacks on cloud systems and infrastructures which cause a DoS or a temporarily loss of the services.

Table 1. Example of open source and commercial intrusion and prevention detection systems

Name	Type	Open Source / Proprietary	Commercial/Free
Snort	NIDS	Open source	Free / Commercial signatures
Suricata	NIDS	Open source	Free
Bro	NIDS	Open source	Free
OSSEC	HIDS	Open source	Free
Kismet	WNIDS	Open source	Free
HP-UX HIDS	HIDS	Proprietary	Commercial

- **Integrity of the Applications' State:** If an attacker can access or modify the state of some files of the applications offered, the expected results of processing will differ from normal states.
- **Security Issues on the Network Level:** Vulnerabilities on the network level affect directly the cloud services. Among the attacks that occur on this level are DNS poisoning attacks, port scanning, IP and ARP spoofing.
- **Data Storage Issues:** Many issues exist on this level. In practice, there are plenty of challenges when talking about data location (on site, in a different country or different continent), data in transit and data recovery, etc.
- **Issues Related to Virtualization:** Usually multi-tenant share the same host using the hypervisor technology. When the number of the tenants increase, the number of vulnerabilities and security concerns increase automatically. With the ability to hack the virtualization system by an attacker, the latter could access every virtual machine created.
- **Access Control and Authentication Issues:** Because the data of the client is treated outside his professional environment. Data ownership problems are the main issues at this level.
- **Trust Issues:** The users of cloud computing services don't have full control of the resources they use. For this, even if the cloud providers integrate trust mechanisms in their services the trust is still fuzzy for most clients.
- **Issues Related to Laws and Auditing of the Cloud Service:** Responding to regulations, customer agreements and laws of every entity should be monitored to fulfil the privacy, the geographic and industry compliances. The multi-tenancy nature of cloud computing makes it difficult to achieve these objectives.

INTERNET OF THINGS SECURITY ISSUES

With the development of IoT products and services, new security issues have been developed and increased. To see the importance of securing IoT environments. On October 30, 2016 Internet was not available for many popular websites including Twitter, PayPal, GitHub, Spotify, etc. The source of the attack was a Trojan which exploited the DNS of the company providing the service to these websites. IoT devices were compromised and used by hackers to perform this attack, resulting in the unavailability of many important websites. By nature, IoT devices have limited CPU processing and RAM capabilities, some of these devices are called constrained. Table 2 shows some operating systems used by IoT devices and their characteristics.

The majority of these systems use different protocols and technologies for communication like CoAP described by Shelby et al. (2014), MQTT by Tang et al.

Table 2. Internet of things operating systems used by constrained devices

OS Name	RAM	Open Soure / Proprietary
Tiny OS	~ 1KB	Open Source
Contiki	~ 2KB	Open Source
Linux	~ 1MB	Open Source
RIOT	~ 1.5KB	Open Source
KasperskyOS	~ 8MB	Proprietary

(2013) and IEEE 802.15.4 standard by Molisch et al. (2004). Because of all these limitations, IoT environments suffer from many security issues like the following:

- **Unencrypted Data:** Not all devices have the capacity to encrypt the network traffic used by it.
- **DoS or DDoS:** Attacking IoT devices is not very hard since the latter don't have all the necessary mechanisms for defending intruders.
- **Physical Issues:** Hackers can hack the core of systems used by the devices and thus causes physical issues (like in Ambient Assisted Environments) and financial loss.
- **Vulnerabilities:** Due to the incapability of IoT devices to automatically update their core systems and fix vulnerabilities existing in the operating system. Some intruders may exploit the known vulnerabilities to hack the IoT environment.

Depending on the technology used in the IoT devices. Shah and Yaqoob (2016) described some of the said technologies like RFID, NFC, M2M, and V2V.

INTEGRATION OF CLOUD COMPUTING SERVICES AND INTERNET OF THINGS

IoT devices in general don't have much storage capacity. For this reason, cloud computing storage could be a better option for storing data of the IoT devices. The integration of cloud platforms with IoT applications is still in development and many startups are created for this purpose. Cubo et al. (2014), Dehury and Sahoo (2016), Xu and Helal (2016) and Botta et al. (2016) did some research on how to integrate cloud platforms with IoT applications.

The Figure 3 shows some start-ups companies which integrate IoT sensors with cloud computing platforms in real world applications.

Figure 3. Example of start-ups companies integrating cloud computing platforms with IoT sensors

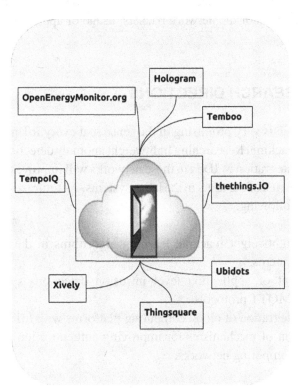

LIGHTWEIGHT ANOMALY DETECTION TECHNIQUES IN IOT APPLICATIONS

Lee et al. (2014) proposed a lightweight IDS scheme which analyses energy consumption. In the proposed technique, every node will monitor its energy consumption and uses some defined prediction models. When irregular energy consumption is identified, the node will be detected as a malicious one. Krontiris et al. (2008) developed a distributed lightweight intrusion detection architecture for sensor networks. The architecture consists of nodes that overhear the neighbors and with collaboration they can detect intrusions. Based on the first known compromised node, the others are considered as collaborators. The first node can follow a protocol to behave as normal one but after a period of time however at some point in time the compromised node should change its behavior and deviate from the protocol. At this point of time, the attacker is detected and the system is alerted. Zonouz et al. (2013) designed a framework which can be used to accomplish and analyze different powerful intrusion detection analysis. The framework is called Secloud and it was designed for small devices like Android with little resource utilization.

In summary, many lightweight anomaly detection techniques could be used from different fields like machine learning, analysis of energy consumption, statistic analysis of some parts of the network packets, usage of application level anomaly detection systems, etc.

FUTURE RESEARCH DIRECTIONS

This research topic is very promising in the sense that every IoT network will need protection from hacking. Researching lightweight anomaly detection and prevention techniques and integration of IDSs in these networks will improve quality of service and will increase trust of the users in the latter systems. As future research directions, we propose the following:

- Usage of lightweight machine learning algorithms in developed intrusion detection systems.
- Development of application level intrusion detections systems based on CoAP and MQTT protocols.
- Efficient integration of cloud computing platforms with IoT devices.
- Development of mechanisms for improving authentication in integrated IoT and cloud computing networks.

CONCLUSION

With the rapid development of cloud computing and IoT technologies, the need for a better exploitation of the resources (data, devices, networks) and protection of the shared data is crucial. Cloud computing services might be a better solution for hosting the data generated by the IoT devices, however malicious users always try to find ways to hack the systems and perform unpermitted actions (hacking, compromising, etc.). For these reasons, lightweight intrusion detection and prevention systems and techniques should be developed to minimize the risks of getting hacked especially in critical systems like those of the bank and e-health.

REFERENCES

Botta, A., de Donato, W., Persico, V., & Pescapé, A. (2016). Integration of Cloud computing and Internet of Things: A survey. *Future Generation Computer Systems*, *56*, 684–700. doi:10.1016/j.future.2015.09.021

Colina, A.L., Vives, A., Zennaro, M., Bagula, A., & Pietrosemoli, E. (2016). Internet of Things In 5 Days.

Columbus, L. (2016). Roundup Of Cloud Computing Forecasts And Market Estimates, 2016. *Forbes*. Retrieved May 27, 2016 from https://www.forbes.com/sites/louiscolumbus/

Cubo, J., Nieto, A., & Pimentel, E. (2014). A Cloud-Based Internet of Things Platform for Ambient Assisted Living. *Sensors (Basel, Switzerland)*, *14*(8), 14070–14105. doi:10.3390/s140814070 PMID:25093343

Dehury, C. K., & Sahoo, P. K. (2016). Design and implementation of a novel service management framework for IoT devices in cloud. *Journal of Systems and Software*, *119*, 149–161. doi:10.1016/j.jss.2016.06.059

Fernandes, D. A. B., Soares, L. F. B., Gomes, J. V., Freire, M. M., & Inácio, P. R. M. (2014). Security issues in cloud environments: A survey. *International Journal of Information Security*, *13*(2), 113–170. doi:10.1007/s10207-013-0208-7

Forrest Stroud. (2016). What Is Everything-as-a-Service (XaaS)? Webopedia Definition. Retrieved August 30, 2016 from http://www.webopedia.com/TERM/E/everything-as-a-service_xaas.html

Foster, I., Zhao, Y., Raicu, I., & Lu, S. (2008). *Cloud Computing and Grid Computing 360-Degree Compared. In 2008 Grid Computing Environments Workshop* (pp. 1–10). IEEE; https://doi.org/10.1109/GCE.2008.4738445

Gascon, H., Orfila, A., & Blasco, J. (2011). Analysis of update delays in signature-based network intrusion detection systems. *Computers & Security*, *30*(8), 613–624. doi:10.1016/j.cose.2011.08.010

Krontiris, I., Giannetsos, T., & Dimitriou, T. (2008). LIDeA: A Distributed Lightweight Intrusion Detection Architecture for Sensor Networks Ioannis. In *Proceedings of the 4th international conference on Security and privacy in communication networks SecureComm '08* (p. 1). New York, New York, USA: ACM Press. doi:10.1145/1460877.1460903

Lee, T.-H., Wen, C.-H., Chang, L.-H., Chiang, H.-S., & Hsieh, M.-C. (2014). A Lightweight Intrusion Detection Scheme Based on Energy Consumption Analysis in 6LowPAN. In *Advanced Technologies, Embedded and Multimedia for Human-centric Computing, LNEE* (Vol. 260, pp. 1205–1213). doi:10.1007/978-94-007-7262-5_137

Mell, P. M., & Grance, T. (2011). The NIST definition of cloud computing. Gaithersburg, MD. doi:10.6028/NIST.SP.800-145

Modi, C., Patel, D., Borisaniya, B., Patel, A., & Rajarajan, M. (2013). A survey on security issues and solutions at different layers of Cloud computing. *The Journal of Supercomputing*, *63*(2), 561–592. doi:10.1007/s11227-012-0831-5

Modi, C., Patel, D., Borisaniya, B., Patel, H., Patel, A., & Rajarajan, M. (2013). A survey of intrusion detection techniques in Cloud. *Journal of Network and Computer Applications*, *36*(1), 42–57. doi:10.1016/j.jnca.2012.05.003

Molisch, A. F., Balakrishnan, K., Chong, C. C., Emami, S., Fort, A., Karedal, J., ... & Siwiak, K. (2004). IEEE 802.15. 4a channel model-final report. *IEEE P802, 15*(04), 0662.

Ou, C.-M. (2012). Host-based intrusion detection systems adapted from agent-based artificial immune systems. *Neurocomputing*, *88*, 78–86. doi:10.1016/j.neucom.2011.07.031

Shah, S. H., & Yaqoob, I. (2016). *A survey: Internet of Things (IOT) technologies, applications and challenges. In 2016 IEEE Smart Energy Grid Engineering (SEGE)* (pp. 381–385). IEEE. doi:10.1109/SEGE.2016.7589556

Shelby, Z., Hartke, K., & Bormann, C. (2014). The constrained application protocol (CoAP).

Tang, K., Wang, Y., Liu, H., Sheng, Y., Wang, X., & Wei, Z. (2013, September). Design and implementation of push notification system based on the MQTT protocol. In *Proceedings of the International Conference on Information Science and Computer Applications (ISCA 2013)* (pp. 116-119). doi:10.2991/isca-13.2013.20

Van Kranenburg, R. (2008). *The Internet of Things: A critique of ambient technology and the all-seeing network of RFID*. Institute of Network Cultures.

Xu, Y., & Helal, A. (2016). Scalable Cloud–Sensor Architecture for the Internet of Things. *IEEE Internet of Things Journal*, *3*(3), 285–298. doi:10.1109/JIOT.2015.2455555

Zonouz, S., Houmansadr, A., Berthier, R., Borisov, N., & Sanders, W. (2013). Secloud: A cloud-based comprehensive and lightweight security solution for smartphones. *Computers & Security*, *37*, 215–227. doi:10.1016/j.cose.2013.02.002

KEY TERMS AND DEFINITIONS

Anomaly: Misbehaviour detected in the network which is different from normal traffic.

Big Data: Refers to large data in enterprise settings. The latter is different from classical datasets and can not be managed, stored, or processed using traditional methods and relational database management systems. Big data uses new types of databases, called NoSQL.

Cloud computing: Cloud computing refers to a virtualized network which offers applications over the Internet. The services are offered from data centres from all over the world or frorm some continents.

Constrained Device: Generally, this is a small device with limited processing and storage capabilities mainly used as a sensor in wireless networks and IoT environments. It often runs on batteries.

Datacentre: A data centre is a facility used for hosting servers of different types and different operating systems in order to access them either locally or remotely by clients.

IDS: Stands for "Intrusion Detection System." It is a device or software meant to monitor the network traffic for anomalous and suspicious activities.

Internet of Things: The Internet of Things, commonly abbreviated "IoT," is a new term that refers to anything connected to Internet like sensors, smartphone, tablets, etc.

Intrusion: Intrusion could be any type of attack or anomalous activity happening on the network.

IPS: Stands for "Intrusion Prevention System." It is similar to the IDS, but it is designed to prevent malicious activities within the network.

Wireless Sensor: Autonomous and distributed device that is using wireless technologies in order to monitor physical or environmental states like lighting, temperature and pressure, etc.

Chapter 11
Cloud Load Balancing and Reinforcement Learning

Abdelghafour Harraz
Mohammed V University, Morocco

Mostapha Zbakh
Mohammed V University, Morocco

ABSTRACT

Artificial Intelligence allows to create engines that are able to explore, learn environments and therefore create policies that permit to control them in real time with no human intervention. It can be applied, through its Reinforcement Learning techniques component, using frameworks such as temporal differences, State-Action-Reward-State-Action (SARSA), Q Learning to name a few, to systems that are be perceived as a Markov Decision Process, this opens door in front of applying Reinforcement Learning to Cloud Load Balancing to be able to dispatch load dynamically to a given Cloud System. The authors will describe different techniques that can used to implement a Reinforcement Learning based engine in a cloud system.

INTRODUCTION

Cloud Computing is the new paradigm in which all nodes having access to the internet are able to communicate together through high speed networks, this creates an internet of things, where the need of managing the communication between servers and clients emerges as a critical problematic in order to avoid congestion and out of service states. Cloud Load Balancing takes on that mission by creating

DOI: 10.4018/978-1-5225-3038-1.ch011

an additional intelligence layer on top of the internet of things to regulate, watch, control and in some cases possibly plan on the resources available and their ability to handle transported traffic.

Cloud load balancing and load balancers in general are classified into two main types, static and dynamic load balancers. Static load balancers handle traffic and load with no special knowledge of the inner characteristics of the traffic being transported, they don't change their behaviour based on runtime in terms of response time, network latency, pick times, resources availability in virtual machines, or other cloud system maintenance operations such as hot or off line virtual machines relocation between data centres, upsizing or downsizing of machines.

Static load balancers are simple to implement, and are not heavy consumer of the resources of the machine in which they sit, they make fast decisions therefore they don't introduce significant latency to the processing chain, they are in most cases transparent in term of adding more service time to the queueing mechanism, but they also hold very little intelligence and they might miss on accurate decision actions in regards of the system they are load balancing.

Dynamic load balancers in the other hand are built with the ability to watch load changes, keep track of it, escalade info to a master node that is responsible of making the load balancing decision, or keeping a local vector of changes in each node, and then decide what is the most accurate actions for the next load balancing iteration. Dynamic load balancers are complex to implement, and are heavy consumer of the resource of the machine in which they sit. Communication between nodes might suffer from network and inter-connexion issues, and in the case when a master node is implemented, this one is a single point of failure and need to be load balanced itself.

In this perspective, the choice of the load balancer to use is a question of what type of traffic is being handled by the cloud system, and how variant it is, to be able to architect the system efficiently, and give a deep insight on how it will behave in the future to be able to plan and control it.

Making the right decision or taking the most accurate action in a given situation regarding a system requires having full knowledge about that system. If we suppose we have knowledge about arrival rate and average service time of a given cloud, we can model it as a queue theory problem and therefore compute and draw a mathematical model of the system to be able to control it in real time to reduce reaching overloaded state with a given certainty.

Since in most cases the system does not expose these kind of information:

- Arrival distribution is hidden by the type of requests made to the cloud and no benchmark can give an exact form of its moments.
- Exit distribution is completely controlled by the current available resources in the cloud.

Figure 1. Execution Chain on a Cloud System

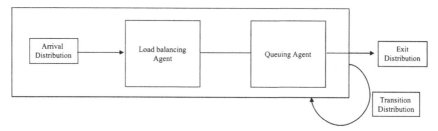

- The transition distribution is supposed to be Markov but the transition probabilities also are in constant changes.

Signal processing theory show that through significant sampling and under some assumption over the sampling frequency, very good approximations and retrieval of an original signal from its noisy version by means of statistical stochastic computation can be achieved. That same principal can be used to expose the hidden characteristics of a cloud system in terms of its input, processing and output distributions.

Therefore, the system is, in general, stochastic by nature and does not behave following a certain a priori known set of rules. One of the approaches to use in that case is to discover the system characteristics by going through the load balancing and queuing processes over multiple episodes of iterations in time and then statistically create a model of the environment. Given that, Reinforcement Learning approaches are a rational candidate to solve this kind of control problems.

In the next sections, the authors will describe what Reinforcement Learning is, and propose a handful of different implementations that were studied throughout the literature to achieve control over systems that present the same symptoms as the problem of load balancing in cloud. The authors will also describe how Reinforcement Learning creates models of environments' characteristics that are initially fully or partially not known, and then describe different techniques that make a Reinforcement Learning agent converge to its optimal policy and how this optimality can be achieved experimentally.

REINFORCEMENT LEARNING

Reinforcement learning is the branch of artificial intelligence techniques that allows to learn what to do when a given situation arises. Reinforcement learning can be added as another way of learning with supervised and unsupervised learning techniques, and it showed that it can have broader applications and broader approach to solve problems.

Supervised learning requires the existence of input and output data, which the teacher must have a full knowledge of their characteristics. The teacher creates the model, and ask the learning agent to do exploration until it understands the provided model. The exploration is made by replaying iteratively the couples $(input, output)$ from the provided data. The idea here is to achieve a good and acceptable model of the world the learner is interacting in, by reducing at each step the error between the output of the model function being constructed for estimation and the real output given by the teacher. This error, under conditions of convergence corresponding to the problem being studied, will result in creating a learner model of the environment being studied through, for example, a binding to a parametrized or weighted transfer function. The transfer function in that case is a lookup and fine tuning entity that is being polished by error reduction.

Unsupervised learning is a technique where the teacher only has an input set of data, but needs to create a model of it characteristics, the learner acts on the data and tries to find hidden models and trends.

Reinforcement learning differs from supervised and unsupervised learning in the way that it works on data, creates a model, and then the model is criticized through a reward system.

In Reinforcement learning, input data is not need, the learner can act on real world situation to learn by trial and error. The idea behind that type of learning is similar to how children learn about and explore new world situations, cache or store them, and then throughout time they only keep the ones that are the most rewarding and satisfactory, and let go of the ones that are the least rewarding. A child that goes to the kitchen and touches the hob, will not try to do it again.

In this sense, in order for Reinforcement learning to work, it needs a set of pre-existing conditions:

- **Markov Decision Process:** The system, on which is applied the Reinforcement Learning, needs to be modelled by a Markov Decision Process with transition distribution $P_{ij}(t)$ to be the probability to transition from state s_i to state s_j when taking action $a_t \in A$.
- **States Set:** The MDP modelling the system is created on top of states space S, in which each state mandatorily needs to be frequently often visited to guarantee correct knowledge of the system by the learning agent.
- **Action Set:** To transition from a state to another, a set of known actions that the learning agent can executes in a given state is needed, this set is noted as A.

- **Reward System:** Reward is how the learning agent understands what the system will be as a consequence of an action it engaged, noted as R.

Markov Decision Process in the Reinforcement Learning problem can:

- Either be fully defined, meaning all transition probabilities are known, or not providing a model of its transitions at all.
- With finite state space or infinite state space
- With all states known or with hidden states. Markov Decision Process with hidden states are called partially observable Markov Decision Process. Partially observable Markov Decision Process suffers from the fact that the Markov aspect is removed, and therefore the theoretical framework describing normal MDPs does not apply anymore.
- Be either episodic processes with an ending state, where the learner has a goal to achieve or an obstacle to avoid. In which case the learning ends once the objective of the episode is reached or the obstacle is hit. Episodic learning can be batched and streamed online in a Monte Carlo fashion of learning, which the authors are going to describe later. This online streaming can be used to capitalize on knowledge gathered during an episode and transmitting it to the next execution of the algorithm. In the same way, the MDP might also not have an ending state, in which case the learning goes forever on a streamed line manner either using online updates at each step or batched update after a given number of transition.

Both Online – update at each time transition -, and batched updates has shown to converge and teach the agent to have enough knowledge about its environment to be able to control and plan on top of it.

Given this set of required conditions, a formal description of how Reinforcement Learning problem solving occurs can be given. Taking action a_i in a state s_i at time i transitions the system to state s_{i+1}, and returns a deferred reward few time lapses later R_{i+1}. The Reinforcement Learning agent objective is to filter the actions it executes on a given state to maximize the global reward it will receive during an episode of execution.

To be able to do that, it needs a way of mapping states or actions states to scalars that define how good or bad is a state or action state. And therefore, maximizing the reward at each transition and more accurately the expected reward received can only be done by labelling the states, or the actions states. This is a very powerful and simple way to criticize the behaviour of the agent, the reward system is a layer added on top of the initial transition distribution $P_{ij}^0 (t)$ of the MDP to drive it toward a better transition distribution $P_{ij}^*(t)$ in terms of the expected gained reward. In a sense, Reinforcement Learning is a lookup algorithm, which iteratively improves the usage of the characteristics of the MDP by the learner to go from poor outcome to better outcome, and consequently gaining better and efficient knowledge of the environment.

If we consider the total reward gained throughout the whole learning process or the whole episode to be given by the following formula:

$$G_t = R_{t+1} + R_{t+2} + R_{t+3} + \dots + R_T$$

and its discounted form:

$$G_t = R_{t+1} + \gamma R_{t+2} + \gamma^2 R_{t+3} + \dots + \gamma^{T-1} R_T = \sum_{t+1}^{T} \gamma^k R_{t+k+1}$$

where γ is a discount factor, inferior to 1, used to discount the influence of future rewards on the current estimation of the global reward.

The objective of the learning agent through Reinforcement Learning is to maximize its expected reward from any given point in time, this is done by choosing the action that is most likely, based on its knowledge, to output the better transitions, not only in terms of the next state, but most importantly regarding the path of states, actions thereafter.

The ensemble of the tags composes what is called a state value function $V(s)$ or a state action value function $Q(s,a)$.

The state value function is considered to be the expectation of the expected reward that the agent will be able to get starting from a given state and it is written as:

$$V(s) = E[G|S = s] = E\left[\sum_{t+1}^{T} \gamma^k R_{t+k+1} | S = s\right]$$

and in the same way the action state value function is considered to be the expected reward that the agent will be able to get starting from a given state and taking a given action:

$$Q(s,a) = E[G|S = s, A = a] = E\left[\sum_{t+1}^{T} \gamma^k R_{t+k+1} | S = s, A = a\right]$$

Figure 2. Backup diagrams for $V(s)$ and $Q(s,a)$

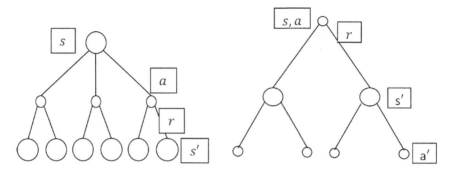

Using basic mathematic computation, the state value function and the action state value function become:

$$V(s) = V(s) + \alpha \left(V(s') - V(s) \right)$$

$$Q(s,a) = Q(s,a) + \alpha \left(r + \gamma max_{a'} Q(s',a') - Q(s,a) \right)$$

where:

- γ is a discount factor inferior to 1 meant to be used to reduce the influence of future rewards on the current decision.
- α is a learning rate that controls the learning speed, in a deterministic environment for example $\alpha = 1$ is optimal.

Example: A very simple example would be to consider a cloud system with two states set $(s_0, s_1) = ($*loaded, not loaded*$)$, two actions set $(a_0, a_1) = ($*do not relay, relay*$)$, and four rewards set $(r_{00}, r_{01}, r_{10}, r_{11}) = ($*0, 100, 0, 100*$)$, if we suppose the system starts at the state s_0, the following transition action value matrix can be drawn, using $\alpha = 0,9$ and $\gamma = 0,2$

After three runs through the Reinforcement Learning algorithms, the results shown in Tables 1-3

The load balancer at each iteration only needs to compute this matrix and execute the action, given a state, that will allow it to maximize its gain. After few runs through the Reinforcement Learning algorithm, the results show that the actions that provides the bigger reward are the one having the bigger action state values.

Figure 3. basic Reinforcement Learning environment

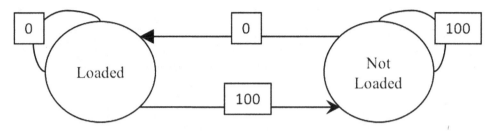

Table 1. Iteration 0

s	a	r	s¹	Q updated	value
s_0	do not relay	100	s_1	$Q[s_0,\ \text{do not send job}] = 0 + 0.2*(100 + 0.9*100 - 0)$	38
s_0	relay	0	s_0	$Q[S_0,\ \text{send job}] = 0 + 0.2*(0 + 0.9*100 - 0)$	18
s_1	do not relay	100	s_1	$Q[S_1,\ \text{do not send job}] = 0 + 0.2*(100 + 0.9*100 - 0)$	38
s_1	relay	0	s_0	$Q[S_1,\ \text{send job}] = 0 + 0.2*(0 + 0.9*100 - 0)$	18

Table 2. Iteration 1

s	a	r	s'	value
s_0	do not relay	100	s_1	68,4
s_0	relay	0	s_0	32,4
s_1	do not relay	100	s_1	68,4
s_1	relay	0	s_0	32,4

Table 3. Iteration 2

s	a	r	s'	value
S_0	do not relay	100	S_1	92,72
S_0	relay	0	S_0	43,92
S_1	do not relay	100	S_1	92,72
S_1	relay	0	S_0	43,92

EXPLORATION VS. EXPLOITATION

One of the most important tasks that a learning agent need to integrate into its processing is load balancing the two operations of exploration and exploitation.

Exploration allows the agent to explore and discover the environment in which it will be acting, it is a mandatory step to be able to visit all states of the MDP, and consequently attach or label them with a value function, that can be exploited later. Exploration also helps the agent to exit local minima of the value function to be able to have a broader view of the environment.

Exploitation is the intended operation that the agent should be executing most of the time once it gets a good knowledge of its environment, it is an execution of actions drawn from the state or state action value function that has been constructed through exploration and exploitation updates throughout the processing.

The agent by definition need be constructed to be greedy in its behaviour, meaning that all the actions that it executes should be an *argmax* of the value function of the current state. This assumption in a sense conflicts with the need of the agent to be exploratory. The solution that is proposed in most literatures and have been proven to be efficient to integrate exploration into the greedy behaviour of the agent is to use a ε-greedy policy to commands the behaviour of the agent regarding how it will choose the next action.

ε-Greedy Policies

A ε-greedy policy is a policy that can be used to generate two types of outcomes:

- Explore with probability μ, in which case the agent will execute an action drawn from its exploration algorithm.
- Exploit with probability $1 - \varepsilon$, in which case the agent will execute an action drawn from its value function.

The recommendations for the μ are that it needs to be high in early stages of the learning to promote exploration iterations, in order to populate the knowledge of the agent. Once the agent starts to have enough information to base its decisions on, μ needs to start decreasing consequently. Even in high time steps μ should not be equal to 0, to let room for the agent to update its policy for any future changes in the environment.

Exploration Algorithm

In the case where the agent through its ε-greedy policy decides to engage an exploration action, it needs to choose randomly an action from the valid action set A, a common way of doing that is to use a Maxwell-Boltzmann distribution defined by:

$$P\left(a|s\right) = \frac{e^{\left(\frac{Q\left(s|a\right)}{T}\right)}}{\sum e^{\left(\frac{Q\left(s|a'\right)}{T}\right)}} a' \in A$$

with T is the temperature, which drives the randomness of the pick to be a uniform law choice or not. High values of T mean all actions have the same chances to get chosen, small values of T lead to a greedier behaviour. Just like ε, the learning should start with high values of T and decrease as the agent gets deeper into the learning.

Example: Suppose our Q matrix for a given state s is:

$$Q\left(s \mid a_1\right) = 1, Q\left(s \mid a_2\right) = 2$$

1.   T = 10 outputs:

$$P\left(a_1 \mid s\right) = 0.48, P\left(a_2 \mid s\right) = 0.52$$

Almost equal probability, a_1 and a_2 are randomly chosen similarly when the agent hits an exploration phase.

2.   T = 1 outputs:

$$P\left(a_1 \mid s\right) = 0.27, \ P\left(a_2 \mid s\right) = 0.73$$

Probabilities are more skewed, a_1 will be chosen more often when at an exploration hit.

3.   T = 0.25 outputs:

$$P\left(a_1 \mid s\right) = 0.02, \ P\left(a_2 \mid s\right) = 0.98$$

Almost always explore a_1.

On/Off Policy Learning

Two types of learning can be distinguished which are on policy and off policy learning, a policy is defined as the distribution that maps actions to states $a = \pi\left(s\right)$.

Both on and off policy learning have an optimal state value function V^* and state action value function Q^* objective that they aim to converge to, this value function is a result of continuous trial and error iterations which update either the value function itself in a greedy way or update a target policy that will criticize the agent behaviour policy.

In the on policy learning the target policy is the policy that generates actions for the agent, in the off-policy learning actions are generated using a behaviour policy. One of the challenges with off policy learning is that data is sampled from the behaviour policy, cause that is what the agent is using to generate actions, while the agent needs to learn about the target policy. This has been well studied and handled by Importance Sampling methods that propose a way of to compute the expected value function of a given distribution π. when samples are generated from another distribution b. Importance sampling estimator is defined as below:

$$\frac{1}{n}\sum_{i=1}^{n}x_i\frac{\pi\left(x_i\right)}{b\left(x_i\right)}\text{ with }x_i\text{ are sampled drawn from }b$$

Another version of the importance sampling estimator is the weighted importance sampling estimator and it is given by:

$$\frac{\sum_{i=1}^{n}x_i\dfrac{\pi\left(x_i\right)}{b\left(x_i\right)}}{\sum_{i=1}^{n}\dfrac{\pi\left(x_i\right)}{b\left(x_i\right)}}\text{ with }x_i\text{ are sampled drawn from }b$$

The normal importance sampling estimator is consistent unbiased estimator, whereas the weighted version is consistent biased estimator, but it shows better convergence performance.

On policy learning happens when the learner has a way to build a policy that it uses to generate action. The updates of the value function use the generated actions and the estimated expected reward the agent will receive. An example of an on-policy technique is Actor critic algorithms.

Actor critic algorithms build a policy that the learner will use to update the parameter of its behaviour policy. Like any negative feedback system, the reward output from the state transition is used to update a target policy in the direction of the performance measure, this update results in a fine tuning of the parameters of the behaviour policy.

A simple example would be the following, let us define the learner behaviour policy as being drawn for the value function $V\left(\theta\right)$, and the target policy π, the learner is trying to improve based on the continuous find tuning of the θ vector parameter from error optimization. So, the update algorithm goes through two operations of updating target policy, reflecting changes onto the behaviour policy and then draw next action for the latter.

Off-policy learning happens when the agent updates its value function based on the greedy immediate action it will take and the future expected reward it estimates it will receive. A good example of an off-policy learning technique is Q learning algorithms.

Q Learning is an off-policy technique that estimates and converges directly to the optimal Q* state action value function, it is independent of the policy followed by the learner and it is by construction a greedy technique, this allows for faster convergences and shows early convergence proof.

Policy Improvement

Reinforcement learning algorithms follow a path of improving the policy from which they generate actions when a state occurs, this is a direct result of the greedy behaviour followed when selecting actions. Let us suppose a policy π is being followed, that is to say that $a_{i+1} = \pi\left(s_i\right)$, if the learning decides to follow policy π' defined as:

$$\pi'\left(s\right) = \begin{cases} \pi\left(s\right), & \text{all } s \neq s_i \\ argmax\left(\pi\left(s_i\right)\right), & s = s_i \end{cases}$$

then $\pi'\left(s\right)$ is at least better than $\pi\left(s\right)$, which means through iterative processing, the agent is able to improve its behaviour policy, and consequently improve its value function.

In the case where $V_\pi\left(s\right) = V_{\pi'}\left(s\right)$, the algorithm can be considered to have reached its optimality for the currently studied environment.

This continuous policy improvement has been studied thoroughly in the literature, and many techniques have been proposed which showed good performance and convergence proof. The authors are going to describe three approaches in this chapter, which are policy improvement using tabular approximation, policy improvement using linear function basis, and policy improvement using neural networks.

Tabular Approximations

This is the most basic and simple way to approximate a value function through an iterative process. The law of large numbers states that the average of a large number of trials should get closer to the expected statistical characteristics of the population as more trials are performed.

Using a matrix representation of the value function based on finite number of states and actions, and then updating the value function using a set of rewards is often helpful in solving basic control and planning problems of reinforcement learning.

Although this type of approximation usually shows fast convergence proof, under required assumptions, and can be used as a proof of implementation of more complex learners, they show very bad performance once the number of states and actions gets big or transition to the continuous domain, in which case a more sophisticated solutions is needed, two methods that can be mentioned to overcome this limitation are neural network as a nonlinear approximation method, and space generator basis functions also called features, with projections to be able to absorb all the variance of the distributions involved in the learning process.

Neural Networks

Neural network gained interest on different classification problems through supervised and unsupervised learning. They are constructed of three type of layers, an input layer, one or multiple hidden layers and output layer. The input of a layer to the next is given as a linear sum over the output of an activation function of the weights and inputs._

The weights play the role of scalar that adjusts to the nature of the problem being studied and once acceptable convergence is reached, the outputted model is considered to be the optimal classifier.

Example: Back Propagation (delta rule) with three layers' neural network (one hidden layer) can be seen in Figure 4.

Using a gradient descent update rule such as delta rule, the outputs can be written as:

$$O = F\left(I * W + B\right)$$

and the weight updates by:

$$W \leftarrow W + L * Change + M * C$$

Figure 4. example of a basic three layers' neural network

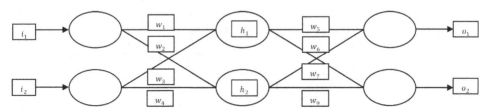

$C \leftarrow Change$

where:

L is the learning rate

$Change = f\left(input\,activated_{neuron}, \delta_{neuron}\right)$

M is the momentum value

C is the momentum coefficient

Simple run of the neural network achieves the following results (see Table 4).

In Reinforcement learning Neural network are used as nonlinear approximation methods of the value function. One of the biggest break through made in recent years that were based on a Q learning based agent with a neural network approximation function was made by DeepMind in which they combined a deep neural network and a Q learning algorithm to create Deep Q learning. The application of Deep Q Learning to playing ATARI keeps exploration enabled at all time with a probability μ, integrates an operation of memory replay through storing transitions in a buffer then used to feed the neural network.

The update of the weight of the deep Q network is done via gradient descent over an objective function. The interaction with the environment is done via plugging directly into the image buffer to collect frames which goes through operations of down scaling in dimensionality before being inputted into the deep Q learning algorithms. The results show that the agent is able to play most games better than a human.

Table 4.

	Input	**Output**		**Input**	**Output**	**Approximation**
training data	[0, 0, 0]	0	test	[0, 0, 0]	0.00071817	0
	[0, 0, 1]	1		[0, 0, 1]	0.99824102	1
	[0, 1, 0]	0		[0, 1, 0]	0.00240537	0
	[0, 1, 1]	1		[0, 1, 1]	0.99834662	1
	[1, 0, 0]	0		[1, 0, 0]	0.00296237	0
	[1, 0, 1]	1		[1, 0, 1]	0.99776186	1
	[1, 1, 0]	0		[1, 1, 0]	0.00167438	0
	[1, 1, 1]	1		[1, 1, 1]	0.99785089	1
		average error achieved	4,00E-05			

In the DeepMind works, a feed forward neural network was used to generate the greediest action corresponding to a given state at each forward pass:

$$a_t = \max_a \left[Q^* \left(\varphi\left(st\right), a; \theta \right) \right]$$

with θ is a vector weights of the neural network. The update of the weights occurs using one of the methods that the authors shall describe in next sections to drive the performance of the approximation toward the error direction like gradient descent, bellman operator error optimization.

Linear Function Approximation

Linear function approximation requires a set of function basis called features, these features will be used in the following way:

$G_t = F\theta_t$ meaning $\nabla_\theta G_t = F$ with G_t is the expected reward from a given point in time

The gradient descent over the parametrization vector is equal to the set of features used, and therefore the choice of the feature set impact directly the learning process and the update that will be injected into θ.

Function basis:

Common function basis used to approximate value function are:

- Radial function basis:

$$\varphi_i = \frac{1}{\sqrt{2\pi\sigma^2}} e^{-\|c_i - x\|^2 / 2\sigma^2}$$

- Polynomial function basis:

$$\varphi_i\left(x\right) = \prod_{j=1}^{d} x_j^{c_{i,j}}$$

with

$$c_{i,j} \in \left[0, n\right]$$

- Fourier basis:

$$
\begin{cases}
1 & if\ i = 0 \\
\cos\left(\dfrac{i+1}{2}\pi x\right) & if\ i > 0,\ i\ odd \\
\sin\left(\dfrac{i}{2}\pi x\right) & if\ i > 0,\ i\ even
\end{cases}
$$

Studies show a significant advantage of using the Fourier basis over the other ones in terms of convergence speed and accuracy. In most cases, depending on prior knowledge over the expected reward to be approximated (being odd or even for example), the Fourier basis can be truncated to only using its *cos* component or *sin* component.

Another type of basis that are used in the Reinforcement Learning linear approximation problem are the Proto-Value Functions, this type of functions is learned while the learning agent is doing its own learning, they are task independent and are learnt from analysing the topology of the state space.

Once the method to construct the basis function set is chosen, the learner supposes the existence of a randomized stationary policy μ_θ (RSP) as a Boltzmann policy, defined by:

$$
\mu_\theta\left(a \mid s\right) = \frac{e^{h_\theta^a(s)}}{\sum_{a' \in A} e^{h_\theta^{a'}(s)}}
$$

with $h_\theta^a\left(s\right)$ is a function that corresponds to action a and is parametrized by a vector θ. This RSP format makes the search for the optimal value of θ that drives μ_θ toward greediness behaviour the main operation to reach increasing expected reward through iterative processing, and therefore create a framework where policy improvement is drawn from. The direct consequence of this method is to look for a better μ_θ at each step for our Reinforcement learning problem that will allow to reach the optimal distributions that maximizes the expected rewards and optimizes the value function.

Performance Measures

Multiple performance measures are being used in Reinforcement Learning, most of them either work directly on the optimization of the value function, or the error in regards of an objective function. Errors like MSPBE (mean-square projected Bellman error), Temporal difference signal and error, loss, cost or total gain have been introduced and studied to optimize the learning.

Bellman Operator

Bellman operators are defined as:

$$(T^\pi f)(s) = r(s, \pi(s)) + \lambda \sum_{s'} p(s'|s, \pi(s)) f(s')$$

the optimal version is defined as:

$$(T^\pi f)(s) = \max_{a \in A} \left[r(s, \pi(s)) + \lambda \sum_{s'} p(s'|s, \pi(s)) f(s') \right]$$

and describes the result when following an optimal policy that selects the action with the highest value at each state. Basic algebraic operations show that the value function is a fixed point of the bellman operator, under a given policy π, we can write the expected reward as:

$$G_t = R_{t+1} + \gamma R_{t+2} + \gamma^2 R_{t+3} + \gamma^T R_T$$

$$G_t = R_{t+1} + \gamma G_{t+1}$$

therefore

$$V^\pi(s) = E\left[G_t | s_t = s\right] = E\left[R_{t+1} + \gamma G_{t+1} | s_t = s\right]$$

$$V^\pi(s) = E\left[R_{t+1} | s_t = s\right] + \gamma E\left[G_{t+1} | s_t = s\right]$$

$$V^{\pi}\left(s\right) = r + \gamma V^{A}\left(s'\right)$$

$$V^{\pi}\left(s\right) = \left(T^{\pi}V\right)\left(s\right)$$

under any iterative greedy improvement of policy π for it to converge toward π^{*} defined as:

$$\pi^{*}\left(s\right) = \operatorname*{argmax}_{a \in A} V^{\pi}\left(s\right)$$

$V^{\pi}\left(s\right)$ will converge toward the optimal $V^{*}\left(s\right)$ which is the unique fixed point of the optimal bellman operator if the learner proceeds in an improvement of the value function using an iterative process described by the following:

$$TV^{n} = V^{n+1} = \gamma PV^{n} + R$$

A line of studies regarding Reinforcement Learning, that use the bellman operator for convergence, use iterative procedure to reduce the distance between the projection of the bellman operator on the basis function set used for the approximation and the value function written in that basis set. The MSPBE and a gradient descent algorithm to optimize the parameters used to project the value function on the space of the linear functions. This approach has a non-linear version that approximate the value function in a small region where it can be studied as linear approximation, in that case the error is being contracted in a compact set.

One of the proposed algorithms in the literature generates features in the direction of the bellman error of the current value estimate, the algorithm creates new features out of a combination of compressed projection, OLS regression and a temporal difference error. The power of the algorithm is a direct result of the works of Parr et al. which show that if a feature set defined as $\psi = \left\{\psi_{1}, \psi_{2}, \ldots, \psi_{m}\right\}$ is considered, the linear approximation in a set define by $\psi = \left\{\psi_{1}, \psi_{2}, \ldots, \psi_{m}, e_{V_{m}}\right\}$, will shrink by γ.

The bellman error has an intimate relationship with the temporal difference error since they have the same expectance, and consequently they are can be used interchangeably in estimation and update of the value function.

Gradient Descent

The Mean-square projected Bellman error is one of the many measures that can be optimized as a performance measure to make the Reinforcement Learning problem converge. Gradient descent based methods are very popular as a way to reduce the error. A general gradient algorithm has been proposed for Temporal Difference learning, with eligibility traces where the objective function to optimize is the MSPBE error. Other works propose a policy gradient based algorithm for both average reward and state formulation of the expected reward.

REINFORCEMENT LEANING TECHNIQUES

Dynamic Programming

Dynamic programming is a basic Learning technique, it is not model free as Reinforcement Learning is, this means that it needs a model of the environment or the process they are interacting with, including having full knowledge of the transition probabilities, and the reward system to be able to find the optimal value function iteratively. Whereas Reinforcement Learning is able to look for and create a model of the environment only by looking into a significant number of samples of transitions.

Dynamic programming, unlike Reinforcement Learning, does need to go through all the path and eventualities, compare findings, and they come up with a solution. This aspect makes dynamic programming less interesting when it comes to solve problems like cloud load balancing due to the ever-changing nature of the traffic fed to the cloud system.

Monte Carlo

One of the Methods that are used Reinforcement Learning is the Monte Carlo method, it consists in approaching the value function using a batched experience sampling that is uses to average the update over an execution episode. Unlike dynamic programming Monte Carlo does not require knowledge about the model or the environment to be estimated. It only needs experience. The Monte Carlo method is a considered to be a special case of the broader Temporal Difference framework.

Temporal Difference

One of the biggest breakthrough in Reinforcement Learning was the creation of temporal difference learning algorithm known as $TD(\lambda)$. These type of algorithms combines online value function update and batch value function update. The idea behind temporal difference is to create a framework for the agent to learn through a combination of a sum of different averages of realizations of the expected reward in time. This means that temporal difference is a general framework that allows to tune a lambda parameter to control the type of the averages taken into consideration in the learning.

To give an example of what is a temporal difference algorithm, let us consider a learning episode of T iterations. TD techniques allows, using the lambda parameter, to either:

Update its value function using one step update, meaning an online update as soon as it receives the reward of a given transition.

Update using a combination of multiple many steps updates, meaning if the choice is to apply the update at three time steps, the update will look like:

$$G_t \leftarrow \left(1 - \lambda\right) G_t^{\text{one step}} + \left(1 - \lambda\right) \lambda G_t^{\text{second step}} + \lambda^2 G_t^{\text{third step}}$$

Using a combination of many average update has a lot of advantages in term of making the learner exploits in an even more efficient way the states transition and reward resulted from them, TD methods do not need a model to learn like dynamic programming, and they do not need to wait until the end of the learning episode like Monte Carlo Techniques do.

The formal mathematical definition of TD(λ) is a direct result of the expected reward that the learner will be able to collect through the learning episode:

$$G_t^{\lambda} = \left(1 - \lambda\right) \sum_{1}^{\infty} \lambda^{n-1} G_t^n$$

in the case of a TD learning with terminal state the expected reward can be written as:

$$G_t^{\lambda} = \left(1 - \lambda\right) \sum_{1}^{T-t-1} \lambda^{n-1} G_t^n + \lambda^{T-t-1} G_t$$

if $\lambda = 0$., the expected reward update is a Monte Carlo update rule with:

$$G_t^\lambda = G_t^{(1)}$$

if $\lambda = 1$ the expected reward update is a one step on line update with:

$$G_t^\lambda = G_t$$

That shows that TD(0) is an on line one step update, and TD(1) is a Monte Carlo update, which makes $\text{TD}(\lambda)$ methods span the complete range of multiple step update by tuning the λ parameter.

Forward and Backward View of Temporal Differences Algorithms

In the current definition, Temporal differences algorithms suppose the existence and the access to future expected rewards, that shall be used to update the value function at the current time steps, this is called TD forward view of the update, Sutton describes it as looking forward in time for all future reward and decide how best to combine them. This approach is only theoretical and is not applicable in real world case scenarios, this is why the temporal differences has a backward view version through what is called eligibility traces.

Eligibility traces allows to attain the same result as the forward view of $\text{TD}(\lambda)$. By only using historical data and they are defined as:

$$Z_t(s) = \begin{cases} \gamma Z_{t-1}(s) & \text{if } s \neq s_t \\ \gamma Z_{t-1}(s) + 1 & \text{if } s = s_t \end{cases}$$

or in another version known as the replacing eligibility traces:

The idea with eligibility traces is to shout the update to the previous transitions. They are a tampon that is used to record the occurrence of an event and its eligibility to undergo changes. Equivalence between eligibility traces and $\text{TD}(\lambda)$ is proved by showing that the multi-step errors and the one step eligibility traces error are equal.

Challenges

The architecture in Figure 5 is an illustration of a cloud system using Reinforcement Learning as a load balancing technique. The mappers will host the Reinforcement Learning agent. Load is being generated by users, and received at the mappers end to be dispatched to processors. Each processor has a known initial resource pool that is shared among all the mappers. At any given point in time, the mappers will have only a perceived view about what the shared resource pool state is, the objective then is to control and plan on top of that perceived knowledge. Therefore, the problem to be solved is to create a learner that can follow, control, plan and construct a model of the cloud system environment noting that the users' load is generated based on distributions not known by any instance of the mappers.

In essence creating a load balancer using Reinforcement Learning as its core component will not be possible if not only restriction of transit time, service time, and availability of resources on the processors are taken into account, but also how one load balancer affects the Reinforcement Learning process in an adjacent load balancer. Should we allow for inter load balancer communication to hold one global state of the environment, in that case what is the entity that shall be responsible of watching for system state changes and reflecting the reward into the value function for update. Or should we allow each load balancer node to have its own value function or a matrix of value functions each one directed toward the perceived behaviour of a given processor to just be responsible of only its perception of the outside world and update of its own value function. The latter case seems to be the preferred but is the one with more degree of freedom.

Figure 5. Cloud system model

M_i *is the load balancer instance that will hold the reinforcement learning agent*

R_i *is the processors in the cloud system*

U_i *is users generating requests toward the cloud system*

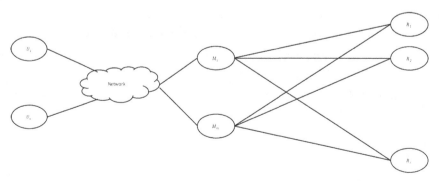

Game theoretical approaches are powerful candidate to handle this type of situation. Game theory created a framework where multiple agent can communicate either collaboratively or non-collaboratively to solve a shared problem. The solution of the problem is assured to exist and it is defined in its basic format as the Nash equilibrium. Reaching the equilibrium is what a load balancing Reinforcement Learning agent will seek to achieve throughout its learning journey.

A second challenge that faces the Reinforcement Learning is the continual changing and variant nature of the load being inputted into the system, this means that the exploration function of the agent needs not to be shut down or marginalized over the exploitation phase.

Another challenge to be considered thoroughly is the way with which the learning agent should be able to perceive and understand its environment. In most of the works made to study and analyse Reinforcement Learning problem, it was question of teaching a robot how to wonder in a given environment with obstacles, this was achieved by equipping the robot with sensors that understand outside world and answers to reward from it. In the DeepMind works, the agent plugs into a serial bus to retrieve images in real time of the game simulator to be able to understand its environment state. In a cloud load balancing problem, the agent only sensors are its network inputs and outputs, so a way to achieve communication and understanding is by using the networks sensors to gather data and organize it in a reward framework.

Once these challenges are overcome, the Reinforcement Learner based load balancer can be used to either control the cloud system to not overload the system by not allowing the load permitted or balanced above a certain limit, or for planning to know how to scale up and down the cloud system for future pick times.

CONCLUSION

Most of the works on cloud load balancing do deep inspection of the behaviour of the system by either keeping track of the states in the load balancing software, or relying on a central node that does the mapping or dispatching of users' requests to the cloud. These approaches are often computationally consuming, introduce point of failures that need to be handled as a separate process in the cloud system lifetime, or not dynamic in time.

Considering the cloud system as a reinforcement learning problem will allow to be independent of how the users' requests are being generated, this means any fed job distribution to the software, or any behaviour seen from adjacent routers will be handled with no need to do additional parametrization; the Reinforcement Learning engine will explore new states and map them to actions, which allows for creating a model free handling of the system that is being studied.

In summary, reinforcement learning techniques are a very good candidate to achieve good performances in cloud load balancing in terms of:

- Reducing the load on processors that are likely to be loaded at the instant of making the load balancing decision.
- Dispatching the correct load to the instances that are likely to have more room for computing resources.
- Attaining an equilibrium where all the system is working optimally in regard of users' requests.
- Proposing a framework for planning and control of the system.

REFERENCES

Barto, A. G., & Duff, M. (1994). Monte Carlo matrix inversion and reinforcement learning. In *Advances in Neural Information Processing Systems* (pp. 687–687).

Bhatnagar, S., Precup, D., Silver, D., Sutton, R. S., Maei, H. R., & Szepesvári, C. (2009). Convergent temporal-difference learning with arbitrary smooth function approximation. In Advances in Neural Information Processing Systems (pp. 1204-1212).

Busoniu, L., Babuska, R., De Schutter, B., & Ernst, D. (2010). *Reinforcement learning and dynamic programming using function approximators* (Vol. 39). CRC press. doi:10.1201/9781439821091

Fard, M. M., & Grinberg, Y. massoud Farahmand, A., Pineau, J., & Precup, D. (2013). Bellman error based feature generation using random projections on sparse spaces. In Advances in Neural Information Processing Systems (pp. 3030-3038).

Glynn, P. W., & Iglehart, D. L. (1989). Importance sampling for stochastic simulations. *Management Science*, *35*(11), 1367–1392. doi:10.1287/mnsc.35.11.1367

Harraz, A., Bissiriou, C., Cherkaoui, R., Zbakh, M. (2016). Study of an adaptive approach for a Cloud system implementation. *Proceedings of 2016 International Conference on Cloud Computing Technologies and Applications CloudTech 2016* (pp. 230-23).

Hecht-Nielsen, R. (1988). Theory of the backpropagation neural network. *Neural Networks*, *1*(Supplement-1), 445–448. doi:10.1016/0893-6080(88)90469-8

Jaakkola, T., Singh, S. P., & Jordan, M. I. (1995). Reinforcement learning algorithm for partially observable Markov decision problems. In *Advances in Neural Information Processing Systems* (pp. 345–352).

Konda, V. R., & Tsitsiklis, J. N. (2003). Onactor-critic algorithms. *SIAM Journal on Control and Optimization, 42*(4), 1143–1166. doi:10.1137/S0363012901385691

Konidaris, G., & Osentoski, S. (2008). Value function approximation in reinforcement learning using the Fourier basis.

Kuleshov, V., & Precup, D. (2014). Algorithms for multi-armed bandit problems. arXiv:1402.6028

Kunz, F. (n. d.). An Introduction to Temporal Difference Learning.

Maei, H. R., & Sutton, R. S. (2010, March). GQ (λ): A general gradient algorithm for temporal-difference prediction learning with eligibility traces. In *Proceedings of the Third Conference on Artificial General Intelligence* (Vol. 1, pp. 91-96). doi:10.2991/agi.2010.22

Mahadevan, S. (2005, August). Proto-value functions: Developmental reinforcement learning. In *Proceedings of the 22nd international conference on Machine learning* (pp. 553-560). ACM.

Mnih, V., Kavukcuoglu, K., Silver, D., Graves, A., Antonoglou, I., Wierstra, D., & Riedmiller, M. (2013). Playing atari with deep reinforcement learning. arXiv preprint arXiv:1312.5602.

Mnih, V., Kavukcuoglu, K., Silver, D., Rusu, A. A., Veness, J., Bellemare, M. G., & Petersen, S. et al. (2015). Human-level control through deep reinforcement learning. *Nature, 518*(7540), 529–533. doi:10.1038/nature14236 PMID:25719670

Parr, R., Painter-Wakefield, C., Li, L., & Littman, M. Analyzing feature generation for value-function approximation. In *Proceedings of the International Conference on Machine Learning*.

Precup, D. (2000). Eligibility traces for off-policy policy evaluation.

Precup, D., Sutton, R. S., & Dasgupta, S. (2001, June). Off-policy temporal-difference learning with function approximation. In ICML (pp. 417-424).

Regalia, P. (1994). *Adaptive IIR filtering in signal processing and control.* CRC Press.

Sutton, R. S., & Barto, A. G. (1998). Reinforcement learning: An introduction. Cambridge: MIT press.

Sutton, R. S., McAllester, D. A., Singh, S. P., & Mansour, Y. (1999, November). Policy gradient methods for reinforcement learning with function approximation. In NIPS (Vol. 99, pp. 1057-1063).

Chapter 12
Mobile Cloud Computing Security Frameworks:
A Review

Anita Dashti
Foolad Institute of Technology, Iran

ABSTRACT

Mobile Cloud Computing (MCC) is a rich technology of mobile that offers cloud resources and network technology features like unlimited storage at any time via Ethernet or internet based on Pay-Per-Use method. In MCC all processes will be done in cloud servers and data is stored there too, thus mobile devices are just a tool for presenting events. MCC technology is completely different from previous traditional network technologies, so nowadays most impossible ways are becoming possible. MCC is a combination of cloud computing and mobile network. Being online and internet network brings some problems for users. One of the most popular challenges in this technology is building a secure architecture in mobile internet platform. Different security frameworks in different contexts of security challenges in MCC are recommended and compared in some common parameters to have better understanding of which one is the best for user's needs.

INTRODUCTION

Mobile cloud computing is a technology that refers to accessing the resources in network whenever and wherever wanted (Gupta, 2012). The popularity of internet network and cloud computing is getting clear to all. Everything is going to be

DOI: 10.4018/978-1-5225-3038-1.ch012

computerized and the popularity of cloud computing helps to have another architecture that inherits from previous technologies. The number of mobile devices are growing every day, thus the needs for mobile applications increases (Gupta, 2012). As well as having advantages using this technology, some significant issues can rise and cause concerns for users who want to migrate to cloud servers. These issues are privacy, accessibility, security, reliability and some other related ones (Reza, 2016). Mobile devices are becoming important as a part of human life which plays an important role that effects the life and makes it more convenient. Cloud computing has helped users to take their information with them everywhere, also helped to access them whenever wanted (Hoang, 2011). Mobile phones were not invented in the last century, but now is rare to find a house without some mobile phone device. Smart phones have become popular in the last 5 years and in 10 people 6 has a smart phone and the rest has a mobile phone device. Technology never leaves its users alone and is coming up fast according to their needs. According to Portio Research the number of mobile phone users will reach 7.5 till the end of 2014 (Al-Hammami, 2015). It means more 3 quarter of the world will choose mobile device to help them during the day, because it's small, light, can make/receive a call, processes data and all the user needs can be done using it. Mobile phone device is considered one of the most common thing in the history of the technology (Al-Hammami, 2015). Today the mobile phone device has become a key point to contact between people, businesses and consumers. Mobile phone devices have changed the way of communication between human beings, also it contributed to the creation of new businesses (Al-Hammami, 2015). After popularity of MCC and increasing growth of mobile devices, limitations of mobile devices caused a kind of migration for mobile users to cloud. This way, it's clear that mobile internet can fix in cloud computing architecture and because MCC is fixed on cloud computing architecture, so it inherits all security issues plus mobile device limitations. Portable devices need less CPU processing ability, storage capacity, battery, bandwidth, smaller monitor and keyboard than a PC. These are called limitations in MCC technology. Too many works have been done for improving security in cloud computing, but because of mobile device limitations all frameworks can't be used in mobile devices (Chaubey, 2016). Mobile device limitations and security issues on the way of using MCC has drew attentions to itself. Many researches have been done to improve security and privacy that causes concerns for all users. Some solutions can run in mobile devices, some run in cloud-side and some can handle both. Because of mobile device limitations cloud-side frameworks are welcomed more than others. In this chapter the main purpose is to introduce different best security frameworks that are focused on data security and third party misuse. Then by comparison of these frameworks all features can be revealed clearly.

Background: Cloud and Mobile Cloud Computing

Cloud computing delivers different kinds of services over the internet by computing resources that are provided dynamically (Gupta, 2012). This technology is popular because it eliminates the limitations. These limitations include computing overhead, different service requirements and other related problems. According to (Mell, Sep. 2011), released in its "Special Publication 800-145", the National Institute of Standards and Technology (NIST) defines cloud computing as "a model for enabling convenient, on-demand network access to a shared pool of configurable computing resources that can be rapidly provisioned and released with minimal management effort or service provider interaction". NIST believes that characteristics of cloud computing are as stated bellow.

- **On-Demand Self-Service:** Users can change cloud services online (add, delete or change storage network and software).
- **Broad Network Access:** The user can access cloud services using smart and portable devices wherever connected to the access point.
- **Resource Pooling:** The user can use required cloud resources anytime and anywhere.
- **Elasticity:** The user can add or remove other users and resources according to the user's needs.
- **Measured Service:** Cloud provider measures storage levels, processing, user accounts and bills accordingly.
- **Pricing:** The cost of used services by user must be paid. This feature is transparent to the user.
- **Quality of Service:** Guarantees, best performance, required resources and availability is provided for users by cloud provider.

Services in cloud computing is in three categories: these three-layered service model are 1- Infrastructure as a Service (IaaS), 2- Platform-as-a-Service (PaaS), 3- Software-as-Service (SaaS) (Bheda, 2013). IaaS supplies processing, storage, networks and other hardware oriented resources (Foster, 2008; Buyya, 2009). Service managers use this service and other users can run a virtual machine to use this kind of applications and software. The cloud provider manages the infrastructure and the user has full control of operating system, applications, storage and also has partial control over network devices. The main advantage of IaaS is free servers, physical data storage and networking (Reza, 2016). PaaS can run applications on the appropriate cloud provider's infrastructure. PaaS runs applications and tools which are supported by cloud provider. Service provider manages the operating system and the infrastructure and user manages required applications on cloud system

(Bahar, 2013). The SaaS runs applications and software that infrastructure and OS management needs, also application configuration will be done by service provider. Business user tend to use this service model. It focuses on end-user requirements (Reza, 2016).

Mobile cloud computing tries to resolve issues caused by limitations of low end computing devices. It's been done by the help of cloud resources and network connectivity. The key features that are expected from MCC is availability, reliability, scalability, security, device independence and low costs (Bahar, 2013).There are three main parts in MCC, the user, Mobile device and cloud provider. The user take the advantages of cloud resources by using mobile device and network connectivity. The user can upload and download information from the cloud, install mobile apps, upgrade OS and applications and use cloud resources via mobile network connections. The cloud provides resources for computing, storage and other related ones (Reza, 2016).

Advantages of Mobile Cloud Computing

Cloud computing is known as a solution for Mobile Computing because of having mobility, communication and portability (Forman, 1994). The advantages of MCC are provided bellow.

1. **Extending Battery Life:** Mobile users always have some problem with battery lifetime. There are some solutions to enhance the CPU performance (Kakerow, 2003; Paulson, 2003) and to manage disk (Davis, 2002; Mayo, 2003) and screen smart to reduce consumption. These solutions need some changes in structure of mobile devices or some hardware changes. These changes increase the cost of mobile devices and is not suitable for all devices. Processing large amount of data causes large amount of power consumption. Computational offloading aims to transfer large computations to the cloud server to eliminate limitations and save energy (Hoang, 2013). According to (Rudenko, 1998; Smailagic, 2002) remote applications save energy significantly, they could find it through several examinations in this context. In (Rudenko, 1998) it is evaluated that offloading of large matrix of computation can save energy up to 45%. Some applications can take advantage of being transferred to cloud servers for computation. For example, offloading image processing reduces 41% energy consumption for a mobile device (kremer, 2001). Also, offloading a mobile game component using Memory Arithmetic Unit and Interface can save energy to 27% for computer games and 45% for a chess game (Cuervo, 2010).

2. **Enhancing Data Storage Capacity and Power of Processing:** Storage capacity is another limitation for mobile devices. So, users can be able to store/access large amount of data on cloud using wireless network (Hoang, 2013). There some examples for this context like Amazon Simple Storage Service that supports data storage service (Amazon, 2013), Image Exchange using large amount of storage service in cloud for mobile users (Vartiainen, 2010). In this technology, immediate upload after capturing is enabled for mobile users. This technology is called image sharing and users are able to access the images from any device. The main advantage of this technology is saving battery power and storage of mobile devices because all image processing and storage is sent to clouds. Flicker (Flicker, 2013) and ShoZu (ShoZu, 2013) are mobile photo sharing application using MCC. Facebook (Facebook, 2013) is a popular social network application that has cloud photo sharing. MCC also helps reducing consumption of time and energy and storage on limited devices.

3. **Improving Reliability:** Storing and processing data and running applications on cloud servers is an effective way to improve the reliability because backups, application data and other information can be stored on several computers and can be accessed from any device. This way the data and application lost is reduced, also MCC helps data security for both CSP and user (Hoang, 2013). For example, the cloud can be protected from any hacks, misuses and unauthorized distribution (Zou, 2010). Also, remote security services can be provided for users in cloud like virus scanning, malicious code detection and authentication (Oberheide, 2008).

MCC also inherits advantages for clouds for mobile services as follows (Hoang, 2013).

1. **Scalability:** Mobile applications' deployment can be scaled to meet the unpredictable user requests because of flexible resource provisioning. CSPs can simply add and expand an application or service without any limitation.

2. **Multi-Tenancy:** CSPs' ability to share resources and costs to support variety of applications and large number of users.

3. **Ease of Integration:** The ability to integrate multiple services from different CSPs easily through the cloud and internet network to meet the user demand.

Security in Mobile Cloud Computing

MCC wants to create an easy way for users to send/receive data to/from the cloud. In this way, users will have their data with them anywhere, and can access them on demand (Bahar, 2013). Some security issues are found on the way of cloud computing, network connectivity and mobile devices. According to (Kekre, 2008) main security issues are: 1) Physical control: when user sends information to the cloud he won't have physical access to them anymore, so it's important to have legal and complete access over the data. 2) Privacy Policy: when user sends information to the cloud he is concern about who can access the information, so he has the right to know who can have the access to which data. 3) Security: user is always concern about data to know whether hackers can misuse the files or they are kept out of sight.

To provide security for data stored on cloud, some security standards must be followed (Bahar, 2013). These standards are like access control, encryption, content security, data authentication and some other related ones (Sahu, 2012). According to (Prasad, 2012; Bahar, 2013; Hoang, 2011; Satyanarayanan, 1996; Oberheide, 2008; Portokalidis, 2010) there are some issues that are related to client-side that means mobile devices. When data is uploaded to the cloud-side, mobile devices are also at risk of being stolen or lost, or man-in-the-middle attacks that means steal the information on the way of being transmitted to the cloud when the data is not encrypted, or being stolen or attacked by and intruder in cloud administrator. There are proposed resolves for these kind of security issues. When mobile device is stolen or lost, data can be wiped from the device via remote location. When man-in-the-middle attack happens, security application and some encryption-based ways can be used (Bheda, 2013; Saravankumar, 2014). And when insider attacks happen, additional security layer must be provided (Reza, 2016).

SECURITY ARCHITECTURE

Cloud computing among top 10 technologies is known as the first and will be accepted by more and more companies and organizations (Hashizume, 2013). Researchers estimated in (Subashini, 2011) that till 2016 up to 12% of software market will use cloud computing and the amount of it will reach 95$ billion. In the following security issues available on three layers infrastructure model are discussed (Hassan Hussein, 2016).

Infrastructure as Services (IAAS) Security Challenges

Services which are provided by CSPs are storage, servers, hardware and other related wireless based services. CSPs own all the equipment and are responsible to house, run and maintain it. In this model pay-per-use method is considered for users. Characteristics and components in IaaS are as the following (Jaiswal, 2014):

- Service Level Agreement (SLA)

- Dynamic scaling
- Automation of administrative tasks
- Utility computing service and billing model
- Internet connective
- Desktop virtualization

Platform as Services (PaaS) Security Challenges

PaaS let users to rent needed hardware over the internet, so they can run application without the need for installing any platform or tools on their local machines. This layer allows users to use cloud-side operating system, hardware and any platform needed. Also, this way user can develop any software using advanced level services (Shekhar, 2014). Advantages that developers can take from PaaS:

- OS can change when needed.
- PaaS allows share information to develop software project wherever needed (Jaiswal, 2014).

Security threads in PaaS are described as following (Hassan Hussein, 2016).

1. **Data Location:** The platform is distributed to several hosts so the location of data is not clear. This way it has more security in comparison with a single host. Data can be duplicated in hosts, so duplication can add more security and availability for user data (Shehri, 2013).
2. **Privileged Access:** PaaS allows software developers to debug. Debug grant access to data and its location to modify values and test results (Devi, 2015).
3. **Distributed Systems:** PaaS file system is distributed. CSP must provide security for all the equipment and user, and user is responsible to take this security (Nerkar, 2012).

Software as Services (SaaS) Security Challenges

SaaS is called software on demand, it means license of the software application will be available once so that users can use it without charge. Services provided by cloud are accessed over the internet. SaaS is deployed for CRM, digital billing, invoicing, human resource management, financials, document management, service desk management and collaboration (Jaiswal, 2014). SaaS services are access over the internet using web browser. Thus, web browser's security affects the security of this technology (Ayoleke, 2011). CSP has to verify users and make sure that they cannot lead to other user's privacy, and user must have security and privacy while using the application (Patell, 2014).

SaaS security challenges are as following (Hassan Hussein, 2016):

- Authentication and authorization
- Data confidentiality
- Availability
- Information security
- Data access
- Data breaches
- Identity management and sign on process

Questions that users ask to get sure security threads are covered are as following (Patell, 2014):

- What metrics can be used for reporting?
- What is the level of access controls?
- Is the provided data can be easily adapted in the internal monitoring tools?
- How important and critical the enterprise data is?

Cloud computing infrastructure has three layers, and each layer has to deal with some related security issues. Issues related to each layer discussed above, so it's clear that the best way to cover security in CC and other technologies that inherit from that, is to consider security in all layers. In the following a three-layered cloud security model is described. In the first layer, user will be authenticated by a suitable authentication techniques. In the second layer, data will be protected by proper identification and data encryption. In the third layer security is provided by secure transmission of data using proper cryptography (Hassan Hussein, 2016).

MAIN FOCUS OF THE CHAPTER

Issues, Controversies, Problems

As discussed in previous sections, mobile cloud computing is now a popular environment and mobile devices are being essential in human life. MCC has some advantages and in this way some disadvantages and problems exist. The most important issue in MCC is security in all aspects of its technology. Everyone has to be aware of them, so that can manage it much easier. Many security frameworks exist that resolve some security aspects of MCC. In the following section it will be discussed.

Security Frameworks in Different Aspects of Mobile Cloud Computing

Despite having security issues in the way of sending/receiving data to/from cloud providers, there are some frameworks that cover different aspects of MCC system. They can all be combined to have a full pack security framework. Security is always a concern when it comes to mobile network. There are always some attackers that want to find a way to access the file. So, every day there will be a new need to provide better security for the proposed system. In the following different security frameworks are provided (Patel, 2015).

1. Data Security Framework in Cloud Computing

This article proposes a mechanism that only legal users can access their own files and other users must have the data owner's permission to access the file. There are some steps for uploading the file on the cloud server. Figure 1 shows uploading steps and figure 2 shows downloading steps (Patel, 2015).

1.1 Uploading Steps

For uploading the user's file to the cloud server, this framework has rules to must be obeyed. All steps are the exact words of (Patel, 2015). In figure 3 encryption process of proposed framework in shown.

Step 1: Select the File "F" and provide the password up to 6 to 20 characters from mobile user.

Step 2: Divide the File "F" in to "N" numbers of equal block size. For symmetric defragmentation, some extra bits should be padded at the end of file if required for equal size.

Step 3: Generate the multiple block keys from given password and also generate the integrity key and symmetric key by using the Hash function on password as well as other unique factors related to user file.

Step 4: Encrypt the individual blocks by using counter mode of operations. The generated multiple block key is used for each different block. The X-OR operation is performed for encryption of each block. The counter is also used to produce the keys as an input for block encryption. In these operations, the multiple block key and counter are increment one by one from previous block to next succeed blocks.

Figure 1. Uploading steps (Patel, 2015)

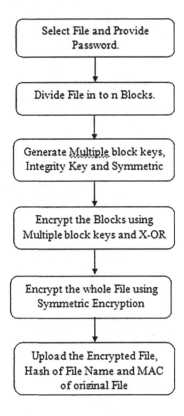

Step 5: Concatenate all blocks to build one file. Encrypt the complete file with symmetric encryption algorithm. The generated symmetric key is used as an encryption key.

Step 6: Mobile user uploads the encrypted File, hash of file name and MAC of original file. Integrity key is applied in MAC for file integrity verification. This complete information will be uploaded to cloud storage servers by mobile users and it will only save the file name.

1.2 Downloading Steps

For downloading the user's file from the cloud server, this framework has rules to must be obeyed. All steps are the exact words of [1]. In figure 4 decryption process of proposed framework in shown.

Figure 2. Downloading steps (Patel, 2015)

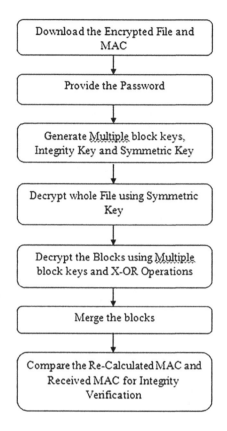

Figure 3. Encryption process of proposed framework (Patel, 2015)

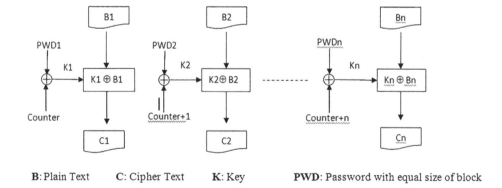

Figure 4. Decryption process of proposed framework (Patel, 2015)

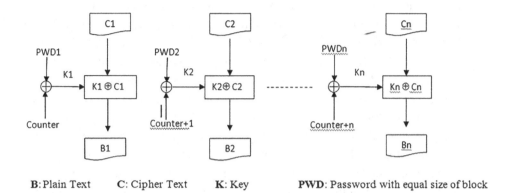

B: Plain Text   **C**: Cipher Text   **K**: Key   **PWD**: Password with equal size of block

Step 1: Mobile user sends the request for file download to Cloud Service Provider (CSP). CSP sends the encrypted file with MAC of original File. Mobile user downloads the encrypted file and MAC.

Step 2: The password is provided by mobile user for generation of various keys. The keys for blocks and for decrypt the encrypted file is generated from provided password.

Step 3: The symmetric key, integrity key and multiple block key are generated from given password by mobile user.

Step 4: The complete encrypted file is decrypted with generated symmetric key and symmetric cryptographic algorithm.

Step 5: Every blocks are decrypted by generated multiple block keys and X-OR operations. The counter mode of operations are used to obtain the original file blocks or plaintext of blocks.

Step 6: Following decryption of every blocks the plaintext of all blocks are produced. Thereafter, merge or concatenate every plaintext blocks for collect the original file.

Step 7: Compare the MAC of received MAC from CSP and re-calculated MAC of original file subsequent to decryption, with generated integrity key.

2. Mobi-Cloud Security Framework for Mobile Computation and Communication

Hoang and co-workers in (Hoang, 2010) proposed a new framework for wireless mobile networks that is called Mobi-Cloud. Each mobile node is considered as a service node that it can be considered either as an intermediate or as a service provider according to its capacity. To reduce the uncertainty caused by the movement of mobile devices, in this model each service node will be considered as a virtual component also each service node will be mapped in cloud side ESSI to make up the computing and communicational limitations of mobile devices. A new service is provided, that is called VTaPD, by using programmable router technology for isolation the flow of information security domains. Mobi-Cloud uses software agents to connect to the cloud services and mobile devices that can run on both mobile devices and cloud platforms. In the cloud, MAI exports all services that can be used by mobile devices. A node manager is responsible for managing, loading and unloading of the ESSI software agents. Resource manager, program manager, VTaPD manager and TMS form the core of SeaaS. By using security as a service (SaaS) Mobi-Cloud system can offer combination of security services according to the mobile devices' requests. Mobi-Cloud interdependent components in a TMS include identity management, key management, effective access control and aware risk assessment. TMS includes managements like identity management, key management, simple access control and risk assessment. Mobi-Cloud uses identity based encryption for assigning keys to user-centric IDs and for access control uses attribute based encryption and for ID management uses ABIDM.

3. Mobile Cloud Framework by Developing Mobi-Cloud

Hoang and co-workers in (Chow, 2010) proposed a secure data process framework in mobile cloud computing that is based on Mobi-Cloud architecture and focuses

Figure 5. Mobi-cloud architecture (Hoang, 2010)

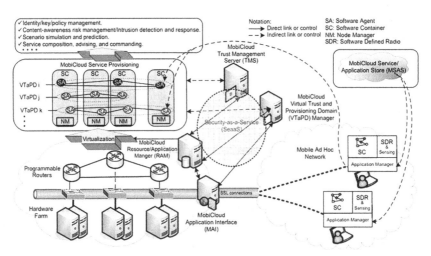

on protecting user data against untrusted CSPs. Mobile cloud consists of three main parts: 1- cloud mobile 2- untrusted cloud domain 3- public cloud service and storage domain. In this system, a TA is considered for managing security keys and mobile user certificates. Also, a secure TA is considered for keys and certificates distribution. According to these assumptions, TA is responsible for establishing ABIDM in mobile cloud IDs and secure management. The user can deduct private key for next secure communications by TA. For sharing the file in a group ABE method is recommended. Consider a user is communicated with a group that have these addresses: {111,110,101,100,011,001}, except these addresses: {000,010}. A local method is used for making the access tree using logical OR (+) in the root. For reducing involved features a date function (m) with BFM method is used and shown in equation 1.

$$M\{001,011,100,110,111\} = B`_1 B`_2 B_3 + B`_1 B_2 B_3 + B_1 B_2 B_3 + B_1 B`_2 B`_3 + B_1 B_2 B_3 + B_1 B_2$$
$$B_3 = B_0 + B_2 \tag{1}$$

Bi and Bi shows values of 0 and 1 in (i)th place. The final access tree includes features $B_0 + B_2$ for making encrypted data secure, and 000 and 010 cannot access the data. As figure 6 shows, this system classifies the data in two levels of 1- critical data 2- normal data, to manage the data in multi-tenancy environment. ESSI is considered as a three root, one for cloud, one for user and the last is for auditing. As figure 7 shows, the input flow in ESSI will be processed in some steps: 1- Data flow is inspected by the classification model that classifies the data as critical data or normal data 2- If the data is classified as normal, the normal data will be sent to the public cloud storage through a masking procedure 3- The Encryption/Decryption/Verification (EDV) module is then used on the critical data and stores the processed data in SS. The masking procedure will be performed to remove private information associated with the user and anonymize the data content.

4. Authentication in Mobile Cloud Computing

In (Chow, 2010) has proposed a policy based authentication in cloud that can manage the authentication of user device in a simple and flexible way. This framework uses a reliable cubic model to manage cloud infrastructure and translates user behavior by implied authentication. Implied authentication uses habits instead of belongings for user authentication. By using a statistical model probable authentication score is given to user device via monitored behavior. Proposed authentication framework compares threshold value and user authentication score to detect legal users. Threshold value depends on program type. In figure 9 the main 4 components of the system is shown. They are 1- data aggregator 2- client device 3- authentication engine 4-

Figure 6. Multi-tenant secure data management in Mobi-Cloud (Chow, 2010)

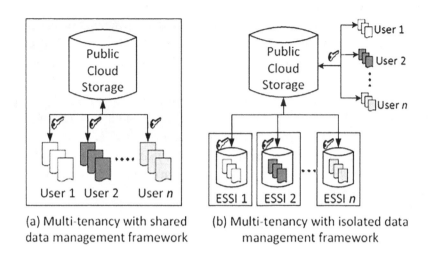

(a) Multi-tenancy with shared data management framework

(b) Multi-tenancy with isolated data management framework

Figure 7. Data processing in ESSIs (Chow, 2010)

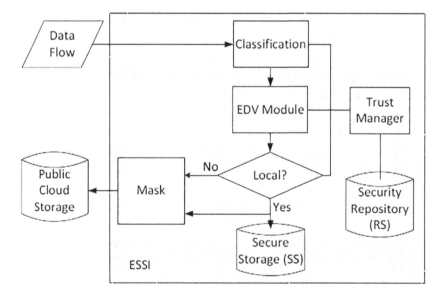

authentication consumer. User device produces important information and operations like SMS, MMS, phone call history, web browser, network information, location information and phone information. The user device keeps this information in a local cache before sending them to the data aggregator. Authentication engine extracts the info(s) from data authentication and corresponding authentication policies to authenticate the user who is using the client device. Authentication consumer part runs authentication policies according to client device's requests, finally authentication consumer responses the user requests according to the authentication engine results. When an authentication consumer receives an access request from a client device, authentication process gets legal. Before sending the request to the authentication engine, authentication consumer registers a policy in authentication engine. This policy consists of three parts: 1- access request 2- gathered requested data stored on data aggregator 3- political rules. Political rules consist of integrity control policy in platform and environment, authentication threshold value and optional authentication if the authentication value was less than threshold. After registering the policies, client device sends access request and details to the authentication engine. Authentication engine retrieves the request and all required data for process from data aggregator and client device, and if all policies are fulfilled it will dedicate the access score to the client device via authentication consumer. This system is designed to detect legal users and can run in trusted third party or CSP.

5. SDSM Secure Data Service Mechanism in Mobile Cloud Computing

jia and co-workers in (Jia, 2011) proposed a secure data service mechanism in mobile cloud computing. SDSM is a secure and user-oriented data service in mobile cloud computing that enables users to enjoy using an outsourced secure data service that has minimum security overload. The main idea of SDSM is that outsourcing is a

Figure 8. System model diagram (Chow, 2010)

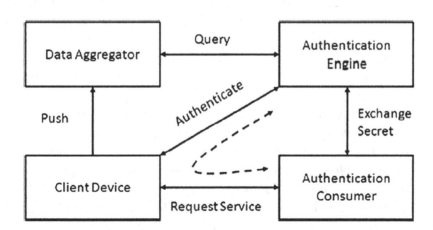

secure way not only for data but also for system security management in mobile cloud computing. Data owners and data subscribers can easily connect to the internet via mobile devices. For preventing from data leaking they share and use encrypted data. Data subscribers must have the decryption permission from data owners. In this framework cloud servers are considered online and with high storage and computing ability. Identity-based encryption scheme is based on mutual mapping and has bijective, indestructibility and calculable features. Two independent functions H_1 and H_2 are used that are shown in relation 2 and 3.

$$h_1: \{0, 1\}^* \rightarrow g_1 \tag{2}$$

$$H_2: G_T \rightarrow G_1 \tag{3}$$

In this protocol, an ID-based re-encryption proxy is used to achieve data confidentiality. PRE schema allows semi-trusted proxies to convert an encrypted file using Alis public key to re-encrypted file with Bob public key. In mobile network, users must be registered in the system with an ID, this way they can acquire corresponding secure key. Mobile users use IB_PRE encryption algorithm for making the data secure in the cloud servers and the cipher text can be decrypted whenever the user wants. Before encryption file 'F' is divided into N blocks. F=(m_1, m_2, m_3, ..., m_n) for m_i blocks, data owner will encrypt them via its security key. In that time, the data owner must produce proxy re-encryption security key for legal users. This proxy re-encryption security key is produced from its corresponding user ID. Proxy re-encryption framework consists of six algorithms that follows: Keygen, Setup‹ Encrypt, Pkeygen, Re-encrypt, Decrypt. 1- Setup (1^λ): the input is a security parameter λ that produces system parameters and master security key. They are all kept secure. 2- Keygen (params, msk, id): gets params, ID $\in \{0,1\}$ and master security key as an input and will produce decryption key sk_{id} corresponding to the user ID. 3- Encrypt(params,id,m): gets set of params, ID $\in \{0,1\}$ and text 'm' that m $\in$ M as an input. The result is C_{id}, m will be encrypted based on ID. 4- Rkgen(params, sk_{id}, id_1,id_2): gets sk_{id}, id_1,id_2 $\in \{0,1\}^*$ as an input and produces re-encryption key $rk_{id1 \rightarrow id2}$. 5- Re-encrypt (params, $rk_{id1 \rightarrow id2}$, c_{id1}): gets C_{id1} based on id_1 and re-encryption key $rk_{id1 \rightarrow id2}$ and produces re-encryption text c_{id2}. 6- Decrypt (params, sk_{id},C_{id}): decrypt C_{id1} using security key sk_{id} and produce text 'm'.

There are five phases in this protocol that will be explained in the following. 1- Setting: In this phase system parameters and secret key will be produced using setup and keygen algorithms. MSK (main secret key) value is s (MSK=s). All mobile users that are registered in the system can have can have a secret key corresponding to this user's ID. In the equation Sk=H1 $(ID_A)^s$, 'S' is just used in user registration process. Data owners can share the data just by giving subscriber's ID. 2- Data encryption: Data 'f' is divided into 'N' parts. $F = (m_1, m_2, ..., m_n)$ runs Encrypt algorithm for every part of data owner's data then creates m_i. $M_i = (m.e(g^s, H1(id_a)^r))$ After encryption of 'F' mobile user loads $F' = (M_1, M_2, ..., M_n)$ to the cloud. 3- Sharing data: In this phase data owner runs Rkgen algorithm and RK key can be used by cloud to convert cipher text 'F' to partner's public key based cipher text. Data owner sends RK to the cloud. This means the cloud will be data management representative from the owner. The cloud can consider RK to allow legal users decrypt their cipher text. 4- Data access: When data partners want to access the file, they will send a request to cloud servers. If cloud server has the RK for it, will confirm the request then runs Keygen algorithm to access RK cipher text. Data partner fetches re-encrypted file and runs Decrypt algorithm on M_i using its secret key like phase 4, to access 'F' content. 5- Updating security policies: User may want to update this user's partners list. This means to grant or grab this user's score to/ from them. This way mobile user can do it without retrieving and decrypting secret text or re-creation of access tree. For updating or deleting a partner, data owner must create a new encryption key.

Comparison of Frameworks

According to frameworks represented in Table 1, (Patel, 2015) is focused on reducing the computational complexity. All CSP's are considered untrusted so in this framework for having information security strong encryption is used. Furthermore, the speed of processing is significant. According to considered features, proposed framework uses three technique encryption for information privacy and security. It also uses Blowfish cryptographic algorithm because of speed importance. Also, storage capacity limitations are considered. User sends information in a secure way to cloud, cloud tries protect the information for the next user call. The framework uses many security keys in this protection type, so in this way third party can't listen to it. In (Hoang, 2010) users must trust the CSP but this is a big matter for users and they are concerned about their sensitive information. This framework defined and assigned VTaPD to the mobile devices, so this has caused big problems in scalability. It uses encryption based on features for data protection. This method needs preset features and needs to rebuild the access tree for updating access policies, thus it brings so much Communicational and computational overhead. In (Hoang, 2011) uses secure data process for mobi-cloud that improves security and user protection using Secure Multi-Tenancy Management Service, reliable management and ESSI data processing model. In this method for providing strong security services, storage module and reliable module range are physically isolated. ESSI makes a security layer for protection of users' private information in multi-tenancy environment that improves data security. It uses encryption based on identity and encryption based on feature to resolve the complexity of access policy and group key updates. If reliable range module is hosted by a third-party scalability issues would arise. And if reliable range module is hosted by other CSPs, it is possible that different CSPs use different APIs, it causes problems that should be considered. In (Chow, 2010) important information is collected and stored in a data collector that influences the users' privacy policy. Mobile users use a data hash function with a key produced by their own for having privacy policy then they send produced information to the data collector. In this way, suspicious cases can be detected without disclosing the users' sensitive information. Mobile users use a data hash function rapidly to gain privacy but it can cause communication delay and energy lost. In (Jia, 2011) proposed a secure data service in cloud computing that outsources security management and data without presenting any information about the user using proxy re-encryption and identity based encryption schemes. It decreases security management overhead by users and communication overhead in re-encryption key size, then the costs decrease. Since changing of the access policy is easy and it doesn't need to retrieve and decrypt the cipher-text, a user can easily get access score just by assigning a re-encryption key from a server. This framework is suitable for high scalable mobile networks. The CSP is considered as a semi-trusted. It does not consider malicious collusion subscribers with cloud servers to find the re-encryption key so the attacker can access the cipher-text.

Evaluation Criteria in Security Frameworks

Data security frameworks or security of inserted and manipulated data is all related to mobile devices and cloud servers. Some important parameters in MCC are selected to compare different security frameworks. In the following description of security criteria that are selected for comparison are provided.

- **Theory:** This parameter defines basic building blocks of security frameworks. They can be mathematical or cryptography principals. The reason for choosing this parameter is to identify computational requirements of security frameworks.
- **Data Security in Cloud:** Just a small number of security frameworks have inserted and manipulated data security in cloud-side. So, it's better to use this parameter to determine the nature of the framework.
- **Integrity:** Users upload their files in cloud servers to increase storage capacity. So, they wouldn't have physical control on them anymore. Therefor there must be a mechanism to ensure the integrity of user's uploaded files. So, this

parameter helps to determine whether the cloud server has this mechanism or not.

- **Scalability:** Scalability shows the ability of the framework to manage and control increasing number of users in the considered way. If the framework could manage and control increased number of users without any reduction or change in physical infrastructure, it would be considered as a scalable framework. If the security framework is dependent on centralized servers that are managed by a third party to provide some security features, the scalability would be considered medium otherwise poor.

- **Authentication:** If a mobile user upload some files on cloud servers to share them with others, there must be a mechanism to approve the file creator. Authentication can help approving the creator. Authentication parameter defines authentication issues in security framework.

- **Device Limitations:** smart phone devices have some limitations. For resolving this problem MCC is recommended. Some frameworks have computation offloading and some have storage offloading. This help mobile devices to send files and processes in cloud-side then receive the results.

- **Accessibility:** Accessibility can be considered in two groups: 1- auto 2- semi-auto. The accessibility is auto when users share uploaded files on cloud servers and legal users can automatically access and decrypt the files without

Table 1. Data security in different MCC frameworks

Jia	Chow	Hoang	Hoang	Patel	Researcher's Name
2011	2010	2011	2010	2015	**Year**
UAE	USA	Arizona	USA	India	**Location**
IDE PRE	Implied Policy Based Authentication	Mobi-Cloud	IDE ABE	Three technique encryption	**Theory**
SDSM	Reliable Cubic Model and Implied Policy	ESSI	ESSI	MAC Hash Blowfish	**Technology**
No	No	Yes	No	Yes	**Data Security in Cloud**
Yes	Yes	Yes	No	Yes	**Privacy Policy**
No	No	Yes	Yes	Yes	**Integrity**
No	Yes	Yes	Yes	Yes	**Authentication**
High	High	High	Medium	High	**Scalability**
Auto	Auto	Auto	Auto	Auto	**Accessibility**
Yes	No	Yes	Yes	Yes	**Device Limitations**
Semi-trusted	Untrusted	Untrusted	Semi-trusted	Untrusted	**Cloud Provider**

owner's permission. The accessibility is semi-auto when the user wants to send private information like passwords and private keys by other tools like E-mail or text message, and accessing the uploaded file needs decryption.

- **Cloud Service Provider:** CSP can be in two states: 1- untrusted 2- semi-trusted. It is impossible to know whether the CSP is completely safe or not. If a framework is untrusted, they will consider all safety aspects. Otherwise they didn't consider all safety aspects.

CONCLUSION

Mobile cloud Computing is becoming more and more popular in computer society. Now in most organizations cloud computing is being used and they are taking the advantage of this technology. In this chapter MCC and security issues in all parts, from infrastructure to front end, and other user concerns for using MCC resources discussed. Some new challenges explained and different proposed security frameworks against risks in MCC reviewed. At the end, significant parameters selected to compare different aspects of security frameworks. The result of this comparison is provided in Table 1.

REFERENCES

Al Shehri, W. (2013). Cloud database database as a service. *International Journal of Database Management Systems, 5*(2).

Amazon. (n. d.). AWS. Retrieved from http://aws.amazon.com/s3/

Ibikunle Ayoleke (2011). Cloud Computing Security Issues and Challenges. *International Journal of Computer Networks*, 3(5).

Bahar, A., Habib, M., & Islam, M. (2013). Security Architecture for Mobile Cloud Computing. *International Journal of Scientific Knowledge*, 3(3), 11–17.

Bheda, H., & Lakhani, J. (2013). Application Processing Approach for Smart Mobile Devices in Mobile Cloud Computing. *International Journal of Software Engineering and Knowledge Engineering*, 3, 1046–1055.

Buyya, R., Yeo, C., Venugopal, S., Broberg, J., & Brandic, I. (2009). Cloud Computing and Emerging IT Platforms: Vision, Hype, and Reality for Delivering Computing. The 5th Utility. *Future Generation Computer Systems*, 25(6), 599–616. doi:10.1016/j.future.2008.12.001

Chaubey, N. K., & Tank, D. M. (2016). Security, Privacy and Challenges in Mobile Cloud Computing (MCC). A Critical Study and Comparison. *International Journal of Innovative Research in Computer and Communication Engineering*, *4*(2).

Chauhan, P.V. (2012). Cloud Computing in Distributed System. *International Journal of Computer Science and Informatics*, *1*(10).

Cuervo, E., Balasubramanian, A., & Dae-ki, C. et al.. *(*2010) MAUI: making smartphones last longer with code offload. In *Proceedings of the 8th International Conference on Mobile systems, applications, and services* (pp. 49–62). doi:10.1145/1814433.1814441

Davis, J. W. (2002). Power benchmark strategy for systems employing power management, In *Proceedings of the IEEE International Symposium on Electronics and the Environment.*

Devi, T., & Ganesan, R. (2015). Platform-as-a-Service (PaaS): Model and SecurityIssues. *Telkomnika Indonesian Journal of Electrical Engineering.*, *15*(1), 151–161.

Dinh, H. T., Lee, C., Niyato, D., & Wang, P. (2013). a survey of mobile cloud computing: Architecture, applications, and approaches. *Wirel. Commun. Mob. Comput*, *13*(18), 1587–1611. doi:10.1002/wcm.1203

Dinh, H. T., Lee, C., Niyato, D., & Wang, P. (2011). A survey of Mobile Cloud Computing: Architecture, Applications, and Approaches. *Wireless Communications and Mobile Computing*, *13*(18), 1587-1611.

Facebook. (n. d.). Retrieved from http://www.facebook.com/

Flickr. (n. d.). Retrieved from http://www.flickr.com/

Forman, G. H., & Zahorjan, J. (1994). The Challenges of mobile computing. *IEEE Computer Society Magazine*, *27*(4), 38–47. doi:10.1109/2.274999

Foster, I., Zhao, Y., Raicu, I., & Lu, S. (2008). Cloud Computing and Grid Computing 360-Degree Compared. In *Proceedings of the Grid Computing Environments Workshop.* doi:10.1109/GCE.2008.4738445

Garcia, A., & Kalva, H. (2011). Cloud transcoding for mobile video content delivery. In *Proceedings of the IEEE International Conference on Consumer Electronics (ICCE).* doi:10.1109/ICCE.2011.5722637

Gupta, P., & Gupta, S. (2012). Mobile Cloud Computing: The Future of Cloud. *International Journal of Advanced Research in Electrical Electronics and Instrumentation Engineering, 1*(3), 134–145.

Hashizume, K., Rosado, D. G., Fernández-Medina, E., & Fernandez, E. B. (2013). An analysis of security issues for cloud computing. *Journal of Internet Services and Applications, 4*(1), 5.

Hoang, D., Zhang, X., Kang, M., & Luo, J. (2010). MobiCloud: Building Secure Cloud Framework for Mobile Computing And Communication. In Proceedings of the Fifth IEEE International Symposium on Service Oriented System Engineering. doi:10.1109/SOSE.2010.20

Hoang, D., Zhou, Z., Le Xu, T. X., & Zhong, Y. (2011). Secure Data Processing Framework for Mobile Cloud Computing. In *Proceedings of the IEEE INFOCOM Workshop on Cloud Computing*. doi:10.1109/INFCOMW.2011.5928886

Hussein, N. H., & Khalid, A. (2016). A survey of Cloud Computing Security challenges and solutions. *International Journal of Computer Science and Information Security, 14*(1).

Jaiswal, P. R., & Rohankar, A. W. (2014). Infrastructure as a Service: Security Issues in Cloud Computing. *International Journal of Computer Science and Mobile Computing, 3*(3), 707–711.

Jia, W., Zhu, H., Cao, Z., Wei, L., & Lin, X. (2011). SDSM: a secure data service mechanism in mobile cloud computing. In *Proceedings of the IEEE Conference on Computer Communications Workshops, INFOCOMWKSHPS*, Shanghai, China.

Kakerow, R. (2003). Low power design methodologies for mobile communication. In *Proceedings of IEEE International Conference on Computer Design: VLSI in Computers and Processors*.

Kekre, H. B., Athawale, A., & Halarnkar, P. N. (2008). Increased Capacity of Information Hiding in LSB's Method for Text and Image. *International Journal of Electrical Computing Systems in Engineering, 2*(4), 246–249.

Kremer, U., Hicks, J., & Rehg, J. (2001) A compilation framework for power and energy management on mobile computers. In *Proceedings of the 14th International Conference on Languages and Compliers for Parallel Computing* (pp. 115–131).

Kumar, K. L. (2010). Cloud computing for mobile users: Can offloading computation save energy. *Computer, 43*(4), 51–56.

Mayo, R. N., & Ranganathan, P. (2003). Energy consumption in mobile devices: why future systems need requirements aware energy scale-down. In *Proceedings of the Workshop on Power-Aware Computing Systems*.

Mell, P., & Grance, T. (n. d.). The NIST definition of Cloud Computing (Vol. 15).

Oberheide, J., Veeraraghavan, K., Cooke, E., Flinn, J., & Jahanian, F. (2008) Virtualized in-cloud security services for mobile devices. In *Proceedings of the 1st Workshop on Virtualization in Mobile Computing (MobiVirt)* (pp. 31–35). doi:10.1145/1622103.1629656

Patell, N.S. (2014). Software as a Service (SaaS): Security issues and Solutions. *International Journal of Computational Engineering Research, 4*(6).

Paulson, L. D. (2003). Low-power chips for high-powered handhelds. *IEEE Computer Society Magazine, 36*(1), 21–23. doi:10.1109/MC.2003.1160049

Portokalidis, G., Homburg, P., Anagnostakis, K., & Bos, H. (2016). Paranoid Android: Versatile Protection for Smartphones. In *Proceedings of the 26th Annual Computer Security Application Conference (ACSAC)*, Los Angeles. doi:10.1145/1920261.1920313

Prasad, R., Gyani, J., & Murti, P. (2012). Mobile Cloud Computing: Implications and Challenge. *Journal of Information Engineering and Applications, 2*(7), 7–15.

Reza, H., & Sonawane, M. (2016). Enhancing Mobile Cloud Computing Security Using Steganography. *Journal of Information Security, 7*(4), 245–259. doi:10.4236/jis.2016.74020

Rudenko, A., Reiher, P., Popek, G. J., & Kuenning, G. H. (1998). Saving portable computer battery power through remote process execution. *Journal of ACM SIGMOBILE on Mobile Computing and Communications Revie, 2*(1).

Sahu, D., Sharma, S., Dubey, V., & Tripathi, A. (2012). Cloud Computing in Mobile Applications. *International Journal of Scientific and Research Publications, 2*(8), 1–9.

Saravankumar, C., & Arun, C. (2014). An Efficient ASCII-BCD Based Steganography for Cloud Security Using Common Development Model. *Journal of Theoretical and Applied Information Technology, 65*, 1992–8645.

Satyanarayanan, M. (1996). Fundamental Challenges in Mobile Computing. In *Proceedings of the 15th Annual ACM Symposium on Principles of Distributed Computing*, Philadelphia. doi:10.1145/248052.248053

Shekhar, J. (2014). An analysis on security concerns and their possible solutions in cloud computing environment. In *Proceedings of the 3rd International Conference on Role of Engineers as Entrepreneurs in Current Scenario.*

Shozu. (n. d.). Index. Retrieved from http://www.shozu.com/portal/index.do

Smailagic, A., & Ettus, M. (2002) System design and power optimization for mobile computers, In *Proceedings of IEEE Computer Society Annual Symposium on VLSI.* doi:10.1109/ISVLSI.2002.1016867

Subashini, S., & Kavitha, V. (2011). a survey on security issues in service delivery models of cloud computing. *Journal of Network and Computer Applications, 34*(1), 1–11. doi:10.1016/j.jnca.2010.07.006

Vartiainen, E., & Mattila, K. V.-V. (2010). User experience of mobile photo sharing in the cloud. In *Proceedings of the 9th International Conference on Mobile and Ubiquitous Multimedia (MUM).* doi:10.1145/1899475.1899479

Zou, P., Wang, C., Liu, Z., & Bao, D. (2010) Phosphor: a cloud based drm scheme with SIM card, In *Proceedings of the 12th International Asia-Pacific on Web Conference (APWEB).* doi:10.1109/APWeb.2010.43

KEY TERMS AND DEFINITIONS

Cloud Computing: Using a network to reach remote servers which are hosted on the Internet to store and process data, instead of traditional methods like a local server or a personal computer.

Data Security: It refers to protection of data digitally to prevent unauthorized access to computers, databases, remote servers and websites. Data security also protects data from corruption, so it is the main priority for all organizations.

Information Privacy: It refers to the user's ability to control when, how, and to what extent information about themselves will be collected, used, and shared with others.

Mobile Cloud Computing: This technology is the combination of three other technologies: 1) Mobile Computing 2) Cloud Computing 3) wireless networks. This combination helps to bring a rich storage and computational resources for mobile users, network operators and cloud computing providers. All have some advantages and disadvantages, so Mobile Cloud Computing inherits all and has its own matters beside others.

Mobile Computing: It is a technology that allows transmission of data, voice and video via a computer or any other wireless enabled device without having to be connected to a fixed physical link. The main concept is to create mobile communication and eliminate mobile hardware limitations.

Pay-Per-Use: In a pay-per-use business model, use of a product or service is metered, and customers are charged when they use the service.

Security Framework: It is a kind of method to resolve some available security issues. There are too many security risks in any aspects of technologies, and researchers try to propose a solution by recommending new methods that is called security framework. When it comes to cloud computing environment, it will be definition of an approach that intends to make computing free from security risks and privacy threats.

Chapter 13

Monitoring and Auditing in the Cloud

Indira K
Thiagarajar College of Engineering, India

Vennila A
Thiagarajar College of Engineering, India

ABSTRACT

The cloud computing is the term which have different services such as storage, servers, and applications which are delivered to an organization's computers and devices through the Internet for both technical and economical reasons. However they are many potential cloud users are reluctant to move to cloud computing on a large scale due to the unaddressed security issues present in cloud computing and so is increased the complexity of the infrastructures behind these services. So in this chapter, the challenges faced on both auditing and monitoring is identified. Accordingly it considers an investigation which uses to produce the major security audit issues present in cloud computing today based on a framework for security subsystems. To overcome the standards of auditing and process of auditing is briefly explained. There are also many platforms that provide cloud services also those domains are listed out with domain based monitoring process.

INTRODUCTION

Cloud Computing has rapidly become a widely adopted paradigm for delivering services over the Internet. Many thought that once the National Institute of Standards and Technology (NIST) came up with a formal definition for cloud computing. The

DOI: 10.4018/978-1-5225-3038-1.ch013

NIST cloud definition has three main components that consists of five key cloud characteristics: On demand self services, Rapid elasticity, Broad network access, Resource pooling and Measured Services. There are four cloud deployment models: Public Cloud, Private cloud, Hybrid Cloud and Community cloud. Finally three cloud service models incorporated: Software as a Service, Platform as a service and Infrastructure as a service. The entire cloud model is shown in Figure 1.

Infrastructure as a Service

Infrastructure as a Service (IaaS) providers allow their customers access to different kinds of infrastructure. The provider typically provides this service by dividing a very large physical infrastructure resource into smaller virtual resources for access by the consumer. Sometimes the service provided is a complete virtual machine with an operating system. In other instances the service provided is simply for storage, or perhaps a bare virtual machine with no operating system. In cases where the operating system or other software is included, the cost of the required license is either amalgamated into the cost for the service, or included as an additional surcharge. IaaS providers are often service providers to other cloud providers (see Integrator).

Platform as a Service

Platform as a Service (PaaS) providers extend the software stack provided by IaaS to include middleware. Middleware generically refers to software such as a DB2 database, or runtime environments such as a Java Runtime Environment (JRE) or a Websphere application server. This middleware is a prerequisite to running more sophisticated applications, and provides a rich operating environment for the

Figure 1. Cloud model

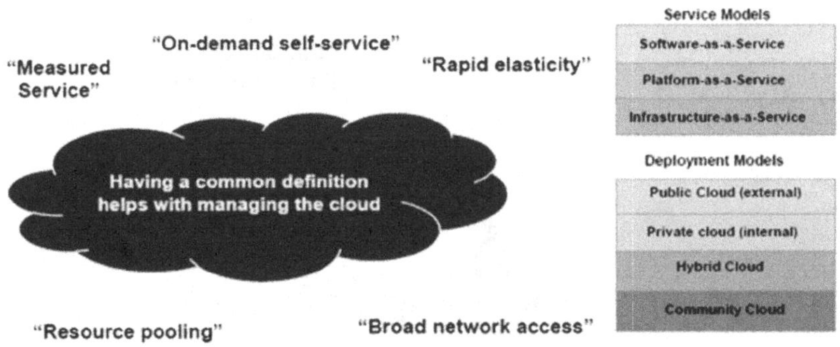

319

application to exploit. PaaS providers have two methods in which they facilitate the extra capacity needed for a large multitenant system.

Software as a Service

Application as a Service, or Software as a Service (SaaS) providers as they are more commonly known, typically provide a rich web-based interface to their customers. The customer, in most cases, is completely abstracted from the nuances of the application running behind the scenes. Tenant separation is often done at the application layer, leaving a common application, platform, and infrastructure layer underneath.

Roles in Cloud Computing

The cloud-computing paradigm defines three key roles. These roles each have different responsibilities and expectations relative to one another. Any party might have multiple roles depending on the context. See Figure 2.

Figure 2. Roles on cloud infrastructure

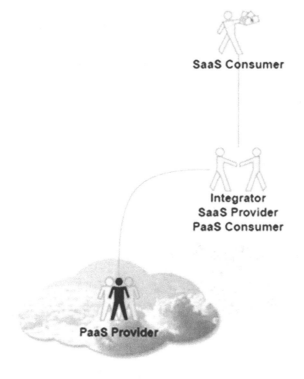

Consumer

Simply defined, a consumer consumes any service that is provided. In Exhibit 1.3, the SaaS provider exposes a SaaS to the SaaS consumer. The consumer is permitted access to this service for a fee of some sort, though in many instances this fee is augmented or replaced through advertising revenue. The consumer has no responsibility, nor access beyond the SaaS provided to them.

Provider

The providers in this case are both the PaaS provider and the SaaS provider. The PaaS provider provides a PaaS to the SaaS provider. The SaaS provider in turn provides an SaaS to the consumer. Ultimately, the provider is anyone who provides a service to one or more consumers.

Integrator

The integrator role is sometimes referred to as a broker. The integrator essentially assembles the services of many providers under a new service.

Challenges in Monitoring

Although there are many benefits to cloud computing, it is not without its own challenges. Traditional computing model shave permitted a high degree of control over compute resources. Cloud computing, by virtue of abstraction, prevents the consumer from having the same level of influence over the computing resource. Of great concern is the ability of consumers to assert quality of service. Quality of service refers to aspects of a service that are not functional (press the red button to submit your form) but are important consideration for example, how quickly (Aceto, 2013) the form submission takes to process. This leads to some of the following challenges with public cloud computing.

Availability

One of the cited benefits to cloud computing is the lowered barrier to entry. This is facilitated financially by sharing a significant amount of infrastructure between consumers. This allows for economies of scale from both a service management and computing resource perspective. Unfortunately, this also causes challenges regarding system availability. A nefarious user within the cloud can adversely affect the performance or availability of other consumers by attempting to over-consume resources. Consider a recent case where law enforcement officials confiscated racks of servers out of a data center as a result of alleged illegal activity from one of the consumers.

Data Residency

Different countries and regions have different requirements regarding how its citizens' information should be handled. In some areas, such as the European Union (EU), there are specific requirements regarding protection of personally identifiable information (PII) of EU residents. In other areas, such as the United States (US), there are directives regarding protected health information (PHI), such as the Health Insurance Portability and Accountability Act (HIPAA). Cloud consumers should consult with their providers regarding the countries in which they operate, and if possible restrict them to a subset that is congruent with their security and compliance requirements.

Performance

Many cloud providers assert a particular level of performance based on the service purchased. The main challenge regarding performance is the customer's recourse for degraded performance. The penalty in an SLA provided by most cloud providers, more often than not, entails a refund of fees for services rendered. For many IaaS services, this is measured in cents per hour. There is no consideration given to the business impact of the service degradation, which may be many orders of magnitude higher. Consider a cloud consumer who might, in turn, provide a stock trading service to their customers with SLA penalties measured in thousands of dollars per second; in such a case, the penalty offered by the cloud provider is wholly inadequate.

Data Evacuation

In cloud environments, data evacuation can be a significant concern. Data evacuation focuses on how sensitive information is cleared from physical storage due to the suspension or deletion of a consumer's resources. This might be a table in a database, a virtual disk on a Storage Area Network (SAN), or virtual memory on suspended disk. In the highly elastic world of cloud computing, memory is usually de-allocated, but not cleared. So a virtual machine containing sensitive information wouldn't be zeroed out prior to deletion, but rather its disk space would be released back to the SAN as is.

Supervisory Access

One of the main challenges with public cloud computing is that the highest level of access to the system, supervisory access, is maintained by the cloud provider. A cloud provider can inspect the activities of every virtual machine in an IaaS cloud. An SaaS provider has access to the information of all tenants in their cloud. This is an important consideration for cloud consumers, especially as it pertains to the storage of highly regulated, confidential, proprietary, or other information deemed appropriate for a limited audience.

Audit

Traditional IT audits typically fall into two main categories: *internal* and *external*. Internal audits refer to work done by an organization's own employees, concern very specific organizational processes, and focus primarily on optimization and risk management. External audits give an outside perspective on an organization's ability to meet the requirements of various laws and regulations. The threats pose new challenges for security auditing, but cloud advocates are responding to them. For instance, groups such as Cloud Security Alliance are urging standardization of cloud confidentiality, integrity, and availability auditing.

Challenges in Auditing

A traditional IT security audit is an examination of an IT group's checks, balances, and controls. Auditors enumerate, evaluate, and test an organization's systems, practices, and operations to determine whether the systems safeguard the information assets, maintain data integrity, and operate effectively to achieve the organization's business goals or objectives. To support these objectives, IT security auditors need data from both internal and external sources.

In addition, cloud computing comes with its own set of security challenges. A cloud infrastructure is the result of a constant three-way negotiation among service organizations, cloud service providers (CSPs), and end users to ensure productivity while maintaining a reasonable degree of security. A CSP should keep data safe from security threats and yet give clients access anywhere with Internet service. In addition, the client organization must verify that the cloud computing enterprise contributes to its business goals, objectives, and future needs. Effective cloud security auditors must be familiar with cloud computing terminology and have a working knowledge of a cloud system's constitution and delivery method. This knowledge ensures auditors pay attention to security factors that might be more important in

Table 1. Cloud specific auditing challenges

Challenge	Traditional IT Security Auditing Practices	Cloud-Specific Challenge	Potential Cloud Security Auditing Solution
Transparency	Data and Information security management system are more accessible	Data and security are managed by a third parity	Service-level agreements should outline CSP policies and assurances while CSPs provide clients with audit results
Encryption	The data owner has control	Cloud service providers(CSPs) might be responsible for encryption	Use a third party and homomorphic encryption
Colocation	This rarely occurs	CSPs heavily depend on this	Standardize and increase oversight
Scale, scope and complexity	These are relatively less	Auditors must be knowledgeable and aware of these differences	Implement continuing education and new certification programs

cloud security auditing processes, including transparency; encryption; colocation; and scale, scope, and complexity (see Table 1).

Encryption

It's unsafe to store sensitive plaintext data anywhere, especially outside a home organization's IT infrastructure. If a cloud is breached, the information in it would be instantly available to hackers. To prevent this, a client could encrypt all its data in-house before sending it to the cloud provider, but this approach introduces the risk of system administrators abusing their privileges. Leaving encryption to the CSP isn't foolproof either: a breach in its storage system might also mean a breach in its encryption and decryption tools. Traditional IT infrastructures face many encryption concerns as well. To help mitigate this cloud specific problem, the Payment Card Industry (PCI) Data Security Standard (DSS) Cloud Special Interest Group (SIG) strongly encourages that cryptographic keys and encryption algorithm information "be stored and managed independently from the cloud service.

Scale, Scope, and Complexity

In cloud computing, one physical machine typically hosts many VMs, which drastically increases the number of hosts to be audited. Unless carefully managed, the sheer number of these VMs could overwhelm IT staff and auditors. However, when standardization is in place (for instance, in the form of master VM images verified for security), the auditing process can go smoother and faster despite cloud computing elements' larger scale. Therefore, it's crucial that cloud security auditors find out where the CSP stores CSU data and information. Colocation due to multitenancy also contributes to the importance of the physical data and information storage location.

CLOUD MONITORING: BASIC CONCEPTS

Cloud monitoring is needed to continuously measure and assess infrastructure or application behaviours in terms of performance, reliability, power usage, ability to meet SLAs, security, etc. (Kutare,2010), to perform business analytics, for improving the operation of systems and applications (Kumar,2006). In this section we introduce a number of concepts at the base of Cloud monitoring that are used to set the context for the following sections, while in Figure 3 we report these concepts in a taxonomy we propose for main aspects of Cloud monitoring we consider in this paper.

Layers

According to the work of the Cloud Security Alliance, a Cloud can be modelled in seven layers: facility, network, hardware, OS, middleware, application, and the user (Spring, 2011). Considering the roles defined in Section 2, these layers can be controlled by either a Cloud Service Provider or a Cloud Service Consumer. They are detailed in the following:

Figure 3. Cloud monitoring-motivations, properties, basic concept, open issues and future directions

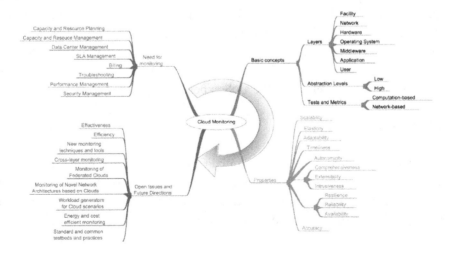

- **Facility:** At this layer, we consider the physical infrastructure comprising the data centers that host the computing and networking equipment.
- **Network:** At this layer, we consider the network links and paths both in the Cloud and between the Cloud and the user.
- **Hardware:** At this layer, we consider the physical components of the computing and networking equipment.
- **Operating System (OS):** At this layer, we consider the software components forming the operating system of both the host (the OS running on the physical machine) and the user (the OS running in the virtual machine).
- **Middleware:** At this layer, we consider the software layer between the OS and the user application. It is typically present only in the Cloud systems offering SaaS and PaaS service models.
- **Application:** At this layer, we consider the application run by the user of the Cloud system.
- **User:** At this layer, we consider the final user of the Cloud system and the applications that run outside the Cloud (e.g. a web browser running on a host at the user's premise).

In the context of Cloud monitoring, these layers can be seen as where to put the probes of the monitoring system. Besides, due to the very high complexity of Cloud systems, it not possible to be sure those certain phenomena are actually observed or not.

Abstraction Levels

In Cloud Computing, we can have both high- and low level monitoring, and both are required (Desprez,2012). High-level monitoring is related to information on the status of the virtual platform. This information is collected at the middleware, application and user layers by Providers or Consumers through platforms and services operated by themselves or by third parties. In the case of SaaS, high-level monitoring information is generally of more interest for the Consumerthan for the Provider (being closely related to the QoS experienced by the former).

Tests and Metrics

Monitoring tests can be divided in two main categories: Computation-based and Network-based (Mei, 2010). Computation based tests are related to monitoring activities aimed at gaining knowledge about and at inferring the status of real or virtualized platforms running Cloud applications.

Computation-Based

Tests are related to the following metrics: server throughput, defined as the number of requests (e.g. web page retrieval) per second; CPU Speed; CPU time per execution, defined as the CPU time of a single execution; CPU utilization, defined as the CPU occupation of each virtual machine (useful to monitor the concurrent use of a single machine by several VMs); memory page exchanges per second, defined as the number of memory pages per second exchanged through the I/O; memory page exchanges per execution, defined as the number of memory pages used during an execution; disk/memory throughput; throughput/ delay of message passing between processes; duration of specific predefined tasks; response time; VM startup time; VM acquisition/release time; execution/access time, up-time.

Network-Based

Tests are related to the monitoring of network-layer metrics. This set includes round-trip time (RTT), jitter, throughput, packet/data loss, available bandwidth, capacity, traffic volume, etc. Using these metrics, several experimental studies in literature compared legacy webhosting and Cloud-based hosting (Aljohani, 2011).

Cloud Monitoring: Properties and Related Issues

In order to operate properly, a distributed monitoring system is required to have several properties that, when considered in the Cloud Computing scenario, introduce new issues. In this section, we define and motivate such properties, analyze the issues arising from them, and discuss how these issues have been addressed in literature (Aceto, 2013). In Figure 2 we report these properties in taxonomy of main aspects regarding Cloud monitoring considered in this paper. In Figure 3 we illustrate the research issues associated with each of the properties considered. This picture shows that, as will be clearer in the following,

1. The research issues to be tackled range in a wide and heterogeneous set, comprising multidisciplinary research areas,
2. Some of these issues are related with more than one property, i.e. their solution may provide multiple benefits.

Scalability

A monitoring system is scalable if it can cope with a large number of probes [55]. Such property is very important in Cloud Computing scenarios due to the large number of parameters to be monitored about a huge number of resources. This importance is amplified by the adoption of virtualization technologies, which allow allocating many virtual resources on top of a single physical resource. Most of the proposed architectures, regardless of the specific low-level or high-level monitored parameters, adopt a subsystem to propagate event announcements (Hasselmeyer, 2010) or rely on agents, which are responsible for performing data collection, filtering and aggregation (Katsaros, 2011). Some architectures further improve scalability by adopting additional optimizations: efficient algorithms for agent deployment and interconnection Content Based Routing (CBR) and Complex Event Processing (CEP) facilities (Romano,2011) lightweight analysis close to the data source, adjustable sampling, time-based filtering, and ad hoc collection and aggregation strategies applied to different partitions of the monitored system.

Elasticity

A monitoring system is elastic if it can cope with dynamic changes of monitored entities, so that virtual resources created and destroyed by expansion and contraction are monitored correctly. Such property, also referred to as dynamism (Hasselmeyer, 2010), implies scalability and adds to it the requirement of supporting on-line upsizing or downsizing of the pool of monitored resources. As opposed to the static nature of previous computing paradigms (e.g. Grid computing), Cloud Computing requires its resources to be dynamic, thus making elasticity an essential property for its monitoring system, as derived from three main drivers: varying assignment of resources to users, varying monitoring requirements for the user, and varying presence of users (multi-tenant scenarios).

Figure 4. Properties of system for cloud monitoring and issues

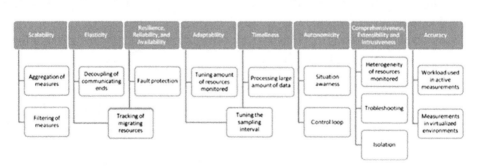

Adaptability

A monitoring system is adaptable if it can adapt to varying computational and network loads in order not to be invasive (i.e. impeding for other activities). Due to the complexity and the dynamism of the Cloud scenarios, adaptability is fundamental for a monitoring system in order to avoid as much as possible a negative impact of monitoring activities on normal Cloud operations, especially when active measurements are involved. Thus, the ability to tune the monitoring activities according to suitable policies is of significant importance to meet Cloud management goals. Providing adaptability is not trivial, because it requires to quickly reacting loading changes, maintaining the right trade-off between precision (e.g. predictable latencies) and invasivity.

Autonomicity

An autonomic monitoring system is able to self-manage its distributed resources by automatically reacting to unpredictable changes, while hiding intrinsic complexity to Providers and Consumers. As Cloud infrastructures are meant to provide on-demand self-service and rapid elasticity while operating continuously with minimal service interruptions, it is extremely important for the monitoring system to be able to react to detected changes, faults and performance degradation, without manual intervention. Resources are monitored using a framework capable of mapping low-level resource metrics (e.g. host up- and down-times) to user defined SLAs (e.g. service availability).

Accuracy

We consider a monitoring system to be accurate when the measures it provides are accurate, i.e. they are as close as possible to the real value to be measured. The accuracy is important for any distributed monitoring system because it can heavily impact the activities that make use of the monitoring information. The first one is related to the workload used to perform the measurements: in order to monitor the Cloud, especially when using active monitoring approaches, it is necessary to apply a suitable stress (e.g. the HTTP GET to a WEB server in the Cloud must arrive with a certain statistical distribution in order to accurately compute the average response time of the WEB server). The second issue is related to the virtualization techniques used in the Cloud: performed measurements may be affected by errors imputable to the virtualization systems that add additional layers between applications and physical resources (e.g. time-related measurements are impaired by the sharing of physical resources such as CPUs, interface cards, and buffers). (Ostermann, 2011) performed also an analysis at user layer, thanks to emulated web browsers issuing requests to servers running in the Cloud.

THE AUDIT PROCESS

Audit is essentially an assurance function that some standard, method, or practice is followed. Depending on the type of audit, the auditor systematically examines evidence for compliance to established criteria. The best practice in effective IT auditing is to start with an understanding of business functions, to identify which IT infrastructure is providing those functions, and to then consider the scope of the audit and controls best suited for that IT function. The same holds true for IT infrastructure and services provided by the cloud. In fact, most cloud providers are using IT systems models similar to those of their clients. These include: securing workstation (access) and server devices, core services (such as identity and authorization), and monitoring and logging functions. Therefore, many of the same controls and control frameworks (like COBIT or NIST) typically used for systems audits are also usable for auditing systems that are hosted or provided by cloud vendors. But as businesses move into cloud environments, certain changes occur that auditors must recognize as the move changes the scope of the audit and introduces new risk to systems. These applications, if not adapted for the cloud, can now be compromised by lack of secure authentication controls and data integrity issues for data at rest or in transit. & Systems that are developed in-house expecting a level of security provided by the corporate network are similarly at risk when moved to a cloud provider.

Control Frameworks for the Cloud

When adopting new technology of any kind, both system owners and internal auditors must consider not only the business justification for adoption but also the risks inherent to the new technology. Control (compliance) frameworks have not yet been well adapted to cloud environments, although most (like COBIT, ITIL, and ISO 27001) are considered sufficient overall and a worthy starting point. There are organizations that have been instrumental in exploring the cloud in relation to security and compliance programs—the most active are currently CSA, NIST, ISACA, and ENISA.1 These organizations have been leading the development of concepts and guidance sufficient to understand, protect, and trust cloud infrastructure. It is advisable to keep up with new publications from these organizations (and many others) to keep abreast of new thought and advice. The most consistent advice from most of these organizations focuses on some core concepts, which include: &

Cloud hosted/based systems cannot be protected in the same manner as traditional corporate systems.

ENISA Cloud Risk Assessment

ENISA is the European Network and Information Security Agency. It is a purely advisory organization, but it has commissioned work on security issues including "Cloud Computing Risk Assessment," published in November 2009. This paper provided one of the first risk assessments of the cloud computing business model and outlines some even handed views on the risks and benefits of cloud computing. In particular, this document provides uniquely specific advice to those organizations that do business in the European Union, or are planning to do so. One of the key findings of this document was the summary of three recommendations (from a risk standpoint) of the cloud computing models.

These were:

1. Building trust in the cloud (a continual issue between vendors and clients)
2. Data protection in large scale environments (incorporating international boundaries, forensics, and incident handling)
3. Engineering (large-scale systems' interoperability, resiliency, and monitoring)

There have been significant efforts on all these fronts by vendors and customers since the publication, which underscores the value of this research.

CSA Guidance

The Cloud Security Alliance (CSA) published Security Guidance for Critical Areas of Focus in Cloud Computing V2.18 in December 2009. This work has become well referenced and considered a solid foundation for approaching security in the cloud. The Domain 4 ("Compliance and Audit") section of this document is most applicable to the discussion in this chapter. CSA points out much of the responsibility for compliance to regulations will have to be borne by the consumer, making the consumer responsible for bridging the information and communications gap with audit function. This is true insofar as the business is responsible for planning and meeting compliance, but discounts the role that the vendor can provide. Nonetheless, review the recommendations of this guidance for tips on addressing compliance concerns with vendors, approaches to legal issues, and a reminder that auditors must be qualified to understand some of the security approaches in cloud computing.

CloudAudit/A6: The Automated Audit, Assertion, Assessment, and Assurance API

The CloudAudit/A6 group is a relatively new organization and a public effort to address audit and compliance of cloud services. Merged with CSA in 2011, it endeavors to create a common method for providers of cloud computing services to automate audit functions of their infrastructure— regardless of service type (IaaS, PaaS, or SaaS) and regardless of platform technology. The goal of this group is to allow cloud consumers to be able to check (audit/assess) remote infrastructure via a common (non-platform-specific) interface/namespace. The advantages of this mechanism would be obvious: Vendors would be able to provide customer access to controls that could meet compliance and security requirements without having to expend as much time on testing and assurance tasks. The consumer and the vendor would not have to specify specific controls if the Cloud Audit/A6 efforts are standard and there could be a mapping of controls to various compliance requirements without having to prescribe specific measures that are platform specific. This organization has extended an invitation for auditors, vendors and consumers to work together via a forum at their web site. As with similar effort at building standards for cloud services, the efforts are a work in progress and it may serve the reader well to stay abreast or to get involved directly.

RECOMMENDED CONTROLS

Controls should be defined and refined based on the needs of the business, both regulatory and security. Some baseline technical and operational controls are likely to be universally applicable and the following exhibit may assist in helping to consider control areas of comparatively high importance. It is provided to assist an organization or auditor in consideration of a variety of core control areas and should not be assumed sufficient for any specific security audit. It assumes internal control is a process, designed to provide reasonable assurance regarding the achievement of objectives in the following three categories:

1. Effectiveness and efficiency of operations
2. Reliability of financial reporting
3. Compliance with laws and regulations

Governmental/Highly Sensitive Data Environment

- Physical location of data

- Data classification (both features and support)
- System data isolation (virtual server versus allocated drive)
- System resource reuse (erase procedures)
- Support or provision for two-factor authentication
- Existing certification to security framework (e.g., ISO 27001, FISMA), scope of systems, and protection profile of that certification

Supply Chain Issues

- Define key services/products outsourced and provided to operations
- Security plan that addresses third-party access to cloud
- Audit of third-party providers (frequency, level)
- Security policy and controls applied (contractually) to third-party providers

Operational Environment

- Change control process/governance
- Remote access policy
- System documentation, operating procedures
- Test bed
- System hardening (technical controls applied to system components)
- Anti-virus/white list controls
- Mobile device controls
- Backup and restore process
- Log management
- Right to audit provisions

Software Assurance

- Quality Assurance and Quality Control process and procedure
- Test plans

Patch Management

- Patch management documentation for all system components and layers of cloud
- architecture
- Test plans
- Update logs

Network Controls

- Levels of isolation in the architecture
- Virtual infrastructure controls
- Specific LAN architecture used (e.g., PVLAN, VLAN tagging) and network layer controls
- used (e.g., DNS control)
- Interoperability (service) support

PAAS: Application Security

- Design of multi tenanted application hosting
- Access control measures
- Vulnerability scanning
- Security features

SAAS: Application Security

- Administrative access controls
- Customized access control

Identity and Access Management: Authorization

- System-wide rights
- Account management plan/methodology
- Segregation of duties/least privilege rules
- Emergency procedures affecting access
- User account management (registration included)

Encryption

- Password and key management
- Incident management (including emergency and key revocation)
- Encryption of data in transit
- Encryption of data at rest
- Encryption management plan (including emergency management process)

Authentication

- Authentication plan (relative to client/vendor agreements)

Mutual Authentication

- Mechanism defined and documented

Identity Management Frameworks

- Identity Management infrastructure plan (including providers and features)

Client Access Control

- Role-based access control planning for multiple roles and possible multiple domains
- Endpoint (customer) system image management
- BUSINESS CONTINUITY MANAGEMENT recovery point objective (RPO) and recovery time objective (RTO) for services
- Emergency procedures, with details on assets, services, and specific processes
- Memos of understanding (MOUs) on emergency procedures

Incident Management and Response

- Detection capabilities/controls
- Communication plan regarding incidents
- Forensics plan
- Reporting frequency/analysis provided
- Privacy controls

Environmental Control Issues

- Risk management plan
- Special controls to address environmental disasters.

Legal Requirements

- Country where cloud provider located (laws and legal agreements)
- Country where cloud infrastructure located (laws and legal agreement)
- Data ownership/responsibility agreements
- Procedures for discovery/e-discovery protections
- Regulatory and other compliance requirements

RISK MANAGEMENT AND RISK ASSESSMENT

The cloud user is strongly advised to perform a risk assessment of any system proposed for the cloud environment. In some cases, the assessment of risk will be performed as part of enterprise risk management and should be adjusted to address specific risks associated with different vendors, specific cloud offerings, existing compliance requirements, and data sensitivity.

Risk Management

Because controls cannot be prescriptive beyond a certain baseline, and because all systems are somewhat different, a risk management process component should be developed for most environments to assure the security and compliance of any system. In many organizations, a governance model is advised to help in management of the risk process. In many cases, compliance programs are expecting to find a risk management process that is documented, supported by management, and able to address the risk assessment and configuration control process at a minimum. In any case, cloud computing introduces a variety of risk scenarios that a risk management process is likely to find challenging such as scope of control, trust (and verification) provisions to contracts, service level agreements (SLAs), and memos of understanding (MOUs). Risk management process documentation should be made available to auditors.

Risk Assessment

A risk assessment is a process wherein the stakeholders try to analyze and agree on a particular threat to a specific system (or component) and the probability of an occurrence. The exercise is sometimes scientific, but often involves an element of guesswork when data points are lacking. For this reason, it is sometimes considered a flawed practice, but it is also the best way to identify and document the threat and mitigation for a particular system at a particular time. The risk assessment itself can be seen as both an activity and a product. The product should be constantly reviewed and protected at the same time. An auditor should be able to review the risk assessment product and observe the risk assessment process. The consideration of risk management and the risk assessment is suited to a solid discussion during the cloud computing audit. The wide range of unique risks facing the organization make this an important subject and depend on the type and model of the cloud solution, the uniqueness of the client environment, and the specifics of data or an application. As we have pointed out above, many of the risks to cloud environments are similar and in some cases the same as traditionally hosted and outsourced IT systems. The auditor will recall and focus on these common items:

- Gaps in control between processes performed by the service provider and the organization
- Compromises of system security and confidentiality
- Solutions selected incorrectly or with significant missing requirements

Discrepancies in contracts and gaps between business expectations and service provider capabilities

- Costly compensating controls
- Reduced system availability and questionable integrity of information
- Poor software quality, inadequate testing, and a high number of failures
- Failures to respond to relationship issues with optimal and approved decisions
- Insufficient allocation of resources
- Inability to satisfy audit/assurance charter and requirements of regulators or external auditors
- Fraud

None of these are common controls, and each is likely to require an independent assessment of risk and mitigation by the sourcing firm. In addition, cloud environments and projects generate new risks due to a number of issues that are somewhat unique to this new computing model. The complexity brought about by dependency on third-party providers brings up unique problems that can be challenging problems that almost always require specific address: vulnerability of communications channels, external interfaces, and reliance on self-imposed controls.

The auditor will often uncover increased risks in cloud data centers because relationships with outside providers are not transparent to his organization. He will grapple with the issues and complexity of local and international laws. Compliance with these laws is difficult, due to the newness of the cloud business model, the potential for data flow through foreign countries, and the likelihood that incident and privacy laws will vary significantly in certain countries. Unique to the industry are a variety of technical challenges with operations that include the needs of the facility to grow rapidly and balance load requirements, the co-location of facilities with other businesses (including competitors), and the untested nature of the business model. The solutions to these issues are typically found in careful planning and recognition that the audit may help you sleep at night.

Legal

Legal agreements are also an important factor in the risk assessment. There are always a number of sources for advice on what should be included in the client provider agreements to mitigate certain risks, and we agree auditors should inspect these documents as part of their risk review. Organizations such as ENISA and others have done a review of some of the legal issues and some of the advice is worth repeating here. Agreements common to any cloud computing scenario most often address the following issues:

1. Data protection requires an understanding of where data is going to reside and what legal protections must be addressed at that residence, especially the privacy and retention conditions. The auditor must make certain that the organization and provider understand what data protections are being promised and what the risks will be to availability and integrity of data.
2. Confidentiality is a significant issue when moving data and applications to the cloud. Agreements should address confidentiality, what protections/ controls are made against inadvertent release of confidential information, and how classification of data will be supported (when applicable) and managed accordingly.
3. Intellectual property is an issue when custom code, data files, and other forms of business data are stored or processed by a cloud provider. Protections should be stated and risks assumed.
4. Professional negligence protections must be addressed. Customers must assess risks and possible mitigations that range from insurance to code protection.
5. Outsourcing services and changes in control of your cloud provider infrastructure can occur without the client being aware. Agreements must make certain that any change of controls is brought to the attention of the client.

IT Governance in the Cloud

Governance is the managerial obligation to:

*   Ensure business value is recognized from IT-enabled business investments.
*   Establish a solid base for a defensible standard of due care.
*   Demonstrate due diligence to that defensible standard20.

Key elements for good governance in risk and control (GRC) for cloud computing and the virtualization technologies that enable cloud computing include:

- Top-down engagement.
- Clear roles and responsibilities.
- Proactive—linked to business plan.
- Business risk-based standard of care clearly articulated.
- Clear methods for buy/build analysis with a complete cost model bought off by all stakeholders.
- "Inspect what you Expect".
- Do not outsource what you could not manage anyway.
- Match the IT model to the company culture21.

The issues in securing (and governing) cloud computing use mirror those of any other IT and InfoSec governance issue: ensuring good security in protecting the access, transmission, and storage of data. Accomplishment of this in a cloud environment is through the use of legal documents mandating compliance with acceptable security standards through service-level agreements. The governance strategies that must be pursued by organizations wishing to participate in the benefits of cloud computing don't differ greatly from those that don't. The major difference is in the degree of vigilance one must assert over the only protection mechanisms available to the client the service agreement.

Managing Service Agreements

The service agreement is a legal contract that guarantees the vendor will provide specified services for a specified rate, subject to certain conditions. It is the specification of conditions that adds value to the service beyond cost. An SLA is an agreement to provide services between a service provider and a service consumer. This is usually done either as a standard element of a contract for services when it exists between organizations, or it may exist as a policy element or informal agreement between organizational units within a larger organization. The top issues in cloud computing service agreements that the governance committee should review are:

- Support for outages
- Assurance of data
- Incident response procedures
- Auditability of security
- Financial restitution for lost business
- Certification of trust

Some of this can be addressed through service agreements, but most cloud vendors will prove unwilling to reimburse a cloud service customer for lost business in the event of an internal outage. External outages, resulting from natural disasters, regional power outages and the like, will continue to be dismissed as acts of God and thus covered only under service fees, if at all. Seldom will a vendor offer to reimburse lost business from these areas.

IMPLEMENTING AND MAINTAINING GOVERNANCE FOR CLOUD COMPUTING

To establish an effective governance strategy for cloud computing, the organization must first select an implementation methodology. If the organization already has a governance structure in place for IT and InfoSec, it can move to the Extending IT Governance to the Cloud section of this chapter.

Implementing Governance as a New Concept

For the organization that has not previously implemented a governance structure, a number of preliminary functions must be handled before governance of the cloud can even be considered. First, a governance structure for IT and Information Security must be established. The following provides an excellent overview of IT and Information Security Governance, and can assist in setting up the governance structure. The key components of the implementation of a new governance structure are highlighted here.

Preliminary Tasks

Before completely investing in the governance process, a series of preliminary tasks should be performed. These tasks allow the organization to lay a solid foundation upon which to build a successful governance program.

Identify the Stakeholders

The first task is to identify those groups that will have a vested interest in the governance structure and who may be directly involved. These groups include:

- Executive management
- Business management and business process owners
- Chief information officer (CIO), IT management, and IT process owners
- IT audit
- Information Security, including risk and compliance

Define the Governance Board

Once the stakeholders are identified, those who should, and who are willing to, serve on a governance board should be identified. Once identified, their primary roles and responsibilities should be defined. According to ISACA, these roles include the following:

- **Board and Executives:** Set direction for the program, ensure alignment with enterprise-wide governance and risk management, approve key program roles and define responsibilities, and give visible support and commitment. Sponsor, communicate, and promote the agreed-upon initiative.
- **Business Management:** Provide appropriate stakeholders and champions to drive commitment and to support the program. Nominate key program roles and define and assign responsibilities.
- **IT Management:** Ensure that the business and executives understand and appreciate the high-level objectives. Nominate key program roles and define and assign responsibilities. Nominate a person to drive the program in agreement with the business.
- **IT Audit:** Agree on the role and reporting arrangements for audit participation. Ensure that an adequate level of audit participation is provided through the duration of the program.
- **[Information Security] Risk and Compliance:** Ensure an adequate level of participation through the duration of the program.24

Review the Key Success Factors

A key success factor, or critical success factor, is something that must go right for the operation to succeed. Absence of these factors can substantially decrease the probability of success in the venture. For IT (and InfoSec) governance, the key success factors are:

- **Top Management Investiture:** More than simply a memo from top management, executive management must demonstrate investiture in the governance structure by meeting and establishing the direction and purpose (mandate) for the governance function. They must demonstrate to the entire organization that they are dedicated to the process.
- **Understanding of the Outcomes and Objectives:** In addition to understanding the impetus of the governance function, all stakeholders in the process must understand why the governance is being done; the business, IT, and InfoSec objectives; and the desired governance outcomes.

- **Change Management:** In order for any change to be effective and established as the new organizational culture, the projected changes to result from the governance effort must be clearly communicated and then enabled.
- **Customization of the Governance Framework to the Organization:** A careful adaptation of any governance framework is required to ensure it meets the needs and ability of the organization. The tailoring of the practices and procedures must be carefully effected to maximize compatibility.
- **Pick the Low-Hanging Fruit:** The project should look for activities that can be quickly implemented with clear benefits realized. Identify those components of the governance project, like an executive briefing on InfoSec issues in the cloud that can be easily and quickly performed, with immediate results realized.25

Adopt a Governance Implementation Methodology

The following governance implementation methodology, taken from ISACA's Implementing and Continually Improving IT Governance can be used to initiate the governance function:

Phase 1 - Initiate the Program: What are the drivers? Phase 1 identifies current change drivers and creates at executive management levels a desire to change that is then expressed in an outline of a business case. Risks associated with implementation of the IT governance program itself will be described in the business case and managed throughout the life cycle. A change driver is an internal or external event, condition or key issue that serves as a stimulus for change. Events, trends (industry, market, or technical), performance shortfalls, software implementations and even the goals of the enterprise can act as change drivers.

Phase 2 - Define Problems and Opportunities: Where are we now? Phase 2 aligns IT objectives with business strategies and risks, and prioritizes the most important IT goals and processes (including controls). COBIT provides a generic mapping of business goals to IT goals to IT processes to help with the selection of goals. Given the defined IT goals, critical processes are defined, managed, and controlled to ensure successful outcomes. Management needs to know its current capability and where deficiencies may exist. This is achieved by a capability maturity model assessment of the asis status of the selected processes and controls.

Phase 3 - Define the Road Map: Where do we want to be? Phase 3 sets a target for improvement followed by a gap analysis to identify potential solutions. Some solutions will be quick wins and others more challenging, long-term tasks. Priority should be given to projects that are easier to achieve and likely to give the greatest benefit. Longer-term tasks should be broken down into manageable pieces.

Phase 4 - Plan the Program: What needs to be done? Phase 4 plans feasible and practical solutions by defining projects supported by justifiable business cases, and developing a change plan for implementation. A well-developed business case will help ensure that the project's benefits are identified and monitored. Val IT provides an example template and guidance for preparation of a business case.

Phase 5 - Execute the Plan: How do we get there? Phase 5 provides for the implementation of the proposed solutions into day-to-day practices, and the establishment of measures and monitoring systems to ensure that business alignment is achieved and performance can be measured. Success requires engagement, awareness and communication, understanding and commitment of top management, and ownership by the affected business and IT process owners.

Phase 6 - Realize Benefits: Did we get there? Phase 6 focuses on sustainable transition of the improved management practices into normal business operations, and monitoring achievement of the improvement by measuring performance metrics and the expected benefits.

Phase 7 - Review Effectiveness: How do we keep the momentum going? Phase 7 reviews the overall success of the initiative, identifies further governance requirements, and reinforces the need for continual improvement. While reporting is not mentioned explicitly in any of the phases, it is a continual thread through all of the phases and iterations.27 The ISACA Governance Methodology is illustrated in Figure 5.

Extending IT Governance to the Cloud

Once the organization has an established governance function, how can this be extended to cloud computing use? The answer is simply to apply the governance framework to the cloud computing decision.

Phase 1 - Initiate the Program: What are the drivers? During this phase, the IT (and InfoSec) Groups must thoroughly research the cloud computing environment, including general advantages and disadvantages. The various stakeholders should be briefed on these items. The question of what drivers are forcing the organization to consider cloud computing must be evaluated.

Phase 2 - Define Problems and Opportunities: Where are we now? Here, the governance board determines if the adoption of cloud computing supports the current organizational business strategies and risks. If the determination is that cloud computing would become an important IT function, it is prioritized with other IT functions, projects, and proposals. The current organizational functions and their shortcomings must be determined in light of a potential cloud computing implementation.

Phase 3 - Define the Road Map: Where do we want to be? The governance board must determine what strategic value will result from cloud computing implementation. What improvements in the organization will result from cloud computing adoption? The level of complexity, time frame for implementation, and challenges associated with cloud computing adoption are considered.

Phase 4 - Plan the Program: What needs to be done? During this phase, a cloud computing investigatory subgroup is appointed, consisting of IT, InfoSec, and business representatives, to evaluate cloud computing vendors and services more thoroughly. It is during this phase, where a complete risk assessment of cloud computing is conducted, given the service agreements from potential vendors. It is here, before any one vendor is selected, that the organization has the most pull in ensuring acceptable levels of protection of data to be stored on vendor systems, as well as in the level of security assessment and transparency

Figure 5. ISACA governance implementation and continuous improvement methodology

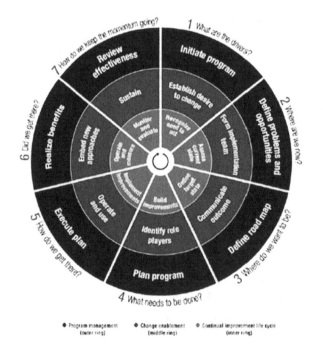

that will be provided to systems leased to the organization. It is also here that the organization would expect the vendors to share information on their own security practices, including personnel and physical security functions.

Phase 5 - Execute the Plan: How do we get there? Once this phase is reached, the organization begins to deploy cloud computing. Closely monitoring the implementation, security and operation of business activities as cloud computing is deployed can serve to negate potential security issues. Throughout this process, the governance board must keep a watchful eye on issues arising from migration, comparing them to the negotiated service agreements, to determine compliance.

Phase 6 - Realize Benefits: Did we get there? Once the organization has completely implemented cloud computing, it must begin a performance measures (metrics) program to monitor and evaluate ongoing operations for

Phase 7 - The Organization Must Determine at this Stage: Did we meet our desired objectives and outcomes? Are we realizing the benefits we expected? Is continual use at this stage justified? Phase 7: Review Effectiveness: How do we keep the momentum going? The maintenance and change phase of the cloud computing implementation is the most critical. On a regular basis the governance board should review the performance measures collected on cloud computing deployment, and make the ongoing decision to either continue cloud computing use or discontinue it, either with a particular vendor or in totality. The governance board has the continual responsibility to monitor and guide the future use of this technology, just as with any deployed technology. However, unlike most deployed technologies, the external trust issues between the organization and its cloud computing vendor creates a level of permanent discomfort that can never be fully resolved. Just as an investor carefully monitors his or her investment portfolio to ensure maximum return on the use of his or her monies, the organization must continually monitor the interaction between the employees using the cloud computing services and the third-party vendor providing them.

FUTURE DIRECTION

Our future research will focus on improving the existing cloud security auditing approaches discussed in this article. Another goal is to identify more challenges that clearly differentiate cloud security auditing from traditional IT security auditing by conducting a formal survey of various stakeholders in the cloud security auditing community. The more comprehensive the list of the cloud security auditing challenges, the more educated cloud security auditors will be and the more thorough and reliable the audit results will be.

Cloud Monitoring: Open Issues and Future Directions

The infrastructure of a Cloud is very complex. This complexity translates into more effort needed for management and monitoring. The greater scalability and larger size of Clouds compared to traditional service hosting infrastructures, involve more complex monitoring systems, which have therefore to be more scalable, robust and fast. Such systems must be able to manage and verify a large number of resources and must do it effectively and efficiently. This has to be achieved through short measurement times and fast warning systems, able to quickly spot and report performance impairments or other issues, to ensure timely interventions such as the allocation of new resources. However, some of them still require considerable effort to achieve the maturity level necessary for their seamless integration in such a complex infrastructure.

Effectiveness

Main open issues reside in the possibility to have a clear view of the Cloud and to pinpoint the original causes of the observed phenomena. To achieve this, improvements are needed in terms of:

1. Custom algorithms and techniques that provide effective summaries, filtering and correlating information coming from different probes.
2. Root cause analysis techniques able to derive the causes of the observed phenomena, spotting the right thread in the complex fabric of the Cloud infrastructure.
3. Very importantly, accurate measures in an environment dominated by virtualized Resources.

Efficiency

Referring to the issues reported in Section 5, main improvements in terms of efficiency are expected for data management. In particular, algorithms and techniques more and more efficient are needed to manage the large volume of monitoring data necessary to have a comprehensive view of the Cloud, quickly and continuously, and without putting too much burden on the Cloud and monitoring infrastructures both in terms of computing and communication resources. The monitoring system should be therefore able to do several operations on data (collect, filter, aggregate, correlate, dissect, store, etc.) respecting strict requirements in terms of time, computational power, and communication overhead.

New Monitoring Techniques and Tools

Effective monitoring techniques should be able to provide, on the one hand, very fine grained measures, and, on the other hand, a synthetic outlook of the Cloud, involving all the variables affecting the QoS and other requirements At the same time, the techniques should not add performance burden to the system (think, for example, to mobile Cloud). Finally, they should be integrated with a control methodology that manages performance of the enterprise system. For all these reasons, new monitoring techniques and tools specifically designed for Cloud Computing are needed.

Cross-Layer Monitoring

The complex structure of Cloud is made of several layers to allow for functional separation, modularity and thus manageability. However, such strong layering poses several limits on the monitoring system, in terms of kinds of analysis and consequent actions that can be performed. These limits include the inability for Consumers to access lower-layer metrics and for Providers to access upper-layer ones. As a consequence, Consumers and Providers make their decisions based on a limited horizon. Overcoming this limitation is very challenging, technology-, privacy and administration-wise.

Cross-Domain Monitoring: Federated Clouds, Hybrid Clouds, Multi-Tenancy Services

Cloud Service Providers offer different types of resources and levels of QoS that can be exploited by cross-domain solutions to improve resource utilization, end-to-end performance, and resiliency. When standardized, the collaboration across multiple Cloud infrastructures is referred to as resource federation; however, such standardization process is still at an early stage. Among different Cloud monitoring infrastructures there is a high heterogeneity of systems, tools, and exchanged information, and monitoring of Federated Clouds is part of ongoing research. Research in the field of security has focused on cross-domain data leakage and its prevention, where the ability to monitor services performance has been considered as a security risk and monitoring is an attack tool, and not for its potential value in evaluating and predicting the performance of a given service.

Monitoring of Novel Network Architectures Based on Cloud

As reported Cloud-based networking is a new way to roll out distributed enterprise networks, via highly resilient, multi-tenant applications that require no capital investment in networking equipment. Unlike traditional hardware-based legacy solutions, Cloud-based networking is extremely simple, enabling enterprises to deploy remote locations in a short time and operate their distributed networks via a Cloud-based application, while providing high levels of centralized control (thanks to protocols like Open- Flow) and network visibility. They are planning to use Software Defined Networks, based on Open Flows, to implement and integrate Cloud-based networks.

CONCLUSION

As we know the cloud platform is prominent in today's world. All the issues on cloud infrastructure are survey on much research work. To achieve those issues and prove trustworthy the chapter have described about auditing the cloud and monitoring the cloud. This chapter we have provided a careful analysis of the state of the art in the field of Cloud monitoring and Cloud auditing. The main activities have discussed in Cloud environment that have strong benefit from auditing and actual need of monitoring. To contextualize and study Cloud properties, we have provided background and definitions for key concepts. It has also derived the main properties that Cloud monitoring systems and Cloud auditing should have, the issues arising from these properties. It has then described the main platforms and services for Cloud monitoring, indicating how they relate with such properties and issues. And some summarization of different method (algorithms technique) and theory which being used to formulate framework and model, derived to provide a better monitoring process in terms properties of a better performance, competitive and efficiency to meet the required SLA, improved the resource performance and lowered the power consumption. Some of the auditing process also discussed to maintain in organization with some standards and procedure to implement. The open issues, challenges and future directions in the field of Cloud monitoring and auditing is provided to provide the security of tag consistency and integrity were achieved.

REFERENCES

Aceto, G., Botta, A., De Donato, W., & Pescapè, A. (2013). Cloud monitoring: A survey. *Computer Networks*, *57*(9), 2093-2115.

Aljohani, A. M., Holton, D. R. W., Awan, I.-U., & Alanazi, J. S. (2011). Performance evaluation of local and cloud deployment of web clusters. In Proceedings of the 2011 14th International Conference on Network-Based Information Systems (NBiS) (pp. 274-278). IEEE. doi:10.1109/NBiS.2011.47

Caron, E., Rodero-Merino, L., Desprez, F., & Muresan, A. (2011). Auto-scaling, load balancing and monitoring in commercial and open-source clouds.

Cannon, D. (2011). *Certified Information Systems Auditor Study Guide* (3rd ed.). Wiley.

Foster, I., Zhao, Y., Raicu, I., & Lu, S. (2008). Cloud computing and grid computing 360-degree compared. In *Proceedings of the Grid Computing Environments Workshop*. doi:10.1109/GCE.2008.4738445

Hasselmeyer, P., & d'Heureuse, N. (2010). Towards holistic multi-tenant monitoring for virtual data centers. In Proceedings of the Network Operations and Management Symposium Workshops (pp. 350–356). doi:10.1109/NOMSW.2010.5486528

Hazarika, B., & Singh, T.J. (2015, January). Survey Paper on Cloud Computing & Cloud Monitoring: Basics. *SSRG International Journal of Computer Science and Engineering, 2*(1), 10-15.

Jansen, W., & Grance, T. (2011, December). *Guidelines on Security and Privacy in Public Cloud Computing*. NIST.

Katsaros, G., Kübert, R., & Gallizo, G. (2011). Building a service-oriented monitoring framework with REST and Nagios. In *Proceedings of the IEEE International Conference on Services Computing (SCC)* (pp. 426–431). doi:10.1109/SCC.2011.53

Kumar, V., Cai, Z., Cooper, B. F., Eisenhauer, G., Schwan, K., Mansour, M., . . . Widener, P. (2006). Implementing diverse messaging models with self-managing properties using IFLOW. In Proceedings of the IEEE International Conference on Autonomic Computing ICAC'06 (pp. 243-252). doi:10.1109/ICAC.2006.1662404

Kutare, M., Eisenhauer, G., Wang, C., Schwan, K., Talwar, V., & Wolf, M. (2010). Monalytics: online monitoring and analytics for managing large scale data centers. In *Proceedings of the 7th International Conference on Autonomic Computing* (pp. 141–150). doi:10.1145/1809049.1809073

Mei, Y., Liu, L., Pu, X., & Sivathanu, S. (2010). Performance measurements and analysis of network I/O applications in virtualized cloud. In *Proceedings of the 2010 IEEE 3rd International Conference on Cloud Computing (CLOUD)* (pp. 59–66).

Mell, P., & Grance, T. (2011). The NIST Definition of Cloud Computing (Special Publication 800-145). NIST.

Mohamaddiah, M. H., Abdullah, A., Subramaniam, S., & Hussin, M. (2014, February). A Survey on Resource Allocation and Monitoring in Cloud Computing. *International Journal of Machine Learning and Computing, 4*(1).

Rochwerger, B., Breitgand, D., Levy, E., Galis, A., Nagin, K., Llorente, I. M., ... & Ben-Yehuda, M. (2009). The RESERVOIR model and architecture for open federated cloud computing. *IBM Journal of Research and Development, 53*(4).

Ryoo, J., Rizvi, S., Aiken, W., & Kissell, J. (2014). Cloud security auditing: challenges and emerging approaches. *IEEE Security & Privacy, 12*(6), 68-74.

Shao, J., & Wang, Q. (2011). A performance guarantee approach for cloud applications based on monitoring. In *Proceedings of the Computer Software and Applications Conference Workshops (COMPSACW)* (pp. 25–30).

Spring, J. (2011). Monitoring cloud computing by layer- Part 2. *IEEE Security and Privacy, 9*(52–55).

Wang, C., Schwan, K., Talwar, V., Eisenhauer, G., Hu, L., & Wolf, M. (2011). A flexible architecture integrating monitoring and analytics for managing large-scale data centers. In *Proceedings of ICAC*. doi:10.1145/1998582.1998605

Chapter 14
Trust Relationship Establishment Among Multiple Cloud Service Provider

Abhishek Majumder
Tripura University, India

Samir Nath
Tripura University, India

Arpita Bhattacharjee
Tripura University, India

Ranjita Choudhury
Tripura University, India

ABSTRACT

Trust relationships among multiple Cloud Service Providers is a concept in which multiple cloud service providers from multiple distributed Identity Provider can access resources of each other, only if they are trusted with their Identity Provider. In this chapter a scheme has been proposed to enhance the security of data in a multi-cloud environment by improving trust relationships among multiple clouds. The scheme is also designed to overcome interoperability problem between different clouds. In the proposed scheme concept of proxy is used. Client organization tries to communicate with multiple cloud service providers through proxy. Client organization send resource request to cloud service providers. On receiving the resource request the cloud service provider collect the authentication confirmation from proxy. Then it sends the reply and data to requested client organization. Numerical analysis and comparative study of the proposed scheme with some of the existing scheme has been carried out.

DOI: 10.4018/978-1-5225-3038-1.ch014

INTRODUCTION

Cloud computing (Armbrust et. al., 2010) is known as a distributing computing, which is used to store client data and application in scattered data centre around the world, so that, client can access their data or grant applications from anywhere just with an internet connection. User's data and information is stored in the cloud data centre. Cloud service provider allows access to applications, operating systems and hardware.

For example, e-mail service like Gmail and Hotmail are type of cloud computing services. In the cloud, users can easily access their email from different browsers and computers just with the help of an internet connection. The emails are hosted in servers, but not stored locally on the client computer.

The cloud service provided to the user may be provided by a single cloud service provider. But the problem with single cloud service provider is the problem of availability. For overcoming this problem, the concept of multiple CSP (AlZain et al., 2012) has come into picture. Though multi cloud computing environment overcomes some of the security problems encountered in single cloud computing environment, but introduction of multi-cloud environment creates some new problems. One of these important issues is lack of trust relationships in Interoperability among multiple cloud service providers. Trust relationship among multiple Cloud Service Providers (CSPs) is a concept in which multiple CSPs from multiple distributed

Figure 1. Cloud computing

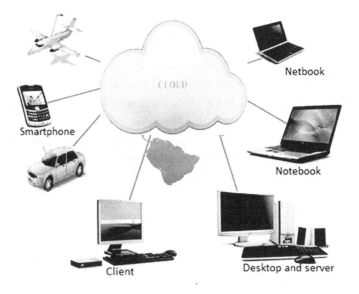

Identity Provider's (IdP) can access resources of each other, only if they are trusted with the Identity Provider's (IdP).

In this chapter, some of the existing schemes that had been designed to provide services to the client in multi clod environment have been discussed. A proxy based scheme has been proposed for multi-cloud environment with the following objectives:

- To enhance the security of data by improving trust relationship between multiple clouds.
- To overcome interoperability problem between different clouds.
- To reduce time consumption by introducing proxy.

MULTI-CLOUD COMPUTING

Popularity of single cloud providers are decreasing days by day, because of unavailable of service and malicious insider. Now-a-days multi-cloud computing have becoming in place of a single cloud computing.

Multi cloud strategy is a combination of two or more cloud services, which is used to avoid the risk of data loss, malicious insider etc. specially, user's data and information are stored in multiple cloud in multi-cloud computing environment.

Switching from single cloud to multi-cloud computing is most essential. Multi-cloud computing controls multiple clouds. Multi-cloud is not only reasonable but also important many reasons given here under.

- **Data Integrity:** Integrity is prevention of improper modification of information (Celesti et al., 2010; AlZain et al., 2011). Since in multi-cloud computing system copy of user data is stored in multiple CSPs, if one CSP get infected, the result from other CSP will contradict with that affected one. Therefore, it is not possible in multi-cloud environment to violet the integrity of the stored data.
- **Service Unavailability:** No compensation will be given by the company if system becomes failure (AlZain et al., 2011; AlZain et al., 2011) in single cloud provider. On the contrary, data is stored in multiple CSPs. So, even with failure of one system there is hardly chance of data loss in multi-cloud computing.
- **Data Intrusion:** In case of a single cloud provider data intrusion (AlZain et al., 2011) may take place. It is not possible to hack, access and modify the accounts password, information and resources in the case of multi-cloud computing environment. As multiple copies of same data are stored in multiple clouds, and retrieval of all of the copies is almost impossible.

- **Data Leakage:** Unauthorized transmission among two-user organization is known as data leakage (Ristenpart et al., 2009). Data leakage may occur in single cloud provider as because the service providers are not trusted to each other. Whereas in the case of multi-cloud trust relationship is the root to avoid any leakage.
- **Authenticity:** Data authentication assures that the returned data is the same as the stored data. Only the authorize users can access any information stored in multi-clouds.
- **Data Confidentiality:** Data Confidentiality (Yau et al., 2010) may be followed up only by the authenticated users of multi-cloud because multiple copies of the same data are stored in multiple distinct clouds with different types of encryption techniques.
- **Trust Relationship Between CSP:** Due to lack of trust relationships among user and cloud service provider no one can put faith on each other, which is a major problem. Trust relationship between multiple CSPs can build up only in multi-cloud computing.

LITERATURE REVIEW

In this section the existing schemes designed for providing cloud services in Multi cloud environment have been discussed.

Interoperability of Identity Management system

Le et al. (2008) introduces Identity Management Model. The theme of interoperability of Identity Management system is identified as follows:

- Cardspace from Microsoft
- Liberty from Liberty Alliance Project.

Windows Cardspace (Chappell et. al., 2006) is designed based on the law of identities and idea of identity meta-system. User-centric approach for digital identity management is windows Cardspace. It provides users secure way to manage their online identities. Windows Cardspace provides user two types of cards, namely:

- Self-issued cards, can be issued by the user himself.
- Managed cards, are accepted by the user but issued by other IdPs.

These cards are also known as information cards. Information card contains meta data which is useful to retrieve the users information at the identity provider side, and thus it establishes trust relationships among the user and identity provider.

Liberty Project is founded in 2001 (Alliance, 2002) and is based on the idea of federated network identity and circle of trust in which service providers and identity providers establish a business relationship among them so that a principal (internet user in Liberty terminology) can perform business transaction in secure environment.

Liberty architecture is based on three frame work:

- ID-FF stands for Liberty Identity-Federation Framework. As its name indicates, this framework provides the specification for identity federation and simplified sign-on. It also supplies mechanisms for the termination of Federation and for single logout.
- ID-WSF stands for Identity-Web Service framework. It provides identity-based web services specification. It also defines a framework for creating, discovering and consuming identity services
- ID-SIS stands for Identity-Services Interface Specification. It is a collection of specifications. It enables network identity services by using ID-FF and ID-WSF.

If a user want to access service provider's resources, the service provider will ask the user to choose an identity provider and the user is redirected to the selected identity provider. This identity provider will require to the user to authenticate him with his account and to give him a security token. His security token will be forwarded

Figure 2. Cardspace interaction and standards

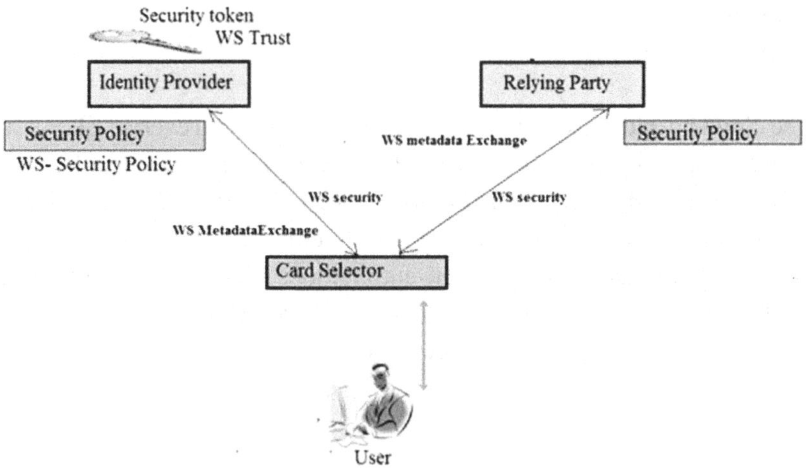

to the service provider. The service provider will verify the token with the identity provider through a secured channel. As soon as the verification is terminated with a positive result, the user will be granted to access service provider's resources. With the belief of identity federation, after authentication, the user can access to any service provider's resource without asking for log-in again within a same circle of trust.

Drawback

It is not easy to find circles of trust due to complicated relationships among actors residing in different circles of trust. It brings out a problem of interoperability at two different levels:

1. Interoperability at the level of web simplified sign-on(SSO) of intraperimeter and of inter-perimeter.
2. Interoperability at the level of attributes sharing.

Proxy Based Model

Mukesh Singhal et al. (2013) proposed proxy based model. It is like firewalls, that carryout operation on the behalf of CSP's and/or client. The main purpose of using proxy is, it does not require prior agreement. The prior agreement means pre-established business.

Agreement between CSP's Proxy based model consists of five strategies:

- Cloud hosted proxy
- Proxy as a service
- Peer to peer proxy
- On premises proxy
- Hybrid proxy infrastructure

In the cloud hosted proxy, proxies are hosted by each and every CSP. As soon as any service request is received by one CSP, the same is forwarded to others through proxy. Proxy is used here for collaboration. Here, the user sends a request to cloud C1. Cloud C1 authentically sends the request to cloud C2 and C3.

Here proxy is considered to be an autonomous cloud itself. Proxy provides services to the clients and CSPs. Whenever a set of CSPs wants to collaborate, it can be managed by PSP (Proxy Service Provider).

Figure 3. Cloud hosted proxy

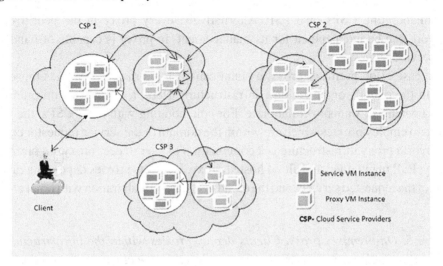

Figure 4. Proxy as a service. (a) Two proxies are employed to interact with CSPs C1 and C2 by the client. (b) C1 requires to discover services from C2 after a client requests a service to C1

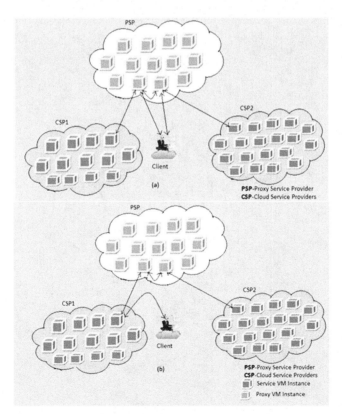

In a peer-to-peer network interaction among the proxies can be done by a group of collaborating CSPs or a PSP. Alternatively, every proxy in the peer-to-peer network can be independent for its management. In proxy is capable of handling the service requests.

In case of on-premises proxy, a client can host and manages proxies those are within the client's organization's infrastructure. Here, a client uses on-premises proxy whenever wants to collaborate. For collaborating with other CSPs, the CSP needs to employ proxies which are within the domain of the service requestor client.

Hybrid proxy infrastructure is a combination of peer to peer proxy, on premises proxy, PSP maintained and cloud hosted proxy. It selects proxies depending on the type of the requested services and the cloud that starts collaboration with other cloud.

Figure 5. On-premises proxy. Clients deploy proxies within the infrastructure of their organization. (a) Two proxies are employed by the client for interaction with CSPs C1 and C2. (b) Service request is initiated with C1, and it discovers that service from C2 is needed

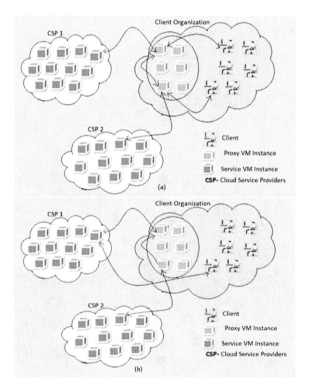

Drawback

The security issues founded in multi-cloud computing environment during the collaboration among multiple clouds are isolation management, data exposure and confidentiality and lack of trust relationships among multiple clouds, etc.

Security and Privacy Model

Jensen Meiko et al. (2013) presented a security and privacy model which provides different security solutions for multi-cloud adoption environment. Security and privacy model meditate on public clouds. It provides four distinct models for multi-cloud architectures.

In this model, different architectural models are introduced for distributing resources to multiple cloud service providers. Four architectural patterns are used:

- Republication of application.
- Partition of application System into tries.
- Partition of Application logic into fragments.
- Partition of application data into fragment.

In the republication of application system, same operation is performed in multiple clouds and a comparison is made between the respective results, which allow users to have the evidence. In this way data integrity is preserve here.

Figure 6. Republication of application system

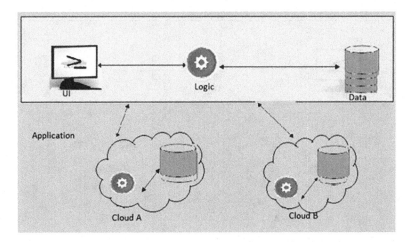

In partition of application system tries data and logic are separated and stored in two different clouds. If the execution of logic and data are performed within the user's system, it will not be possible for the application provider to know about the outcome of the execution. In this model, data and logic are separated, so there may not be any risk of data leakage.

Data confidentiality is preserved in partition of application logic into fragments because the application logic is distributed among two clouds. The sharing of the computational load is lying with entrusted cloud, that is, public cloud and the part of critical share is laying with trusted cloud, that is private cloud.

Figure 7. Partition of application system into tries

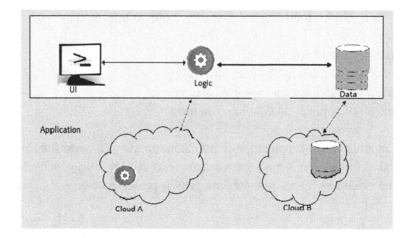

Figure 8. Partition of application logic into fragments

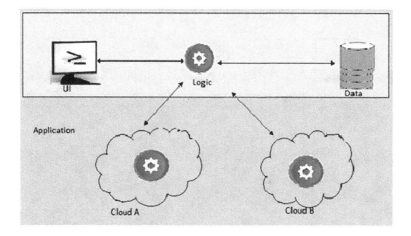

Figure 9. Partition of application data into fragments

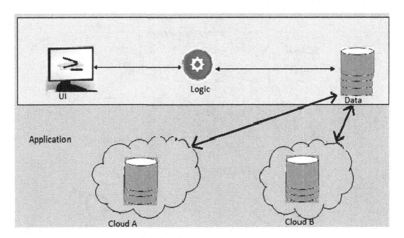

Data confidentiality is also preserved by partitioning of application data into fragments. Since the application data is divided into two parts, they are stored in two different clouds. Therefore, the clouds will not able to access full data.

Drawback

The complaint reoperation of logic and data is only possible if the application provider does not receive the customer's data in any case. Processing needs to take place in a secure environment. This can be present in the customer's own premises. But this almost annihilates the benefits of outsourcing, cost reduction, and seamless scalability of using cloud computing, because the customer needs to provision sufficient and complaint resources by himself. Alternatively, the application logic can also take place in a different tier of the complaint storage cloud, or on a different cloud with similar compliance level.

The drawback is the customer has to fully trust those cloud service providers that receive all information, logic and data. This somewhat contradicts the initial motivation of this multi-cloud approach. The disadvantageous in terms of confidentiality is every cloud provider learns everything about the application logic and data.

Depsky Model

Bassani et al. (2013) presented a simple model for multi-cloud system. It is a virtual storage cloud system. It consists of different clouds to build a cloud-of-clouds. By using multi-cloud provider the availability and confidentiality of data is preserved in the storage.

Figure 10. Depsky model

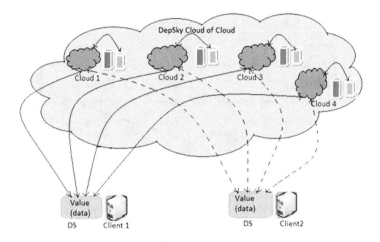

This system model is based on four clouds. All of these are storage clouds and being used independently. As this model uses the concept of secret sharing algorithm, therefore data can be encrypted before storing in the cloud.

Drawback

Data need to be manipulated in virtual machine of cloud providers, which will not happen if the data has been encrypted.

Multi Cloud Database Model

Mohammed A. AlZain et al. (2011) proposed multi cloud database model (MCDB), which stated the data security and privacy issues of cloud computing, such as data intrusion, data integrity, service availability etc. MCDB model uses the concept of multi cloud service provider and secret sharing algorithm (Shamir, 1979). Some security risk like malicious insider and failing of cloud services can be overcome by this model.

MCDB model uses the concept of multi share technique (AlZain et al., 2011), in which multiple copies of the user's data are stored into multiple distinct clouds. Therefore, it avoids the drawbacks of single cloud, and minimizes the security risk from malicious insider. Database management system manages and controls the operations between the clients and the CSP. The components of different layers of MCDB are shown in Table 1. Overview of MCDB components are shown in Table 2.

Table 1. MCDB layer

Layer Name	Component
Presentation Layer	User, HTTP Server
Application Layer	Servlet Engine
Management Layer	DBMS, CSP and data storage

Table 2. Overview of MCDB component

Component	Description
User	End user's web browser is accountable for displaying user interface.
HTTP Server	HTTP server manages the communication between the application and the browser. Execution of the application from the server side generates user interface
Servlet Engine	Servlet engine uses JDBC protocol to communicate with the data source
DBMS (Data source)	DBMS is responsible for rewriting the user's query, generating polynomial values, handling the user's query to each CSP and then receiving the result from CSP.
CSP and Dara Storage	CSP is responsible for storing the data in its cloud storage, that is divided into n shares and then returning the relevant shares to the DBMS that consists of the user's query result

INTER-CLOUD IDENTITY MANAGEMENT INFRASTRUCTURE MODEL

Celesti et. al. (2010) proposed Inter-cloud Identity Management Infrastructure (ICIMI) Model. This model is useful to overcome the Identity Management (IdM) and authentication issues in a cloud federation scenario. Here cloud is distinguished into two types: home cloud and foreign cloud. Home cloud is a cloud service provider which forwards service request to the foreign cloud. The foreign cloud in turn accepts the request from the home cloud and provides the corresponding response to the requested services. The concept of single sign-on (SSO) authentication (Hursti, 1997) and digital identities are used in this model.

The following logical components are used in this model:

1. **End-User:** It is a person or a software/hardware which deserves a particular digital identity and who interacts with an on-line application.

Figure 11. MCDB model

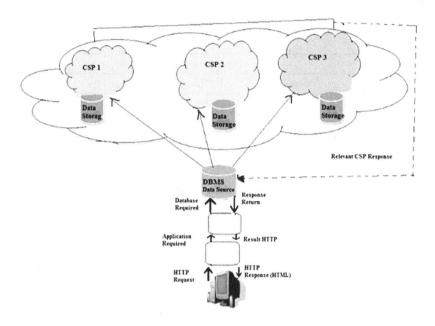

2. **User Agent:** In the common case of the human interaction, it can be a browser or another software application.
3. **Service Provider (SP):** It is a system, or administrative domain. Identity provider provides information to the service provider and the service provider shall have to rely on the information of identity provider.
4. **Identity Provider (IdP) or Asserting Party:** It is a system or administrative domain, who provides information about the user's authentication.

In Figure 12, cloud A is considered to be home cloud and cloud B, C, and D as foreign cloud. Cloud A sends resource request to the cloud B, C, and D and an authentication task is performed in the IdPs of the respective foreign clouds.

To access the resources from foreign cloud B, C and D, home cloud A requires creating an account on IdP X and IdP Z respectively. When home cloud A wants to access resources from cloud B and cloud C, clouds B and C forwards the same request to their IdP X. IdP X then verify the identity of home cloud A. If home cloud A is authenticated, only the requested resource is delivered to the home cloud A. The same is also applicable in case of foreign cloud C.

Figure 12. Inter-cloud identity management infrastructure

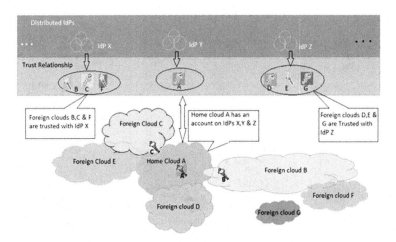

Proposed Scheme

It is already known that to establish a trust relationship among multiple CSPs a prior agreement is required. Therefore, use of proxy enables user to make a trust relationship without any prior agreements. In the proposed scheme, Pearson's correlation algorithm is used to select the foreign cloud which will be providing services.

In Figure 13, it is assumed that client Organization is trusted with IdP X and CSP 1 CSP 2 is trusted with IdP Y. Here, client organization is considered to be Home cloud and CSP1 & CSP 2 is considered to be foreign cloud.

Figure 13. Communication between home cloud and foreign cloud

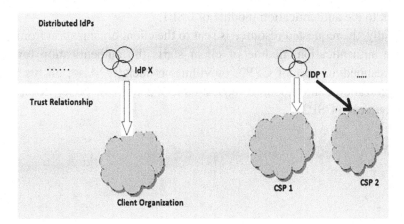

Figure 14. Trust relationship establishment

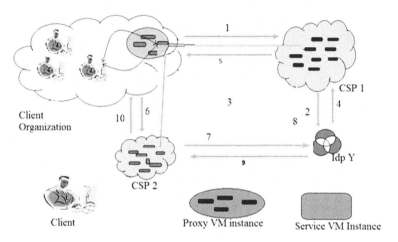

Steps of the proposed scheme are given as follows

1. The authentication module of client starts the authentication toward the corresponding peer of CSP1 providing its identity. Also, clients in client organization send resource request to CSPl through proxy, to access the resources in CSP1

2. The authentication module of CSP 1 forwards the authentication request to the IdP Y.

3. An authentication interaction between the authentication module of CSPl & the IdP Y is initiated, and it will lead to the generation of a security context for the client in the client organization.

4. IdP Y sends the attributes (i.e., the credentials needed for executing local authentication) associated to the authenticated client in the client organization back to the authentication module of CSP1.

5. Finally, the requested resource is sent to the client organization from CSP1.

6. The authentication module of client starts the authentication toward the corresponding peer of CSP2, providing its identity. Also, clients in client organization send resource request to CSP2 through proxy, to access the resources in CSP2.

7. The authentication module of CSP2 forwards the authentication request to the IdP Y.
8. Since a security context already exists for client organization, so generation of security context will not be performed.
9. The attributes for authenticating client with CSP2 will be directly sent to the authentication module of CSP2.
10. Finally, the requested resource is sent to the proxy of the client organization from CSP2.

NUMERICAL ANALYSIS

In this scheme the concept of proxy is used because, proxy provides the facility for collaboration between the cloud service providers without the need of any prior agreement. The proposed scheme uses Pearson's Correlation to select the foreign cloud.

Pearson's Correlation is denoted by r. Correlation between two variables say X and Y are represented by

$$r_i = \frac{\sum XY_i}{\sqrt{\sum X^2 \sum Y_i^2}}$$

$$= \frac{\text{covarience of } (x,y)}{\sqrt{\text{covarience of } x}\sqrt{\text{covarience of } y}}$$

where, $X = x - \bar{x}, Y = y - \bar{y}$ i.e., X and Y are the deviations measured from their respective means.

Let, HC and F (F_1, F_2, F_3, F_4 and F_5) are the quantifiable parameters of home cloud and foreign cloud.

In this analysis one home cloud and five foreign clouds is considered. Let both of them are trusted. Suppose parameters of home cloud and foreign clouds are as follows:

$$
\begin{array}{llll}
& CPU & Working \\
& Speed & Time \\
& (GHz) & (AM \ / \ PM) \\
HC = & [2.8 \quad 2 & 12 & 3] \\
F1 = & [1.4 \quad 1 & 12 & 2.5] \\
F2 = & [1.9 \quad 1.5 & 10 & 2.4] \\
F3 = & [2.5 \quad 3 & 8 & 4] \\
F4 = & [3.0 \quad 4 & 8 & 4] \\
F5 = & [2.7 \quad 2.8 & 6 & 3.2] \\
& RAM & Transmission \\
& (GB) & rate \, (B \ / \sec)
\end{array}
$$

Relation (r_1) between Home cloud (HC) and Foreign cloud (F_1) can be calculated in the following way:

The mean of quantifiable parameters of HC, $\bar{x} = \dfrac{\sum HC}{n} = \dfrac{(2.8+2+12+3)}{4} = 4.95$

The mean of quantifiable parameters of F_1, $\bar{y} = \dfrac{\sum F1}{n} = \dfrac{(1.4+1+12+2.5)}{4} = 4.225$

where, n = the total number of quantifiable parameters of Home cloud and Foreign cloud.

Now,

$$
r_1 = \frac{\sum XY}{\sqrt{\sum X^2 Y^2}} = \frac{73.765}{\sqrt{66.83*81.8075}} = 0.997626681
$$

Table 3.

HC	F_1	X = HC - 4.95	Y= F_1 - 4.225	X²	Y²	X*Y
2.8	1.4	-2.15	-2.825	4.6225	7.980625	6.07375
2	1	-2.95	-3.225	8.7025	10.400625	9.51375
12	12	7.05	7.775	49.7025	60.450625	54.81375
3	2.5	-1.95	-1.725	3.8025	2.975625	3.36375
19.8	16.9	0	0	66.83	81.8075	73.765

Relation (r_2) between Home cloud (HC) and Foreign cloud (F_2) can be calculated in the following way:

The mean of quantifiable parameters of HC, $\bar{x} = \dfrac{\sum HC}{n} = \dfrac{(2.8+2+12+3)}{4} = 4.95$

The mean of quantifiable parameters of F_2, $\bar{y} = \dfrac{\sum F_2}{n} = \dfrac{(1.9+1.5+10+2.4)}{4} = 3.95$

Now,

$$r_2 = \frac{\sum X\,Y}{\sqrt{\sum X^2 Y^2}} = \frac{31.93}{\sqrt{66.83 * 18.861}} = 0.905398981$$

Relation (r_3) between Home cloud (HC) and Foreign cloud (F_3) can be calculated in the following way:

The mean of quantifiable parameters of HC, $\bar{x} = \dfrac{\sum HC}{n} = \dfrac{(2.8+2+12+3)}{4} = 4.95$

The mean of quantifiable parameters of F_3, $\bar{y} = \dfrac{\sum F_3}{n} = \dfrac{(2.5+3+8+4)}{4} = 4.375$

Now,

$$r_3 = \frac{\sum X\,Y}{\sqrt{\sum X^2\,Y^2}} = \frac{34.375}{\sqrt{66.83 * 18.6875}} = 0.972705504$$

Relation (r_4) between Home cloud (HC) and Foreign cloud (F_3) can be calculated in the following way:

The mean of quantifiable parameters of HC, $\bar{x} = \dfrac{\sum HC}{n} = \dfrac{(2.8+2+12+3)}{4} = 4.95$

Table 4.

HC	F2	X= HC - 4.95	Y= F$_2$ - 3.95	X^2	Y^2	X*Y
2.8	1.9	-2.15	-2.05	4.6225	4.2025	4.4075
2	1.5	-2.95	-2.45	8.7025	6.0025	7.2275
12	10	7.05	6.05	49.7025	6.0025	17.2725
3	2.4	-1.95	-1.55	3.8025	2.4025	3.0225
19.8	15.8	0	0	66.83	18.61	31.93

Table 5.

HC	F_3	X= HC - 4.95	Y= F_3- 4.375	X^2	Y^2	X*Y
2.8	2.5	-2.15	-1.875	4.6225	3.515625	4.03125
2	3	-2.95	-1.375	8.7025	1.890625	4.05625
12	8	7.05	3.625	49.7025	13.140625	25.55625
3	4	-1.95	-0.375	3.8025	0.140625	0.73125
19.8	17.5	0	0	66.83	18.6875	34.375

The mean of quantifiable parameters of F_4, $\bar{y} = \dfrac{\sum F_4}{n} = \dfrac{(3.0+4+8+4)}{4} = 4.75$

Now,

$r_4 = \dfrac{\sum X\,Y}{\sqrt{\sum X^2\,Y^2}} = \dfrac{30.35}{\sqrt{66.83*14.75}} = 0.966667137$

Relation (r_5) between Home cloud (HC) and Foreign cloud (F_5) can be calculated in the following way:

The mean of quantifiable parameters of HC, $\bar{x} = \dfrac{\sum HC}{n} = \dfrac{(2.8+2+12+3)}{4} = 4.95$

The mean of quantifiable parameters of F_5 $\bar{y} = \dfrac{\sum F_5}{n} = \dfrac{(2.7+2.8+6+3.2)}{4} = 3.675$

Now,

$r_5 = \dfrac{\sum XY}{\sqrt{\sum X^2 Y^2}} = \dfrac{21.995}{\sqrt{66.83*7.3475}} = 0.99258667$

Table 6.

HC	F_4	X= HC - 4.95	Y=F_4- 4.75	X^2	Y^2	X*Y
2.8	3.0	-2.15	-1.75	4.6225	3.0625	3.7625
2	4	-2.95	-0.75	8.7025	0.5625	2.2125
12	8	7.05	3.25	49.7025	10.5625	22.9125
3	4	-1.95	-0.75	3.8025	0.5625	1.4625
19.8	19	0	0	66.83	14.75	30.35

Table 7.

HC	F_s	X= HC - 4.95	Y.= F5- 3.675	X^2	Y^2	X*Y
2.8	2.7	-2.15	-0.975	4.6225	0.950625	2.09625
2	2.8	-2.95	-0.875	8.7025	0.765625	2.58125
12	6	7.05	2.325	49.7025	5.405625	16.39125
3	3.2	-1.95	-0.475	3.8025	0.225625	0.92625
19.8	14.7	0	0	66.83	7.3475	21.995

There must need to arrange the values of relation(r) in descending order, like as given under:

$r_1 = 0.997626681$, $r_2 = 0.905398981$, $r_3 = 0.972705504$, $r_4 = 0.966667137$, $r_5 = 0.99258667$

Antonio Celesti et al. (2010) propose one mathematical analysis process, in which they use Weighted Euclidean Distance formula for analysis. According to their analysis, only those foreign clouds whose SLA matches with the SLA of home cloud are able to share or access resources from each other. But the problem is that, those foreign clouds whose SLA does not match with the home cloud SLA will not be able to share resources. They may have the requested resource that a particular home cloud is looking for.

Let,

$$F = (4) = \begin{bmatrix} 14 & 1 & 12 & 2.5 \\ 1.9 & 1.5 & 10 & 2.4 \\ 2.5 & 3 & 8 & 4 \\ 3.0 & 4 & 8 & 4 \\ 2.7 & 2.8 & 6 & 3.2 \end{bmatrix}$$

where, F is the K X N matrix in which only the matched foreign clouds are present.

The entries shown in the given matrix are supposed to be the quantifiable parameters of those foreign clouds. The formula for calculating the distance between the home cloud and a particular foreign cloud is,

$$d_i = \sqrt{\sum_{j=0}^{N} W_j \left(p^i_j - h_j \right)^2}$$

where,

P_j^i = i-th row and j-th column of matrix F and is considered as a vector.
d_i = Distance between home cloud and i-th foreign cloud.
h_j = Vector of N quantifiable parameters of home cloud.
W_j = The vector whose N elements w_j represent the weight associated to the j-th term of Euclidean distance. It is related to SLA.

They uses the concept of Kronecker delta (Δ_i) and calculates i-th row of matrix F by $p^i = \Delta_i \bullet F$. According to Kronecker delta,

$\Delta_i = 0, if\ i \neq j$

$= 1, if\ i = j$

Therefore,

$$\Delta_1 = \begin{bmatrix} 1 & 0 & 0 & 0 & 0 \end{bmatrix}$$

$$\Delta_1 = \begin{bmatrix} 0 & 1 & 0 & 0 & 0 \end{bmatrix}$$

$$\Delta_1 = \begin{bmatrix} 0 & 0 & 1 & 0 & 0 \end{bmatrix}$$

$$\Delta_1 = \begin{bmatrix} 0 & 0 & 0 & 1 & 0 \end{bmatrix}$$

$$\Delta_1 = \begin{bmatrix} 0 & 1 & 0 & 0 & 1 \end{bmatrix}$$

let,

$$H = \begin{bmatrix} 2.8 & 2 & 12 & 3 \end{bmatrix}$$

and

$$W = \begin{bmatrix} 5 & 10 & 15 & 20 \end{bmatrix}$$

now,

$$p^1 = \begin{bmatrix} 1.4 & 1 & 12 & 2.5 \end{bmatrix}$$

$$p^2 = \begin{bmatrix} 1.9 & 1.5 & 10 & 2.4 \end{bmatrix}$$

$$p^3 = \begin{bmatrix} 2.5 & 3 & 8 & 4 \end{bmatrix}$$

$$p4 = \begin{bmatrix} 3.0 & 4 & 8 & 4 \end{bmatrix}$$

$$p^5 = \begin{bmatrix} 2.7 & 2.8 & 6 & 3.2 \end{bmatrix}$$

According to the Weighted Euclidean distance formula, distance between home cloud and foreign cloud is calculated as,

$$d_i = \sqrt{\sum_{j=0}^{N} W_j \left(p_j^i - h_j \right)^2}$$

$$\begin{aligned} d_1 &= \sqrt{W_1 \left(p_1^1 - h_1 \right)^2 + W_2 \left(p_2^1 - h_2 \right)^2 + W_3 \left(p_3^1 - h_3 \right)^2 + W_4 \left(p_4^1 - h_4 \right)^2} \\ &= \sqrt{5 \left(1.4 - 2.8 \right)^2 + 10 \left(1 - 2 \right)^2 + 15 \left(12 - 12 \right)^2 + 20 \left(2.5 - 3 \right)^2} \\ &= \sqrt{24.8} \end{aligned}$$

$$d_1 = 4.979959839$$

$$\begin{aligned} d_2 &= \sqrt{W_1 \left(p_1^2 - h_1 \right)^2 + W_2 \left(p_2^2 - h_2 \right)^2 + W_3 \left(p_3^2 - h_3 \right)^2 + W_4 \left(p_4^2 - h_4 \right)^2} \\ &= \sqrt{5 \left(1.9 - 2.8 \right)^2 + 10 \left(1.5 - 2 \right)^2 + 15 \left(10 - 12 \right)^2 + 20 \left(2.4 - 3 \right)^2} \end{aligned}$$

$$d_2 = 8.587782019$$

$$d_3 = \sqrt{W_1\left(p_1^3 + h_1\right)^2 + W_2\left(p_2^3 + h_2\right)^2 + W_3\left(p_3^3 + h_3\right)^2 + W_4\left(p_4^3 + h_4\right)^2}$$
$$= \sqrt{5\left(2.5 - 2.8\right)^2 + 10\left(3 - 2\right)^2 + 15\left(8 - 12\right)^2 + 20\left(4 - 3\right)^2}$$

$d_3 = 16.44536409$

$$d_4 = \sqrt{W_1\left(p_1^4 + h_1\right)^2 + W_2\left(p_2^4 + h_2\right)^2 + W_3\left(p_3^4 + h_3\right)^2 + W_4\left(p_4^4 + h_4\right)^2}$$
$$= \sqrt{5\left(3.0 - 2.8\right)^2 + 10\left(4 - 2\right)^2 + 15\left(8 - 12\right)^2 + 20\left(4 - 3\right)^2}$$

$d_4 = 17.32628062$

$$d_5 = \sqrt{W_1\left(p_1^5 + h_1\right)^2 + W_2\left(p_2^5 + h_2\right)^2 + W_3\left(p_3^5 + h_3\right)^2 + W_4\left(p_4^5 + h_4\right)^2}$$
$$= \sqrt{5\left(2.7 - 2.8\right)^2 + 10\left(2.8 - 2\right)^2 + 15\left(6 - 12\right)^2 + 20\left(3.2 - 3\right)^2}$$

$d_5 = 23.39337513$

Now, all the results of the distance are needed to be arranged in ascending order, like, $d_1 = 4.979959839$, $d_2 = 8.587782019$, $d_3 = 16.44536409$, $d_4 = 17.32628062$, $d_5 = 23.39337513$.

According to Euclidean distance the values of the vector di are sorted in ascending order, like d_1, d_2, d_3, d_4 and d_5. Minimum distanced home cloud and foreign cloud will share resources with each other. Here, value of d_1 is the minimum. Therefore, the resource transmission will take place between the home cloud and first foreign cloud. And the rest of the transmission will follow the same procedure.

According to Pearson's correlation the values of relation (r) are sorted in descending order, like r_1, r_2, r_3, r_4, r_5. This means that, maximum correlation between home cloud and foreign cloud will share resources with each other. Here, value of r_1 is the maximum. Therefore, the resource transmission will take place between the home cloud and first foreign cloud. Next will occur between home cloud and fifth foreign cloud, home cloud and third foreign cloud, home cloud and fourth foreign cloud, and lastly between home cloud and second foreign cloud.

ADVANTAGES OF USING CORRELATION

By using Pearson's correlation, it became possible to give chance to every trusted cloud to share their resources with each other without checking their policies. Since the concept of proxy is used, there is no need to create any prior agreements (SLA) among multiple cloud service providers. The numerical analysis is completely based on the quantifiable parameters of every trusted cloud. Quantifiable parameter means RAM (total memory needed), CPU speed, working time, transmission rate, etc. Correlation will reduce the time needed to check the agreements between two or more different clouds.

CONCLUSION AND FUTURE SCOPE

There are some security risks and issues in single cloud computing environment which can be overcome by introducing the concept of multi-cloud computing environment. But multi-cloud computing environment also have some security problems, some of those are interoperability, trust relationship among multiple CSPs, malicious insider etc. To establish trust relationship among multiple CSPs prior legal agreement is required, but this legal agreement varies CSP to CSP.

In this chapter a proxy based trust relationship establishment technique has been proposed to overcome the problem of pre-agreement in federated cloud environment. The proposed scheme uses Pearson's correlation mechanism to select the foreign cloud. The proposed scheme does not consider the scalability of the system. Therefore, scalability of the proposed scheme remains as future work.

REFERENCES

Liberty Alliance. (2002). Liberty alliance project. Retrieved from http://www. project liberty.org

AlZain, M. A., & Pardede, E. (2011, January). Using multi shares for ensuring privacy in database-as-a-service. In *Proceedings of 44th Hawaii International Conference on System Sciences* (pp. 1-9). doi:10.1109/HICSS.2011.478

AlZain, M. A., & Pardede, E. (2011, December). Using Multi Shares for Ensuring Privacy in Database-as-a-Service. In *Proceedings of 44th Hawaii International Conference on System Sciences* (pp. 1-9). doi:10.1109/HICSS.2011.478

AlZain, M. A., Pardede, E., Soh, B., & Thom, J. A. (2012, January). Cloud computing security: from single to multi-clouds. In *Proceedings of 45th Hawaii International Conference on System Science (HICSS)* (pp. 5490-5499). doi:10.1109/HICSS.2012.153

AlZain, M. A., Soh, B., & Pardede, E. (2011, December). Mcdb: using multi-clouds to ensure security in cloud computing. In *Proceedings of Ninth International Conference on Dependable, autonomic and secure computing (DASC)* (pp. 784-791). doi:10.1109/DASC.2011.133

Armbrust, M., Stoica, I., Zaharia, M., Fox, A., Griffith, R., Joseph, A. D., & Rabkin, A. et al. (2010). A view of cloud computing. *Communications of the ACM*, *53*(4), 50–58. doi:10.1145/1721654.1721672

Bessani, A., Correia, M., Quaresma, B., André, F., & Sousa, P. (2013). DepSky: dependable and secure storage in a cloud-of-clouds. *ACM Transactions on Storage*, *9*(4), 12:1-12:33.

Bohli, J. M., Gruschka, N., Jensen, M., Iacono, L. L., & Marnau, N. (2013). Security and privacy-enhancing multicloud architectures. *IEEE Transactions on Dependable and Secure Computing*, *10*(4), 212–224. doi:10.1109/TDSC.2013.6

Celesti, A., Tusa, F., Villari, M., & Puliafito, A. (2010, July). How to enhance cloud architectures to enable cross-federation. In *Proceedings of 3rd International Conference on Cloud Computing* (pp. 337-345). doi:10.1109/CLOUD.2010.46

Celesti, A., Tusa, F., Villari, M., & Puliafito, A. (2010, June). Security and cloud computing: Intercloud identity management infrastructure. In *Proceedings of 19th IEEE International Workshop on Enabling Technologies: Infrastructures for Collaborative Enterprises* (pp. 263-265).

Chappell, D., ... (2006). Introducing Windows CardSpace. Retrieved 15.02.17 from https://msdn.microsoft.com/en-us/library/aa480189.aspx

Hursti, J. (1997, November). Single sign-on. In *Proc. Helsinki University of Technology Seminar on Network Security*.

Le, H. B., & Bouzefrane, S. (2008, October). Identity management systems and interoperability in a heterogeneous environment. In *Proceedings of the International Conference on of Advanced Technologies for Communications* (pp. 239-242). doi:10.1109/ATC.2008.4760564

Ristenpart, T., Tromer, E., Shacham, H., & Savage, S. (2009, November). Hey, you, get off of my cloud: exploring information leakage in third-party compute clouds. In *Proceedings of the 16th ACM Conference on Computer and Communications Security* (pp. 199-212). doi:10.1145/1653662.1653687

Shamir, A. (1979). How to share a secret. *Communications of the ACM*, *22*(11), 612–613. doi:10.1145/359168.359176

Singhal, M., Chandrasekhar, S., Ge, T., Sandhu, R., Krishnan, R., Ahn, G. J., & Bertino, E. (2013). Collaboration in multicloud computing environments: Framework and security issues. *Computer*, *46*(2), 76–84. doi:10.1109/MC.2013.46

Yau, S. S., & An, H. G. (2010). Confidentiality Protection in Cloud Computing Systems. *International Journal of Software Informatics*, *4*(4), 351–365.

ADDITIONAL READING

Abadi, D., Madden, S., & Ferreira, M. (2006, June). Integrating compression and execution in column-oriented database systems. *In Proceedings of the International Conference on Management of Data* (pp. 671-682). doi:10.1145/1142473.1142548

Abraham, I., Chockler, G., Keidar, I., & Malkhi, D. (2006). Byzantine disk paxos: Optimal resilience with Byzantine shared memory. *Distributed Computing*, *18*(5), 387–408. doi:10.1007/s00446-005-0151-6

Abu-Libdeh, H., Princehouse, L., & Weatherspoon, H. (2010, June). RACS: a case for cloud storage diversity. In *Proceedings of the 1st ACM Symposium on Cloud Computing* (pp. 229-240). doi:10.1145/1807128.1807165

Adam, N. R., & Worthmann, J. C. (1989). Security-control methods for statistical databases: A comparative study. *ACM Computing Surveys*, *21*(4), 515–556. doi:10.1145/76894.76895

Agrawal, D., El Abbadi, A., Emekci, F., & Metwally, A. (2009, March). Database management as a service: Challenges and opportunities. In *Proceedings of IEEE 25th International Conference on Data Engineering* (pp. 1709-1716).

Alrodhan, W. A., & Mitchell, C. J. (2008, March). A client-side CardSpace-Liberty integration architecture. In *Proceedings of the 7th symposium on Identity and trust on the Internet* (pp. 1-7).

Amazon. (2006, October). Amazon Web Services. Web services licensing agreement.

Anthes, G. (2010). Security in the cloud. *Communications of the ACM, 53*(11), 16–18. doi:10.1145/1839676.1839683

Ateniese, G., Burns, R., Curtmola, R., Herring, J., Kissner, L., Peterson, Z., & Song, D. (2007, October). Provable data possession at untrusted stores. In *Proceedings of the 14th ACM Conference on Computer and Communications Security* (pp. 598-609).

Bernstein, D., & Vij, D. (2010, November). Intercloud security considerations. In *Proceedings of the Second International Conference on Cloud Computing Technology and Science (CloudCom).* (pp. 537-544).

Birman, K., Chockler, G., & van Renesse, R. (2009). Toward a cloud computing research agenda. *ACM SIGACT News, 40*(2), 68–80. doi:10.1145/1556154.1556172

Bowers, K. D., Juels, A., & Oprea, A. (2009, November). HAIL: A high-availability and integrity layer for cloud storage. In *Proceedings of the 16th ACM Conference on Computer and Communications Security* (pp. 187-198). doi:10.1145/1653662.1653686

Brunette, G., & Mogull, R. (2009). Security guidance for critical areas of focus in cloud computing. *Cloud Security Alliance.*

Buyya, R., Yeo, C. S., & Venugopal, S. (2008, September). Market-oriented cloud computing: Vision, hype, and reality for delivering it services as computing utilities. In *Proceedings of the 10th IEEE International Conference on High Performance Computing and Communications* (pp. 5-13).

Cachin, C., Haas, R., & Vukolic, M. (2010). Dependable storage in the Intercloud (Research Report RZ, 3783).

Cachin, C., Keidar, I., & Shraer, A. (2009). Trusting the cloud. *ACM SIGACT News, 40*(2), 81–86. doi:10.1145/1556154.1556173

Cachin, C., & Tessaro, S. (2006, June). Optimal resilience for erasure-coded Byzantine distributed storage. In *Proceedings of the International Conference on Dependable Systems and Networks* (pp. 115-124). doi:10.1109/DSN.2006.56

Castro, M., & Liskov, B. (1999, February). Practical Byzantine fault tolerance. *Operating Systems Review, 99*, 173–186.

Chandrasekhar, S., Chakrabarti, S., Singhal, M., & Calvert, K. L. (2010). Efficient proxy signatures based on trapdoor hash functions. *IET Information Security*, *4*(4), 322–332. doi:10.1049/iet-ifs.2009.0204

Chockler, G., Guerraoui, R., Keidar, I., & Vukolic, M. (2009). Reliable distributed storage. *Computer*, *42*(4), 1–7. doi:10.1109/MC.2009.126

Concordia project. (n. d.). Retrieved from http://projectconcordia.org/index.php/Main_Page

Feldman, A. J., Zeller, W. P., Freedman, M. J., & Felten, E. W. (2010, October). SPORC: Group Collaboration using Untrusted Cloud Resources. In OSDI (Vol. 10, pp. 337-350).

Garfinkel, S. (2007). An evaluation of amazon's grid computing services: EC2, S3, and SQS (Technical Report TR-08-07). *Harvard University*.

Garfinkel, S. L. (2003). Email-based identification and authentication: An alternative to PKI? *IEEE Security and Privacy*, *99*(6), 20–26. doi:10.1109/MSECP.2003.1253564

Goh, E. J., Shacham, H., Modadugu, N., & Boneh, D. (2003, February). SiRiUS: Securing Remote Untrusted Storage. In *Proceedings of Network and Distributed System Security Symposium* (Vol. 3, pp. 131-145).

Goodson, G. R., Wylie, J. J., Ganger, G. R., & Reiter, M. K. (2004, June). Efficient Byzantine-tolerant erasure-coded storage. In *Proceedings of International Conference on Dependable Systems and Networks* (pp. 135-144).

Grosse, E., Howie, J., Ransome, J., Reavis, J., & Schmidt, S. (2010). Cloud computing roundtable. *IEEE Security and Privacy*, *8*(6), 17–23. doi:10.1109/MSP.2010.173

Hammer-Lahav, E. (2010). The OAuth 1.0 protocol.

Hendricks, J., Ganger, G. R., & Reiter, M. K. (2007, October). Low-overhead byzantine fault-tolerant storage. In *Proceedings of 21st ACM SIGOPS symposium on Operating systems principles*. (pp. 73-86). doi:10.1145/1294261.1294269

Higgins Project. (n. d.). Retrieved from http://www.eclipse.org/higgins/

Hui, M., Jiang, D., Li, G., & Zhou, Y. (2009, March). Supporting database applications as a service. In *Proceedings of 25th International Conference on Data Engineering* (pp. 832-843).

Jin, J., Ahn, G. J., Hu, H., Covington, M. J., & Zhang, X. (2011). Patient-centric authorization framework for electronic healthcare services. *Computers & Security, 30*(2), 116–127. doi:10.1016/j.cose.2010.09.001

Juels, A., & Kaliski, B. S. Jr. (2007, October). PORs: Proofs of retrievability for large files. In *Proceedings of the 14th ACM conference on Computer and Communications Security* (pp. 584-597). doi:10.1145/1315245.1315317

Kamara, S., & Lauter, K. (2010, January). Cryptographic cloud storage. In *Proceedings of the International Conference on Financial Cryptography and Data Security* (pp. 136-149). doi:10.1007/978-3-642-14992-4_13

Krawczyk, H., Canetti, R., & Bellare, M. (1997). HMAC: Keyed-hashing for message authentication.

Kuznetsov, P., & Rodrigues, R. (2010). BFTW 3: Why? when? where? workshop on the theory and practice of byzantine fault tolerance. *ACM SIGACT News, 40*(4), 82–86. doi:10.1145/1711475.1711494

Lamport, L., Shostak, R., & Pease, M. (1982). The Byzantine generals problem. *ACM Transactions on Programming Languages and Systems, 4*(3), 382–401. doi:10.1145/357172.357176

Loscocco, P. A., Smalley, S. D., Muckelbauer, P. A., Taylor, R. C., Turner, S. J., & Farrell, J. F. (1998, October). The inevitability of failure: The flawed assumption of security in modern computing environments. In *Proceedings of the 21st National Information Systems Security Conference* (Vol. 10, pp. 303-314).

Mahajan, P., Setty, S., Lee, S., Clement, A., Alvisi, L., Dahlin, M., & Walfish, M. (2011). Depot: Cloud storage with minimal trust. *ACM Transactions on Computer Systems, 29*(4), 1–16. doi:10.1145/2063509.2063512

Maheshwari, U., Vingralek, R., & Shapiro, W. (2000, October). How to build a trusted database system on untrusted storage. In *Proceedings of the 4th conference on Symposium on Operating System Design & Implementation.*

Maler, E., & Reed, D. (2008). The venn of identity: Options and issues in federated identity management. *IEEE Security and Privacy, 6*(2), 16–23. doi:10.1109/MSP.2008.50

Malinen, J. (2006, Autumn). Windows Cardspace. In *Proceedings of the Seminar on Network Security, Helsiki University of Technology.*

Malkhi, D., & Reiter, M. (1998). Byzantine quorum systems. *Distributed Computing, 11*(4), 203–213. doi:10.1007/s004460050050

Martin, J. P., Alvisi, L., & Dahlin, M. (2002, October). Minimal byzantine storage. In *Proceedings of the International Symposium on Distributed Computing* (pp. 311-325).

Mell, P., & Grance, T. (2009). *Perspectives on cloud computing and standards.* NIST.

Merkle, R. C. (1980, April). Protocols for public key cryptosystems. In *Proceedings of the IEEE Symposium on Security and Privacy* (pp. 122-122).

Microsoft Windows Cardspace. (n. d.). Retrieved from http://netfx3.com/content/WindowsCardspaceHome.aspx

Mykletun, E., Narasimha, M., & Tsudik, G. (2006). Authentication and integrity in outsourced databases. *ACM Transactions on Storage, 2*(2), 107–138. doi:10.1145/1149976.1149977

Ortiz, S. (2011). The Problem with Cloud Computing Standardization. *Computer, 44*(7), 13–16. doi:10.1109/MC.2011.220

Papamanthou, C., Tamassia, R., & Triandopoulos, N. (2008, October). Authenticated hash tables. In *Proceedings of the 15th ACM conference on Computer and Communications Security* (pp. 437-448).

Papazoglou, M. P., & van den Heuvel, W. J. (2011). Blueprinting the cloud. *IEEE Internet Computing, 15*(6), 74–79. doi:10.1109/MIC.2011.147

Pease, M., Shostak, R., & Lamport, L. (1980). Reaching agreement in the presence of faults. *Journal of the ACM, 27*(2), 228–234. doi:10.1145/322186.322188

Perez, R., Sailer, R., & van Doorn, L. (2006, July). vTPM: virtualizing the trusted platform module. In *Proceedings of 15th Conference on USENIX Security Symposium* (pp. 305-320).

RedHat. (n. d.). Critical: openssh security update. Retrieved from https://rhn.redhat.com/errata/RHSA-2008-0855.html

Rocha, F., & Correia, M. (2011, June). Lucy in the sky without diamonds: Stealing confidential data in the cloud. In *Proceedings of IEEE/IFIP 41ˢᵗ International Conference on Dependable Systems and Networks Workshops* (pp. 129-134).

Rochwerger, B., Breitgand, D., Epstein, A., Hadas, D., Loy, I., Nagin, K., & Tofetti, G. et al. (2011). Reservoir-when one cloud is not enough. *Computer*, *44*(3), 44–51. doi:10.1109/MC.2011.64

Santos, N., Gummadi, K. P., & Rodrigues, R. (2009). Towards Trusted Cloud Computing. *HotCloud*, *9*(9), 1–5.

Sarno, D. (2009). Microsoft says lost sidekick data will be restored to users. *Los Angeles Times*.

Schneider, F. B., & Zhou, L. (2005). Implementing trustworthy services using replicated state machines. In Replication (pp. 151-167). Springer Berlin Heidelberg. doi:10.1109/MSP.2005.125

Shraer, A., Cachin, C., Cidon, A., Keidar, I., Michalevsky, Y., & Shaket, D. (2010, October). Venus: Verification for untrusted cloud storage. In *Proceedings of the ACM Workshop on Cloud Computing Security Workshop* (pp. 19-30).

Subashini, S., & Kavitha, V. (2011). A survey on security issues in service delivery models of cloud computing. *Journal of Network and Computer Applications*, *34*(1), 1–11. doi:10.1016/j.jnca.2010.07.006

Sun. (n. d.). Amazon S3 silent data corruption. Retrieved from http://blogs.sun.com/gbrunett/entry/amazon_s3_silent_data_corruption

Takabi, H., Joshi, J. B., & Ahn, G. J. (2010). Security and privacy challenges in cloud computing environments. *IEEE Security and Privacy*, *8*(6), 24–31. doi:10.1109/MSP.2010.186

Van Dijk, M., & Juels, A. (2010). On the impossibility of cryptography alone for privacy-preserving cloud computing. In *Proceedings of HotSec* (pp. 1–8). .

Viega, J. (2009). Cloud computing and the common man. *Computer*, *42*(8), 106–108. doi:10.1109/MC.2009.252

Vukolić, M. (2010). The Byzantine empire in the intercloud. *ACM SIGACT News*, *41*(3), 105–111. doi:10.1145/1855118.1855137

Wu, R., Ahn, G. J., & Hu, H. (2012, January). Towards HIPAA-compliant healthcare systems. In *Proceedings of the 2nd International Health Informatics Symposium* (pp. 593-602).

Xiong, L., Chitti, S., & Liu, L. (2007). Preserving data privacy in outsourcing data aggregation services. *ACM Transactions on Internet Technology*, *7*(3), 17, es. doi:10.1145/1275505.1275510

Zhang, Y., & Joshi, J. (2009). Access control and trust management for emerging multidomain environments. In Handbooks in Information Systems (Vol. 4, pp. 421–452). Emerald Group Publishing.

KEY TERMS AND DEFINITIONS

Cloud Client: A cloud client contains software and/or hardware that rely on the cloud for providing services. It is designed to provide cloud services only. Without the connectivity with the cloud the cloud client is totally useless.

Cloud Computing Security: The collection of policies and control technologies used to comply with the rules of regulatory authorities and to protect infrastructure, data, information and application associated with the cloud computing environment is known as cloud computing security.

Cloud Service Provider: A Cloud service provider (CSP) is a company which provides infrastructure, network services, business applications or platform through the cloud. A data center hosts the services of the cloud. Users access cloud services through network connectivity. Major advantages of using CSP are its low cost and scalability. The individuals or the companies need not setup and maintain their own infrastructure for supporting the internal applications and services. They can purchase the required resources from a CSP in a very less price. CSP shares the infrastructure for providing services to the clients. CSP mainly provides three categories of services: Software as a Service (SaaS), Platform as a Service (PaaS) and Infrastructure as a Service (IaaS). In SaaS CSP provides access to the application software. In case of PaaS, a platform for hosting or developing application is provided by CSP. In IaaS CSP provides a computing infrastructure or entire network to the client. The differentiation between them is not distinct because many CSPs provide multiple types of services to their clients. For instance, one can go to a CSP, such as Rackspace, for hosting a website and purchase either IaaS or PaaS.

Identity Provider: An Identity provider (IdP), is an entity having the following functionalities: For interaction with the system, the IdP provides identifiers to the users. If the identifier produced by the user is known to the IdP, it recognizes and asserts the system. It also provides all the information that it knows about the user.

Multiple Cloud Computing: Multiple cloud computing is an environment where services from two or more clouds are used to reduce the risk of data loss or down time because of component failure in any of the cloud computing environment.

Proxy: It is a dedicated server or a software system which is running within a computer. It works as an intermediate device between the client and another server to which the clients wants to send a request for some service. In this mechanism, the client requests for the required services to the proxy. The proxy now acts as a client and sends that request to the server for the service. The server sends reply to the proxy which in turn will be returned to the client. The primary advantage of using proxy is that it enhances the security of the communication and can use cache for faster response.

Trust Relationship: Let D be the truster and E be the trustee. X represent successful performance in context K claimed by E. The trust relationship means that if E believes X in context K, then D also believes X in that in the same context.

Compilation of References

Aarti, A. G., & Anjali, D. (2015). Big Data Security Issues and Challenges in Cloud Computing. *Asian Journal of Convergence in Technology*.

Abbasi, H., Wolf, M., Eisenhauer, G., Klasky, S., Schwan, K., & Zheng, F. (2010). Datastager: Scalable data staging services for petascale applications. *Cluster Computing*, *13*(3), 277–290. doi:10.1007/s10586-010-0135-6

Abdulaziz, A. (2012). Cloud Computing for Increased Business Value. *International Journal of Business and Social Science*, *3*(1), 234-239.

Aceto, G., Botta, A., De Donato, W., & Pescapè, A. (2013). Cloud monitoring: A survey. *Computer Networks*, *57*(9), 2093-2115.

Adhikari, M., & Roy, D. (2016). Green computing. In G. Deka, G. Siddesh, K. Srinivasa, & L. Patnaik (Eds.), *Emerging research surrounding power consumption and performance issues in utility computing* (pp. 84–108). Hershey, PA: IGI Global. doi:10.4018/978-1-4666-8853-7.ch005

Agarwal, S., Ghosh, A., & Nath, A. (2016). Green Enterprise Computing- Approaches Towards a Greener IT. *Presented at the International Journal of Innovative Research in Advanced Engineering (IJIRAE)*.

Ahmed, H., Ismail, M., & Hyder, M. (2014). Performance Optimization of Hadoop Cluster Using Linux Services. In *Proceedings of the 7th IEEE International Multi Topic Conference: Collaborative and Sustainable Development of Technologies* (pp. 167-172). doi:10.1109/INMIC.2014.7097331

Ahrens, J., Hendrickson, B., Long, G., Miller, S., Ross, R., & Williams, D. (2011). Data-intensive science in the US DOE: Case studies and future challenges. *Computing in Science & Engineering*, *13*(6), 14–24.

Ahuja, S. P., & Muthiah, K. (2016). Survey of state-of-art in green cloud computing. *International Journal of Green Computing*, *7*(1), 25–36. doi:10.4018/IJGC.2016010102

Al Shehri, W. (2013). Cloud database database as a service. *International Journal of Database Management Systems, 5*(2).

Al-Hudhaif, S., & Alkubeyyer, A. (2011). E-commerce adoption factors in Saudi Arabia. *International Journal of Business and Management*, *6*(9), 122–133. doi:10.5539/ijbm.v6n9p122

Ali, M., Khan, S. U., & Vasilakos, A. V. (2015). Security in cloud computing: Opportunities and challenges. *Information Sciences*, *305*(1), 357–383. doi:10.1016/j.ins.2015.01.025

Alizadeh, M., Hassan, W. H., Behboodian, N., & Karamizadeh, S. (2013). A brief review of mobile cloud computing opportunities. *Research Notes in Information Science*, *12*, 155–160.

Aljohani, A. M., Holton, D. R. W., Awan, I.-U., & Alanazi, J. S. (2011). Performance evaluation of local and cloud deployment of web clusters. In Proceedings of the 2011 14th International Conference on Network-Based Information Systems (NBiS) (pp. 274-278). IEEE. doi:10.1109/NBiS.2011.47

Allenotor, D., & Thulasiram, R. K. (2008). Grid resources pricing: A novel financial option based quality of service-profit quasi-static equilibrium model. In *Proceedings of the 8th ACM/IEEE International Conference on Grid Computing*, Tsukuba, Japan. doi:10.1109/GRID.2008.4662785

Alshaer, H. (2015). An overview of network virtualization and cloud network as a service. *International Journal of Network Management*, *25*(1), 1–30. doi:10.1002/nem.1882

AlZain, M. A., & Pardede, E. (2011, January). Using multi shares for ensuring privacy in database-as-a-service. In *Proceedings of 44th Hawaii International Conference on System Sciences* (pp. 1-9). doi:10.1109/HICSS.2011.478

AlZain, M. A., Pardede, E., Soh, B., & Thom, J. A. (2012, January). Cloud computing security: from single to multi-clouds. In *Proceedings of 45th Hawaii International Conference on System Science (HICSS)* (pp. 5490-5499). doi:10.1109/HICSS.2012.153

AlZain, M. A., Soh, B., & Pardede, E. (2011, December). Mcdb: using multi-clouds to ensure security in cloud computing. In *Proceedings of Ninth International Conference on Dependable, autonomic and secure computing (DASC)* (pp. 784-791). doi:10.1109/DASC.2011.133

Amazon Elastic Computing Cloud. (2017, January 3). Retrieved from http://www.aws.amazon.com/ec2

Amazon. (n. d.). AWS. Retrieved from http://aws.amazon.com/s3/

Anandharajan, T., & Bhagyaveni, M. (2014). Minimum power performance-based virtual machine consolidation technique for green cloud datacenters. *International Journal of Green Computing*, *5*(1), 24–43. doi:10.4018/ijgc.2014010103

Anuradha, V. P., & Sumathi, D. (2014). A survey on resource allocation strategies in cloud computing. In *Proceedings of the International Conference on Information Communication and Embedded Systems*, (pp. 1-7). doi:10.1109/ICICES.2014.7033931

Apache Hadoop. (2017, January 20). Retrieved from http://hadoop.apache.org

APACHE HIVE. (2017, February 10). Retrieved from http://hive.apache.org/

Apache Mahout. (2017, February 1). What is Apache Mahout? Retrieved from http://mahout.apache.org

Compilation of References

Apache Spark Web site. (2016, December 28). Lightning-fast cluster computing. Retrieved from http://Spark.apache.org/

Apache Wiki. (2017, January 1). Apache Hadoop. Retrieved from http://wiki.apache.org/hadoop/

Apache ZooKeeper. (2017, February 9). Retrieved from http://zookeeper.apache.org/

Araya, D. (2010). ICTs and the Green Economy.

Armbrust, M., Fox, A., Griffith, R., Joseph, A., Katz, R., Konwinski, A., & Zaharia, M. et al. (2010, April). A view of cloud computing. *Communications of the ACM, 53*(4), 50–58. doi:10.1145/1721654.1721672

Avanzi, R. M., Savas, E., & Tillich, S. (2005). Energy-efficient software implementation of long integer modular arithmetic. In *Proceedings of 7th Workshop on Cryptographic Hardware and Embedded Systems*, Edinburg, Scotland.

Avita, K., Mohammad, W., & Goudar, R. H. (2013). Big Data: Issues, Challenges, Tools and Good Practices. In *Proceedings of Contemporary Computing (IC3)* (pp. 404-409).

Avita, K., Mohammad, W., & Goudar, R. H. (2013). Big Data: Issues, Challenges, Tools and Good. In *Proceedings of the International Conference on Contemporary Computing* (pp. 404-409).

Aymerich, F. M., Fenu, G., & Surcis, S. (2008, August). An approach to a Cloud Computing network. In Proceedings of the First International Conference on the Applications of Digital Information and Web Technologies ICADIWT '08 (pp. 113-118). doi:10.1109/ICADIWT.2008.4664329

Bahar, A., Habib, M., & Islam, M. (2013). Security Architecture for Mobile Cloud Computing. *International Journal of Scientific Knowledge, 3*(3), 11–17.

Baliga, J., Ayre, R., Hinton, K., & Tucker, R. S. (2010). Green Cloud computing: Balancing energy in processing, storage and transport. *Proceedings of the IEEE, 99*(1), 149–167.

Banerjee, S., Sing, T. Y., Chowdhury, A. R., & Anwar, H. (2013). Motivations to adopt green ICT: A tale of two organizations. *International Journal of Green Computing, 4*(2), 1–11. doi:10.4018/jgc.2013070101

Baran, D. (n. d.). Cloud computing basics. *Webguild.org*. Retrieved November 11, 2016 from http://www.webguild.org/2008/07/cloud-computing-basics.php

Barto, A. G., & Duff, M. (1994). Monte Carlo matrix inversion and reinforcement learning. In *Advances in Neural Information Processing Systems* (pp. 687–687).

Bekaroo, G., Bokhoree, C., & Pattinson, C. (2016). Impacts of ICT on the natural ecosystem: A grassroot analysis for promoting socio-environmental sustainability. *Renewable & Sustainable Energy Reviews, 57*, 1580–1595. doi:10.1016/j.rser.2015.12.147

Beloglazov, A., Buyya, R., Lee, Y. C., & Zomaya, A. (2011). A taxonomy and survey of energy-efficient data centers and cloud computing systems. In M. Zelkowitz (Ed.), *Advances in Computers*. Amsterdam: Elsevier.

387

Bessani, A., Correia, M., Quaresma, B., André, F., & Sousa, P. (2013). DepSky: dependable and secure storage in a cloud-of-clouds. *ACM Transactions on Storage, 9*(4), 12:1-12:33.

Bhadra, S., & Kundu, A. (2016). Introducing eco friendly corporate system: A green approach. *International Journal of Green Computing, 7*(1), 1–24. doi:10.4018/IJGC.2016010101

Bhatnagar, S., Precup, D., Silver, D., Sutton, R. S., Maei, H. R., & Szepesvári, C. (2009). Convergent temporal-difference learning with arbitrary smooth function approximation. In Advances in Neural Information Processing Systems (pp. 1204-1212).

Bheda, H., & Lakhani, J. (2013). Application Processing Approach for Smart Mobile Devices in Mobile Cloud Computing. *International Journal of Software Engineering and Knowledge Engineering, 3*, 1046–1055.

Bianchini, R., & Rajamony, R. (2004). Power and energy management for server systems. *Computer, 37*(11), 68–74.

Blue and Green Tomorrow. (n. d.). Benefits of green cloud computing. Retrieved Dec 12, 2016 from http://blueandgreentomorrow.com/environment/benefits-of-cloud-computing-for-green enterprises/S

Bobby, S. (2015). A greener approach to computing and save energy. *International Journal of Advance Research in Science and Engineering.*

Bobor, V. (2006). Efficient Intrusion Detection System Architecture Based on Neural Networks and Genetic Algorithms.

Bohli, J. M., Gruschka, N., Jensen, M., Iacono, L. L., & Marnau, N. (2013). Security and privacy-enhancing multicloud architectures. *IEEE Transactions on Dependable and Secure Computing, 10*(4), 212–224. doi:10.1109/TDSC.2013.6

Borko, F. (2010). Cloud Computing Fundamentals. In F. Borko & E. Armando (Eds.), *Handbook of Cloud Computing* (pp. 24–40). Boca Raton: Springer.

Botta, A., de Donato, W., Persico, V., & Pescapé, A. (2016). Integration of Cloud computing and Internet of Things: A survey. *Future Generation Computer Systems, 56*, 684–700. doi:10.1016/j.future.2015.09.021

Brandon, G. (n. d.). Ultimate Guide and List of Cloud Computing Security Companies, Vendors, Services, Issues and Solutions. Secure your Cloud. Cloudnewsdaily.com. Retrieved January 15, 2017 from http://cloudnewsdaily.com/cloud-security/

Busoniu, L., Babuska, R., De Schutter, B., & Ernst, D. (2010). *Reinforcement learning and dynamic programming using function approximators* (Vol. 39). CRC press. doi:10.1201/9781439821091

Buyya, R., Ranjan, R., & Calheiros, R. N. (2010). Intercloud: Utility-oriented federation of cloud computing environments for scaling of application services. In Algorithms and architectures for parallel processing (pp. 13-31). Springer.

Buyya, R., Yeo, C. S., & Venugopal, S. (2008). Market-oriented Cloud computing: Vision, hype, and reality for delivering it services as computing utilities. In *Proceedings of the 10th IEEE International Conference on High Performance Computing and Communications.* doi:10.1109/HPCC.2008.172

Buyya, R., Yeo, C., Venugopal, S., Broberg, J., & Brandic, I. (2009). Cloud Computing and Emerging IT Platforms: Vision, Hype, and Reality for Delivering Computing. The 5th Utility. *Future Generation Computer Systems, 25*(6), 599–616. doi:10.1016/j.future.2008.12.001

Cannady, J. (2010). Artificial Neural Networks for Misuse Detection. In *Proceedings of the National Information Systems Security Conference.*

Cannon, D. (2011). *Certified Information Systems Auditor Study Guide* (3rd ed.). Wiley.

Cao, F., Zhu, M. M., & Wu, C. Q. (2015). Green cloud computing with efficient resource allocation approach. In X. Liu & Y. Li (Eds.), *Green services engineering, optimization, and modeling in the technological age* (pp. 116–148). Hershey, PA: IGI Global. doi:10.4018/978-1-4666-8447-8.ch005

Carlyle, A. G., Harrell, S. L., & Smith, P. M. (2010). Cost-effective HPC: The community or the cloud? In *Proceedings of the IEEE International Conference on Cloud Computing Technology and Science* (pp. 169–176). doi:10.1109/CloudCom.2010.115

Caron, E., Rodero-Merino, L., Desprez, F., & Muresan, A. (2011). Auto-scaling, load balancing and monitoring in commercial and open-source clouds.

Cecere, G., Corrocher, N., Gossart, C., & Ozman, M. (2014). Technological pervasiveness and variety of innovators in green ICT: A patent-based analysis. *Research Policy, 43*(10), 1827–1839. doi:10.1016/j.respol.2014.06.004

Celesti, A., Tusa, F., Villari, M., & Puliafito, A. (2010, July). How to enhance cloud architectures to enable cross-federation. In *Proceedings of 3rd International Conference on Cloud Computing* (pp. 337-345). doi:10.1109/CLOUD.2010.46

Celesti, A., Tusa, F., Villari, M., & Puliafito, A. (2010, June). Security and cloud computing: Intercloud identity management infrastructure. In *Proceedings of 19th IEEE International Workshop on Enabling Technologies: Infrastructures for Collaborative Enterprises* (pp. 263-265).

Chabarek, J., Sommers, J., Barford, P., Estan, C., Tsiang, D., & Wright, S. (2008). Power Awareness in Network Design and Routing. In *Proceedings of 27th IEEE INFOCOM*. doi:10.1109/INFOCOM.2008.93

Chan, T. (2010). Inside the Australian Govt. ICT sustainability plan 2010-2015.

Chang, H.-Y., Lu, H.-C., Huang, Y.-H., Lin, Y.-W., & Tzang, Y.-J. (2013). Novel auction mechanism with factor distribution rule for cloud resource allocation. *The Computer Journal.*

Chappell, D., ... (2006). Introducing Windows CardSpace. Retrieved 15.02.17 from https://msdn.microsoft.com/en-us/library/aa480189.aspx

Chase, J. S., Anderson, D. C., Thakar, P. N., Vahdat, A. M., & Doyle, R. P. (2001). Managing energy and server resources in hosting centers. In *Proceedings of 18th ACM Symposium on Operating Systems Principles (SOSP '01)*, Banff, Canada. doi:10.1145/502034.502045

Chaturvedi, M., Malik, S., Aggarwal, P., & Bahl, S. (2011). Privacy & Security of Mobile Cloud Computing. *Ansal University Sector, 55*.

Chaubey, N. K., & Tank, D. M. (2016). Security, Privacy and Challenges in Mobile Cloud Computing (MCC). A Critical Study and Comparison. *International Journal of Innovative Research in Computer and Communication Engineering, 4*(2).

Chauhan, P.V. (2012). Cloud Computing in Distributed System. *International Journal of Computer Science and Informatics, 1*(10).

Chavan, S., Shah, K., Dave, N., & Mukherjee, S. (2004). Adaptive neuro-fuzzy intrusion detection systems. In Proceedings of the IEEE international conference on information technology: coding and computing (ITCC'04) (pp. 70-74). doi:10.1109/ITCC.2004.1286428

Chen, C. P., & Zhang, C. Y. (2014). Data-intensive applications, challenges, techniques and technologies: A survey on Big Data. *Information Science, 275*, 314–347. doi:10.1016/j.ins.2014.01.015

Chen, H., Zhu, X., Guo, H., Zhu, J., Qin, X., & Wu, J. (2015). Towards energy-efficient scheduling for real-time tasks under uncertain cloud computing environment. *Journal of Systems and Software, 99*, 20–35. doi:10.1016/j.jss.2014.08.065

Chen, X., Li, J., & Susilo, W. (2012). Efficient fair conditional payments for outsourcing computations. *IEEE Transactions on Information Forensics and Security, 7*(6), 1687–1694. doi:10.1109/TIFS.2012.2210880

Chetan, S., Kumar, G., Dinesh, K., Mathew, K., & Abhimanyu, M. A. (2010). Cloud computing for mobile world. Retrieved from chetan.ueuo.com

Chitahranjan, K., & Kala, K. A. (2013). A review on hadoop-HDFS infrastructure extensions. In *Proceedings of the IEEE Conference on Information and Communication Technologies* (pp. 132-137).

Chitra, S. (2011). Adopting green ICT in business. In B. Unhelkar (Ed.), *Handbook of research on green ICT: Technology, business and social perspectives* (pp. 643–651). Hershey, PA: IGI Global. doi:10.4018/978-1-61692-834-6.ch047

Cloud Hosting Web. (2017, January 3). CLoud Computing and Hybrid Infrastructure from GoGrid. Retrieved from http://www.gogrid.com

Cloud Security Alliance (CSA). (n. d.). *Security best practices for cloud computing*. Retrieved February 05, 2017 from https://cloudsecurityalliance.org/

Colina, A.L., Vives, A., Zennaro, M., Bagula, A., & Pietrosemoli, E. (2016). Internet of Things In 5 Days.

Columbus, L. (2016). Roundup Of Cloud Computing Forecasts And Market Estimates, 2016. *Forbes*. Retrieved May 27, 2016 from https://www.forbes.com/sites/louiscolumbus/

Computer Weekly. (n. d.). Security implications of green IT. Retrieved Dec 12, 2016 from http://www.computerweekly.com/feature/The-security-implications-of-green-IT

CSO. (n. d.). *CSO Online survey*. Retrieved January 5, 2017 from https://eforms.cso.ie/

Cubo, J., Nieto, A., & Pimentel, E. (2014). A Cloud-Based Internet of Things Platform for Ambient Assisted Living. *Sensors (Basel, Switzerland)*, *14*(8), 14070–14105. doi:10.3390/s140814070 PMID:25093343

Cuervo, E., Balasubramanian, A., & Dae-ki, C. et al.. *(*2010) MAUI: making smartphones last longer with code offload. In *Proceedings of the 8th International Conference on Mobile systems, applications, and services* (pp. 49–62). doi:10.1145/1814433.1814441

Curtis, D., & Lingarchani, A. (2011). Green ICT system architecture frameworks. In B. Unhelkar (Ed.), *Handbook of research on green ICT: Technology, business and social perspectives* (pp. 446–458). Hershey, PA: IGI Global. doi:10.4018/978-1-61692-834-6.ch032

Dastjerdi, A. V., Tabatabaei, S. G. H., & Buyya, R. (2012). A dependency-aware ontology-based approach for deploying service level agreement monitoring services in cloud. *Software, Practice & Experience*, *42*(4), 501–518. doi:10.1002/spe.1104

Data hadoop tutorial Web site. (2017, January 30). Hadoop HDFS. Retrieved from https://datahadooptutorial.blogspot.com/2016/11/hadoop-architecture.html

Davis, J. W. (2002). Power benchmark strategy for systems employing power management, In *Proceedings of the IEEE International Symposium on Electronics and the Environment*.

Dean, J., & Ghemawat, S. (2008). MapReduce: Simplified Data Processing on Large Cluster. *Communications of the ACM*, *51*(1), 107–113. doi:10.1145/1327452.1327492

Dehury, C. K., & Sahoo, P. K. (2016). Design and implementation of a novel service management framework for IoT devices in cloud. *Journal of Systems and Software*, *119*, 149–161. doi:10.1016/j.jss.2016.06.059

Depavath, H. (2008). Emerging trends in Green IT.

Deshmukh, A. A., Jothish, M., & Chandrasekaran, K. (2015). Green routing algorithm for wired networks. *International Journal of Green Computing*, *6*(2), 16–29. doi:10.4018/IJGC.2015070102

Deshpande, Y., & Unhelkar, B. (2011). Information systems for a green organisation. In B. Unhelkar (Ed.), *Handbook of research on green ICT: Technology, business and social perspectives* (pp. 116–130). Hershey, PA: IGI Global. doi:10.4018/978-1-61692-834-6.ch008

Devi, T., & Ganesan, R. (2015). Platform-as-a-Service (PaaS): Model and SecurityIssues. *Telkomnika Indonesian Journal of Electrical Engineering.*, *15*(1), 151–161.

Dhanalakshmi Y & Ramesh Babu I (2008). Intrusion Detection Using Data Mining Along Fuzzy Logic and Genetic Algorithms. *International Journal of Computer Science and Network Security, 8*(2).

di Salvo, A. L. A., Agostinho, F., Almeida, C. M. V. B., & Giannetti, B. F. (2017). Can cloud computing be labeled as "green"? Insights under an environmental accounting perspective. *Renewable & Sustainable Energy Reviews, 69*, 514–526. doi:10.1016/j.rser.2016.11.153

Dinh, H. T., Lee, C., Niyato, D., & Wang, P. (2011). A survey of Mobile Cloud Computing: Architecture, Applications, and Approaches. *Wireless Communications and Mobile Computing, 13*(18), 1587-1611.

Dinh, H. T., Lee, C., Niyato, D., & Wang, P. (2013). A survey of mobile cloud computing: architecture, applications, and approaches. *Wireless communications and mobile computing, 13*(18), 1587-1611.

Dinh, H. T., Lee, C., Niyato, D., & Wang, P. (2013). a survey of mobile cloud computing: Architecture, applications, and approaches. *Wirel. Commun. Mob. Comput, 13*(18), 1587–1611. doi:10.1002/wcm.1203

Din, N., Haron, S., & Ahmad, H. (2013). The level of awareness on the green ICT concept and self directed learning among Malaysian Facebook users. *Procedia: Social and Behavioral Sciences, 85*, 464–473. doi:10.1016/j.sbspro.2013.08.375

Divyakant, A., Sudipto, D., & El Abbadi, A. (2011). Big data and cloud computing: current state and future opportunities. In *Proceedings of the International Conference on Extending Database Technology* (pp. 530–533).

Dolgikh, A., Birnbaum, Z., Chen, Y., & Skormin, V. (2013). Behavioral Modeling for Suspicious Process Detection in Cloud Computing Environments. In Proceedings of the 2013 IEEE 14th International Conference on In Mobile Data Management (MDM) (Vol. 2, pp. 177-181). doi:10.1109/MDM.2013.90

Duan, Q., Yan, Y., & Vasilakos, A. V. (2012). A survey on service-oriented network virtualization toward convergence of networking and cloud computing. *IEEE eTransactions on Network and Service Management, 9*(4), 373–392. doi:10.1109/TNSM.2012.113012.120310

Egbuta, I. C., Thomas, B., & Al-Hasan, S. (2014). The contribution of teleworking towards a green computing environment. In E. Ariwa (Ed.), *Green technology applications for enterprise and academic innovation* (pp. 218–232). Hershey, PA: IGI Global. doi:10.4018/978-1-4666-5166-1.ch014

Eid, H.F., Darwish, A., Hassanien, A., & Tai-Hoon, K. (2011). Intelligent Hybrid Anomaly Network Intrusion Detection System. In Communication and networking (pp. 209-218).

Eid, H.F., Darwish, A., Hassanien, A., & Tai-Hoon, K. (2011). Intelligent Hybrid Anomaly Network Intrusion Detection System. In Communication and Networking (pp. 209-218).

Ejarque, J., Álvarez, J., Sirvent, R., & Badia, R. M. (2012). Resource Allocation for Cloud Computing: A Semantic Approach. In *Open Source Cloud Computing Systems: Practices and Paradigms: Practices and Paradigms*.

Ergu, D., Kou, G., Peng, Y., Shi, Y., & Shi, Y. (2013). The analytic hierarchy process: Task scheduling and resource allocation in cloud computing environment. *The Journal of Supercomputing, 64*(3), 835–848. doi:10.1007/s11227-011-0625-1

Facebook. (n. d.). Retrieved from http://www.facebook.com/

Fan, J., Han, F., & Liu, H. (2014). Challenges of Big Data analysis. *National science review, 1*(2), 293-314.

Fard, M. M., & Grinberg, Y. massoud Farahmand, A., Pineau, J., & Precup, D. (2013). Bellman error based feature generation using random projections on sparse spaces. In Advances in Neural Information Processing Systems (pp. 3030-3038).

Fernandes, D. A. B., Soares, L. F. B., Gomes, J. V., Freire, M. M., & Inácio, P. R. M. (2014). Security issues in cloud environments: A survey. *International Journal of Information Security, 13*(2), 113–170. doi:10.1007/s10207-013-0208-7

FlexiScale. (2017, January 5). Cloud Computing and Hosting. Retrieved from http://www.flexiscale.com

Flickr. (n. d.). Retrieved from http://www.flickr.com/

Forman, G. H., & Zahorjan, J. (1994). The Challenges of mobile computing. *IEEE Computer Society Magazine, 27*(4), 38–47. doi:10.1109/2.274999

Forrest Stroud. (2016). What Is Everything-as-a-Service (XaaS)? Webopedia Definition. Retrieved August 30, 2016 from http://www.webopedia.com/TERM/E/everything-as-a-service_xaas.html

Foster, I., Zhao, Y., Raicu, I., & Lu, S. (2008). *Cloud Computing and Grid Computing 360-Degree Compared. In 2008 Grid Computing Environments Workshop* (pp. 1–10). IEEE; https://doi.org/10.1109/GCE.2008.4738445

Foster, I., Zhao, Y., Raicu, I., & Lu, S. (2008). Cloud Computing and Grid Computing 360-Degree Compared. In *Proceedings of the Grid Computing Environments Workshop GCE '08*. doi:10.1109/GCE.2008.4738445

Freeh, V. W., Pan, F., Kappiah, N., Lowenthal, D. K., & Springer, R. (2005). Exploring the energy-time trade-off in MPI programs on a power-scalable cluster. In *Proceedings of the 19th IEEE International Parallel and Distributed Processing Symposium*, CA, USA doi:10.1109/IPDPS.2005.214

Furht, B., & Escalante, A. (2010). *Handbook of Cloud Computing*. Springer. doi:10.1007/978-1-4419-6524-0

Furuta, H., Kameda, T., Fukuda, Y., & Frangopol, D. (2004). Life-cycle cost analysis for infrastructure systems: Life cycle cost vs. safety level vs. service life. In *Life-cycle performance of deteriorating structures: Assessment, design and management* (pp. 19–25).

Gahlawat, M., & Sharma, P. (2016). Green, energy-efficient computing and sustainability issues in cloud. In R. Kannan, R. Rasool, H. Jin, & S. Balasundaram (Eds.), *Managing and processing big data in cloud computing* (pp. 206–217). Hershey, PA: IGI Global. doi:10.4018/978-1-4666-9767-6.ch014

Gandomi, A., & Haider, M. (2015). Beyond the hype: Big data concepts, methods, and analytics. *International Journal of Information Management*, *35*(2), 137–144. doi:10.1016/j.ijinfomgt.2014.10.007

Ganesh, K., & Anbuudayasankar, S. P. (2013). *International and interdisciplinary studies in green computing* (pp. 1–238). Hershey, PA: IGI Global. doi:10.4018/978-1-4666-2646-1

Garcia, A., & Kalva, H. (2011). Cloud transcoding for mobile video content delivery. In *Proceedings of the IEEE International Conference on Consumer Electronics (ICCE)*. doi:10.1109/ICCE.2011.5722637

Garfinkel, T., & Rosenblum, M. (2003). A Virtual Machine Introspection Based Architecture for Intrusion Detection. In *Proceedings of Network and Distributed Systems Security Symposium* (pp. 191-206).

Garg, M., Gupta, S., Goh, M., & Desouza, R. (2010). Sustaining the green information technology movement. In N. Bajgoric (Ed.), *Always-on enterprise information systems for business continuance: Technologies for reliable and scalable operations* (pp. 218–230). Hershey, PA: IGI Global. doi:10.4018/978-1-60566-723-2.ch013

Garg, P., & Sharma, V. (2013). Secure data storage in mobile cloud computing. *International Journal of Scientific & Engineering Research*, *4*(4), 1154–1159.

Garg, S. K., & Buyya, R. (2013). An environment for modeling and simulation of message-passing parallel applications for cloud computing. *Software, Practice & Experience*, *43*(11), 1359–1375. doi:10.1002/spe.2156

Gascon, H., Orfila, A., & Blasco, J. (2011). Analysis of update delays in signature-based network intrusion detection systems. *Computers & Security*, *30*(8), 613–624. doi:10.1016/j.cose.2011.08.010

Gasmelseid, T. M. (2016). On the decision criteria for "greening" information systems. In V. Ponnusamy, N. Zaman, T. Low, & A. Amin (Eds.), *Biologically-inspired energy harvesting through wireless sensor technologies* (pp. 187–200). Hershey, PA: IGI Global. doi:10.4018/978-1-4666-9792-8.ch009

Gawanmeh, A., Alomari, A., & April, A. (2017). Optimizing Resource Allocation Scheduling in Cloud Computing services. *Journal of Theoretical and Applied Information Technology*, *95*, 31–39.

Gawanmeh, A., & April, A. (2016). A Novel Algorithm for Optimizing Multiple Services Resource Allocation. *International Journal of Advanced Computer Science and Applications, 7*(6), 428–434. doi:10.14569/IJACSA.2016.070655

Ge, Y., & Wei, G. (2010). Ga-based task scheduler for the cloud computing systems. In *Proceedings of the International Conference on Web Information Systems and Mining* (Vol. 2, pp. 181-186). doi:10.1109/WISM.2010.87

Ghemawat, S., Gobioff, H., & Leung, S. T. (2003). The Google file system. In *Proceedings of the 19th Symposium on Operating Systems Principles* (pp. 29-43).

Gleeson, E. (2009). Computing industry set for a shocking change. *Moneyweek.com.* Retrieved January 10, 2010 from http://www.moneyweek.com/investment-advice/computing-industry-set-for-ashocking-change-43226.aspx

Glynn, P. W., & Iglehart, D. L. (1989). Importance sampling for stochastic simulations. *Management Science, 35*(11), 1367–1392. doi:10.1287/mnsc.35.11.1367

Google. (2017, January 2). Google App Engine. Retrieved from http://code.google.com/appengine

Guan, B., Wu, J., Wang, Y., & Khan, S. U. (2014). CIVSched: A communication-aware inter-VM scheduling technique for decreased network latency between co-located VMs. *IEEE Transactions on Cloud Computing, 2*(3), 320–332. doi:10.1109/TCC.2014.2328582

Guo, F., Yu, L., Tian, S., & Yu, J. (2015). A workflow task scheduling algorithm based on the resources fuzzy clustering in cloud computing environment. *International Journal of Communication Systems, 28*(6), 1053–1067. doi:10.1002/dac.2743

Guo, W., Gong, J., Jiang, W., Liu, Y., & She, B. (2010). OpenRS-Cloud: A remote sensing image processing platform based on cloud computing environment. *Science China: Technological Sciences, 53*(Suppl. 1), 221–230. doi:10.1007/s11431-010-3234-y

Gupta, I. (n. d.). *Cloud Computing Concepts.* Retrieved February 02, 2017 from https://www.coursera.org/learn/cloud-computing

Gupta, P., & Gupta, S. (2012). Mobile Cloud Computing: The Future of Cloud. *International Journal of Advanced Research in Electrical Electronics and Instrumentation Engineering, 1*(3), 134–145.

Gupta, P., & Gupta, S. (2012). Mobile cloud computing: The future of cloud. *International Journal of Advanced Research in Electrical. Electronics and Instrumentation Engineering, 1*(3), 134–145.

Gupta, V., & Rajput, I. (2013). Enhanced data security in cloud computing with third party auditor. *International Journal of Advanced Research in Computer Science & Software Engineering, 3*(2), 341–345.

Gurumurthi, S., Stan, M.R., & Sankar, S. (2009). Using intra-disk parallelism to build energy-efficient storage systems. *IEEE Micro, 29*(1), 50-61.

Hadoop HDFS Web site. (2017, February 8). HDFS Users Guide. Retrieved from http://hadoop. apache.org/docs/r2.4.1/hadoop-project-dist/hadoop-hdfs/HdfsUserGuide.html

Hai, J., Shadi, I., Tim, B., Wei, G., & Dachuan, H. (2010). Cloud Types and Services. In F. Borko & E. Armando (Eds.), *Handbook of Cloud Computing* (pp. 356–376). Boca Raton: Springer.

Han, J., & Kamber, M. (2006). *Data Mining Concepts and Techniques* (2nd ed.). Morgan Kaufmann Publishers.

Hanne, F. Z. (2011). Green IT: Why Developing Countries Should Care. *International Journal of Computer Science Issues*, *8*(4).

Harraz, A., Bissiriou, C., Cherkaoui, R., Zbakh, M. (2016). Study of an adaptive approach for a Cloud system implementation. *Proceedings of 2016 International Conference on Cloud Computing Technologies and Applications CloudTech 2016* (pp. 230-23).

Hashem, I. A., Yaqoob, I., Anuar, N. B., Mokhtar, S., Gani, A., & Khan, S. U. (2015). The rise of big data on cloud computing: Review and open research issues. *Information Systems*, *47*, 98–115. doi:10.1016/j.is.2014.07.006

Hashizume, K., Rosado, D. G., Fernández-Medina, E., & Fernandez, E. B. (2013). An analysis of security issues for cloud computing. *Journal of Internet Services and Applications*, *4*(1), 5.

Hasselmeyer, P., & d'Heureuse, N. (2010). Towards holistic multi-tenant monitoring for virtual data centers. In Proceedings of the Network Operations and Management Symposium Workshops (pp. 350–356). doi:10.1109/NOMSW.2010.5486528

Hazarika, B., & Singh, T.J. (2015, January). Survey Paper on Cloud Computing & Cloud Monitoring: Basics. *SSRG International Journal of Computer Science and Engineering, 2*(1), 10-15.

Hecht-Nielsen, R. (1988). Theory of the backpropagation neural network. *Neural Networks*, *1*(Supplement-1), 445–448. doi:10.1016/0893-6080(88)90469-8

Hernandez, A. A., & Ona, S. E. (2016). Green IT adoption: Lessons from the Philippines business process outsourcing industry. *International Journal of Social Ecology and Sustainable Development*, *7*(1), 1–34. doi:10.4018/IJSESD.2016010101

Hill, Z., Li, J., Mao, M., Ruiz-Alvarez, A., & Humphrey, M. (2011). Early observations on the performance of Windows Azure. *Scientific Programming, 19*(2-3), 121-132.

Hoang, D., Zhang, X., Kang, M., & Luo, J. (2010). MobiCloud: Building Secure Cloud Framework for Mobile Computing And Communication. In Proceedings of the Fifth IEEE International Symposium on Service Oriented System Engineering. doi:10.1109/SOSE.2010.20

Hsueh, S. C., Lin, J. Y., & Lin, M. Y. (2011, June). Secure cloud storage for convenient data archive of smart phones. In *Proceedings of IEEE 15th International Symposium on Consumer Electronics (ISCE)*. (pp. 156-161). doi:10.1109/ISCE.2011.5973804

Huang, D., Yi, L., Song, F., Yang, D., & Zhang, H. (2014). A secure cost-effective migration of enterprise applications to the cloud. *International Journal of Communication Systems, 27*(12), 3996–4013. doi:10.1002/dac.2594

Huang, D., Zhou, Z., Xu, L., Xing, T., & Zhong, Y. (2011, April). Secure data processing framework for mobile cloud computing. In *Proceedings of IEEE Conference on Computer Communications Workshops (INFOCOM WKSHPS).* (pp. 614-618). doi:10.1109/INFCOMW.2011.5928886

Hursti, J. (1997, November). Single sign-on. In *Proc. Helsinki University of Technology Seminar on Network Security.*

Hurwitz, J. (2013). *Big data for dummies.* Wiley Hoboken.

Hussein, N. H., & Khalid, A. (2016). A survey of Cloud Computing Security challenges and solutions. *International Journal of Computer Science and Information Security, 14*(1).

Hutchinson, C., Ward, J., & Castilon, K. (2009). Navigating the next-generation application architecture. *IT Professional, 11*(2), 18–22. doi:10.1109/MITP.2009.33

Hu, W., & Kaabouch, N. (2012). *Sustainable ICTs and management systems for green computing* (pp. 1–495). Hershey, PA: IGI Global. doi:10.4018/978-1-4666-1839-8

Ibikunle Ayoleke (2011). Cloud Computing Security Issues and Challenges. *International Journal of Computer Networks, 3*(5).

Ibrahim, L. (2010). Anomaly network intrusion detection system based on distributed time-delay neural network. *Journal of Engineering Science and Technology, 5*(4), 457-471.

InformationWeek Report. (2014). *Return of the Silos.* Retrieved December 10, 2017 from http://www.oracle.com/us/products/ondemand/collateral/cloud-executive-strategy-1559197.pdf

InformationWeek Report. (n. d.). *Cloud at the Crossroads: OAUG Survey on Application Delivery Strategies.* Retrieved January 13, 2017 from http://www.ebizroundtable.com/CORE/Presentations/2014 _Summer/On_Ramp_to_the_Clouds-APS_and_OMCS.pdf

Info-tech. (2009). Green IT: Why Mid-Size Companies Are Investing Now.

Intl.aliyun. (n. d.)Error! Hyperlink reference not valid.. *VPC/ECS.* Retrieved December 17, 2016 from intl.aliyun.com: https://intl.aliyun.com/help/doc-detail/34221.html

Inukollu, V. N., Arsi, S., & Ravuri, S. R. (2014). Security issues associated with big data in cloud computing. *International Journal of Network Security & Its Applications, 6*(3), 45-56.

Isaias, P., Issa, T., Chang, V., & Issa, T. (2015). Outlining the issues of cloud computing and sustainability opportunities and risks in European organizations: A SEM study. *Journal of Electronic Commerce in Organizations, 13*(4), 1–25. doi:10.4018/JECO.2015100101

Issa, T., Tolani, G., Chang, V., & Issa, T. (2015). Awareness of sustainability, green IT, and cloud computing in Indian organisations. In X. Liu & Y. Li (Eds.), *Green services engineering, optimization, and modeling in the technological age* (pp. 269–287). Hershey, PA: IGI Global. doi:10.4018/978-1-4666-8447-8.ch011

Itani, W., Kayssi, A., & Chehab, A. (2010, December). Energy-efficient incremental integrity for securing storage in mobile cloud computing. In *Proceedings of International Conference on Energy Aware Computing (ICEAC)* (pp. 1-2). doi:10.1109/ICEAC.2010.5702296

Jaakkola, T., Singh, S. P., & Jordan, M. I. (1995). Reinforcement learning algorithm for partially observable Markov decision problems. In *Advances in Neural Information Processing Systems* (pp. 345–352).

Jaiswal, P. R., & Rohankar, A. W. (2014). Infrastructure as a Service: Security Issues in Cloud Computing. *International Journal of Computer Science and Mobile Computing, 3*(3), 707–711.

Jansen, W., & Grance, T. (2011, December). *Guidelines on Security and Privacy in Public Cloud Computing.* NIST.

Jayanthi, S., & Babu, S. (2015). Green Cloud Computing - Resource Utilization with Respect to SLA and Power Consumption. *International Journal of Computer Science and Mobile Applications.*

Jena, R. K. (2013). Green computing to green business. In P. Ordóñez de Pablos (Ed.), *Green technologies and business practices: An IT approach* (pp. 138–150). Hershey, PA: IGI Global. doi:10.4018/978-1-4666-1972-2.ch007

Jena, R. K., & Dey, D. G. (2013). Green computing: An Indian perspective. In S. Siqueira (Ed.), *Governance, communication, and innovation in a knowledge intensive society* (pp. 40–50). Hershey, PA: IGI Global. doi:10.4018/978-1-4666-4157-0.ch004

Jensen, M., Schwenk, Gruschka N. & Iacono L. (2009). On Technical Security Issues in Cloud Computing. In *Proceedings of the IEEE International Conference on Cloud Computing.* doi:10.1109/CLOUD.2009.60

Jeyarani, R., Nagaveni, N., Sadasivam, S. K., & Rajarathinam, V. R. (2011). Power aware meta scheduler for adaptive VM provisioning in IaaS cloud. *International Journal of Cloud Applications and Computing, 1*(3), 36–51. doi:10.4018/ijcac.2011070104

Ji, C., Li, Y., Qiu, W., Awada, U., & Li, K. (2012). Big Data Processing in Cloud Computing Environments. In *Proceedings of the International Symposium on Pervasive Systems, Algorithms and Networks* (pp. 17-23). doi:10.1109/I-SPAN.2012.9

Jia, W., Zhu, H., Cao, Z., Wei, L., & Lin, X. (2011). SDSM: a secure data service mechanism in mobile cloud computing. In *Proceedings of the IEEE Conference on Computer Communications Workshops, INFOCOMWKSHPS,* Shanghai, China.

Jia, W., Zhu, H., Cao, Z., Wei, L., & Lin, X. (2011, April). SDSM: a secure data service mechanism in mobile cloud computing. In *Proceedings of IEEE Conference on Computer Communications Workshops (INFOCOM WKSHPS)* (pp. 1060-1065).

Jorge, L. R., Oneto, L., & Anguita, D. (2015). Big Data Analytics in the Cloud: Spark on Hadoop vs MPI/OpenMP on Beowulf. *Procedia Computer Science*, *53*, 121-130.

Jutras, C. (2011). *QAD on demand gives manufacturers the tools they need to become global*. Aberdeen Research Group.

Juve, G. E., Deelman, K. V., Mehta, G., Berriman, B., Berman, B. P., & Maechling, P. (2009). Scientific workflow applications on Amazon EC2. In *Proceedings of the 5th IEEE International Conference on e-Science* (pp. 59-65).

Kakerow, R. (2003). Low power design methodologies for mobile communication. In *Proceedings of IEEE International Conference on Computer Design: VLSI in Computers and Processors*.

Kamani, K., Kathiriya, D., Virparia, P., & Parsania, P. (2011). Digital green ICT: Enabling eco-efficiency and eco-innovation. In B. Unhelkar (Ed.), *Handbook of research on green ICT: Technology, business and social perspectives* (pp. 282–289). Hershey, PA: IGI Global. doi:10.4018/978-1-61692-834-6.ch019

Kamiya, S.N. (2013). Green Cloud Computing Resource Managing Policies a Survey.

Kanaker, H., Saudi, M., & Marhusin, M. (2014). Detecting Worm Attacks in Cloud Computing Environment: Proof of Concept. In *Proceedings of the IEEE 5th Control and System Graduate Research Colloquium (ICSGRC)* (pp. 253-256).

Kanaker, H. M., Saudi, M. M., & Marhusin, M. F. (2015, February). A systematic analysis on worm detection in cloud based systems. *Journal of Engineering and Applied Sciences (Asian Research Publishing Network)*, *10*(2).

Kantarci, B., Foschini, L., Corradi, A., & Mouftah, H. T. (2015). Design of energy-efficient cloud systems via network and resource virtualization. *International Journal of Network Management*, *25*(2), 75–94. doi:10.1002/nem.1838

Kasemsap, K. (2015a). The role of cloud computing adoption in global business. In V. Chang, R. Walters, & G. Wills (Eds.), *Delivery and adoption of cloud computing services in contemporary organizations* (pp. 26–55). Hershey, PA: IGI Global. doi:10.4018/978-1-4666-8210-8.ch002

Kasemsap, K. (2015b). The role of cloud computing in global supply chain. In N. Rao (Ed.), *Enterprise management strategies in the era of cloud computing* (pp. 192–219). Hershey, PA: IGI Global. doi:10.4018/978-1-4666-8339-6.ch009

Kasemsap, K. (2016). Examining the roles of virtual team and information technology in global business. In C. Graham (Ed.), *Strategic management and leadership for systems development in virtual spaces* (pp. 1–21). Hershey, PA: IGI Global. doi:10.4018/978-1-4666-9688-4.ch001

Kasemsap, K. (2017). Advocating sustainable supply chain management and sustainability in global supply chain. In M. Khan, M. Hussain, & M. Ajmal (Eds.), *Green supply chain management for sustainable business practice* (pp. 234–271). Hershey, PA: IGI Global. doi:10.4018/978-1-5225-0635-5.ch009

Kasemsap, K. (2017a). Sustainability, environmental sustainability, and sustainable tourism: Advanced issues and implications. In N. Ray (Ed.), *Business infrastructure for sustainability in developing economies* (pp. 1–24). Hershey, PA: IGI Global. doi:10.4018/978-1-5225-2041-2.ch001

Kasemsap, K. (2017b). Environmental management and waste management: Principles and applications. In U. Akkucuk (Ed.), *Ethics and sustainability in global supply chain management* (pp. 26–49). Hershey, PA: IGI Global. doi:10.4018/978-1-5225-2036-8.ch002

Katsaros, G., Kübert, R., & Gallizo, G. (2011). Building a service-oriented monitoring framework with REST and Nagios. In *Proceedings of the IEEE International Conference on Services Computing (SCC)* (pp. 426–431). doi:10.1109/SCC.2011.53

Kaushik, R. T., Cherkasova, L., Campbell, R., & Nahrstedt, K. 2010. Lightning: selfadaptive, energy-conserving, multi-zoned, commodity green Cloud storage system. In *Proceedings of the 19th ACM International Symposium on High Performance Distributed computing (HPDC '10).* New York, NY, USA: ACM. doi:10.1145/1851476.1851523

Kekre, H. B., Athawale, A., & Halarnkar, P. N. (2008). Increased Capacity of Information Hiding in LSB's Method for Text and Image. *International Journal of Electrical Computing Systems in Engineering*, 2(4), 246–249.

Kern, E., Dick, M., Naumann, S., & Hiller, T. (2015). Impacts of software and its engineering on the carbon footprint of ICT. *Environmental Impact Assessment Review*, 52, 53–61. doi:10.1016/j.eiar.2014.07.003

Kesswani, N., & Jain, S. K. (2017). Schematic classification model of green computing approaches. In *Nature-inspired computing: Concepts, methodologies, tools, and applications* (pp. 1643–1650). Hershey, PA: IGI Global. doi:10.4018/978-1-5225-0788-8.ch063

Khaba, M. V., & Santhanalakshmi, M. (2013). Remote Data Integrity Checking in Cloud Computing. *International Journal on Recent and Innovation Trends in Computing and Communication*, 1(6), 553–557.

Khan, S. (2013). A survey on scheduling based resource allocation in cloud computing. *International Journal For Technological Research In Engineering*.

Khan, A. N., Kiah, M. M., Khan, S. U., & Madani, S. A. (2013). Towards secure mobile cloud computing: A survey. *Future Generation Computer Systems*, 29(5), 1278–1299. doi:10.1016/j.future.2012.08.003

Khan, N., Shah, A., & Nusratullah, K. (2017). Adoption of virtualization in cloud computing: A foundation step towards green computing. In *Nature-inspired computing: Concepts, methodologies, tools, and applications* (pp. 1693–1700). Hershey, PA: IGI Global. doi:10.4018/978-1-5225-0788-8.ch066

Khan, S., Honnutagi, A. R., & Khan, M. S. (2015). Development of a research framework for green IT enablers using interpretive structural modelling. *International Journal of Green Computing*, 6(1), 1–13. doi:10.4018/IJGC.2015010101

Khatri, T. S., & Jethava, G. B. (2012, November). Survey on data Integrity Approaches used in the Cloud Computing. *International Journal of Engineering Research and Technology, 1*(9), 1–6.

Khosravi, A., & Buyya, R. (2017). Energy and carbon footprint-aware management of geo-distributed cloud data centers: A taxonomy, state of the art, and future directions. In N. Kamila (Ed.), *Advancing cloud database systems and capacity planning with dynamic applications* (pp. 27–46). Hershey, PA: IGI Global. doi:10.4018/978-1-5225-2013-9.ch002

Kiranjit, P., & Bhabani, S. P. (2016). Introduction to Big Data Analysis. In *Techniques and Environments for Big Data Analysis Parallel, Cloud, and Grid Computing* (pp. 11-30).

Kołodziej, J., Khan, S. U., Wang, L., & Zomaya, A. Y. (2015). Energy efficient genetic-based schedulers in computational grids. *Concurrency and Computation, 27*(4), 809–829. doi:10.1002/cpe.2839

Konda, V. R., & Tsitsiklis, J. N. (2003). Onactor-critic algorithms. *SIAM Journal on Control and Optimization, 42*(4), 1143–1166. doi:10.1137/S0363012901385691

Konidaris, G., & Osentoski, S. (2008). Value function approximation in reinforcement learning using the Fourier basis.

Kremer, U., Hicks, J., & Rehg, J. (2001) A compilation framework for power and energy management on mobile computers. In *Proceedings of the 14th International Conference on Languages and Compliers for Parallel Computing* (pp. 115–131).

Krontiris, I., Giannetsos, T., & Dimitriou, T. (2008). LIDeA: A Distributed Lightweight Intrusion Detection Architecture for Sensor Networks Ioannis. In *Proceedings of the 4th international conference on Security and privacy in communication networks SecureComm '08* (p. 1). New York, New York, USA: ACM Press. doi:10.1145/1460877.1460903

Kuleshov, V., & Precup, D. (2014). Algorithms for multi-armed bandit problems. arXiv:1402.6028

Kumar, K., Feng, J., Nimmagadda, Y., & Lu, Y.-H. (2011). Resource allocation for real-time tasks using cloud computing. In *Proceedings of the International Conference on Computer Communications and Networks*, (pp. 1-7). doi:10.1109/ICCCN.2011.6006077

Kumar, V., Cai, Z., Cooper, B. F., Eisenhauer, G., Schwan, K., Mansour, M., . . . Widener, P. (2006). Implementing diverse messaging models with self-managing properties using IFLOW. In Proceedings of the IEEE International Conference on Autonomic Computing ICAC'06 (pp. 243-252). doi:10.1109/ICAC.2006.1662404

Kumar, D., Sahoo, B., & Mandal, T. (2016). Heuristic task consolidation techniques for energy efficient cloud computing. In *Web-based services: Concepts, methodologies, tools, and applications* (pp. 760–782). Hershey, PA: IGI Global. doi:10.4018/978-1-4666-9466-8.ch034

Kumar, K. L. (2010). Cloud computing for mobile users: Can offloading computation save energy. *Computer, 43*(4), 51–56.

Kunz, F. (n. d.). An Introduction to Temporal Difference Learning.

Kutare, M., Eisenhauer, G., Wang, C., Schwan, K., Talwar, V., & Wolf, M. (2010). Monalytics: online monitoring and analytics for managing large scale data centers. In *Proceedings of the 7th International Conference on Autonomic Computing* (pp. 141–150). doi:10.1145/1809049.1809073

Le, H. B., & Bouzefrane, S. (2008, October). Identity management systems and interoperability in a heterogeneous environment. In *Proceedings of the International Conference on of Advanced Technologies for Communications* (pp. 239-242). doi:10.1109/ATC.2008.4760564

Lee, T.-H., Wen, C.-H., Chang, L.-H., Chiang, H.-S., & Hsieh, M.-C. (2014). A Lightweight Intrusion Detection Scheme Based on Energy Consumption Analysis in 6LowPAN. In *Advanced Technologies, Embedded and Multimedia for Human-centric Computing, LNEE* (Vol. 260, pp. 1205–1213). doi:10.1007/978-94-007-7262-5_137

Lee, C., Wang, P., & Niyato, D. (2015). A real-time group auction system for efficient allocation of cloud internet applications. *IEEE Transactions on Services Computing, 8*(2), 251–268. doi:10.1109/TSC.2013.24

Lenk, A., Klems, M., Nimis, J., Tai, S., & Sandholm, T. (2009). What's inside the Cloud? An architectural map of the Cloud landscape. In *Proceedings of the 2009 ICSE Workshop on Software Engineering Challenges of Cloud Computing CLOUD '09* (pp. 23–31). IEEE Computer Society, Washington, DC, USA. doi:10.1109/CLOUD.2009.5071529

Li, W. (2004). Using genetic algorithm for network intrusion detection. In *Proceedings of the United States Department of Energy Cyber Security Group*.

Li, W. (2004, January). Using genetic algorithm for network intrusion detection. *Proceedings of the United States Department of Energy Cyber Security Group*.

Liberty Alliance. (2002). Liberty alliance project. Retrieved from http://www.project liberty.org

Li, C. (2015). Hybrid cloud service selection strategy: Model and application of campus. *Computer Applications in Engineering Education, 23*(5), 645–657. doi:10.1002/cae.21634

Lin, W.-Y., Lin, G.-Y., & Wei, H.-Y. (2010). Dynamic auction mechanism for cloud resource allocation. In *Proceedings of the International Conference on Cluster, Cloud and Grid Computing* (pp. 591-592). doi:10.1109/CCGRID.2010.92

Liu, L., Wang, H., Liu, X., Jin, X., He, W. B., Wang, Q. B., & Chen, Y. (2009) *GreenCloud: A New Architecture for Green Data Center.*

Liu, T., & Chen, Y. (2010). Retrospective Detection of Malware Attacks by Cloud Computing. In *Proceedings of the International Conference on Cyber-Enabled Distributed Computing and Knowledge Discovery* (pp. 510-517). doi:10.1109/CyberC.2010.99

Liu, J., Huang, X., & Liu, J. K. (2015). Secure sharing of personal health records in cloud computing: Ciphertext-policy attribute-based signcryption. *Future Generation Computer Systems, 52*, 67–76. doi:10.1016/j.future.2014.10.014

Lu, W., & Traore, I. (2004). Detecting new forms of network intrusion using genetic programming. In *Proceedings of the Conference on Evolutionary Computation* (pp. 475-494). doi:10.1111/j.0824-7935.2004.00247.x

Lu, L. H. (2012). Assessing MapReduce for Internet Computing: A Comparison of Hadoop and BitDew-MapReduce. In *Proceedings of the 2012 ACM/IEEE 13th International Conference on Grid Computing* (pp. 76-84). IEE Computer Society. doi:10.1109/Grid.2012.31

Maei, H. R., & Sutton, R. S. (2010, March). GQ (λ): A general gradient algorithm for temporal-difference prediction learning with eligibility traces. In *Proceedings of the Third Conference on Artificial General Intelligence* (Vol. 1, pp. 91-96). doi:10.2991/agi.2010.22

Maenhaut, P. J., Moens, H., Ongenae, V., & de Turck, F. (2016). Migrating legacy software to the cloud: Approach and verification by means of two medical software use cases. *Software, Practice & Experience*, *46*(1), 31–54. doi:10.1002/spe.2320

Mahadevan, S. (2005, August). Proto-value functions: Developmental reinforcement learning. In *Proceedings of the 22nd international conference on Machine learning* (pp. 553-560). ACM.

Mair, J., Huang, Z., & Zhang, H. (2012). Energy-aware scheduling for parallel applications on multicore systems. In N. Kaabouch & W. Hu (Eds.), *Energy-aware systems and networking for sustainable initiatives* (pp. 38–58). Hershey, PA: IGI Global. doi:10.4018/978-1-4666-1842-8.ch003

Malakata M. (2014). Safari.com to tackle Kenya's growing e-waste problem.

Mane, Y. D., & Devadkar, K. K. (2013). Protection concern in mobile cloud computing–a survey. *IOSR Journal of Computer Engineering*, *3*, 39-44.

Manvi, S. S., & Shyam, G. K. (2014). Resource management for Infrastructure as a Service (IaaS) in cloud computing: A survey. *Journal of Network and Computer Applications*, *41*, 424–440. doi:10.1016/j.jnca.2013.10.004

Manyika, J., Chui, M., Brown, B., Bughin, J., Dobbs, R., Roxburgh, C., & Byers, A. H. (2011). *Big data: The next frontier for innovation, competition, and productivity*. McKinsey Global Institute.

Mardamutu, K., Ponnusamy, V., & Zaman, N. (2016). Green energy in data centers. In V. Ponnusamy, N. Zaman, T. Low, & A. Amin (Eds.), *Biologically-inspired energy harvesting through wireless sensor technologies* (pp. 234–249). Hershey, PA: IGI Global. doi:10.4018/978-1-4666-9792-8.ch012

Marhusin, M.F. (2012). Improving the Effectiveness of Behaviour-based Malware Detection [doctoral dissertation]. UNSW, Canberra. Retrieved from http://www.unsworks.unsw.edu.au/primo_library/libweb/action/dlDisplay.do?vid=UNSWORKS&docId=unsworks_10868. 2012.

Martignoni, L., Paleari, R., & Bruschi, D. (2009, December 14-18). A framework for behavior-based malware analysis in the cloud. In *Proceedings of the 5th International Conference (ICISS)* (pp. 1-15). doi:10.1007/978-3-642-10772-6_14

Martinez, C., Echeverri, G., & Sanz, A. (2010, November). Malware Detection based on Cloud Computing integrating Intrusion Ontology representation. In *Proceedings of the 2010 IEEE Latin-American Conference on Communications (LATINCOM)*. doi:10.1109/LATINCOM.2010.5641013

Mavridis, I., & Karatza, H. (2017). Performance evaluation of cloud-based log file analysis with Apache Hadoop and Apache Spark. *Journal of Systems and Software, 125,* 133–151. doi:10.1016/j.jss.2016.11.037

Mayo, R. N., & Ranganathan, P. (2003). Energy consumption in mobile devices: why future systems need requirements aware energy scale-down. In *Proceedings of the Workshop on Power-Aware Computing Systems.*

Mayo, R. N., & Ranganathan, P. (2005). Energy consumption in mobile devices: Why future systems need requirements-aware energy scale-down. In *Proceedings of 3rd International Workshop on Power-Aware Computer Systems,* San Diego, CA, USA doi:10.1007/978-3-540-28641-7_3

McGraw, G., & Morrisett, G. (2000). Attacking Malicious Code. *IEEE Software, 17*(5), 33-41.

McWhorter, R. R., & Delello, J. A. (2016). Green computing through virtual learning environments. In *Professional development and workplace learning: Concepts, methodologies, tools, and applications* (pp. 837–864). Hershey, PA: IGI Global. doi:10.4018/978-1-4666-8632-8.ch047

Mehdi, B., & Mukesh, S. (2015). The Role of Cloud Computing Architecture in Big Data. In *Pedrycz* (pp. 275–295). Information Granularity, Big Data, and Computational Intelligence.

Mei, Y., Liu, L., Pu, X., & Sivathanu, S. (2010). Performance measurements and analysis of network I/O applications in virtualized cloud. In *Proceedings of the 2010 IEEE 3rd International Conference on Cloud Computing (CLOUD)* (pp. 59–66).

Mell, P. M., & Grance, T. (2011). The NIST definition of cloud computing. Gaithersburg, MD. doi:10.6028/NIST.SP.800-145

Mell, P., & Grance, T. (2011). The NIST Definition of Cloud Computing (Special Publication 800-145). NIST.

Mell, P., & Grance, T. (n. d.). The NIST definition of Cloud Computing (Vol. 15).

Mell, P., & Grance, T. (2009). *The NIST Definition of Cloud computing.* National Institute of Standards and Technology.

Mell, P., & Grance, T. (2011). *The NIST Definition of Cloud.* NIST Spec.

Menzel, M., Ranjan, R., Wang, L., Khan, S. U., & Chen, J. (2014). CloudGenius: A hybrid decision support method for automating the migration of web application clusters to public clouds. *IEEE Transactions on Cloud Computing, 64*(5), 1336–1348. doi:10.1109/TC.2014.2317188

Microsoft. (2017, January 2). Windows Azure. Retrieved from http://www.microsoft.com/azure

Minarolli, D., & Freisleben, B. (2013). Virtual Machine Resource Allocation in Cloud Computing via Multi-Agent Fuzzy Control. In *Proceedings of the Int. Conference on Cloud and Green Computing* (pp. 188-194). doi:10.1109/CGC.2013.35

Mnih, V., Kavukcuoglu, K., Silver, D., Graves, A., Antonoglou, I., Wierstra, D., & Riedmiller, M. (2013). Playing atari with deep reinforcement learning. arXiv preprint arXiv:1312.5602.

Mnih, V., Kavukcuoglu, K., Silver, D., Rusu, A. A., Veness, J., Bellemare, M. G., & Petersen, S. et al. (2015). Human-level control through deep reinforcement learning. *Nature*, *518*(7540), 529–533. doi:10.1038/nature14236 PMID:25719670

Modi, C., Patel, D., Patel, H., Borisaniya, B., Patel, A., & Rajarajan, M. (2013). A survey of intrusion detection techniques. Cloud, 36(1), 42–57.

Modi, C., Patel, D., Borisaniya, B., Patel, A., & Rajarajan, M. (2013). A survey on security issues and solutions at different layers of Cloud computing. *The Journal of Supercomputing*, *63*(2), 561–592. doi:10.1007/s11227-012-0831-5

Modi, C., Patel, D., Borisaniya, B., Patel, H., Patel, A., & Rajarajan, M. (2013). A survey of intrusion detection techniques in Cloud. *Journal of Network and Computer Applications*, *36*(1), 42–57. doi:10.1016/j.jnca.2012.05.003

Mohamaddiah, M. H., Abdullah, A., Subramaniam, S., & Hussin, M. (2014, February). A Survey on Resource Allocation and Monitoring in Cloud Computing. *International Journal of Machine Learning and Computing*, *4*(1).

Mohan, V. M., & Satyanarayana, K. V. (2015). Efficient task scheduling strategy towards qos aware optimal resource utilization in cloud computing. *Journal of Theoretical \& Applied Information Technology, 80*.

Molisch, A. F., Balakrishnan, K., Chong, C. C., Emami, S., Fort, A., Karedal, J., ... & Siwiak, K. (2004). IEEE 802.15. 4a channel model-final report. *IEEE P802, 15*(04), 0662.

Moradi, M., & Zulkernine, M. (2004). A Neural Network Based System for Intrusion Detection and Classification of Attacks. In *Proceedings of the 2004 IEEE International Conference on Advances in Intelligent Systems Theory and Applications.*

Moreno, I. S., & Xu, J. (2013). Energy-efficiency in cloud computing environments: Towards energy savings without performance degradation. In S. Aljawarneh (Ed.), *Cloud computing advancements in design, implementation, and technologies* (pp. 18–36). Hershey, PA: IGI Global. doi:10.4018/978-1-4666-1879-4.ch002

Nagele, T. (2013). *MapReduce Framework Performance Comparison*. Radboud University Nijmegen.

Nimje, A. R. V. T. Gaikwad, H. N. Datir (2013). Green Cloud Computing: A Virtualized Security Framework for Green Cloud Computing. *Presented at the International Journal of Advanced Research in Computer Science and Software Engineering.*

Oberheide, J., Veeraraghavan, K., Cooke, E., Flinn, J., & Jahanian, F. (2008). Virtualized In-Cloud Security Services for Mobile Devices. In *Proceedings of the 1st Workshop on Virtualization in Mobile Computing*, Breckenridge. doi:10.1145/1622103.1629656

Osones. (2017, January 26). Openstack Formation User. Retrieved from https://osones.com/formations/openstack-user.html

Ou, C.-M. (2012). Host-based intrusion detection systems adapted from agent-based artificial immune systems. *Neurocomputing, 88*, 78–86. doi:10.1016/j.neucom.2011.07.031

Palanivel, K., & Kuppuswami, S. (2017). Green and energy-efficient computing architecture for e-learning. In *Nature-inspired computing: Concepts, methodologies, tools, and applications* (pp. 1668–1692). Hershey, PA: IGI Global. doi:10.4018/978-1-5225-0788-8.ch065

Palankar, M. R., Iamnitchi, A., Ripeanu, M., & Garfinkel, S. (2008). Amazon S3 for Science Grids: a Viable Solution? In *Proceedings of ACM International Workshop on Data-aware Distributed Computing* (pp. 55-64).

paloaltonetworks. *Secure the network*. Retrieved January 02, 2017 from https://www.paloaltonetworks.com/products/secure-the-network/subscriptions/minemeld

Pandya, S. S. (2014). Green Cloud computing.

Parr, R., Painter-Wakefield, C., Li, L., & Littman, M. Analyzing feature generation for value-function approximation. In *Proceedings of the International Conference on Machine Learning*.

Patel, Y. S., Jain, K., & Shukla, S. K. (2016). A Brief Survey on Benchmarks and Research Challenges for Green Cloud Computing. *Presented at the National Conference on Advancements in Computer & Information Technology*.

Patell, N.S. (2014). Software as a Service (SaaS): Security issues and Solutions. *International Journal of Computational Engineering Research, 4*(6).

Patil, P. S., & Kharade, J. (2016). A Study on Green Cloud Computing Technologies. *Presented at the International Journal of Innovative Research in Computer Communication Engineering*.

Pattinson, C., Oram, D., & Ross, M. (2013). Sustainability and social responsibility in raising awareness of green issues through developing tertiary academic provision: A case study. In R. Colomo-Palacios (Ed.), *Enhancing the modern organization through information technology professionals: Research, studies, and techniques* (pp. 284–294). Hershey, PA: IGI Global. doi:10.4018/978-1-4666-2648-5.ch020

Paulson, L. D. (2003). Low-power chips for high-powered handhelds. *IEEE Computer Society Magazine, 36*(1), 21–23. doi:10.1109/MC.2003.1160049

Philipson, G. (2013). A framework for green computing. In K. Ganesh & S. Anbuudayasankar (Eds.), *International and interdisciplinary studies in green computing* (pp. 12–26). Hershey, PA: IGI Global. doi:10.4018/978-1-4666-2646-1.ch002

Pohlheim, H. (2003). Genetic and Evolutionary Algorithms: Principles, Methods and Algorithms. Retrieve from http://www.pg.gda.pl/~mkwies/dyd/geadocu/algindex.html

Ponemon. (2017). *Ponemon Survey 2017*. Retrieved December 14, 2017 from https://www.ponemon.org/

Porritt, J. (2010). Green IT a global benchmark".

Portokalidis, G., Homburg, P., Anagnostakis, K., & Bos, H. (2016). Paranoid Android: Versatile Protection for Smartphones. In *Proceedings of the 26th Annual Computer Security Application Conference (ACSAC)*, Los Angeles. doi:10.1145/1920261.1920313

Pragya, M. G. (2015). A Review on Energy Efficient Techniques in Green Cloud Computing. *International Journal of Advanced Research in Computer Science and Software Engineering*.

Prasad, A., & Rao, S. (2014). A mechanism design approach to resource procurement in cloud computing. *IEEE Transactions on Cloud Computing*, *63*(1), 17–30. doi:10.1109/TC.2013.106

Prasad, R., Gyani, J., & Murti, P. (2012). Mobile Cloud Computing: Implications and Challenge. *Journal of Information Engineering and Applications*, *2*(7), 7–15.

Prashant, D. (2014). Greening the Cloud Computing.

Precup, D. (2000). Eligibility traces for off-policy policy evaluation.

Precup, D., Sutton, R. S., & Dasgupta, S. (2001, June). Off-policy temporal-difference learning with function approximation. In ICML (pp. 417-424).

Purcell, B. M. (2014). Big Data Using Cloud Computing. *Journal of Technology Research*, 1-8.

Qaisar, S., & Khawaja, K. (2012). *Cloud Computing: Network/Security Threats and Countermeasures. Interdisciplinary Journal of Contemporary Research*, *3*(9), 1323–1329.

Qi, H., & Gani, A. (2012, May). Research on mobile cloud computing: Review, trend and perspectives. In *Proceedings of Second International Conference on Digital Information and Communication Technology and it's Applications (DICTAP)* (pp. 195-202).

Quinton, C., Romero, D., & Duchien, L. (2016). SALOON: A platform for selecting and configuring cloud environments. *Software, Practice & Experience*, *46*(1), 55–78. doi:10.1002/spe.2311

Rackspace. (2017, February 5). Web Hosting by Rackspace Hosting. Retrieved from http://www.rackspace.com

Radu, L. D. (2014). GreenICTs potential in emerging economies. *Procedia Economics and Finance*, *15*, 430–436. doi:10.1016/S2212-5671(14)00473-0

Rahman, N. (2016). Toward achieving environmental sustainability in the computer industry. *International Journal of Green Computing*, *7*(1), 37–54. doi:10.4018/IJGC.2016010103

Raisinghani, M. S., & Idemudia, E. C. (2016). Green information systems for sustainability. In U. Akkucuk (Ed.), *Handbook of research on waste management techniques for sustainability* (pp. 212–226). Hershey, PA: IGI Global. doi:10.4018/978-1-4666-9723-2.ch011

Rana, P. (2010). Green Computing Saves Green. *International Journal of Advanced Computer and Mathematical Sciences*, *1*(1), 45–51.

Ranganathan, P. (2010). Recipe for efficiency: principles of power-aware computing. Communication, 53(4), 60–67.

Regalia, P. (1994). *Adaptive IIR filtering in signal processing and control*. CRC Press.

Ren, K., & Lou, W. (2009). Ensuring Data Storage Security in Cloud Computing. Retrieved From http://www.ece.iit.edu/~ubisec/IWQoS09.pdf

Ren, W., Yu, L., Gao, R., & Xiong, F. (2011). Lightweight and compromise resilient storage outsourcing with distributed secure accessibility in mobile cloud computing. *Tsinghua Science and Technology*, *16*(5), 520–528. doi:10.1016/S1007-0214(11)70070-0

Reza, H., & Sonawane, M. (2016). Enhancing Mobile Cloud Computing Security Using Steganography. *Journal of Information Security*, *7*(4), 245–259. doi:10.4236/jis.2016.74020

RightScale. (n. d.). *RightScale State of the cloud survey*. Retrieved February 04, 2017. Retrieved from http://www.rightscale.com/

Ristenpart, T., Tromer, E., Shacham, H., & Savage, S. (2009, November). Hey, you, get off of my cloud: exploring information leakage in third-party compute clouds. In *Proceedings of the 16th ACM Conference on Computer and Communications Security* (pp. 199-212). doi:10.1145/1653662.1653687

Rochwerger, B., Breitgand, D., Levy, E., Galis, A., Nagin, K., Llorente, I. M., ... & Ben-Yehuda, M. (2009). The RESERVOIR model and architecture for open federated cloud computing. *IBM Journal of Research and Development*, *53*(4).

Roodt, S., & de Villiers, C. (2012). Teaching green information technology inside and outside the classroom: An undergraduate case-study in the South African context. *International Journal of Innovation in the Digital Economy*, *3*(3), 60–71. doi:10.4018/jide.2012070106

Rudenko, A., Reiher, P., Popek, G. J., & Kuenning, G. H. (1998). Saving portable computer battery power through remote process execution. *Journal of ACM SIGMOBILE on Mobile Computing and Communications Revie*, *2*(1).

Ruebsamen, T., & Reich, C. (2012). Enhancing mobile device security by security level integration in a cloud proxy. In *Proceedings of Third International Conference on Cloud Computing, GRIDs and Virtualization* (pp. 159-168).

Ryoo, J., Rizvi, S., Aiken, W., & Kissell, J. (2014). Cloud security auditing: challenges and emerging approaches. *IEEE Security & Privacy*, *12*(6), 68-74.

Ryoo, J., & Choi, Y. (2011). A taxonomy of green information and communication protocols and standards. In B. Unhelkar (Ed.), *Handbook of research on green ICT: Technology, business and social perspectives* (pp. 364–376). Hershey, PA: IGI Global. doi:10.4018/978-1-61692-834-6.ch026

Sabry, N., & Krause, P. (2013). Optimal green virtual machine migration model. *International Journal of Business Data Communications and Networking, 9*(3), 35–52. doi:10.4018/jbdcn.2013070103

Sagar, M. S., Singh, B., & Ahmad, W. (2013). Study on Cloud Computing Resource Allocation Strategies. *International Journal of Advance Research and Innovation, 1*, 107–114.

Saha, S., Pal, S., & Pattnaik, P. K. (2016). A Novel Scheduling Algorithm for Cloud Computing Environment. In *Computational Intelligence in Data Mining* (Vol. 1, pp. 387–398). Springer. doi:10.1007/978-81-322-2734-2_39

Sahu, D. P., Singh, K., & Prakash, S. (2015). Resource Allocation and Provisioning in Computational Mobile Grid. *International Journal of Applied Evolutionary Computation, 6*(2), 1–24. doi:10.4018/ijaec.2015040101

Sahu, D., Sharma, S., Dubey, V., & Tripathi, A. (2012). Cloud Computing in Mobile Applications. *International Journal of Scientific and Research Publications, 2*(8), 1–9.

Salesforce. (2017, January 8). Salesforce CRM. Retrieved from http://www.salesforce.com/platform

Samadi, Y., Zbakh, M., & Tadonki, C. (2016). Comparative study between Hadoop and Spark based on Hibench benchmarks. In *Proceedings of the 2nd International Conference on Cloud Computing Technologies and Applications (CloudTech16)* (pp. 267- 275).

Sanduja, S., Jewell, P., Aron, E., & Pharai, N. (2015). Cloud computing for pharmacometrics: Using AWS, NONMEM, PsN, grid engine, and sonic. *CPT: Pharmacometrics & Systems Pharmacology, 4*(9), 537–546. PMID:26451333

SAP Business By Design. (2017, January 15). Retrieved from www.sap.com/sme/solutions/businessmanagement/businessbydesign/index.epx

Saravankumar, C., & Arun, C. (2014). An Efficient ASCII-BCD Based Steganography for Cloud Security Using Common Development Model. *Journal of Theoretical and Applied Information Technology, 65*, 1992–8645.

Sasikala, P. (2013). Architectural strategies for green cloud computing: Environments, infrastructure and resources. In S. Aljawarneh (Ed.), *Cloud computing advancements in design, implementation, and technologies* (pp. 218–242). Hershey, PA: IGI Global. doi:10.4018/978-1-4666-1879-4.ch016

Satyanarayanan, M. (1996). Fundamental Challenges in Mobile Computing. In *Proceedings of the 15th Annual ACM Symposium on Principles of Distributed Computing*, Philadelphia. doi:10.1145/248052.248053

Sean, M., Zhi, L., Subhajyoti, B., Juheng, Z., & Anand, G. (2011). Cloud computing: The business perspective. *Decision Support Systems, 51*(1), 176–189. doi:10.1016/j.dss.2010.12.006

Senthilnathan, P., & Kalaiarasan, C. (2013). A joint design of routing and resource allocation using qos monitoring agent in mobile ad-hoc networks. *Journal of Theoretical & Applied Information Technology, 55.*

Shahin, A. A. (2014). Polymorphic Worms Collection in Cloud Computing. *International Journal of Soft Computing, Mathematics and Control.*

Shah, S. H., & Yaqoob, I. (2016). *A survey: Internet of Things (IOT) technologies, applications and challenges. In 2016 IEEE Smart Energy Grid Engineering (SEGE)* (pp. 381–385). IEEE. doi:10.1109/SEGE.2016.7589556

Shaikh, R. & Sasikumar, M. (2012). *Security Issues in Cloud Computing: A survey. International Journal of Computer Applications, 44*(19), pp. 4–10.

Shamir, A. (1979). How to share a secret. *Communications of the ACM, 22*(11), 612–613. doi:10.1145/359168.359176

Shao, J., & Wang, Q. (2011). A performance guarantee approach for cloud applications based on monitoring. In *Proceedings of the Computer Software and Applications Conference Workshops (COMPSACW)* (pp. 25–30).

Shau, S. K., Jena, L., & Satapathy, S. (2015). Big Data Security issues and challenges in Cloud Computing Environment. *International Journal of Innovations in Engineering and Technology, 6*(2), 297-306.

Shekhar, J. (2014). An analysis on security concerns and their possible solutions in cloud computing environment. In *Proceedings of the 3rd International Conference on Role of Engineers as Entrepreneurs in Current Scenario.*

Shelby, Z., Hartke, K., & Bormann, C. (2014). The constrained application protocol (CoAP).

Shivalkar, P., & Tripathy, B. (2015). Rough set based green cloud computing in emerging markets. In M. Khosrow-Pour (Ed.), *Encyclopedia of information science and technology* (3rd ed., pp. 1078–1087). Hershey, PA: IGI Global. doi:10.4018/978-1-4666-5888-2.ch103

Shojafar, M., Cordeschi, N., & Baccarelli, E. (2016). Resource scheduling for energy-aware reconfigurable Internet data centers. In Q. Hassan (Ed.), *Innovative research and applications in next-generation high performance computing* (pp. 21–46). Hershey, PA: IGI Global. doi:10.4018/978-1-5225-0287-6.ch002

Shozu. (n. d.). Index. Retrieved from http://www.shozu.com/portal/index.do

Shuai, Z., Shufen, Z., Chen, X., & Huo, X. (2010). Cloud Computing Research and Development Trend. In *Proceedings of the Second International Conference on Future Networks ICFN '10* (pp. 93–97).

Singh, A., Dutta, K., & Singh, A. (2014). Resource Allocation in Cloud Computing Environment using AHP Technique. *International Journal of Cloud Applications and Computing, 4*(1), 33–44. doi:10.4018/ijcac.2014010103

Singh, A., Mishra, N., Ali, S. I., Shukla, N., & Shankar, R. (2015). Cloud computing technology: Reducing carbon footprint in beef supply chain. *International Journal of Production Economics*, *164*, 462–471. doi:10.1016/j.ijpe.2014.09.019

Singhal, M., Chandrasekhar, S., Ge, T., Sandhu, R., Krishnan, R., Ahn, G. J., & Bertino, E. (2013). Collaboration in multicloud computing environments: Framework and security issues. *Computer*, *46*(2), 76–84. doi:10.1109/MC.2013.46

Singh, S., & Gond, S. (2017). Green computing and its impact. In *Nature-inspired computing: Concepts, methodologies, tools, and applications* (pp. 1628–1642). Hershey, PA: IGI Global. doi:10.4018/978-1-5225-0788-8.ch062

Smailagic, A., & Ettus, M. (2002) System design and power optimization for mobile computers, In *Proceedings of IEEE Computer Society Annual Symposium on VLSI*. doi:10.1109/ISVLSI.2002.1016867

Smeitink, M., & Spruit, M. (2013). Maturity for sustainability in IT: Introducing the MITS. *International Journal of Information Technologies and Systems Approach*, *6*(1), 39–56. doi:10.4018/jitsa.2013010103

Smith, J., & Nair, R. (2003). *Virtual Machines: Versatile Platforms for Systems and Processes*. Los Altos, CA: Morgan Kaufmann.

Song, W., & Xiao, Z. (2013). An Infrastructure-as-a-Service cloud: On-demand resource provisioning. In X. Yang & L. Liu (Eds.), *Principles, methodologies, and service-oriented approaches for cloud computing* (pp. 302–324). Hershey, PA: IGI Global. doi:10.4018/978-1-4666-2854-0.ch013

Son, S., Jung, G., & Jun, S. C. (2013). An SLA-based cloud computing that facilitates resource allocation in the distributed data centers of a cloud provider. *The Journal of Supercomputing*, *64*(2), 606–637. doi:10.1007/s11227-012-0861-z

Soyata, T., Ba, H., Heinzelman, W., Kwon, M., & Shi, J. (2013). Accelerating mobile cloud computing: A survey. In *Communication Infrastructures for Cloud Computing* (pp. 175-197). Hershey, PA: IGI Global.

Spring, J. (2011). Monitoring cloud computing by layer- Part 2. *IEEE Security and Privacy*, *9*(52–55).

Srinivasa, K. (2012). *Application of Genetic Algorithms for Detecting Anomaly in Network Intrusion Detection Systems*. In *CCSIT 2012* (pp. 582–591). doi:10.1007/978-3-642-27299-8_61

Stavrinides, G. L., & Karatza, H. D. (2015). A cost-effective and QoS-aware approach to scheduling real-time workflow applications in PaaS and SaaS clouds. In *Proceedings of the 3rd International Conference on Future Internet of Things and Cloud (FiCloud'15)* (pp. 231-239). doi:10.1109/FiCloud.2015.93

Stephen, K., Frank, A., Alberto, J. E., & William, M. (2013). Big Data: Issues and Challenges Moving Forward. In *Proceedings of the 46th Hawaii International Conference on System Sciences* (pp. 995-1004).

Subashini, S., & Kavitha, V. (2011). a survey on security issues in service delivery models of cloud computing. *Journal of Network and Computer Applications*, *34*(1), 1–11. doi:10.1016/j.jnca.2010.07.006

Sugam, S. (2016). Expanded cloud plumes hiding Big Data ecosystem. *Future Generation Computer Systems*, 59, 63–92.

Su, M., Yu, G., & Lin, C. (2009). A real-time network intrusion detection system for large-scale attacks based on an incremental mining approach. *Computers & Security*, *28*(5), 301–309. doi:10.1016/j.cose.2008.12.001

Suryawanshi, K. (2012). Green ICT implementation at Professional Education Institutions.

Sutton, R. S., McAllester, D. A., Singh, S. P., & Mansour, Y. (1999, November). Policy gradient methods for reinforcement learning with function approximation. In NIPS (Vol. 99, pp. 1057-1063).

Sutton, R. S., & Barto, A. G. (1998). Reinforcement learning: An introduction. Cambridge: MIT press.

Talia, D. (2013). *Toward cloud-based big-data analytics*. IEEE Computer Science.

Tang, K., Wang, Y., Liu, H., Sheng, Y., Wang, X., & Wei, Z. (2013, September). Design and implementation of push notification system based on the MQTT protocol. In *Proceedings of the International Conference on Information Science and Computer Applications (ISCA 2013)* (pp. 116-119). doi:10.2991/isca-13.2013.20

Taruna, S. (2014). Green Computing in Developed and Developing Countries.

Teng, F., & Magoulès, F. (2010). A new game theoretical resource allocation algorithm for cloud computing. In *Advances in Grid and Pervasive Computing* (pp. 321–330). Springer. doi:10.1007/978-3-642-13067-0_35

Thakur, P. K., & Verma, A. (2015). Process batch offloading method for mobile-cloud computing platform. *Journal of Cases on Information Technology*, *17*(3), 1–13. doi:10.4018/JCIT.2015070101

The Green Grid. (2010). About the green grid. Retrieved from http:/www.the greengrid.org/about-thegreen-grid

Thongmak, M. (2013). A systematic framework for sustainable ICTs in developing countries. *International Journal of Information Technologies and Systems Approach*, *6*(1), 1–19. doi:10.4018/jitsa.2013010101

Tillapart, P., Thumthawatworn, T., & Santiprabhob, P. (2002). Fuzzy intrusion detection system. *AU JT*, *6*(2), 109–114.

Truelove, J., & Brumley, D. (2010). Split Screen: Enabling Efficient, Distributed Malware Detection. In *Proceedings of School of Computer science at Research Showcase @ CMU Conference*.

Van Kranenburg, R. (2008). *The Internet of Things: A critique of ambient technology and the all-seeing network of RFID*. Institute of Network Cultures.

Vartiainen, E., & Mattila, K. V.-V. (2010). User experience of mobile photo sharing in the cloud. In *Proceedings of the 9th International Conference on Mobile and Ubiquitous Multimedia (MUM)*. doi:10.1145/1899475.1899479

Velayudham, A., Gohila, G., Hariharan, B., & Ramya Selvi, M. (2014). A Novel Coalition Game Theory Based Resource Allocation And Selfish Attack Avoidance In Cognitive Radio Ad-hoc Networks. *Journal of Theoretical \& Applied Information Technology, 64*.

Vieira, C., & Schulter, A. (2010). Intrusion detection techniques in grid and cloud computing environment. *IT Professional, 12*(4), 38-43.

Vinothina, V., Sridaran, R., & Ganapathi, P. (2012). A survey on resource allocation strategies in cloud computing. *International Journal of Advanced Computer Science and Applications, 3*, 97–104. doi:10.14569/IJACSA.2012.030616

Voderhobli, K. (2015). An SNMP based traffic characterisation paradigm for green-aware networks. In V. Chang, R. Walters, & G. Wills (Eds.), *Delivery and adoption of cloud computing services in contemporary organizations* (pp. 340–357). Hershey, PA: IGI Global. doi:10.4018/978-1-4666-8210-8.ch014

Vriens, P. (n. d.). *What could be a valid definition of DevOps?* Retrieved October 15, 2016, from https://devops.stackexchange.com

Wagener, G., State, R., & Dulaunoy, A. (2008). Malware behaviour analysis. *Journal of Virology, 4*(4), 279-287.

Walker, E., Brisken, W., & Romney, J. (2010). To lease or not to lease from storage clouds. *Computer, 43*(4), 44–50. doi:10.1109/MC.2010.115

Wang, B., Li, H., Liu, X., Li, X., & Li, F. (2014). Preserving identity privacy on multi-owner cloud data during public verification. *Security and Communication Networks, 7*(11), 2104–2113. doi:10.1002/sec.922

Wang, C., Schwan, K., Talwar, V., Eisenhauer, G., Hu, L., & Wolf, M. (2011). A flexible architecture integrating monitoring and analytics for managing large-scale data centers. In *Proceedings of ICAC*. doi:10.1145/1998582.1998605

Wang, H., & Huo, D. (2014). Green cloud computing: Site selection of data centers. In S. Srinivasan (Ed.), *Security, trust, and regulatory aspects of cloud computing in business environments* (pp. 202–214). Hershey, PA: IGI Global. doi:10.4018/978-1-4666-5788-5.ch012

Wang, Z., & Su, X. (2015). Dynamically hierarchical resource-allocation algorithm in cloud computing environment. *The Journal of Supercomputing*.

Wei, G., Vasilakos, A. V., Zheng, Y., & Xiong, N. (2010). A game-theoretic method of fair resource allocation for cloud computing services. *The Journal of Supercomputing, 54*(2), 252–269. doi:10.1007/s11227-009-0318-1

Wikibooks. (2002). The computer revolution/computers and environment/disposal/recycling. Retrieved from http://en.wikibooks.org/wiki/The_Computer_Revolution/Computers_and_Environment/Disposal/Recycling

Williams, J., & Curtis, L. (2008). Green: The new computing coat of arms? *IT Professional Magazine, 10*(1), 12.

Wu, Y., Cegielski, C. G., Hazen, B. T., & Hall, D. J. (2013). Cloud computing in support of supply chain information system infrastructure: Understanding when to go to the cloud. *Journal of Supply Chain Management, 49*(3), 25–41. doi:10.1111/j.1745-493x.2012.03287.x

Xiao, T., Qu, G., Hariri, S., & Yousif, M. 2005. An Efficient Network Intrusion Detection Method Based on Information Theory and Genetic Algorithm. In *Proceedings of the 24 th IEEE International Performance Computing and Communications Conference (IPCCC)*, Phoenix, AZ, USA.

Xiao, Z., Song, W., & Chen, Q. (2013). Dynamic resource allocation using virtual machines for cloud computing environment. *IEEE Transactions on Parallel and Distributed Systems, 24*(6), 1107–1117. doi:10.1109/TPDS.2012.283

Xu, Y., & Helal, A. (2016). Scalable Cloud–Sensor Architecture for the Internet of Things. *IEEE Internet of Things Journal, 3*(3), 285–298. doi:10.1109/JIOT.2015.2455555

Xuan, X. (2012). From cloud computing to cloud manufacturing. *Robotics and Computer-integrated Manufacturing, 28*(1), 75–86. doi:10.1016/j.rcim.2011.07.002

Yang, J., Wang, H., Wang, J., Tan, C., & Yu, D. (2011). Provable data possession of resource-constrained mobile devices in cloud computing. *JNW, 6*(7), 1033–1040. doi:10.4304/jnw.6.7.1033-1040

Yang, M., Kuo, C., & Yeh, Y. (2011). Dynamic rightsizing with quality-controlled algorithms in virtualization environments. *International Journal of Grid and High Performance Computing, 3*(2), 29–43. doi:10.4018/jghpc.2011040103

Yau, S. S., & An, H. G. (2010). Confidentiality Protection in Cloud Computing Systems. *International Journal of Software Informatics, 4*(4), 351–365.

Yuvaraj, M. (2015). Green libraries on cloud computing platform. In M. Khosrow-Pour (Ed.), *Encyclopedia of information science and technology* (3rd ed., pp. 3901–3911). Hershey, PA: IGI Global. doi:10.4018/978-1-4666-5888-2.ch384

Zaharia, M., Chowdhury, M., Michael, J., & Shenker, I. (2010). Spark: Cluster Computing with Working Sets. In *Proceedings of the 2nd USENIX conference on Hot topics in cloud computing* (pp. 10-10).

Zahariev, A. (2009). *Google App Engine*. Otaniemi: Helsinki University of Technology.

Zhang, Q., Cheng, L., & Boutaba, R. (2010). Cloud computing: state-of-the-art and research challenges. *Journal of Internet Services and Applications, 1*(1), 7–18.

Zhang, J., Huang, H., & Wang, X. (2016). Resource provision algorithms in cloud computing: A survey. *Journal of Network and Computer Applications, 64*, 23–42. doi:10.1016/j.jnca.2015.12.018

Zhang, J., & Liang, X. J. (2012). Promoting greenICT in China: A framework based on innovation system approaches. *Telecommunications Policy, 36*(10/11), 997–1013. doi:10.1016/j.telpol.2012.09.001

Zheng, X., & Cai, Y. (2010). Optimal server allocation and frequency modulation on multi-core based server clusters. *International Journal of Green Computing, 1*(2), 18–30. doi:10.4018/jgc.2010070102

Zhou, Z., & Huang, D. (2012, October). Efficient and secure data storage operations for mobile cloud computing. In *Proceedings of 8th international conference and 2012 workshop on systems virtualiztion management (svm), Network and service management (cnsm)* (pp. 37-45).

Zissis, D., & Lekkas, D. (2012). Addressing cloud computing security issues. *Future Generation Computer Systems, 28*(3), 583–592. doi:10.1016/j.future.2010.12.006

Zonouz, S., Houmansadr, A., Berthier, R., Borisov, N., & Sanders, W. (2013). Secloud: A cloud-based comprehensive and lightweight security solution for smartphones. *Computers & Security, 37*, 215–227. doi:10.1016/j.cose.2013.02.002

Zou, P., Wang, C., Liu, Z., & Bao, D. (2010) Phosphor: a cloud based drm scheme with SIM card, In *Proceedings of the 12th International Asia-Pacific on Web Conference (APWEB)*. doi:10.1109/APWeb.2010.43

Zunnurhain K & Vrbsky S (2010). Security Attacks and Solutions in Clouds. In *Proceedings of the Service Aggregated Linked Sequential Activities (SALSAHPC)*.

Zyskind, G., & Nathan, O. (2015). Decentralizing privacy: Using block chain to protect personal data. In *Proceedings of the Security and Privacy Workshops (SPW)* (pp. 180–184).

About the Contributors

Kashif Munir received his BSc degree in Mathematics and Physics from Islamia University Bahawalpur, Pakistan in 1999. He received his MSc degree in Information Technology from University Sains Malaysia in 2001. He also obtained another MS degree in Software Engineering from University of Malaya, Malaysia in 2005. He completed his PhD in Informatics from Malaysia University of Science and Technology, Malaysia. His research interests are in the areas of Cloud Computing Security, Software Engineering, and Project Management. He has published journal, conference papers and book chapters. Munir has been in the field of higher education since 2002. After an initial teaching experience with courses in Stamford College, Malaysia for around four years, he later relocated to Saudi Arabia. He worked with King Fahd University of Petroleum and Minerals, KSA from September 2006 till December 2014. He moved into University of Hafr Al-Batin, KSA in January 2015.

* * *

Harraz Abdelghafour is a PhD Student at ENSIAS (National School of Computer Science and System Analysis) at Mohammed V University, Rabat, Morocco since 2015. His research interests include load balancing, Big data, Cloud computing and Artificial Intelligence.

A. Sheik Abdullah is working as an Assistant Professor, in the Department of Information Technology, Thiagarajar College of Engineering, Madurai, Tamil Nadu, India. He completed his B.E (Computer Science and Engineering), at Bharath Niketan Engineering College, and M.E (Computer Science and Engineering) at Kongu Engineering College under Anna University, Chennai. He has been awarded as gold medalist for his excellence in the degree of Post Graduate. He is pursuing his Ph.D. in the domain of Medical Data Analytics, and his research interests include Medical Data Research, E-Governance and Big Data. He has handled various E-Governance projects such as automation system for tracking community certificate, birth and death certificate, DRDA and income tax automation systems. He has published research articles in various reputed journals and International Conferences. He has been assigned as a reviewer in Various reputed journals such as European Heart Journal, Proceedings of the National Academy of Sciences, Physical Sciences (NASA) and so on. He has received the Honorable chief minister award for excellence in E-Governance for the best project in E-Governance. Currently he is working towards the significance of the medical data corresponding to various diseases and resolving its implications through the development of various algorithmic models.

Ali Alwadi is a student in Computer Engineering Department. Ali has a Bachelor in Computer Engineering from Yarmouk University in Jordan, and a Master degree from Auckland University of Technology in New Zealand. He is currently a Technical Consultant in Auckland. Main research areas: IoT, Radio Frequency, embedded systems.

Alain April is a full professor of Software Engineering at the University of Québec (ETS). With more than 30 years of healthcare, finance/banking and telecommunications, my specific expertise is in: Big Data, Cloud Computing, database and BI, machine learning, software quality assurance, maintainability and IT process mapping/conformity. She is comfortable with practical applications, the use of open source technology and technology transfer to industry. Winner of the ISO award for higher education in standardization (in 2011), currently a Canadian representative on two ISO committees: wg9 -BigData and SC38 - cloud computing/distributed systems. She has also published books on Software Maintenance Management and Software Quality Assurance.

Arpita Bhattacharjee received her B.Tech degree in Information Technology from B.P Poddar Institute of Management and Technology, Kolkata and M.Tech degree in Computer Science & Engineering from Tripura University, Suryamaninagar.

An Braeken obtained her MSc Degree in Mathematics from the University of Gent in 2002. In 2006, she received her PhD in engineering sciences from the KULeuven at the research group COSIC (Computer Security and Industrial Cryptography). In 2007, she became professor at Erasmushogeschool Brussel in the Industrial Sciences Department. Prior to joining the Erasmushogeschool Brussel, she worked for almost 2 years at a management consulting company BCG. Her current interests include cryptography, security protocols for sensor networks, secure and private localization techniques, and FPGA implementations.

Prachi Chaturvedi completed his B.E. at ITM Universe Gwalior and is also pursuing his M.TECH from MITS.

Rachid Cherkaoui Received his BSc degree in Computer Engineering from Abdelmalek Essaadi University, Morocco in 2012, and his MSc degree in Computer Science from Ibn Tofail University, Morocco in 2014. Currently he is a PhD candidate in Computer Engineering at the National School of Computer Science and Systems Analysis, Mohammed V University. His research interests include network security, intrusion and anomaly detection in cloud computing and IoT environments, big data and machine learning.

Priyanka Chinnaiah is currently doing her M.E Computer Science and Information Security in Thiagarajar College of Engineering, Madurai, Tamil Nadu, India. Her area of interest is Cloud Computing.

Ranjita Choudhury received his B.E. degree in Computer Science & Engineering from Maharashtra Institute of Technology, Aurangabad and M.Tech degree in Computer Science & Engineering from Tripura University, Suryamaninagar.

Avijit Das received his B.E. degree in Computer Science & Engineering from Tripura Institute of Technology, Narsingarh and M.Tech degree in Computer Science & Engineering from Tripura University, Suryamaninagar.

Amjad Gawanmeh, is an assistant professor, Khalifa University, UAE., and an affiliate Assistant professor, Concordia University Montreal, Canada. He received the M.S. and the Ph.D degrees from Concordia University, Montreal, Canada, 2003 and 2008. He worked as a researcher for the Hardware Verification Group at Concordia University between 2000 and 2008. He worked for Applied Science University in Jordan from 2008 until 2010 as an assistant professor. His research interests are verification of hardware systems, security systems, and healthcare systems, modeling and analysis of complex systems such as CPS, performance analysis of complex systems, reliability of as medical system, and reliability of CPS. He is associate edit for IEEE Access, and a reviewer for several journals in IEEE, Elsevier, and Wiley. He has co-chaired several conferences such as WiMob 2015, and workshops organized in conferences such as Healthcom, WiMob. He has served on the TPC for key conference such as Globecom, ICC, PIMRC, ICCVE, WCNC, and Infocom workshops. He is an IEEE member.

Amine Haouari received a Master Degrees in Information Systems Engineering and computer science from the Faculty of Science and Technology of Tangier. Currently he is working as a data analyst in the field of BIG DATA with Hewlett-Packard and evolved to data analyst in the field of BIG DATA. He is a PhD student within the Information Security Research Team (ISeRT) at University Mohamed V, exactly in the National Higher School of IT (Rabat-Morocco-). His research interests include the security of transactions in the cloud computing environment, Big Data, containers and cryptography.

K. Indira is working as a assistant professor for the past five year in TCE and she is doing research in "Personalized Ranking System in Multi-Cloud System". She is published IGI Book Chapter in the title of "Resource scheduling in Multi cloud Environment, Monitoring cloud Audit and Green Cloud Computing" and area of interest is Performance and Quality analysis in Multi-Cloud Environment. she is awarded as Microsoft Technical Associate in C# and .NET Framework Environment.

B. Jeyapriya is Student of II Year M.E. Computer Science and Information Security at Thiagarajar College of Engineering. Her research interest includes Cryptography and Cloud Computing.

Kijpokin Kasemsap received his BEng degree in Mechanical Engineering from King Mongkut's University of Technology, Thonburi, his MBA degree from Ramkhamhaeng University, and his DBA degree in Human Resource Management from Suan Sunandha Rajabhat University. Dr. Kasemsap is a Special Lecturer in the Faculty of Management Sciences, Suan Sunandha Rajabhat University, based in Bangkok, Thailand. Dr. Kasemsap is a Member of the International Economics Development and Research Center (IEDRC), the International Foundation for Research and Development (IFRD), and the International Innovative Scientific and Research Organization (IISRO). Dr. Kasemsap also serves on the International Advisory Committee (IAC) for the International Association of Academicians and Researchers (INAAR). Dr. Kasemsap is the sole author of over 250 peer-reviewed international publications and book chapters on business, education, and information technology. Dr. Kasemsap is included in the TOP 100 Professionals–2016 and in the 10th edition of 2000 Outstanding Intellectuals of the 21st Century by the International Biographical Centre, Cambridge, England.

Abhishek Majumer received his B.E. degree in Computer Science & Engineering from National Institute of Technology, Agartala and M.Tech. degree in Information Technology from Tezpur University, Assam in 2006 and 2008, respectively. He is currently working as an Assistant Professor in the Department of Computer Science & Engineering, Tripura University (A Central University), Suryamaninagar, India. His areas of interest are Wireless Network and Cloud Computing.

Samir Nath received his B.E. degree in Computer Science & Engineering from Tripura Institute of Technology, Agartala and M.Tech degree in Computer Science & Engineering from Tripura University, Suryamaninagar. He is currently working as Junior Research Fellow in a project funded by Ministry of Electronics and Communication Technology, Govt. of India.

R. Parkavi, working as Assistant Professor, Department of Information Technology, Thiagarajar College of Engineering, Madurai, Tamil Nadu, India. She completed her B.Tech (Information Technology), at Sree Sowdambika College of Engineering, and M.E (Computer Science and Engineering) at Thiagarajar College of Engineering and done Post Graduate Project in Cloud Computing Security. She started her research in Mobile Learning.

Sazia Parvin is a data and system security researcher at the School of Business, UNSW, Canberra. Her research interests include network security, trust management, cyber systems, cloud computing, big data analytics, system software and intelligent information systems. Her research is published in various top ranked publications. She has published over 38 research papers in her fields of interest as journals and international conferences. She is an Associate Editor for International Journal of Computer System Science and Engineering (IJCSSE) and International Journal of Engineering Intelligent Systems (IJEIS). She has more than 7 years of experience in information system's design and development in various business environments. She holds 7 years of extensive teaching experience in Software and Computer Engineering discipline. She has achieved several prestigious Research Grants from Australia and South Korea. She is also the recipient of the 'Gold Medal' Bachelor of Computer Science and Engineering Award from Jahangirnagar University in 2004 for her outstanding performance (First Class First Position) in that academic year.

K. S. Suriya did her Bachelors of Engineering in Computer Science and Engineering from Kalasalingam Institute of Technology in 2015. She is completed her Master of Engineering in Computer Science and Information Security at Thiagarajar College of Engineering in 2017. Her research interests include Data mining, Cryptography and Network Security.

M. Thangavel is an Assistant Professor, Department of Information Technology, Thiagarajar College of Engineering, Madurai. He is currently pursuing his Ph.D. degree under Information & Communication Engineering – Cloud Security at Madras Institute of Technology, Anna University. He completed his M.E in Computer Science & Engineering at J.J College of Engineering. His research interests are Cryptography Network security, Compiler Design and Data Structures.

Abdellah Touhafi obtained his bachelor's degree in Electronics, option: Computer systems at IHAM Antwerp. He has a Master's degree in Electronics from the VUB Brussels and a PhD in Applied Sciences: Scalable Run-Time Reconfigurable Computing Systems also at the VUB. He currently is a full-time professor at the VUB and the leader of the Rapptor Lab.

A. Vennila completed her B.Tech in Information Technology. Currently, she is pursuing her M.E in Computer Science and Information security at Thiagarajar College of Engineering, Madurai. She is doing her final year project on Recommendation System under distributed system domain.

Samadi Yassir received his MS in IT Telecom Networks at ENSIAS (National School of Computer Science and System Analysis) at Mohammed V University-Souissi, Rabat Morocco in 2015. He is currently a Ph.D. student in department of computer science, laboratory CEDOC ST2I, ENSIAS, Rabat, Morocco. His research interests include load balancing, distributed systems, big data management in workflow systems, and cloud computing.

Mostapha Zbakh received his PhD in computer sciences from Polytechnic Faculty of Mons, Belgium, in 2001. He is currently a Professor at ENSIAS (National School of Computer Science and System Analysis) at Mohammed V University, Rabat, Morocco since 2002. His research interests include load balancing, Parallel and distributed systems, HPC, Big data and Cloud computing.

Index

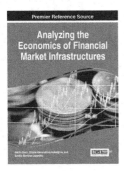

Stay Current on the Latest Emerging Research Developments

Become an IGI Global Reviewer for Authored Book Projects

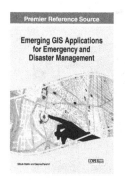

Premier Reference Source

Emerging GIS Applications for Emergency and Disaster Management

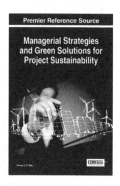

Premier Reference Source

Managerial Strategies and Green Solutions for Project Sustainability

Premier Reference Source

Comparative Approaches to Using R and Python for Statistical Data Analysis

Premier Reference Source

Solutions for High-Touch Communications in a High-Tech World

The overall success of an authored book project is dependent on quality and timely reviews.

In this competitive age of scholarly publishing, constructive and timely feedback significantly decreases the turnaround time of manuscripts from submission to acceptance, allowing the publication and discovery of progressive research at a much more expeditious rate. Several IGI Global authored book projects are currently seeking highly qualified experts in the field to fill vacancies on their respective editorial review boards:

Applications may be sent to:
development@igi-global.com

Applicants must have a doctorate (or an equivalent degree) as well as publishing and reviewing experience. Reviewers are asked to write reviews in a timely, collegial, and constructive manner. All reviewers will begin their role on an ad-hoc basis for a period of one year, and upon successful completion of this term can be considered for full editorial review board status, with the potential for a subsequent promotion to Associate Editor.

If you have a colleague that may be interested in this opportunity, we encourage you to share this information with them.

 InfoSci®-OnDemand

Continuously updated with new material on a weekly basis, InfoSci®-OnDemand offers the ability to search through thousands of quality full-text research papers. Users can narrow each search by identifying key topic areas of interest, then display a complete listing of relevant papers, and purchase materials specific to their research needs.

Comprehensive Service

- Over 81,600+ journal articles, book chapters, and case studies.
- All content is downloadable in PDF format and can be stored locally for future use.

No Subscription Fees

- One time fee of $37.50 per PDF download.

Instant Access

- Receive a download link immediately after order completion!

Database Platform Features:

- Comprehensive Pay-Per-View Service
- Written by Prominent International Experts/Scholars
- Precise Search and Retrieval
- Updated With New Material on a Weekly Basis
- Immediate Access to Full-Text PDFs
- No Subscription Needed
- Purchased Research Can Be Stored Locally for Future Use

"It really provides an excellent entry into the research literature of the field. It presents a manageable number of highly relevant sources on topics of interest to a wide range of researchers. The sources are scholarly, but also accessible to 'practitioners'."

– Lisa Stimatz, MLS, University of North Carolina at Chapel Hill, USA

"It is an excellent and well designed database which will facilitate research, publication and teaching. It is a very very useful tool to have."

– George Ditsa, PhD, University of Wollongong, Australia

"I have accessed the database and find it to be a valuable tool to the IT/IS community. I found valuable articles meeting my search criteria 95% of the time."

– Lynda Louis, Xavier University of Louisiana, USA

Recommended for use by researchers who wish to immediately download PDFs of individual chapters or articles.

www.igi-global.com/e-resources/infosci-ondemand

Printed in the United States
By Bookmasters